The Arms Production Dilemma

P9-AOQ-647

CSIA Studies in International Security

Steven E. Miller and Teresa Johnson Lawson, editors

Published by CSIA

1. *Soviet Nuclear Fission: Control of the Nuclear Arsenal in a Disintegrating Soviet Union*, Kurt M. Campbell, Ashton B. Carter, Steven E. Miller, and Charles A. Zraket (1991)

2. *Cooperative Denuclearization: From Pledges to Deeds*, Graham Allison, Ashton B. Carter, Steven E. Miller, and Philip Zelikow, eds. (1993)

Published by Brassey's, Inc.

3. *Russian Security After the Cold War: Seven Views from Moscow*, Teresa Pelton Johnson and Steven E. Miller, eds. (1994)

4. *Arms Unbound: The Globalization of Defense Production*, David Mussington (1994)

5. *Damage Limitation or Crisis? Russia and the Outside World*, Robert D. Blackwill and Sergei A. Karaganov, eds. (1994)

Published by The MIT Press

6. *Shaping Europe's Military Order: The Origins and Consequences of the CFE Treaty*, Richard A. Falkenrath (1994)

7. *The Arms Production Dilemma: Contraction and Restraint in the World Combat Aircraft Industry*, Randall Forsberg, ed. (1994)

The Arms Production Dilemma

Contraction and Restraint in the World Combat Aircraft Industry

Editor
Randall Forsberg

CSIA Studies in International Security No. 7

The MIT Press
Cambridge, Massachusetts
London, England

Distributed by The MIT Press, Cambridge, Massachusetts, and London, England.

Library of Congress Cataloging-in-Publication Data

The arms production dilemma: contraction and restraint in the world combat aircraft
industry / edited by Randall Forsberg.
      p.   cm.—(CSIA studies in international security; no. 7)
   Includes bibliographical references (p.).
   ISBN 0-262-06176-7.—ISBN 0-262-56085-2 (paper)
   1. Aircraft industry—Military aspects—United States. 2. Arms transfers—United
States. I. Forsberg, Randall. II. Series.
HD9711.U6A84   1994
338.4'76234'0973—dc20   94-38178
                                                                               CIP

Book designed by Miriam Avins
Cover designed by Jeffrey Kälin

10   9   8   7   6   5   4   3   2   1

Printed in the United States of America

Contents

Tables and Figures

Appendix Tables

A list of abbreviations and other conventions used in the text and Appendix tables is given on the first page of the Appendix.

Preface

This book is a product of the efforts of many individuals. The authors have not merely prepared articles for an edited volume, but worked through a series of outlines, drafts, and discussions to contribute parts of an integrated and cohesive whole. Their effort reflects their commitment to the goals of the International Fighter Study (IFS), a multi-year study in which the authors serve not only as scholars, but also as interpreters of diverse national situations and perspectives.

Jonathan Cohen and Andrew Peach, research fellows at the Institute for Defense and Disarmament Studies (IDDS), have done yeoman's work for the entire IFS group, compiling and analyzing data on worldwide combat aircraft production, trade, and holdings. They were assisted in that effort by several IDDS interns, including Eric Desautels, Steve Torrisi, Lucy Chester, and Andreas Staab. The basic global research conducted at IDDS was supplemented the authors' contributions concerning their respective countries, and by Elisabeth Sköns' generous provision of detailed global data on arms trade values compiled by the SIPRI Arms Production and Transfer project.

The Russian analysts at the Principal Research Institute of the Russian Air Force and the Center for Operational and Strategic Analysis of the Supreme Staff of the Russian Air Force, who conducted the background research for Chapter 2, merit recognition for their thorough and informative work.

I speak for all the authors in thanking our exceptionally fine editor and book designer, Miriam Avins. Her rapid, insightful work and the support of Steven Miller and Teresa Johnson Lawson, editors of the CSIA Studies in International Security, made it possible to publish our findings in a concise, timely, and accessible form. I must take responsibility for any factual errors or blunders of presentation that may have slipped through our abbreviated editorial process.

We appreciate the assistance of Karen Motley at CSIA, Matteo Luccio, Elaine Gold, Katarina Forsberg, Steve Lilly-Weber, and Emily

Morrison at IDDS, and Helen Snively, all of whom cheerfully supported the project in various ways. Jeffrey Boutwell of the American Academy of Arts and Sciences and staff members of the Berlin-based Berghof Foundation for Peace and Conflict Research, the London-based King's College Centre for Defence Studies, and IDDS helped make the project's international meetings productive and pleasant.

We gratefully recognize and thank the Carnegie Corporation of New York and the John D. and Catherine T. MacArthur Foundation, whose substantial financial support has made the International Fighter Study possible. The Ploughshares Fund provided seed funding for the project, which has also received generous support from the W. Alton Jones Foundation, the Joyce Mertz-Gilmore Foundation, New-Land Foundation, the CS Fund, the Berghof Foundation, Mrs. Joan Warburg, and Hayward R. Alker, Jr.

Contributors

Randall Forsberg is the Executive Director of the Institute for Defense and Disarmament Studies (IDDS) in Cambridge, Massachusetts, and an officer of the Center for Science and International Affairs, Kennedy School of Government, Harvard University. Starting at the Stockholm International Peace Research Institute (SIPRI) in 1968, she was assistant editor of the first *SIPRI Yearbook* (*1968/69*) and an author for the next nine editions (*SIPRI Yearbook 1969/70–1979*). In the early 1980s she founded and helped lead the Nuclear Weapons Freeze Campaign, and she received a MacArthur Foundation Fellowship. She has edited and contributed to several books, and has published in *International Security*, *Scientific American*, the *Bulletin of Atomic Scientists*, and the *Boston Review*. She is a board member of the Arms Control Association and an advisory board member of the Institute for Global Cooperation and Conflict.

Ulrich Albrecht is Professor of Peace and Conflict Studies in the Political Science Department of the Free University of Berlin, and acting director of the University's Institute for International Politics and Regional Studies. He holds degrees in aeronautical engineering, economics and political science. In 1990 he was head of planning in the East German Ministry for Foreign Affairs, and he participated in the "2+4" negotiations on German unification. He has studied the post–World War II role of German engineers in the USSR and Latin America. His most recent book is *The Soviet Armaments Industry* (1993).

Alexei Arbatov is a member of the Russian Duma (Parliament), a Senior Fellow of the Institute of World Economics and International Relations of the Russian Academy of Sciences, and founder and Director of the Center for Geopolitical and Military Forecasts in Moscow. In 1993, he was a visiting scholar at the Center for Science and International Affairs, Kennedy School of Government, Harvard University. His most recent book is *Nuclear Weapons Reductions and Limitations— Strategic Views from the Second Tier: The Nuclear Weapons Policies of France, Britain and China* (1994).

François Chesnais is Professor of Economics at the University of Paris-Nord. For 20 years, he was a senior economist at the Organization for Economic Cooperation and Development (OECD). His publications include *Compétitivité internationale et dépenses militaires* (Économica, 1990, with Claude Serfati); *L'armement en France: Genese, ampleur et coût d'une industrie* (Éditions Nathan, 1992, with Claude Serfati); "The French National System of Innovation," in Richard R. Nelson, ed., *National Innovation Systems* (Oxford University Press, 1993); and *La mondialisation du capital* (Syros, forthcoming).

Michael Clarke has been the Executive Director of the Centre for Defence Studies, University of London, since 1990. Earlier he was a lecturer at the Universities of Wales (Aberystwyth), Manchester, and Newcastle-on-Tyne. He has also been a guest fellow at the Brookings Institution and an associate fellow at the Royal Institute of International Affairs in London. His books include *British External Policymaking in the 1990s* (1992), and he is editor of *New Perspectives on Security* (1992) and *Britain's Defence Choices for the 1990s* (1993).

Jonathan Cohen is a Research Fellow at the Institute for Defense and Disarmament Studies in Cambridge, Massachusetts, where he studies the conventional arms trade. He holds degrees in political science and history from Tufts University. He co-authored, with Randall Forsberg, "The Global Arms Market: Prospects for the Coming Decade," a paper presented at a February 1993 Brookings Institution conference on the future of the U.S. and Russian arms industries.

Marco De Andreis is a Senior Fellow and the Director of International Security Studies at the Centro Studi di Politica Internazionale (CeSPI, Center for the Study of International Politics) in Rome. He has been a resident fellow at the Institute for East-West Studies in New York and a foreign policy fellow at the University of Maryland School of Public Affairs. Most recently he edited *National Defense Structures and Common Defense in Europe*, and co-authored *The Nuclear Weapon Complex of the Former Soviet Union* (both forthcoming).

Philip Gummett is Professor of Government and Technology Policy at the University of Manchester, UK. He specializes in defense industrial and technology policy, with particular reference to Western Europe, and has published extensively on this subject, as well as on more general themes of British and European science and technology policy. He has served as an adviser to the British Parliament, the European Commission, the European Parliament, and other public bodies.

Sergei Kortunov is a Department Head in the Directorate on Nonproliferation, Disarmament, and Technical Cooperation of the Russian Foreign Ministry, where he helped formulate Russian arms trade policy. He has a Ph.D. from Moscow State Institute for International Relations. He participated in the Strategic Arms Reduction Talks (START) and in the negotiations on Intermediate-range Nuclear Forces and Short-range Nuclear Forces (INF-SNF) and on chemical weapon disarmament. Formerly, he was Counselor of the Directorate on Arms Limitation and Disarmament in the Soviet Foreign Ministry.

Peter Lock is a Senior Researcher at the Free University of Berlin. He was previously Research Coordinator of the Berghof Institute for Peace and Conflict Research and Assistant Professor at the Institute for Political Science of the University of Hamburg. He has served as a consultant to the United Nations Security Council, OECD, UNESCO and the World Council of Churches. He is Editor-in-Chief of *Militärpolitik Dokumentation*. His recent publications in English include *The Restructuring of Arms Production in Western Europe,* co-edited with Michael Brzoska (1992); "The evolution of the arms trade," *Le monde en développement* (1993); and "The Systemic Bed-Rock of Transition," *Journal of Peace Research* (1994).

Alexander Ozhegov is the head of the Economic Research Department at the Russian Bank for Reconstruction and Development. Previously, he was Senior Researcher at the Analytical Center on Science and Industrial Policy of the Ministry of Science and Technology Policy of the Russian Federation. He has published extensively on the topics of investment, structural change in the economy, and defense industry conversion.

Andrew Peach is a Research Fellow at the Institute for Defense and Disarmament Studies in Cambridge, Massachusetts, where he studies U.S. and European air forces and aerospace industries. He has a degree in international politics and economics from Middlebury College.

Giulio Perani is Research Director of the Military Spending and Arms Production Project at Achivio Disarmo in Rome. He has conducted research for the European Commission, the Italian National Research Council, ENEA, and CeSPI. His books and articles include *L'industria militare in Italia* (1991), "The Lagging Restructuring in Italy," in *Restructuring of Arms Industries in Western Europe* (1992), and *Ambienti per l'industria militare italiana* (1993).

Judith Reppy is Associate Professor of Peace Studies in the Center of International Studies at Cornell University, and Director of Cornell's Peace Studies Program. She has published extensively on defense economics and conversion and is the co-editor, with Philip Gummett, of *The Relations Between Defence and Civil Technologies* (1988). Her recent research has focused on the economic impact of military spending and the implications of global changes in defense industries for science and technology policy and, more generally, for economic conversion.

Claude Serfati is Maître de Conférences at the University of Versailles-Saint-Quentin and a member of the research laboratory ORINTE. Recent and forthcoming publications include *L'armement en France: Genese, ampleur et coût d'une industrie* (1992, with François Chesnais); "The French Case," in P. Gummett and J. Stein, eds., *Construction, Conversion and Control of Defense Technological Capabilities in Europe;* and *Croissance, Innovation et Production d'Armes* (forthcoming).

Elisabeth Sköns is a Research Fellow with the Project on Arms Production and Arms Transfers at the Stockholm International Peace Research Institute (SIPRI), and a regular contributor to the *SIPRI Yearbook*. Her most recent publications include "Western Europe: Internationalization," in *Arms Industry Limited* (Oxford University Press, 1993); "Weapon Supplies to Trouble Spots," a background paper prepared for the UN Development Program's *Human Development Report 1994* (Oxford University Press, 1994); and "The Internationalization of the Arms Industry" in the American Academy of Political and Social Science *Annals* (September 1994).

Fredrik Wetterqvist is First Secretary at the Swedish Ministry for Foreign Affairs. He holds degrees in political science from Augustana College and the University of Uppsala. He was previously on the research staff of the Stockholm International Peace Research Institute and the Swedish National Defence Research Establishment (FOA). His recent FOA publications include *French Security and Defence Policy: Current Developments and Future Prospects* (1990); *The War in the Persian Gulf* (1991); and *The Independent European Programme Group and European Defence Industrial Co-operation* (1992).

Susan Willett is a Defense Economist at the Centre for Defence Studies, University of London, where she is responsible for a research and networking program on defense procurement, defense industries, and arms trade. She was previously a Research Associate at Ruskin College, studying European technology and innovation, and a Research Officer at Birkbeck College working on French and British defense procurement and production. She is a NATO-registered conversion expert, and she is on the board of the Council for Arms Control. Her recent publications include "United Kingdom: Strategies for Adjustment in the Post–Cold War Era," in *Towards a Peace Economy: The Oxford Manifesto*, P. Ingram and R. Williamson, eds. (June 1994); and "The Restructuring of the UK and European Defence Industrial Base," *Defence Economics* (1993).

Chapter 1

Randall Forsberg

Introduction: Competitive Arming or Cooperative Arms Control?

The Cold War focused attention on the military aspect of security. The risk of deliberate aggression by East or West was exceedingly small, but the two sides' huge nuclear and conventional forces posed a serious danger that a small incident could escalate into a world war. Today there is no risk of an all-out East-West war. The dissolution of the Warsaw Pact, the disintegration of the former Soviet Union, the unification of Germany, and the end of Communist Party control in Eastern Europe have created a 700-mile-wide "firebreak" between Russia and the West; and a lack of fuel, spare parts, and infrastructure has weakened the remaining Russian armed forces.

Equally important, the perceived reasons for conflict between East and West have vanished. Countries on both sides of the old divide now define security issues in economic and political terms: replacing recession in the West and economic disaster in the East with economic stability and growth, strengthening democratic institutions in the East and stopping the spread of fascism and ultra-nationalism in the West, minimizing disruptive mass migrations, and resolving renewed ethnic and nationalist conflicts. With respect to military security, the main concern on both sides is stopping the proliferation of nuclear weapons and of missiles and aircraft capable of carrying nuclear weapons.

Randall Forsberg is the Executive Director of the Institute for Defense and Disarmament Studies (IDDS) in Cambridge, Massachusetts, and an officer of the Center for Science and International Affairs, Kennedy School of Government, Harvard University.

The industrial nations' shared security interests have created an unprecedented opportunity to develop security policies based on co-operation instead of competition or confrontation. With cooperative arms control and confidence-building measures, the most heavily armed industrial nations—the United States, Russia, Britain, France, Germany, and Japan—could greatly increase their own security and that of other nations. They could reduce the burden of military spending, obstruct the remilitarization of great-power relations, undertake security guarantees that would minimize and perhaps stop proliferation, improve multilateral peacekeeping and peacemaking, and strengthen respect for the rule of law.

In principle these nations could eliminate most of the nuclear and conventional forces they still maintain for mutual deterrence. In addition, after developing ground rules for peacemaking, they could rely on multilateral action, rather than unilateral intervention, to deter or end regional conflicts. These two steps would allow the industrial nations to make deep cuts in their military forces and spending,[1] and "mothball" most arms industries, impeding resurgent militarism among the great powers. These steps would also facilitate efforts to restrict arms exports by allowing the same limits to be applied to arms acquisition in arms-producing and arms-importing countries. If combined with regional arms reductions, restraints on arms transfers would increase regional stability, facilitate multilateral peacekeeping, and allow further military cuts in the industrial nations. Such changes, in turn, would reduce the incentives for nuclear proliferation.

But there are serious obstacles to East-West and North-South co-operation on military security matters. It will be difficult to reverse the long-standing assumption of conflicting interests, and to build a consensus on the military implications of shared security interests. Some nations may be able to move more quickly than others toward greater cooperation; in the interim, there will be pressure for arms exports to keep arms industries afloat. If the governments of the major arms-producing nations yield to this pressure, their exports are likely to create new military threats that will obstruct progress toward cooperative demilitarization.

---

[1] At present, the United States spends about $260 billion (bn) per year on the military; Britain, France, Germany, and Japan each spend $30–45 bn; and Russia probably spends about $100 bn. In contrast, all developing nations combined spend only about $170 bn.

This book presents the first findings of the International Fighter Study, a multinational study of cooperative arms control and confidence-building measures that would minimize military capabilities for cross-border attack and rapid mobilization and strengthen multilateral peacemaking and peacekeeping. As an illustrative case, the project looks at the future of air warfare and potential restraints on the deployment, production, and export of advanced combat aircraft. It focuses on a relatively self-contained area of warfare and weaponry to facilitate discussion of broader issues that need urgent attention, yet are not amenable to a quick consensus:

- How far and how fast should the nations of East and West reduce the large standing conventional armed forces that were formerly maintained primarily for use against each other? For example, how many of their roughly 24,500 combat aircraft should they retire within the next few years?
- If the main purpose of their forces is now to deter and end regional wars, shouldn't the industrial nations cooperate to minimize the risk of such wars? They could, for example, limit arms exports, foster regional arms reductions and restructuring, and prepare for joint regional peacemaking and peacekeeping.
- How might the industrial countries maintain a defense industrial base without exports—and what sort of base do they need to insure against unforeseen threats?

The following sections discuss the links among force size, arms production, arms export, and industrial base issues; the reasons for focusing on combat aircraft in studying these links; and the process by which the International Fighter Study is exploring the issues. The chapter concludes with a brief guide to the subsequent chapters.

Linked Issues Facing the Primary Arms Producers: Force Levels, Production, and Trade

In the past, U.S. and Soviet analysts treated the issues of force size, arms production, arms exports, and the defense industrial base as largely separate and independent. Now that forces and spending are dropping sharply, however, it has become clear that choices in these areas are interdependent—a fact long recognized by the smaller producers of advanced weaponry, Britain, France, Germany, Sweden, and Italy. One reason is that the main peacetime use of defense industries is not to build ever-expanding arsenals, but to replace aging weapon systems worn out in training and exercises. Since most weapon systems have a service life of 20–30 years, one-for-one replacement of aging systems requires peacetime arms production at an average annual rate equivalent to 1/20th–1/30th (3 percent to 5 percent) of the total inventory of a given type of weaponry. But if the standing forces are sharply reduced, then after the oldest weapons are withdrawn, there will still be a surplus of newer weapons not yet due for retirement. As a result, no production for replacement purposes will be needed for some years. The deeper the cuts in the standing forces, the longer will be the period before replacement production is required. Replacement production could be suspended for 5, 10, or even 20 years. This is now the case for nearly all types of weaponry in the United States and for most types in Russia.[2]

For the arms-producing nations, this link between production requirements and force size and age creates a problem when forces decline and inventories are new. From the viewpoints of expense and security, the optimal response would be to shut down arms plants until inventories grow old and replacement weapons are needed. But governments cannot simply lay off workers with specialized knowledge and skills and then expect to rehire them at short notice years later when their special expertise is needed again. The same is true for the special equipment and tools needed for arms production, and for the network of subcontractors that supply materials and parts. No "industrial reserve" system has yet been developed or instituted to keep know-how, plant, equipment, and infrastructure available for remobilization within a year or two. Moreover, government officials argue, a "warm" defense industrial base (that is, factories with active assembly lines and production processes) is needed not only to replace aging equipment, but also to insure against unforeseen military threats.

---

[2] The authors of Chapter 2 argue that the breakup of the former USSR (Union of Soviet Socialist Republics) gave the republics on the periphery much of the newest weaponry, leaving Russia with older systems and an urgent need for new production. But data reviewed in Chapter 12 suggest that Russian Air Force interest in new production may derive more from the desire to field new technology and keep defense plants open than from limits on the useful life of the systems now in service.

To keep arms production lines open when there is no domestic demand for replacement weaponry, governments have turned to two strategies. First, in the United States, the government is funding the procurement of weapon systems that the Secretary of Defense and other officials openly admit are not needed for security, but are being produced solely to maintain firms and workers with specialized skills.[3] Second, all the industrial arms producers are promoting arms exports to developing countries as a way to employ arms production capacity and sustain profits and jobs.

These two strategies are extremely costly in financial and human resources for both industrial and developing nations. They are also counterproductive: they tend to create or exacerbate the very threats that the defense industrial base is meant to guard against. About three-quarters of all international transfers of major weapons go to the key players in regional conflicts: China and Taiwan, North and South Korea, India and Pakistan, Israel, Syria, Saudi Arabia, and Iran, and Greece and Turkey. And such exports have a long history of exacerbating regional conflicts and fueling regional arms races.

This points to a second problematic link in current arms policies: the forces and defense industries needed by the industrial countries are largely a function of regional arms build-ups created by their own arms exports. Governments justify the still-large conventional forces maintained by the United States and Russia and the smaller but not greatly reduced forces of the other advanced weapon producers on two grounds: they must be prepared to intervene with force in potential major regional wars in the Middle East or Asia; and they must guard against the possible future deterioration of relations among the great powers, that is, the United States, Russia, Britain, France, Germany, China, and Japan.

In addition to exacerbating regional threats, the combination of active defense industrial bases (supported by arms exports) and large standing forces increases the risks of great-power conflict. Naturally, fears of renewed military confrontation among the great powers are

---

[3] The two most egregious examples are the planned 1996 funding of a $2 bn nuclear-powered attack submarine to be produced in Groton, Connecticut, and the ongoing funding of a $44 bn B-2 program to preserve a bomber production line. In later chapters, the authors argue that the British, French, and German governments are also funding weapons not needed for security merely to keep arms industries going—but in those cases, this is not openly admitted by the responsible government officials.

heightened by the peacetime maintenance of large armed forces with substantial offensive potential, particularly when such forces are backed up by active production plants that could quickly equip larger forces and keep them resupplied in time of war.

Both potential future threats—new capabilities for regional aggression and renewed great-power confrontation—could be addressed more effectively by cooperative arms control than by competitive arming and arms exports. The United States, Russia, and the countries of Europe (joined later by China and Japan) could undertake several steps to build confidence and prevent renewed great-power military confrontation. They could, for example, reduce the size of their armed forces and restructure the forces that remain to minimize the potential for cross-border aggression. By eliminating the capability for a massive surprise attack, such reductions and restructuring would greatly reduce fears of great-power conflict. Moreover, further cuts in standing forces would delay the need for replacement production and permit all the primary arms producers to shift from a "warm" to a "cool" defense industrial base. This change, combined with the reductions and defense-oriented restructuring in forces, would place economic, political, and technical hurdles in the path of a regressive great-power leader, inclined to use armed aggression as a means of advancing national interests.

At the same time, shifting to a "cool" industrial base would preclude the development of new regional threats by putting the same limit on arms acquisition by producers and importers. In the past, efforts to restrain arms exports have failed because importers have argued successfully that such restraints unfairly discriminate against countries that have not developed their own arms industries. If the primary producers mothball their arms industries, they could apply an equal and nondiscriminatory limit to arms acquisition by producers and importers alike.

If the United States, Russia, and the other main arms producers suspended production of major weapon systems, they would have to develop new methods for preserving industrial know-how. They could store information concerning production specifications and techniques in computer databases and on videotapes, earmark converted plants for potential future use, and establish an industrial reserve corps to maintain specialized skills. Converting from "warm" defense industrial bases with open production lines to "cool" bases without such lines would prevent or significantly delay rearmament; it would provide years, instead of months, in which to stop and reverse a serious deterioration in great-power relations; and it would give the potential victims of aggression years of warning, if needed, to strengthen their defenses.

In sum, the links among force size, the industrial base, and arms exports can either undermine or strengthen security. With a traditional, competitive approach to security, the links exacerbate security problems. Exports used to preserve arms production lines as insurance against future threats are the only source of new regional threats; and maintaining large standing forces plus open production lines maximizes the risk of renewed great-power military confrontation.

In contrast, a cooperative approach to security could turn the links between force size, production, and export to advantage:

- By heading off new regional threats, limits on exports would permit deep cuts in standing forces.
- Force cuts would provide a period of 20–30 years before production of replacement weapons might be needed.[4]
- If a moratorium or low limits on exports were combined with a moratorium or low limits on production for domestic use, this would remove the main political obstacle to export limits.
- Cutbacks in standing forces and a shift from a "warm" to a "cool" industrial base would minimize the risk of a rapid slide toward renewed great-power military confrontation or war.

A Case Study of Combat Aircraft

Advanced combat aircraft form an excellent subject for a study of the links between deployment, production, and trade. Long-range fighter-attack aircraft are a prime candidate for confidence-building reductions and defense-oriented restructuring. Such aircraft form the backbone of the aerospace industry, which is the predominant sector of defense industries. And combat aircraft represent the bulk of international arms transfers, measured in cost.

---

[4] The estimates for the longer periods when replacement would not be needed assume that weapons retired before the end of their useful service lives (when forces are cut) are reactivated to maintain the size of the forces when active systems reach retirement age. (See Chapter 5.)

FORCE REDUCTION ISSUES

Advanced combat aircraft are offense-capable systems whose deployment tends to erode confidence and increase fears of war. Because they can travel far from home, over any terrain, and drop nuclear, conventional, or chemical munitions with pinpoint accuracy, advanced combat aircraft are the component of modern conventional forces with the greatest versatility, range, and power for offensive operations. But their very power and versatility make them the most threatening and potentially destabilizing form of weaponry after nuclear and chemical weapons and ballistic missiles.

There are excessively large inventories of combat aircraft, particularly in the United States and Russia. Thousands of advanced combat aircraft have been procured by the United States and Russia for use in a major East-West war. To reduce the risk that relations between Russia and the West will be re-militarized, it would be helpful for the United States and Russia to undertake global-scope cuts in these forces. By reducing the potential threat of air attack that each side poses to the other, such cuts would help build confidence and obstruct reactionary efforts to redraw the Cold War lines of confrontation.

In addition to the United States and Russia, European countries could make deep cuts in the conventional forces that will remain after implementation of the Treaty on Conventional Armed Forces in Europe (CFE). Air forces were scarcely touched in the CFE talks due to the global reach of tactical aircraft, the interlocking land and naval roles of land- and carrier-based aircraft, the strategic air defense role of some combat aircraft, and potential regional threats in the Middle East, South Asia, and the Far East, and along the Sino-Russian border. These issues, which could not be addressed in the European context, could be discussed and resolved in the context of global arms reductions.[5]

Combat aircraft are also key to post–Gulf War North-South security relations. The Gulf War was a unique showcase for the military advantages that can occasionally be obtained through technological superiority in weaponry, particularly in the air. This has led U.S. officials to stress air superiority in designing forces for potential future

---

[5] Post-CFE talks on global conventional arms reductions were first broached in Jonathan Dean and Randall Forsberg, "CFE and Beyond: The Future of Conventional Arms Control," *International Security*, Vol. 17, No. 1 (Summer 1992).

conflicts in the Third World. But since the main arms producers supply nearly all Third World aircraft, their exports are creating the future challenges to their own tactical air forces. This costly, destabilizing, self-defeating policy could be replaced by stabilizing agreed cutbacks in the long-range, offensive tactical air power of both industrial and developing nations.

DEFENSE PRODUCTION ISSUES

Advanced combat aircraft play a central role in arms production both technically and economically. The aerospace sector, which is the dominant area of specialized military technology, is led by advances in front-line combat aircraft and related attack and defense missiles. This sector accounts for the single largest fraction of the procurement budgets of the industrial nations. In addition, fighter-attack aircraft are the most expensive system exported in large numbers; and measured by cost, combat aircraft and related systems dominate the arms export market.

ARMS EXPORT ISSUES

Advanced combat aircraft exports play a key role in the spread of independent nuclear and conventional arms industries, and in regional arms races. Because of their symbolic role and technological complexity, fighter-attack aircraft represent the leading edge of military technology introduced into Third World nations. The spread of independent arms industries typically starts with the introduction of low-performance fighter or attack aircraft, which are smaller, lighter, slower, and simpler. That is followed by imports of higher-performance aircraft. Next, such aircraft are produced under license. Then an indigenous production line is developed. In several countries this process has been followed or accompanied by steps to develop nuclear weapons and ballistic missiles. Stopping the spread of advanced combat aircraft would slow the spread of high-tech military infrastructure, and prevent the growth of threats that create incentives for the acquisition of nuclear weapons.

In regional conflicts in the Middle East, South Asia, and East Asia, combat aircraft and associated attack and defense systems have long been the main focus of regional arms races. With the United States and other Western countries supplying one side in a conflict, and Russia (formerly the Soviet Union) and China supplying the other, regional opponents have measured their relative strength in large part as a function of the numbers and technological capabilities of their imported combat aircraft. In fact, some U.S. and British officials have recently gone so far as to argue that new aircraft and related systems under development in their countries are needed in order to offset the technology they expect will be incorporated in new systems that Russia may develop and sell to countries in the Middle East.[6]

Finally, combat aircraft are amenable to study. They are physically large and generally kept in the open, where they can be spotted from satellites. Little effort is made to conceal or obscure their existence, and they are relatively easy to track as they are shipped around the world or produced in various countries. This makes it possible to compile a relatively complete, reliable account of holdings and exports of such systems.

The International Fighter Study

In the International Fighter Study, scholars and analysts from the world's most heavily armed nations are studying the security policies of their own nations and developing proposals for cooperative arms control and confidence-building measures that could give their countries greater security at lower cost. Their proposals are reviewed by the group as a whole, discussed with policy makers and advisers in their own nations, and debated in conferences that bring together policy makers from all the nations involved.

The project is divided into two main phases. Phase One involves research and policy development in the world's primary arms-producing and exporting nations: the United States, Russia, France, Britain, Germany, Italy, and Sweden. These seven nations are the only countries that independently design, develop, and produce technologically-advanced major weapon systems. As a result, they alone

---

[6] The Secretary of Defense's 1994 *Annual Report to the President and the Congress*, p. xiv, argues that technological improvements in U.S. tactical air forces are required in large part because new Russian and French fighters may be in production and exported shortly after 2000, increasing the capabilities of potential U.S. regional opponents. Similarly, in an interview with the author, British Ministry of Defence procurement officials argued that the advanced air superiority capabilities of the Eurofighter 2000 will be needed to counter new Russian fighters (not yet developed) that could be exported to parties in regional conflicts.

are responsible for new developments at the leading edge of military technology. In addition, they alone are responsible for the global spread of advanced weaponry. They manufacture about 80 percent of all advanced weapon systems exported around the world, and they give licenses for the production of the remaining 20 percent, for which they provide complete technical specifications and some components. Because of their unique role in the production and export of advanced weaponry, these countries alone face the linked choices regarding force size, arms production, arms exports, and defense industrial capacity discussed earlier.

Phase One project participants began by preparing background studies on their respective nations' current and expected future air forces and air force strategy, aircraft development and procurement, production capacity, and exports. At the same time, researchers at the Institute for Defense and Disarmament Studies (IDDS) prepared a global overview of combat aircraft inventories, production, and trade.[7] This book presents the results of those background studies. Extensive supporting reference material appears in a companion volume, *IDDS Almanac 1994.*[8]

Next, Phase One participants prepared papers on cooperative policy options that might permit stabilizing, confidence-building cuts in the deployment, production, and export of combat aircraft in the main arms-producing nations. These papers have been revised and expanded in light of comments from other project participants, and they are being used as the basis for national and international dialogues on the idea of cooperative international restraints on conventional arms deployment, production, and trade. The policy papers will be published in a later volume.

Phase Two of the project, which began in late 1994, involves partners from countries outside Europe that are secondary combat aircraft producers and major actual or potential importers. Secondary producers manufacture combat aircraft that are either based on older air-

---

[7] To assess the extent to which trends in combat aircraft reflect trends in conventional arms more generally, IDDS researchers also surveyed global tank inventories, production, and trade. The patterns of production and trade in the two areas were similar, suggesting that the combat aircraft results are indicative of general trends. See Randall Forsberg and Jonathan Cohen, "The Global Arms Market: Prospects for the Coming Decade," Cambridge, Mass.: IDDS, February 9, 1994.

[8] *IDDS Almanac 1994: World Combat Aircraft Holdings, Production, and Trade* (Cambridge, Mass.: IDDS, forthcoming).

craft designed by the primary producers, or else limited to the low end of the range of aircraft performance in speed, payload, range, maneuverability, avionics, and weaponry. The current secondary producers are Brazil, China, India, Japan, and Taiwan. Of these, only China is a major exporter, selling basic systems to other developing countries such as Pakistan, Iran, and Bangladesh. The major actual or potential combat aircraft importers are, in addition to the secondary producers, Greece, Egypt, Iran, Israel, Pakistan, Saudi Arabia, South Korea, Syria, and Turkey.[9]

With the continued involvement of the Phase One partners, Phase Two research and discussion will address an overlapping set of issues—factors that influence import demand and the spread of indigenous arms industries. Independent scholars in the new countries involved will prepare background studies on their own nations' current policies. These studies will assess the relative importance of various sources of demand for arms, including regional conflicts, the desire for independence in arms supplies, prestige, civilian industrial development, and other possible commercial factors. Next, new and old project partners will develop policy proposals for arms control and confidence-building measures designed to head off new regional arms build-ups and arms races.

Studies of the Primary Producers

As a backdrop for assessing the pros and cons of potential future arms control and confidence-building measures, this volume looks at the current security policy, armed forces, arms industry, and arms production and exports of countries that independently develop, produce, and export technologically advanced weapon systems: Russia, the United States, Britain, Germany, Italy, France, and Sweden. While the country studies focus on combat aircraft, national policies regarding combat aircraft strategy, holdings, production, and export do reflect national approaches to conventional forces more generally.

---

[9] Excluded from the list are three countries with small air forces that have firm and potential orders for 30–65 combat aircraft (Finland, Malaysia, and Switzerland), and 12–14 other countries with firm and potential orders for fewer than 30 combat aircraft. Also excluded are three past and potential future major importers: Iraq and Libya, which are under UN arms embargoes; and North Korea, which lacks the funds for large orders.

For each country, the background study attempts to cover five policy areas:

- The role of combat aircraft in the country's overall security policy and military strategy.
- The current size, composition, squadron assignment, and age of combat aircraft in the inventory, and the projected future number and types of combat aircraft in service.
- The planned rate of production and acquisition of aircraft to equip the domestic air force(s), with notes on any expected short-fall or surplus of aircraft needed to meet planned force levels.
- The current and projected size of the national combat-aircraft producing industry in terms of employment and revenue, and the plans for keeping the industry employed when domestic demand for new production aircraft is low.
- Government policy and industry strategy regarding exports of combat aircraft, prospective future exports, and their impact on domestic arms industries.

The chapters attempt to show how military strategy, planned future force levels, and the age of systems in the current inventory affect the domestic demand for new production; how that demand affects the arms industries; and the extent to which governments or firms in arms-producing countries are trying to use exports to sustain arms industries during a period of declining or nonexistent domestic demand. The planned future force levels, new production, and exports provide a baseline against which cooperative reductions in forces and limits on production and export can be measured.

The Russian study, directed by Alexei Arbatov, is presented in Chapters 2–4. The extraordinarily rapid pace of change in Russian armed forces and arms industries, the amount of information published here for the first time, and Russia's pivotal role in the future security policies and arms industries of other nations all warranted special attention.

Chapter 2 covers Russian security policy and military strategy, with stress on the role of combat aircraft, and the current and planned future combat aircraft inventory and new procurement. This paper was prepared by Russian Air Force analysts and then edited by Arbatov, who added a commentary. Similarly, Chapter 4, which deals with arms exports and export policy, again stressing combat aircraft, was prepared by Sergei Kortunov, the Russian Foreign Ministry official charged with facilitating arms exports, and edited with a commentary by Arbatov. Events in Russia are so fast-moving and information has been classified so long that independent analysts cannot find essential information solely in published sources. Inviting informed officials to prepare background papers and independently critiquing these papers offered an effective alternative. Chapter 3, on the Russian military aircraft industry and efforts to convert the bulk of its capacity to civilian production, is by Alexander Ozhegov, an independent economist.

For Chapters 5–10, on all of the other primary arms producers, the background chapters were prepared in collaborative efforts involving two or three independent analysts. In most cases, the material on security policy, military strategy, and future force structure was prepared by one analyst (Michael Clarke for Britain, Jonathan Cohen for Germany, Andrew Peach for France, Marco De Andreis for Italy, Elisabeth Sköns for Sweden, and Randall Forsberg and Andrew Peach for the United States). Material on arms industries and export policy was prepared by the other authors (Susan Willett and Philip Gummett for Britain, Ulrich Albrecht and Peter Lock for Germany, François Chesnais and Claude Serfati for France, Giulio Perani for Italy, Elisabeth Sköns and Fredrik Wetterqvist for Sweden, Judith Reppy and Andrew Peach for the United States).

The emphases of the national studies vary considerably, in large part due to differences in national security environments and concerns. The chapters on the United States and Sweden, where force levels are ostensibly determined as a function of perceived threats and desired responses, and where the rate of procurement of new systems is clearly tied to force levels and equipment age, give more or less equal attention to the five issue areas set out above. In contrast, the chapters on Britain, Germany, and France focus on the costs and means of preserving a national arms industry, and the reasons for doing so, apart from perceived military threats, planned force levels, and procurement needs. In none of these large West European countries is military spending or force size explicitly linked to a perceived military threat from Russia or elsewhere. Instead, force size and procurement requirements seem to derive from a policy of slowly but steadily reducing forces compared with their Cold War levels. In Italy, as in Sweden, air defense is the central strategic concern of the Air Force, and related force requirements are somewhat more closely related to specific perceived threats—in Sweden from Russia, and in Italy from countries in the Mediterranean region. These differing emphases evoke the diverse obstacles to cooperative restraints on armaments that would be likely to arise in the course of cooperative security talks.

Chapter 11 briefly surveys the "receiving end" of the world arms trade, with sections on regions and countries that are current or potential major weapon importers, and in some cases secondary arms producers. This chapter does not aim to convey the full range of the security concerns of the arms-importing nations (which will be the focus of Phase Two of the study). The more limited purpose is to provide and document the bases for IDDS projections of the scale of the world export market for combat aircraft in 1994–2000 and beyond. Andrew Peach and Jonathan Cohen reviewed the security policies and planned procurement of countries capable of placing large import orders, and estimated potential additional import orders that might be placed over the next decade, over and above firm orders already placed for deliveries during this period.

Chapter 12 attempts to draw the global picture that emerges from the studies of arms-producing and arms-importing nations. The chapter suggests that by 2000, worldwide arms production and transfers are likely to have fallen by 90 percent compared with their scale in 1978–1982. It also shows that during the 1990s both the United States and Russia will produce more arms for export than for domestic use for the first time in history.

These two points underscore the urgency and importance of finding new approaches to the linked issues of force size, production, and export. Without exports, domestic demand in the primary arms-producing countries would not be sufficient to maintain a "warm" defense industrial base. This is already true in the United States and Russia, and it may soon be the case in Europe. Yet the defense base is being maintained as a form of insurance against possible future military threats that exports and active arms industries exacerbate. By spelling out the details of the arms-production dilemma, this book lays a foundation for research and debate on constructive solutions.

Chapter 2

*Edited and with a
commentary by
Alexei Arbatov*

Russian Air Strategy and Combat Aircraft Production: A Russian Air Force View

Since the end of the Cold War, Russia's political environment has improved, but its strategic situation has deteriorated. This deterioration is mainly a product of three factors. First, Russia has lost its former "first strategic echelon," that is, its forward defense in Central Europe. Second, the former second echelon of defense has shrunk; Belarus and Ukraine had been part of this echelon. Third, the armed forces lost their forward-based infrastructure, control systems, maintenance facilities, and air defense capabilities. Military districts that had been well to the rear of the forward lines of defense are now on the frontier, and a large portion of the best military units, weaponry, and equipment are now located in newly-created, foreign independent states. As a result, the relative military strength of the United States and European NATO countries has increased, and they are now more able to launch airborne strikes against vital Russian urban-industrial, command-and-control, and military targets from any direction.

The information in this chapter was assembled by several military analysts from the Principal Research Institute of the Russian Air Force and the Center for Operational and Strategic Analysis of the Supreme Staff of the Russian Air Force. Alexei Arbatov restructured the presentation of the material, and provided a commentary at the conclusion of the chapter. The views in the body of the chapter should not be construed as reflecting the opinion of the editor or the Center for Geopolitical and Military forecasts; the editor has tried to preserve the philosophy of the Russian Air Force.

Alexei Arbatov is a member of the Russian Parliament (Duma), a senior fellow at the Institute of World Economics and International Relations of the Russian Academy of Sciences, and founder and Director of the Center for Geopolitical and Military Forecasts in Moscow.

Most of the former East European allies of the USSR, the Baltic states, and possibly Ukraine are hoping to join NATO, while some former Soviet republics in Central Asia and the Caucasus are increasingly oriented toward Islamic neighbors, such as Iran, Turkey, and Afghanistan.

One benefit of the current international environment is progress in arms control; for example, in accordance with the Treaty on Conventional Armed Forces in Europe (CFE), NATO states will reduce their ground forces and combat aircraft by about 20 percent. Nonetheless, the United States and many other nations still regard military power as the dominant factor in world politics. For instance, Britain, France, and China have not participated in the nuclear arms reduction process; China conducted a nuclear explosion in 1993; the membership of "the nuclear club" may increase to about 20 states by the year 2000; and NATO is seeking to widen its sphere of influence, as illustrated in its agreement to use its combat aircraft in an effort to stop fighting in the former Yugoslavia.

The West continues to put a high priority on preserving and enhancing its combat capabilities. It will develop and produce new weapon systems and will emphasize the overall qualitative superiority of Western armed forces. Increased reliance on technology is intended to transform the very nature of combat and to neutralize the opponent's counter-actions at a low cost in relation to the size of the forces employed, the casualties, and the equipment losses. The war in the Persian Gulf demonstrated the effectiveness of this approach.

Russia still regards itself as one of the great powers, and it aspires to keep this position. Of course, the task of defending the state's interests and creating effective, mobile, properly-equipped armed forces, including air forces, can be carried out only if Russia possesses formidable economic, industrial, and technological potential. It is extremely important to meet these requirements in peacetime, and they would be all the more crucial in time of war.

Russia's Strategic Situation and New Military Position

Russia is not under direct military threat today, but military dangers still exist. According to the newly-adopted military doctrine, dangers outside Russia could stem from a number of sources: territorial claims, local wars and armed conflicts near Russia's borders, the possibility that nuclear or other weapons of mass destruction will be used, the proliferation of such weapons all over the world, attempts to undermine strategic stability and to interfere in Russia's internal affairs, the suppression of the rights and freedoms of Russian citizens and Russian ethnic minorities abroad, or attacks on Russian facilities and forces on the territories of other countries. Dangers could also be created by the extension of military blocs and alliances to the detriment of Russia's military security, or by international terrorism.

Military dangers can become direct military threats. According to the current doctrine, this could result from the concentration of troops near Russian borders, changing the existing balance of power; assaults on sites and facilities located along Russia's frontier, or other border conflicts; the training of armed units on the territory of other states for the purpose of penetrating the territory of Russia and its allies; the actions of other states aimed at hampering the smooth functioning of Russia's strategic nuclear forces and their maintenance systems or the system of state and military command and control; or the introduction of foreign troops into the territory of the countries that border Russia without the authorization of the UN or regional collective security organizations and without Russia's agreement.

Russia's strategic position has also been affected by the military, political, and economic conditions inside Russia. The Confederation of Independent States (CIS) encountered considerable difficulty along the route toward its consolidation, in part because not all of the former Soviet republics became members. The social, political, and financial instability in Russia, the disruption of economic networks, the "brain drain," and other processes have all led to a decrease in the economic, industrial, and scientific-technical assets of the country.

Expenditures for the armed forces as a whole and for the Air Force of the Russian Federation (AFRF) in particular have been greatly reduced, and the modernization of the Air Force with new types of aircraft, equipment, and weapons has been delayed and reduced. Part of the military aircraft scientific and industrial base has been lost, since some design bureaus and military production plants are located on the territory of newly-created independent states. Moreover, the whole aircraft industrial complex is no longer capable of functioning autonomously, as it should.

The former Soviet system of values, including the prestige of military service, is largely gone. The society is splintered and increasingly stratified, which is tremendously damaging to the armed forces. The disruption has obstructed recruitment for AFRF units and has caused havoc in the life of military and aircraft personnel. Personnel problems have been exacerbated by the proliferation of weapon types, which has impeded training (especially in the Air Force) and is likely to reduce the efficiency and combat-readiness of aircraft units.

In November 1993, Russia adopted a new military doctrine that reflects its current political and strategic position. While the old military doctrine emphasized stopping and repelling aggression, the new doctrine has two new tasks: deterring aggression, and supporting international peacekeeping operations. To fulfill the demands of the new doctrine, a new approach to the design of the armed forces is needed. Rather than increasing the forces' size, it is essential to focus on qualitative improvements, a proper balance in the diversity of armaments, compatibility between weapons and control and maintenance systems, and increasing the prestige of military service in general and the pilot's profession in particular.

The Russian military believes that its armed forces must be able to ward off any threat emanating from any direction. The most economical way to achieve this would be to create, in a timely way, relatively small well-equipped armed forces with a powerful strategic reserve. This would require a fundamentally new approach to Russia's military-technical policy. The chief aim should be the qualitative improvement of weapons and military equipment, based on the most up-to-date scientific-technical achievements and the most advanced technologies. Also of utmost importance are further fundamental research, and the application of its results in the manufacture of military aircraft, munitions, and equipment.

In addition to procuring high-quality weapons and equipment, the armed forces should reduce their excessive variety of types and classes of weapons to simplify maintenance and training of commanders, pilots, and support personnel. The procurement system should be reorganized and streamlined to exclude excessively long development, redundancy, and the mass production of only slightly improved system modifications. Such adjustments should make it possible to procure weapons that can effectively respond to real threats to national security within the requirements of defense sufficiency.

Finally, the military should aim to create a single system of warfare assets. Depending on the priorities of the missions, the subsystems that constitute the large system could include information sources on ground, air and naval targets; precision-guided weapon systems; highly effective counter-air weapons and systems; air defense suppression systems; nighttime and all-weather combat operations assets; and real-time reconnaissance and monitoring of the current operational environment, matched to adequate command-and-control structures and facilities.

RUSSIA'S NEW MILITARY DOCTRINE AND THE ROLE OF
THE AIR FORCE
According to the new military doctrine, the Air Force has the following major tasks:
1. *To prevent armed conflicts and deter aggression:*
- Conduct air reconnaissance and provide timely disclosure of preparations for an armed attack;
- Maintain the structure and condition of the air strategic nuclear forces so that they can inflict the planned damage level on an aggressor in any given situation;
- Maintain the combat capacity of general-purpose aircraft groups and the Air Force reserves so that they can repulse any aggression of a regional nature; and
- Patrol the border, jointly with the troops of the Air Defense.[1]

The availability of a strong Air Force, and the high level of its combat capacity and combat readiness are deterrent factors that help prevent military conflict on any scale.
2. *To stop and repel aggression:*
- Conduct air reconnaissance;
- Repel attacks from the air (including cruise missile attacks) from any direction, in close cooperation with the Air Defense troops and the air forces of allied states;
- Suppress the air forces of the enemy on land;
- Defend Russian and allied troop concentrations and rear infrastructure from air attacks and aerial reconnaissance by the enemy;

---

[1] The Soviet armed forces were divided into five branches: ground forces, air forces, navy, strategic rocket forces, and air defense forces. Russia inherited this structure, with its inherent problems of overlapping functions between the air forces, the air defense forces, and the anti-aircraft artillery of the ground forces. The changes discussed in the section below on command and control structures and systems are partly an attempt to deal with those problems.

- Transport mobile units, other troops, arms, military supplies and equipment;
- Participate in landing operations;
- Provide air escorts to the mobile forces, airborne and amphibious landing troops, other troops, and the Navy;
- Disrupt the political and military command-and-control systems of the enemy;
- Defeat the enemy's troops, naval forces, and airborne and amphibious landing units; and
- Destroy the enemy's reserves, interdict lines of communication, and conduct deep strikes against rear facilities and other targets.

In the event of aggression, the Russian Air Force, either alone or with the air forces of allied states, would take an active part in repelling the attack and defeating the enemy. As in the past, there is some chance that an attack might be mounted directly against Russia as a result of a gradual or sudden growth of international tension, but a war would more likely result from the gradual involvement of Russia in a military conflict that began in a neighboring country or countries. An attack might start like World War II, with an offensive air operation (today it would be a combined air-land-naval operation) accompanied by a ground-troop invasion of Russian territory. Alternatively, a war might start with massive air- and sea-launched multiple strikes conducted over an extended period and followed later by a land force invasion.

3. To support international peacekeeping operations:
- Deliver humanitarian aid and evacuate civilians by air; and
- Impose air blockades on regions in conflict to ensure compliance with and enhance the effectiveness of international sanctions.

International peacekeeping and peacemaking operations require making certain preparations in advance. The air forces of the United States and some NATO countries in Europe plan such operations carefully, and have already started conducting them in Bosnia-Herzegovina.

The military conflicts of recent decades show the growing importance of air- and space-based forces in armed conflict, and the increasingly central role of air forces. This is the product of four major factors. First, the success of ground operations increasingly depends on air force missions, from achieving air supremacy until the moment the enemy surrenders. Second, there is often a need to react quickly to changes in the situation on the ground. Air power can organize all available forces and bring the entire brunt of military might to bear in an area. Third it is vital to attack an aggressor country throughout the entire depth of its troops' deployments. Fourth, airborne smart weapon systems, particularly precision-guided weapons, offer a wide variety of highly effective combat options. In addition, the new military doctrine maintains the Air Force's traditional role of ensuring the mobility of the other branches of the armed forces. Transport aircraft and their fighter escorts are an essential element in creating mobile forces for use in local wars and other conflicts.

Their unique characteristics make air forces useful in military conflicts across virtually the entire range of intensity. (They are less useful for the most minor tasks, such as stopping groups of armed bandits.) The long range and large combat radius of combat aircraft enable them to start from bases at distant airfields, which are difficult to attack, and then land at other airfields that are also beyond the enemy's reach.[2] In theory, the great range of combat aircraft permits their rapid transfer from one theater to another, making it possible to apply massive power at decisive moments in a conflict. Such flexibility is crucial for the defense of Russian territory, with its vast expanse, decreasing inventory of combat aircraft, urgent need to allocate economic resources to support and maintenance facilities, and uncertainty about the potential origins and combinations of future threats.

Because of their flexibility, rapid reaction time, and range, air forces are the most effective way to destroy targets in combined arms operations, especially in support of the ground forces.[3]

Accurate, long-range air-to-ground and air-to-air missiles will make it possible to block an adversary's air force, establish air supe-

---

[2] As admirably displayed in 1993 by the Russian Air Force exercise "Voskhod-98," an aircraft's range can be extended remarkably if it can refuel in the air. But to refuel a large number of aircraft in the air requires a fleet of tanker aircraft, which Russia lacks.

[3] Recent research has shown that ground forces can hit only one-third of targets located at a depth of up to 120 km from the forward line of battle, while attack aircraft on their own can destroy two-thirds of targets located at a depth of more than 120 km, as well as one-third of those in the frontal zone.

Technological advances have increased the opportunities and need for the Air Force. Increasingly, the Air Force must help the Air Defense force provide cover for the ground forces and for targets in the rear. This is the result of the new "stealthy" aircraft and missiles, which are difficult to track and intercept with land-based anti-aircraft systems.

riority above one's own forces, and deliver long-range strikes from beyond the effective zone of the opponent's ground- or sea-based air defense complexes. Offensive tactics may also be employed for attacking reinforcements and installations in the rear with long-range air missiles, and for suppressing hostile radar, command systems, and logistic facilities.

The latest generation of aircraft can fly at any time of day or night, in all weather conditions, and successfully attack targets that might hinder the initiation or conduct of military operations on land and at sea.

THE NEED FOR A HIGHLY MOBILE AIR FORCE

With large reductions in Russian ground forces and equipment, the range of tasks assigned to the Air Force is unchanged, but the number of targets it must cover has grown. While the tasks assigned to the Air Force in cases of large-scale, high-intensity warfare are particularly formidable, there is every reason to believe that the Air Force can also play a decisive role in local or regional wars. The use of multinational tactical combat aircraft units in the Persian Gulf War supports this conclusion.

As the immediate risk of large-scale war recedes, Russia and the United States assume that the main risk in the near future is of wars of low and medium intensity. The redesign of the armed forces and the Air Force must proceed on this assumption—but the possibility of high-intensity conflicts must also be also taken into account, partly because low-intensity conflicts are not sufficiently demanding to define the size or technology of the Russian Air Force.

According to the new military doctrine, the Air Force will participate in all three groups of tasks set for the armed forces (two of which, the first and the third, were not included in former doctrines). To perform all its assigned tasks in joint and independent operations, the Air Force must be equipped with up-to-date weapons and technology and have a balanced structure. Yet at the same time, the Air Force budget will be considerably reduced.

In addition, Russia's most important military and industrial installations are now vulnerable to strikes from all directions even by conventional weapons. Setting up a zonal, all-azimuth Air Defense system would be prohibitively expensive, and land-based air defense complexes cannot be rapidly redeployed. Thus, to balance its needs and resources, Russia seeks to create a highly mobile Air Force, build-

ing on its existing air units. The time has come to abandon the
outdated "infantry-tank" strategy. Enemy targets should be destroyed by precision-guided weapons, delivered mainly by the Air
Force, instead of counting on a "fire wall." Ground troop actions
should be based on the results of Air Force operations, instead of
binding the latter to support the conduct of land warfare.

Threat Assessments of Russia's Contingency Planners

The Russian Ministry of Defense and the Air Force High Command
have based their contingency planning on the assumption that political and military developments in the 1990s and 2000s could lead to
several scenarios of military confrontation or armed conflict in which
Russia might become involved.

NORTHWESTERN AND WESTERN STRATEGIC DIRECTIONS
Under certain circumstances, NATO might try to employ force to
settle Russian internal conflicts, to deny Russia its legitimate interests,
or even to seize parts of its territory to undercut strategic positions or
for post-conflict bargaining.

If tension has lasted at least 50 days, NATO could deploy some
of its forces at forward positions, including on the territory of Central
and Eastern Europe, the Baltic states, and adjacent sea waters.
NATO's preparations would be quicker and easier if the states in
these areas joined NATO in advance. These areas would provide
NATO with reinforcements from East European armies and with the
highly-developed military infrastructure that remained after the dissolution of the Warsaw Treaty Organization.

From the start of military operations, NATO would initiate
intensive offensive air and naval operations. If these were successful it
would undertake offensive air-land operations to seize the Kalin-
ingrad region and, in a rapid advance through Belarus and Ukraine,
reach Russia's frontiers. This would create a direct threat of air strikes
and ground force penetration deep into the Leningrad and Moscow
military districts to deter Russian counterstrikes or a counteroffensive.
The urban-industrial and administrative heartland of Russia, its infrastructure, military production, war stocks, reinforcement and redeployment capabilities, early warning and command-and-control
systems, and the bulk of Russia's strategic nuclear deterrent would

then become vulnerable to massive conventional air and missile attacks.

In such a situation, from the outset of hostilities the aviation group in the Northwestern strategic region would participate in operations to repel the adversary's air attacks, prevent amphibious landings, and destroy the opponent's naval and air formations in the area. In this scenario, Russian Western aviation groups (air armies), reinforced by groups from other Russian regions, would participate in blocking the adversary's forward units, disorganizing its rear areas and second echelons, and conducting deep strikes against key command-and-control, military, and industrial sites; it would also carry out its own operations to weaken the adversary's air force in the air and on the ground and to support friendly ground forces in defense and counteroffensive operations.

THE SOUTHWESTERN STRATEGIC DIRECTION

Turkey and Iran are trying to weaken the position of Russia in the Transcaucasus in order to strengthen their own positions and bring under their influence the predominantly Muslim populations of Azerbaijan, the North Caucasus, and some other areas. Their success would lead to the isolation of Armenia and Georgia, and severe destabilization of Russia's southern regions. An escalation of war between Armenia and Azerbaijan or the complete disintegration of Georgia might provoke massive military intervention from Russia, Turkey, and Iran in various possible sequences and combinations.

Turkey, with possible indirect support from its NATO allies, could launch an attack independently or in conjunction with military actions in Europe. It would launch a land offensive supported by air and naval formations. Russia might resist such an attack first by a special operation of the Russian North Caucasus (Southwestern) air group, and later by combined force military actions supporting frontal defensive operations.

THE SOUTHERN STRATEGIC DIRECTION

In the Central Asian region, the governments of Turkey, Iran, Afghanistan, and Pakistan are trying to increase their influence over the states of Central Asia and Kazakhstan in order to weaken the Russian role there and create a "single Islamic region." It is quite possible, therefore, that in the event of military conflict in Europe or in the Transcaucasus, or as a separate action, one or more of these states might try to change their borders by force.

The armed forces of Turkey, Iran, Afghanistan, and Pakistan, supported by local guerrillas, could try to seize strategically important assets and areas. To oppose them, a coalition of the armed forces of Tajikistan, Uzbekistan, Kazakhstan, and Russia, which would provide the bulk of forces and perform command functions, would conduct defensive operations. Russian aircraft from the North Caucasus and Ural-Volga military districts would carry out a wide range of missions, primarily providing air cover and support to the defending forces and interdicting lines of communication, and reconnaissance.

THE FAR EASTERN STRATEGIC DIRECTION
In the Far East, the main problem stems from the territorial claims of Japan on the Russian Southern Kurile Islands. A sharp reduction in the numerical strength and readiness of Russian ground and air forces in the Far Eastern military district and of the Russian Pacific Fleet, combined with the almost complete demilitarization of the Southern Kurile Islands, in contrast to the steady growth in Japanese military power, could tempt Japan to solve the problem of the "Northern Territories" by military means. It is significant that Japan is an ally of the United States, which defends Japan's interests elsewhere in Asia and the Pacific and supports Japan's claims to the islands.

After a relatively long period of tension, which could be used to form groups of forces and prepare for offensive air and amphibious naval operations, Japan could launch an attack in alliance with the United States. The principal objectives would be the seizure of the Kuriles and Sakhalin Island—"sealing" the Russian Pacific fleet in ports and adjacent waters—and the destruction of Russian forces and military sites and installations in the Far East.

In such a situation the Russian Air Force would attack U.S. aircraft carriers, provide air defense for the ground forces, and support the ground forces in their anti-amphibious and frontal defensive operations.

The situation on the Korean peninsula remains tense. There is a high risk of war between the People's Republic of North Korea and the Korean Republic, which relies on U.S. and Japanese support. The United States supports Seoul because it provides U.S. forces with a bridgehead in Asia, and China and Japan consider the prospect of a strong, united Korea an obstacle to their own increased influence in the sub-region. Thus, a conflict on the Korean peninsula could rapidly involve the United States, Japan, and China in military action, creating a direct threat to industrial, urban, and military assets in the Maritime province of Russia.

THE EAST-SIBERIAN STRATEGIC DIRECTION

China has not finally and totally renounced claims to certain frontier areas in the territories of Kazakhstan, Kirgizstan, Tajikistan, and Russia. For example, articles regularly appear in the Chinese press demanding a revision of the recently-concluded agreement with Russia on boundaries in the Far East, and since there is no freedom of the press in China, these claims cannot be dismissed as the private opinions of their authors. Thus, it is possible that a crisis might arise that could lead to frontier conflicts or local wars.

If there were a conflict between Russia and China, because of Russia's long frontier, the insufficient size of its ground forces, its lack of strategic depth, and the vulnerability of its military infrastructure and lines of communication, the Russian Air Force would focus on intense deep-strike missions in addition to close air support. These missions would target high-value military, communications, command-and-control, and industrial sites in China. Reinforcement of this area would be slow and difficult for Russia, and front-line defense hardly possible given China's ability to massively reinforce its forward troops and concentrate at breakthrough points. Hence, the role of the Air Force would be absolutely crucial, especially early, before reinforcements arrived and began to engage the penetrating forces in maneuver defense. To some degree, the AFRF would implement retaliatory strikes; its capability to perform this mission serves as a conventional deterrent to aggression.

THE AIR FORCES' DUTIES

Although the tactical air forces would perform many standard functions in all regions, there are differences in the requirements for operations in different strategic directions, due to the regions' diverse geography, capabilities of opposing forces, strategic situations on the ground and at sea, basing and maintenance infrastructures, and reinforcement prospects.

The Northwestern and Far Eastern directions are distinguished by vast areas of ocean and sea. A broad range of naval and amphibious forces would probably be used in combat operations, including hostile carrier-borne aircraft. The AFRF would coordinate its operations with shore-based naval aviation, Navy, and Air Defense forces. Its primary missions would be to attack hostile amphibious forces en route and during landings, to strike at surface ships (mainly aircraft carriers and transport and amphibious ships), to give air cover to Russian ships within the combat radius of fighters, to provide an extended perimeter defense of shore facilities (jointly with Air Defense), and to give close air support to friendly amphibious and airborne landings.

In the Far East, where the main areas of operation would be the Kuriles, Sakhalin, and an opponent's bridgeheads at Kamchatka and in the Maritime province, Air Force operations would be conducted over a number of semi-enclosed shore and sea areas dispersed across an extremely broad front. The limited number of Russian airfields in this region would limit the dispersal, redeployment, and reinforcement of the air forces. Operations over the vast sea areas would hamper command-and-control and ground battle management, so that airborne warning and control systems and air-refueling capabilities would be especially important. Long-range strikes against Japan's industrial and military facilities would be of quite limited effectiveness; Japanese and U.S. air defenses are dense and sophisticated, and Russia has a limited number of aircraft with a sufficient range. Any failure by the Air Defense to defend Russia's scanty land-based military sites, including airfields, or by the Navy to destroy aircraft carriers would greatly undercut the operations of the AFRF. Reinforcements would hardly be feasible or helpful for the AFRF in this case. Russian setbacks at an early stage in the conflict or protracted conflict would bring dire military consequences.

The Western, Southwestern, Southern (and, in part, East-Siberian) directions are conspicuous for the newly-created "buffer" areas that separate the armed forces of Russia from its potential opponents. These areas include the Central and East European states, Mongolia, and the former Soviet republics. The depth of the buffer zones is 500–1,200 km in the West and Southwest, up to 1,700 km in the South, and 600–700 km across Mongolia. These zones offer a crucial stabilizing factor: they provide a long advance warning of potential aggression. On the other hand, since Russian military control over the buffer areas would be extremely advantageous in defending against aggression, and hostile control so detrimental, during a crisis these zones might invite the early intrusion of military forces from one side or the other, leading to an inadvertent escalation of conflict. Indeed, such action could become the main focus of conflict.

One possible response to this vulnerability would be for air forces to begin air strikes over the buffer zones long before ground forces are directly engaged in battle. In this case, the air forces would be operating independently from other armed services, fighting for air superiority against adversary air forces in the air and at airfields. Over Eastern Europe, the AFRF would be at a disadvantage; NATO air forces would be able to quickly re-deploy to forward bases in Eastern Europe, and NATO generally has longer-range and better air-to-surface missile attack capabilities. In contrast, the Russian Air Force would mostly fly fighters, in cooperation with Air Defense forces, aiming to protect Russian territory from air strikes and extend the point where hostile aircraft are engaged to the "buffer zones." Operations of Russian frontal strike aircraft would be hampered by their relatively short ranges and limited air-refueling capabilities. Employment of medium- and long-range bombers would lead to unacceptable rates of attrition; NATO's air defense is dense, and Russia's escort fighters could not fly in the area because of their short range.

Thus, Russia would need quick reinforcement by the air forces from other regions, with the possible exception of the Far Eastern group. However, the Western part of Russia has too few suitable airfields, and those available do not have enough aircraft shelters. This could lead to an unacceptable concentration of aircraft in the open on the ground, where they could incur heavy losses from air strikes. To alleviate this problem and extend the combat range of the AFRF, access to Belarussian and Ukrainian airfields and infrastructure would be vital.

The Southwestern direction is characterized by high mountain ridges, narrow valleys, and few and vulnerable communication lines. These conditions rigidly confine ground force maneuvers, which are extremely vulnerable to air strikes, hampering both offensive and counter-offensive operations. Thus, air forces may have a decisive role in blocking hostile penetration and providing close support to troops, although the terrain and weather could severely limit operations of any aircraft other than close-support Su-25s and combat helicopters. The Russian Air Force would operate from North Caucasus airfields, and would be highly effective in slowing down and sometimes paralyzing hostile forces until Russian ground forces can be brought to the combat area. Reinforcements would not be needed for the AFRF; it could quickly gain air superiority. Moreover, the Air Force would be capable of effective strikes against Turkish or Iranian airfields and other military targets lacking an adequate air defense, and the Air Force would have no problem in eliminating the naval and amphibious forces of potential opponents in the Black and Caspian seas.

The Southern direction presents greater possibilities to employ long- and medium-range aircraft over the "buffer zone" to strike isolated targets that are weakly defended by air defenses. The mountainous terrain (similar to Afghanistan) makes strikes by heavy aircraft hardly effective enough to justify their expense. Combined operations of airborne forces, helicopters, and tactical aircraft would be the most efficient form of combat in mountains and deserts. However, because of range limitations and coordination problems, this would require the redeployment of air forces from other regions, and would present enormous obstacles in terms of basing, maintenance, supplies, and command and control.

In sum, at present the Air Force structure, its mix of aircraft and weapon types, the industrial support, the deployment pattern, basing infrastructure, maintenance capabilities, command, control, communications, and intelligence (C3I) systems, and redeployment capabilities are woefully inadequate to respond to the regional contingencies of the new military doctrine.

The Reform Agenda

The rapid reform of the Russian Federation's armed forces is a matter of great importance and urgency. They must be brought into line with real threats and with the economic resources of the state. With this purpose in mind, a three-stage process of restructuring the armed forces has been worked out and is being implemented.

The first stage, which took place in 1992, was to define a new structure and enact laws that regulate the activities of the Army and the Navy. In the second stage, which will last until 1996, the main efforts will be to complete five tasks:

- to form groups of forces on Russian territory according to their purpose and missions;
- to complete the withdrawal to Russia of the forces stationed beyond its frontiers;
- to reduce the armed forces to the level decided upon;

- to continue the transition to a system of mixed recruitment; and
- to establish a basic structure for the armed forces after 1995. This stage is the most important part of the reform process.

In the final stage, which will take place from 1995 to 2000, the armed forces will be reorganized, the transition to a system of mixed recruitment will be completed, and new groups of forces and new military infrastructure will be established on the territory of the Russian Federation. The organization of the armed forces will be strengthened by the formation of compatible structures for forces operating in the same or adjoining regions, using the same or closely-related weapons and military equipment, and carrying out related or integrated missions. The improved organization of the armed services and their branch structures should enhance the efficiency of command systems, avoid redundant functions, reduce the probability of mutual obstruction, simplify the coordinated action of the forces and, ultimately, lead to a reduction in the number of types of weapons and equipment.

The plan for the structural reform of the armed forces of the Russian Federation includes changes in the number of armed services, their relative roles and size, their internal composition, force levels, deployment policies, and strategic and operational planning. Such sweeping changes are needed for several reasons:

First, the military property and assets of the former armed forces of the USSR were divided among its successor states, leaving the Russian Federation with aircraft from the second strategic echelon. The most combat-ready, mission-capable and best manned and equipped units—including 30–40 percent of the latest, fourth-generation aircraft—had been based outside Russia. Thus, the proportion of Air Force equipment with fly-by-wire controls and the survivability of aircraft on the ground have been considerably decreased.

Second, in the past, the first priority had been to develop the infrastructure of territory with first strategic echelon forces, while infrastructure on Russian territory was of secondary significance. Of the most modern airfields, 44 in Central and Eastern Europe and 94 in the other former Soviet republics have been lost, leaving Russia with about 90 airfields. Of these, fewer than half may be first-class; even these require considerable enhancement with support, shelters, and maintenance facilities.

Third, for developing countries, air power represents a "conventional deterrent" which in the future may play the same role that nuclear weapons play now. The plans and policies of the political and military leadership of the principal Western countries reflect their profound belief in this proposition, and their understanding of the role of air power in warfare and national security. As the capabilities of combat aircraft have developed, the importance of air forces in ensuring security and military power has grown commensurably. In many ways, the effectiveness of air strikes will determine the subsequent military operations of the warring sides. Hence, combat aircraft are regarded as an ultimate weapon, particularly in the first hours of war. Naturally, the opponent's combat aircraft are a first priority target for destruction with offensive strikes.

In addition, as noted earlier, air transport enables ground forces to rapidly and flexibly react to threats from any direction. Such flexibility is important for any great power, but absolutely crucial for Russia with its vast territory, uncertain future threats and contingencies, widely-separated potential theaters of military operations, inadequate rail and road networks, and very unevenly distributed industrial, maintenance, and supply infrastructures.

The plan for restructuring the AFRF addresses these needs. It is constrained by two limitations: first, Russian combat aircraft holdings in Europe should not exceed the ceiling established by the CFE Treaty; and second, the number of Air Force personnel must be commensurate with the personnel strengths of the armed forces of industrialized Western nations.

Some organizational innovations planned for the structure of the Air Force include:

- The formation of the new air command system at the operational and strategic levels;
- A reduction in the number of air armies, divisions, and regiments;
- The development of an appropriate Air Force basing and maintenance system. This involves creating permanent, well-protected, technically sophisticated basing, storage, and maintenance facilities in the central part of Russia; and organizing highly mobile air formations that can reinforce the regional aircraft groups, permitting a reduction in regional headquarters, basing, and maintenance costs.
- In 1993–1994 the general reorganization of the Air Force is to be completed, with all formations, units, and institutions placed under one of four air commands: long-range, front-line, military-transport, or reserves and training.

This structure will permit an efficient, centralized system for controlling the Air Force both in peacetime and in case of a military conflict, and will reduce the management apparatus, including the Air Force Commands in the military districts, by 15–20 percent. The establishment of frontal aviation and reserves and training commands will be an important step toward improving operational control over the troops. The functions of the Frontal Aviation Command will include organizing the military training of units following a single pattern for air combat operations and planning for aircraft maintenance during a war. The Reserves and Training Command will concentrate on training pilots; maintaining reserve aircraft, weapons, and equipment in adequate condition to be quickly restored to service; and crash-course training of flight personnel and engineering staff during periods of mobilization. Placing these functions under a single leadership will permit the most effective training of Air Force reserves both in peacetime and in case of a military conflict.

The restructuring of the Air Force ought to be carried out simultaneously with the restructuring, reduction, and redeployment of Russia's armed forces as a whole. However, the government cannot afford this simultaneous restructuring because of the deep economic crisis and industrial collapse, high inflation, competing military and civilian priorities, and the transformation of the economy. Moreover, excessively rapid demobilization of the existing command structures, support units, and maintenance pipelines could lead to a loss of control over the forces.

Implementing the AFRF Reform

Several very important areas of the AFRF reform require major effort and funding. These are basing infrastructure and regional deployment; reserves, training, and storage; command and control structure and systems; air force mobility and airlift capabilities; and industrial production and repair capacities and the associated issue of future force levels.

AFRF BASING, INFRASTRUCTURE, AND DEPLOYMENT PROBLEMS
Air Force units and formations must use airfields, matériel reserves, command posts, radar stations, communication systems, and local resources. The complex of these infrastructure components in a certain

region or area forms a basing system. Basing systems should promote a high level of combat-readiness and ensure the shortest flight time to targets. They should also prevent the destruction of aircraft on air-fields and ensure stable control, uninterrupted coordination, and effective maintenance. A basing system must support the specific functions and tasks assigned to the specific types of aircraft. The air-field network constitutes the core of the basing system; it includes the complex of main and alternative airfields, maneuver airfields, infras-tructure components, communication links, depots and storage facil-ities, etc., that comprise airfield junctions and regions.

Unfortunately, the AFRF's current deployment is defined much more by the basing infrastructure of Russia when it was part of the USSR than by new contingency planning, Air Force reforms, or the new military doctrine.

About 70 percent of AFRF aircraft, including training, reserve, and transport planes, are deployed in the European part of Russia, where 15 percent are assigned to the Northwestern strategic direction, 25 percent to the Western, and 30 percent to the Southwestern direction. Of the 30 percent that lie beyond the Ural Mountains, 10 percent are oriented toward China or Central Asia, and 20 percent toward the Far East. For combat aircraft, the ratio west and east of the Urals is 60:40. For long-range aviation, including medium-range bombers, the ratio is 40:60; for frontal aviation 65:35, and for transport aviation 80:20. (For information on Air Force aircraft as a share of all Russian military aircraft, see Table 2.1, and for information on the types of aircraft in service with the Air Force, the Air Defense, the Naval Air, and Strategic Force, see Table 2.2.)

This deployment is distorted. More aircraft are needed in the North Caucasus military district, oriented to the Transcaucasus, Tur-key, and Iran. Fewer aircraft would suffice for the Northwestern and Far Eastern directions. With centrally located basing areas and pre-positioned war matériel in the main strategic directions, a larger pro-portion of the Air Force could be stationed at invulnerable central bases from which aircraft could be redeployed to threatened regions.

In addition to problems of distribution, Russia's basing system barely meets the requirements of modern operations. The disin-tegration of the Soviet Union, the division of military property among the newly created independent states, and the current economic crisis in Russia have been particularly damaging to the European part of Russia. About two-thirds of all aircraft are located only 200–300 km from Russia's borders; within this region, long-range and military-transport aircraft are concentrated at an unacceptably small number of bases.

Table 2.1. Russian Combat Aircraft by Service and Deployment

	Deployed in Russia			Deployed Abroad			Total Holdings		
	Europe	Asia	Total	Europe	Asia	Total	Europe	Asia	Total
CFE Types									
Air Force									
In Russia	1,260	800	2,060	220	0	220	1,480	800	2,280
In former Soviet Republics	0	0	0	120	0	120	120	0	120
Air Defense Force									
In Russia	610	430	1,040	0	0	0	610	430	1,040
In former Soviet Republics	0	0	0	0	0	0	0	0	0
Naval Air Force									
Fighter/attack	207	25	232	63	0	63	270	25	295
Medium bombers	62	100	162	94	0	94	156	100	256
Strategic Force									
Medium bombers	210	295	505	0	0	0	210	295	505
In Storage	1,050	450	1,500	0	0	0	1,050	450	1,500
Total	3,399	2,100	5,499	497	0	497	3,896	2,100	5,996
Holdings reported at the CFE information exchange, December 15, 1993:							**3,921**		
Non-CFE Types									
Strategic Force									
Strategic bombers	59	88	147	0	0	0	59	88	147
Naval Air Force									
Strategic bombers	81	30	111	0	0	0	81	30	111
Total	140	118	258	0	0	0	140	118	258
Total Holdings	**3,539**	**2,218**		**497**	**0**	**497**	**4,036**	**2,218**	**6,254**

Source: "IDDS Almanac 1994." (The Air Force's 2,280 aircraft deployed in Russia are estimated by Alexei Arbatov. The other holdings are estimated by IDDS.)

Notes: Russian combat aircraft holdings are split between those based in European Russia (all military districts west of the Urals and the Northern and Baltic fleets) and those based in Asian Russia (all military districts east of the Urals and the Pacific fleet). Russian forces deployed abroad are in former Soviet Republics or in former Warsaw Pact countries.

"CFE Types" include fighter, attack, interceptor, and medium-bomber aircraft. (For a complete listing of aircraft covered by the CFE Treaty, see "IDDS Almanac 1994.") Strategic bombers not covered by the CFE Treaty are counted above as "Non-CFE Types." For a complete listing of Russia's combat aircraft holdings by type, see Table 2.2.

Table 2.2. Russian Combat Aircraft by Service and Type

| | Air Force | | Air | Naval | Strategic | | |
	Russia	Abroad	Defense	Air	Force	Stored	Total
CFE Types							
MiG-29	450						450
MiG-23	420		390			400	820
MiG-31	340						340
MiG-27	320			30		240	590
Su-24	320	80		127		100	627
Su-27	190		240				190
MiG-25	80	40	200			150	270
Su-17	80			50		250	380
Su-25	80			88		100	268
Su-15			210				0
Tu-26				173	180	40	393
Tu-16				72	180		252
Tu-22				21	95	20	136
Yak-28					40		40
MiG-21						200	200
Non-CFE Types							
Tu-95				61	147		208
Tu-142				50			50
Total	**2,280**	**120**	**1,040**	**672**	**642**	**1,500**	**5,214**

Source: "IDDS Almanac 1994." (The Air Force's 2,280 aircraft deployed in Russia are estimated by Alexei Arbatov. The other holdings are estimated by IDDS.)
Note: Three hundred forty MiG-31s formally assigned to the Air Defense are counted with the Air Force's holdings due to their dual fighter-attack/interceptor capability.

As aircraft previously stationed abroad have been withdrawn to Russian territory, basing density has greatly increased. The lack of reinforced concrete shelters has made it much more difficult to protect aircraft at airfields; and the prolonged use of concrete air strips has made their operating condition critical. Hardened shelters and earthen walls on airfields protect only 50 percent of the frontal aircraft, 70 percent of the long-range aircraft, and 30 percent of the military-transport aircraft. Once all aircraft return from abroad, only 35 percent of aircraft on airfields will be protected. A program to prepare airfields for the stationing of strategic bombers has been virtually halted, as has the construction of administrative and technical service buildings on airfields.

The integrity of the structure of the state communication network has been destroyed and the capabilities of command-and-control systems in all the strategic regions significantly lowered. The existing system of storage sites can store less than 50 percent of the accumulated stocks. The store houses are not reliably protected against enemy action, and many are obsolete and do not meet safety requirements. The aircraft repair facilities cannot repair four types of aircraft, one type of helicopter, and 14 types of aircraft engines currently in use by the Air Force. About 500 million rubles (in 1991 prices) would be needed to fully provide for repair and maintenance.

About 45 percent of airfields with runways of 1,800 meters or longer urgently need repair and reconstruction. In addition, the creation of Air Force groups in new basing regions necessitates new construction of properly equipped airfields with reinforced concrete shelters, barracks, housing, and air force control and maintenance systems.

In 1993, only 40 percent of the needed housing construction was financed, even though 26,000 Air Force officers lack the most basic housing; this number will rise to 40,000 when all of the former Soviet troops are withdrawn from abroad.

There are many obstacles to the resolution of these problems—first and foremost, the government's lack of financial resources. Yet these problems must be resolved to maintain current levels of combat readiness and fighting capacity, let alone increase them. A promising method is to create aircraft basing regions. The idea is to provide the whole complex of services, including operational, technical, and support services, for both the aircraft that are located in a given region on a permanent basis and those which may be redeployed in a given direction during a crisis. The core of the new aircraft basing regions must be new air bases developed at the main existing airfields for long-range, front-line, and military-transport aviation located more than 300 km from Russian borders. The distinctive characteristic of the new bases will be their ability to perform diverse and universal functions related to operational, technical and rear services. They will be able to maintain all types of front-line aircraft, as well as long-range and military-transport aircraft at airfields earmarked for these roles.

Such air bases will be the hub of aircraft basing regions or junctions, and will promote the smooth functioning of all the airfields attached to them. The bases should be able to accommodate permanently five or six squadrons (two regiments) of frontal aircraft, and should be prepared to support units and formations of strategic and transport aircraft. They should be able to carry out all the functions needed for the combat, technical, and logistic maintenance of units equipped with any type of aircraft used by the frontal aviation. They will require permanent, efficient supply and maintenance facilities.

In the case of full-scale maneuvers, civilian airfields would be included in the aircraft basing regions, which could provide all servicing. In addition, Russia should conclude bilateral and multilateral agreements with the CIS states for basing Russian Air Force units on their territory and facilitating a comprehensive system of Air Force control and maintenance.

To increase the effectiveness of reserve aircraft maintenance, the main airfields must be equipped with universal centralized systems for refueling and electrical power; the communication systems at the airfields must be linked to the network of trunk lines; and the reserve units must be provided with up-to-date computer systems and a unified land-based means of air control. While combat units must be cut by half, maintenance units should be reduced by no more than 20 percent to establish a proper balance.

To enhance the maneuverability, mobility, and flexibility of the Air Force, the main commands must be separated from the units of technical, maintenance, and other operational services, including radio-technical, chemical, and meteorological services, and units responsible for protection against weapons of mass destruction. These separated units can be incorporated into the structure of the Supreme High Command of the Air Force, aircraft basing regions, or air bases.

By 1995, new air armies will be formed in several new strategic regions, particularly in the Western and Southwestern directions, so that one air army (or group) will form part of the armed forces in each strategic direction: Northwest, West, Southwest, South, East Siberia, and Far East. These air armies will be assigned missions of reconnaissance, air cover, and support, as well as close air support of friendly ground troops and deep strikes against the enemy's rear. Their combat forces will vary with the importance of the strategic region and the character of warfare and Air Force missions there. These air armies will enable the Air Force to perform missions in local wars and regional conflicts. To wage a larger regional war, comparable to the Gulf War, the air armies will need substantial reinforcement from the other regional air armies of Russia and from storage bases.

TRAINING AND RESERVES

The experience of World War II and of more recent local and regional wars has shown that it is nearly impossible to accomplish even regional tasks without highly trained combat aircraft reserves. This is especially important in view of the reductions in the Russian Air Force. The AFRF needs a new system for developing and training reserves, as well as a new mobilization system, adapted to the current foreign and internal situation.

A first-line reserve will be formed relatively soon, building on units withdrawn from abroad and aircraft taken from units being demobilized. This will be a well-trained reserve that can be deployed in any strategic direction. A second-line reserve will consist of aircraft that are maintained in a combat-ready state at special storage bases for reserve aircraft. It will take some time to create this reserve force; it requires the formation of command structures, additional coordination between air regiments of different branches, and preparation for carrying out combat missions. Other reserve forces may be created as well, based on the existing centers and training colleges of the Air Force. For example, military transport aircraft can be reinforced by heavy transport aircraft from the Ministry of Air Transportation, which can carry troops and light weapons.

Formerly, all such plans were laid out in documents that were constantly up-dated; such plans were also rehearsed in practice. Today, organizational and financial difficulties have made it difficult to implement this reserve system. Nonetheless, the future of the Russian Air Force depends on the reform of the training system. The most urgent task is to bring the number and structure of Air Force training schools into line with current needs. Schools that do not play a decisive role in the training system as a whole must be closed, and admission of first-year students must be suspended, so that the necessary reductions are more gradual and less painful. Senior students will either continue their studies where they are or be transferred to other schools in their fields of interest. Training in specialties that were previously handled abroad will be started at some schools (the Tambov and Irkutsk High Air-Engineering Schools, the former Yeysk High Military Pilots' School, the Chelyabinsk High Military Air Navigators' School).

The list of specialties should be reviewed—it seems excessively long. Specialties and qualifications should be as close to their civilian counterparts as possible so that officers who retire can more easily find jobs.

In the future it will be necessary to create a unified system of aircraft and personnel training. In some special schools (which provide general education as well) teenagers will receive initial flight training, providing a good base for entering a military college. (Two such schools were opened in 1990 in Yeysk and Barnaul.) In aviation schools, a five-year course is planned: the first three and a half years will be devoted to fundamental theoretical education and physical training; then the students will learn flight skills using special training planes. It will also be necessary to retrain former graduates to use new weapons and equipment. As at present, special training air centers will serve this purpose.

The need to build aviation reserves has created a need for bases for reserve aircraft. These will be oriented toward the long-term conservation of aircraft, and preparation to complement the aviation units and formations to be newly formed.

At present, the Air Force has about 1,000 combat and combat-trainer aircraft of different types stationed at reserve bases. When fully manned and provided with ground facilities and matériel assets, each base will be capable of preparing the aircraft for one aviation regiment in about a week. At present, the capacity for preparing aircraft is much lower; the bases are far from fully manned or fully equipped. Many airplanes are being cannibalized; equipment and spare parts are stolen on a large scale in the absence of proper guarding and accounting. Still more aircraft are quickly degrading beyond repair without proper protection from the weather. The Central Asian storage areas, with their dry and even climate, were lost; storage areas in Siberia and the European part of Russia are among the worst imaginable places for sophisticated aircraft.

In the future, reserve bases should become Centers for the Preparation of Reserves, and should be equipped with training, supply and maintenance facilities, and adequate stores. Proper attention and resources devoted to this issue could have a major, beneficial effect on the Air Force's posture in 10–15 years, given the greatly reduced production of new aircraft and the limited resources available to keep aircraft combat ready and to cover the personnel and operational costs of active duty pilots and support personnel who are engaged in extensive flight training.

COMMAND AND CONTROL: STRUCTURE AND SYSTEMS

The disintegration of the Soviet Union and the creation of the CIS led to the disruption of the Air Force command architecture. Former Air Force Commander-in-Chief Air Marshal E. Shaposhnikov was appointed as Commander-in-Chief of the CIS Combined Armed Forces (CAF), which included the Air Force of the former USSR. Nonetheless, air force units were soon re-subordinated to the ministries of defense of the newly-created states where they were located, except in Russia. Russia's independent armed forces were created in the spring of 1992, creating a conflict in the authority between the Commonwealth's CAF and Russia's Ministry of Defense. A year later the CAF was disbanded, and the air forces deployed on Russia's territory were unequivocally placed under the command of the Russian Ministry of Defense and AFRF. This opened the way for the organizational and technical reform of the Air Force.

Reductions in AFRF force levels, the need for flexible redeployment, and the requirements of modern air warfare make command-and-control systems ever more important. As the Gulf War demonstrated, superior command-and-control is decisive and acts as a great force-multiplier, particularly for air forces. The command-and-control system must be stable, permanent, rapid, secret, and always ready for combat. A central command provides unified guidance of the unit staffs and structures that are directly involved in the command and control of the air forces. However, decentralization must be possible if top command posts are put out of action, or if communications between command posts are suppressed.

Flexibility and stability of command and control can be achieved using a wide network of stationary and mobile command posts, interchangeable command systems, anti-jamming devices and redundant command-and-communication channels, and reserve and decoy command-and-control posts. Readiness and speed can be achieved by permanently manning command posts and using an automated warning and information system; in addition, during war, staff at all levels should be able to rapidly deploy command structures.

These tasks can only be accomplished if the current command-and-control system of the Air Force is reformed and further developed. Both organizational and technical improvements are needed. Organizational changes are needed in the subsystems commanding and controlling the combat forces and assets, the supply and maintenance forces and facilities, personnel training, scientific research, and other areas.

The reduction of the AFRF will affect the organization of command and control. While air armies, units, and inventories will have to be transferred from one theater to another, command-and-control assets (communications, technical services, and automated systems) generally lack mobility since the possibility of moving them by air is extremely limited. The only solution to this problem would be to organize and deploy the Air Force's combat command and control systems and assets along territorial lines. Air armies, units, and individual aircraft would use the local system of command-and-control posts, whose staffs would be well acquainted with the theater and trained in the command and control of all aircraft used by the AFRF. This would eliminate the need for command-and-control personnel to adapt to new conditions, simplify combined action with the Air Force units, and alleviate the need to transport technical assets.

When the regional basing principle is adopted, command and control of supply and maintenance forces and facilities will also be organized on territorial lines. An important improvement in Air Force command and control will be a reduction of the number of links in the command system; it will use a corps-brigade-squadron structure, instead of the old army-division-regiment-squadron structure.

Air Force command and control may also be enhanced by equipping command-and-control posts at all levels with advanced technical communication assets, regulations for technical servicing, and automated control. A priority is to develop a single automated command-and-control system for the entire Air Force. This should include command-and-control subsystems for the strategic, frontal, military transport, and reserve aviation and training. In the future, when the Armed Forces of the Russian Federation are streamlined into a triad, an additional command-and-control subsystem will be established for Air Defense formations.

A single automated command-and-control system for the Air Force is already being developed. However, the introduction of an integrated system of this kind, with subsystems oriented toward branch commands, could hamper the transition to territorial combat command-and-control systems capable of controlling the aircraft of all branches in any strategic region. An even greater problem is the cost; it will be quite expensive to build a new command-and-control system and to modernize the existing automated system. At present, only 4 percent of the funds allocated to the AFRF modernization are earmarked for this purpose.

An automated system depends on a data bank of various forms of information, including radar data, and reliable communication channels to ensure the transmission of this information. Given the low quality of wire communication channels, the inadequate space links (less than 30 percent of what is needed), the obsolete radio communication assets, equipped with too few anti-jamming devices, the lack of protection of communication nodes, and the poor state of the radar systems used for aircraft control, it is essential to hasten the construction of a new integrated automated radar perimeter along Russia's borders. Also, it would be prudent to modernize communication nodes with a better anti-jamming capacity, to provide the aircraft units (including individual aircraft) with space communication assets, and to re-equip all the strategic regions with a system of hardened command-and-control posts and communication nodes.

MOBILITY AND AIRLIFT

Mobility is probably the highest priority for the Russian armed forces; it may also be the most difficult and costly aspect of Russia's military reform.[4] Since the Air Force is by far the most mobile armed service, the need for mobility implies that the Air Force will play a much greater role in the armed forces, but also creates serious problems and competing demands within the AFRF.

For the Air Force, mobility takes three main forms: the mobility of the combat aircraft themselves; the availability of transit routes and basing infrastructure in the areas of redeployment; and the Air Force's ability to transport other components of the armed services.

The mobility of frontal aviation aircraft is a serious problem mainly because close support strike aircraft, fighters, and fighter-bombers—in particular the older aircraft (the Su-25, MiG-23, Su-17, and MiG-27)—have short ranges and cannot refuel in the air. If they are to be redeployed to distant locations they must have intermediate airfields for refueling and maintenance; such airfields may not always be available or properly supplied. Frontal bombers (such as the Su-24) have a much longer range, but only the later models are equipped for air-refueling. New fourth-generation fighters (the MiG-29 and Su-

---

[4] To some extent, the issues of mobility are addressed above in discussions of basing and command-and-control reorganization.

27), and fighters and frontal aircraft of the next generation (the Su-27M, which is also called the Su-35, and the Su-34), will be superbly suited for inter-theater mobility, but for economic reasons, they will not be introduced fast enough to solve the problem in the 1990s. Moreover, a shortage of tanker aircraft will restrict the mobility of new and next-generation frontal aircraft. Thus, it is hard to choose among larger appropriations for tanker aircraft, combat aircraft, and transport aircraft.

A more difficult aspect of achieving high mobility is the transportation of maintenance, storage, and supply facilities. For instance, with adequate refueling one air regiment (30–40 airplanes) can redeploy its aircraft in several hours, but moving its support facilities would take 400 railcars 15 to 30 days or 500 sorties of military-transport aircraft, which is not feasible since they must transport troops and weapons. Hence, regional deployment areas must have advance storage and maintenance facilities available for supporting aircraft.

In addition, the AFRF must establish several inter-regional air routes to connect Russia's Western and Eastern regions. These will be used for large-scale redeployment of frontal aviation and air transportation of troops and equipment among different regions. All supplies and technical reserves must be prepared in advance at the main airfields along these air routes. The airfields must be provided with the whole complex of engineering assistance and navigation aids. Such airfields will constitute prototypes of the future multipurpose air bases, which would perform various combat-support, technical, and rear maintenance functions for aircraft of all types. The creation of such air bases would increase the mobility of the Air Force units, and ultimately reduce maintenance expenses.

The missions to be assigned to military-transport aviation, especially during periods of high political tension and in the early phases of war, far exceed present capabilities. All Russian strategic transport aviation is now capable of lifting only one paratroop division in two sorties. Russia's transport aircraft assets currently include about 200 Il-76, 30 An-124 ("Ruslan"), 50 An-22 ("Antei"), and around 130 tactical transport airplanes (An-72, An-26, and An-12). Airlift capabilities must be increased at least three-fold to provide the mobility envisioned by the new doctrine.

The Il-106 aircraft, with its enhanced lift capacity, range, and air-refueling capability, is one solution to the problem. Its aggregate lift capacity will be three times that of the Il-76 aircraft. (Production of the Il-76 is being discontinued because they were manufactured in Tashkent, the capital of Uzbekistan.) To triple lift capacity in a decade, Russia would have to produce 28–30 of the Il-106 type per year after 2000, when it is expected to enter serial production. However, this level would completely deprive the Air Force of funds to modernize its other branches and would lead to a steep decline in its force levels and operational capabilities.

PRODUCTION, PROCUREMENT, AND REPAIR CAPACITIES
The military-technical policy of the Air Force is at present directed at the development and procurement of highly effective, economical and competitive prototypes of aircraft and weapons, the optimal mix of flying platforms and weapon systems, coordinated development of command-and-control systems and assets and of supply and main-tenance systems.

Russia inherited about 60 percent of the Soviet Union's air force, including a relatively large share of aged aircraft, compelling it to form basically new aviation groups and units, especially in the West.[5] Eighty percent of the military aircraft production industry remained in Russia—enough to sustain the production level of the early 1990s. However, most procurement programs have been hit by drastic cuts in the funding of research, development, experimental design, and pro-duction of combat aircraft. Overall, experimental prototypes of aircraft and weapons and scientific research projects were cut by 70 percent from the end of the Cold War. In 1991, aircraft procurement had already been cut by 46 percent for frontal aviation and by 41 percent for bombers and transports. In 1992 the defense budget was cut to 25–30 percent of the 1991 level (all figures, here and below, in constant prices). Moreover, due to increases in outlays for personnel costs, housing, and retirement, weapons procurement dropped from 39 percent of the budget in 1990 to 18 percent in 1992. As a result, funding for procurement of frontal aviation aircraft in 1992 was only 21 percent of the 1991 level, while that for bombers and transports was 36 percent. In 1993 funds for procurement of frontal aviation

---

[5] The other CIS republics inherited 37 percent of the USSR's MiG-29s, 23 percent of its Su-27 fighters, 43 percent of its Il-76 transport planes, and the bulk of its Tu-95Ms and Tu-160 heavy bombers. None of these republics can maintain these sophisticated machines; many cannot even fly them.

aircraft were reduced by another 31 percent, and in 1994 funding will be cut another 23 percent.

As a result, whereas in the early 1980s the USSR produced an average of 400–450 frontal aviation aircraft and 100 heavy military airplanes each year, in 1993–1994 only a total of 20–23 fighters, fighter-bombers, and strike aircraft are being purchased for the Air Force, Air Defense, and Navy combined. Production of the Su-24, Su-25, and MiG-29 was stopped; production of the MiG-31 was brought down to single numbers; and procurement of the latest models of the Su-27 will probably drop below 14–16 aircraft per year. Procurement of the Tu-160, Tu-142, and Tu-95 has also been halted.

About 340 long-range MiG-31 interceptors belong to the Air Defense, but if the two services are merged—a move that is now under intensive debate—these would constitute a large and modern portion of the AFRF forces, and would materially affect its deployment and operational planning and procurement requirements.

Given the limited service life of older aircraft, by the year 2000 the AFRF will be equipped with TU-160 and TU-95MS strategic bombers, TU-22M medium-range bombers, Su-24 frontal bombers, MiG-29 and Su-27 fighters, Su-25 close support ground attack aircraft, reconnaissance aircraft of frontal and strategic aviation, and An-124 and Il-76 military transport planes.

The procurement funds allocated for 1993–1994 are not sufficient even for the normal planned replacement of aircraft lost through peacetime attrition, to say nothing of replacing obsolete aircraft with contemporary models. This is illustrated by the changing allocations for aerospace research and development bureaus and aircraft building industries, and by the percentage of the capacity of military design bureaus and major production plants occupied with defense contracts. If the trend is not reversed soon, the aircraft building industries may collapse after 1995, and Russia's command of advanced military-aerospace technology may be lost after 1996. It would then require decades to restore the production capacity and level of military technology that, through concentrated national effort since the early 1930s, have made the USSR and then Russia one of the world's leading aerospace powers.

Modernization will be impeded by the fact that a number of production facilities lie beyond Russia's borders. The factories that produce military-transport aircraft (Il-76, An-70, and An-72) and their engines are in Ukraine and Uzbekistan; there is now some difficulty in obtaining supplies of spare parts and electronic equipment for the aircraft. For the time being, these problems can be solved through inter-state agreement, but Russia must manufacture new aircraft and components of these types itself.

Another problem is that only 61 percent of the military aircraft repair facilities of the former USSR are located in Russia. Unique repair workshops have been lost to newly sovereign states. For instance, air-to-surface missiles were repaired only in Estonia. About 60 percent of Su-24 aircraft usually underwent repairs in Lithuania; Su-25s were repaired exclusively in Lithuania and Georgia, and TU-95s only in Ukraine. An effort is now being made to alleviate this problem by organizing aircraft repair at Russian plants, but shortages of funds and supplies make it impossible to make all the necessary repairs.

The goals of the Air Force modernization program are shaped by a mass withdrawal of obsolete aircraft over the next 10 years, new strategic and operational requirements, and advances in technology. The combat capability of the fighter aviation will be enhanced by the modernizations to the Su-27 and MiG-29 aircraft. Modernization of the Su-27 is expected to increase its combat capability by 40 percent. The next generation of fighter-bomber, the Su-27M, should enter production in 1994 or 1995; its combat advantage will be 2.5 times that of current aircraft of this type (Su-17 and MiG-27) and 6-8 times that of prior-generation aircraft (MiG-23). The main problem with current fighter-bombers is their relatively short combat radius. The new Su-27M, which can strike targets 1,500 km behind the front line, will eliminate this deficiency and provide the capacity to reach targets throughout the whole depth of the theater operation. With the use of long-range missiles, the combat radius of the Su-27M may be increased to 2,500 km and with mid-air refueling to at least 4,500 km. In addition, it can fly missions at any time of day and night, under all weather conditions. It will also have low-observability features that facilitate penetration of enemy air defenses, and thus will not require fighter escorts.

After 2000, the combat effectiveness of frontal aviation will be enhanced by the introduction of a new multi-role close support aircraft as a follow-on to the current Su-25 attack airplanes. The new aircraft will have low-observability features, an on-board defense complex providing fire protection, and the capability to identify both ground and air targets. It will be equipped with multiple launchers for air-to-air and air-to-ground rockets, as well as state-of-the-art takeoff and landing gear and maintenance equipment. An outstanding feature of this aircraft is its great versatility in engaging ground and air targets. This is particularly important when the requirements for strike and assault forces may vary at different stages of a conflict. This aircraft would be able to hit air, ground and near-shore naval targets with equal effectiveness.

By 2000, the introduction of the Su-34, a new two-seat multi-role frontal bomber, will greatly enhance the capabilities of tactical and middle-range bombers across the whole spectrum of the theater ranges, radically improving the inter-theater mobility of the AFRF. Its range without external fuel tanks will be about 4,000 km. External tanks and in-flight refueling will make its range practically unlimited. At present, to re-deploy a tactical aircraft from the Far East to Central Asia may require as long as a week, due to sparse intermediate airfields, shortages of fuel supplies, and the pilots' need for rest. In contrast, the Su-34 will be able to re-deploy in one day, and its pilots can alternately rest in flight. Its fully computerized and redundant navigation and targeting system will provide pinpoint strike accuracy and 250 km stand-off attack capability. The aircraft is equipped with a terrain-contour matching system and can fly at 1,400 km per hour at low altitude. Increased maneuverability is provided by forward fins. For protection against anti-aircraft guns, the pilot's cabin has armor plating. The overall Su-34 combat capability will exceed that of the Tu-22 aircraft by 2.7 times and that of the Su-24 even more. It will eventually replace frontal bombers, medium-range bombers, and naval missile-carrying medium-range aircraft.

Unfortunately, a lack of funds to purchase modified fourth-generation aircraft (Su-27, MiG-31, and MiG-29) and to introduce sufficient numbers of fifth-generation planes (Su-27M, Su-34, and Su-25 follow-on) in a timely way will lead to a reduction in AFRF force levels to numbers far below the planned reductions. Inadequate funding for maintenance, repair and the development of basing infrastructure and storage, as well as mass retirement of officers and draft evasion may draw down the forces still further, undercutting the Air Force's ability to perform its assigned missions in the 1990s and beyond.

At present, the frontal aviation division of the Russian Air Force has 2,280 combat aircraft. Only 43 percent are fourth-generation aircraft introduced in the 1980s, which will remain in service until 2010–2015. The rest were produced in the 1970s and are to be withdrawn completely by the end of this decade or the first years of the next. Only the most recent models of the fourth-generation aircraft (Su-24M and Su-25M), given proper maintenance, might stay in service till 2010–2015. Thus, even if procurement continues at the present level in the 1990s and grows after the year 2000—neither of which is assured—AFRF holdings would decline from the present 2,280 to about 1,670 airplanes in 1997, 1,440 in 2000, 1,330 in 2005, 1,140 in 2010, and 870 by 2015.

This forecast ignores peacetime attrition, which is about 1.2 percent for the latest-generation aircraft and 2 percent for the older aircraft. These comparatively low attrition rates are explained by a drastic reduction in pilot flight training. In 1993–2000 cumulative attrition may lead to a loss of about 60 third-generation aircraft. The cumulative 1993–2015 attrition of fourth- and fifth-generation aircraft may come to 215 planes. It is difficult to incorporate AFRF attrition rates into the forecasted force levels, however, since many aircraft are retired before the end of their service life and transferred to base storage or simply parked at airfields without being flown. Moreover, Russian data on the subject are not public; nor are they always comparable to Western figures.[6]

The generally approved goal of the AFRF—to maintain its frontal aviation at the level of defense sufficiency—would not be feasible given the current procurement funding and yearly production. The only aircraft that may be produced in some quantity are new models of the Su-27, the new Su-27M, and, after the year 2000, the Su-34 frontal bomber, and a follow-on to the Su-25. As for the MiG-31, its production, if any, will barely compensate for annual attrition.

In order to maintain an inventory of 2,000 fighter and attack aircraft while replacing withdrawn MiG-23s, MiG-25s, MiG-27s, and Su-17s, Russia would have to produce annually, on average, 110–115 aircraft over the period 1994–2000. In 2000–2010, yearly production could drop to 60 planes, since the bulk of the force would be composed of relatively modern systems (MiG-29s, MiG-31s, and Su-27s), and only the withdrawn Su-24s and Su-25s would be replaced. But in 2010–2015, the annual production rate would have to rise to 80–85

---

[6] The Russian count is based on the average flying time per crash for each type of aircraft.

per year to fill a growing gap created by the removal of most MiG-31s, MiG-29s, and Su-27s. Russia's defense budget will not support these needed rates of production, especially in 1994–2000. Lower procurement during this period will shrink the frontal aviation force to about 1,440 aircraft—far below the 2,000 goal. To restore the desired force level by 2010, annual production would have to be higher than 110 aircraft throughout 2000–2010. This is scarcely possible even if Russia recovers from its economic and financial crisis by then.

The problem of maintaining the planned frontal aviation force level and sustaining sufficient production is aggravated by the need to fund production of other AFRF aircraft, including Tu-22M3 medium bombers, Il-106 heavy lift planes, and tanker aircraft; Su-27s and MiG-31s for Air Defense; new shore-based naval aircraft; helicopters for the ground forces; and various support aircraft for all the armed services.

These problems are deeply intertwined with economic reforms and domestic and foreign policies; they cannot be solved by any AFRF planning or budgeting. These issues are fundamentally a matter of national priorities, and must be addressed at the highest levels of the Ministry of Defense, and by the president, the Security Council, and the Federal Assembly of the Russian Federation.

Editor's Comment: Military Reform and the Air Force

The key issues concerning the future of the Russian Air Force are by no means confined to this service. In various forms and ways they are common to all of the armed services of the Russian Federation, and in a more general way to the whole of Russia's defense policy and the conduct of military reforms in 1992–1994.

The first and most fundamental deficiency in the current military reform program is Moscow's deep relaxation of political control over the military, leaving the armed forces virtually on their own during a time of profound changes within the armed forces and in their political, ideological, strategic and economic environment. The general disintegration of Russia's administrative structures and the growing autonomy of bureaucratic institutions have affected the defense establishment most; this is especially dangerous for a society that is making a transition to a market economy and democratic political system. Moreover, it has produced great confusion and misman-agement of the military reforms, created enormous additional hardships and complications for the Russian military, and undercut proper organization of retraining and housing for demobilized cadres, as well as hampered the orderly reduction and redeployment of forces, the resolution of military controversies with other republics, and the conversion of part of the defense industries. In the absence of a consistent foreign policy or budgetary guidance, the military reform is implemented largely through ad hoc adaptation of traditional military institutions, concepts, and functions to the severe budget lim-itations and new demographic, social, and ideological environment. The armed services and the General Staff departments are trying to preserve as much as possible of their strategic doctrines, deployment patterns, weapon holdings and missions at the expense of readiness, training, maintenance, and capabilities to perform new tasks.

The above military assessment of the strategic situation in the world and regional contingencies clearly reflects the natural proclivity of the military (by no means only the Russian military) to retain as much as possible of its traditional strategic roles and operational missions, giving only lip service to the new post–Cold War security realities. The military's interest in self-preservation determines its policy on force structure and force deployment (within maintenance and budgetary limitations) and drives threat assessment, rather than proceeding from threat analysis to deployment needs, force levels, and budget requirements. To an extent this is typical of all bureau-cratic organizations, but in Russia it has recently been elevated to almost an absolute degree, due to its domestic disintegration and unprecedented security uncertainties.

The dubious and shallow declarations of the top leaders and Foreign Ministry that Russia does not have any enemies or opponents abroad (a thesis that was included in the new military doctrine) put the military in a confusing position. Since an actual or potential ad-versary is always concrete, with its specific forces and geostrategic position, such political "guidance" leaves the military with a bad choice: not to prepare for war at all (placing in question its very exis-tence), or to plan for war with all states that are near Russia, have their forces within reach of its territory, or may even remotely dispute Russia's interests. Naturally, the military has chosen the second option.

The military's inability to choose among numerous competing priorities has led it to spread its limited resources thinly, undermining its defense capabilities in all areas. But making such a choice entails substantial risks and is alien to huge bureaucratic institutions in general. It can be done only outside the defense establishment by a determined political leadership that is not afraid of responsibility.

Despite all the declarations that the United States, NATO, and the West are no longer Russia's enemies, but rather partners and even potential allies, Russia's military requirements (in particularly those of the Air Force) are still primarily driven by contingency planning for major war with the United States and its allies in the West and with the United States–Japanese coalition in the East. In a very simplified way it may be suggested that the drastic changes of 1985–1994 have prompted the military to change the relative priority of the West as a potential opponent from 80 percent to 60 percent. Probably the same is true of the Western contingency planners with regards to Russia.

The simple logic is that while NATO may not be an opponent now, it could be in the future. And since "they" possess huge military power, it is only prudent for Russia to hedge against uncertainty and retain defense capabilities and operational plans of its own. The sacred rule of the Cold War was that military capabilities, not political intentions, are to be taken into account; capabilities take many years to shift, while intentions may change overnight. This is still very much the thinking of U.S. defense planners and even more (although less publicly) of their Russian partners.

Hence, for all the drastic political changes of recent years, nothing has really changed in the fundamental military approaches to contingency planning. The only factors seriously affecting this planning are Russia's economic and financial crisis, the disbanding of the Warsaw Pact and disintegration of the Soviet Union, and the retreat of its military power from the center of Europe to within 400–500 km from the Kremlin. The Moscow Military District has become a front-line area of defense for the first time in many centuries.

This approach to contingency planning has created a dilemma. On the one hand, Russia cannot hope to seriously challenge the West militarily, to say nothing of the West united with former Soviet Warsaw Pact allies and some of the former USSR republics. Nothing but nuclear weapons could equalize this inequality of forces. Even if Russia keeps its frontal air forces at the level of 2,000 aircraft, they would be no match for NATO air power. The Russian military always considered NATO air power superior to its own, even when the Warsaw Pact provided 6,200 airplanes in Europe, the forward edge of the battle area was 1,500 km further west, and it enjoyed triple superiority over the West in ground forces and weapons. Planning a war with the West makes Russia's defense requirements virtually open-ended: whatever share of the limited resources is allocated to this contingency, the AFRF cannot even come close to a minimally sufficient defense capability, as is persuasively demonstrated by the above military assessments.

On the other hand, beside NATO (and a United States–Japanese alliance in the East) there is no conceivable contingency involving Russia's armed forces in the "near abroad" or immediately adjacent zones in the Southwest and South that could justify sustaining 2,000 or even 1,500 frontal aircraft. China might be an exception; it potentially presents a great military threat to Russia directly or to Kazakhstan, Kirgizstan, Tajikistan and Mongolia, which are important to Russia from a security point of view. But whether this hypothetical threat becomes actual depends to a very large extent on Russia's present massive arms and military technology sales to China, as well as its future relations with the "buffer" states and particularly Japan. In any event, this contingency belongs to the next decade and cannot justify the present force levels, especially since 60 percent of all AFRF assets and 65 percent of the frontal aviation are deployed at the Western strategic directions.

Actually, the present "strategic directions," which allegedly correspond to new security requirements, do not look much different from the old military districts and planned theaters of combat action, shrunk proportionately to the shrinkage of the Soviet empire. The same is true of force deployment and resource allocation among geographic regions, missions, and armed services. Mobility is a good concept, but it would not be very necessary under the present plans to preserve high force levels and substantial force deployments in six subregional theaters.

Obviously, a very different policy is needed for the military reform in general and the Air Force reform in particular. A radical redeployment and restructuring of the armed forces is required by the new security environment and contingencies. The European part of the former USSR, including Russia, was traditionally the area of most dense force concentration (on average about three-quarters of general purpose forces). It must become primarily the region of rear supply, storage and reserve forces location. This goes against expediency—infrastructure is needed and personnel prefer the west—but it fits the new strategic and political realities.

It is up to the political leadership to order the military not to plan a war with the United States, NATO or Japan. (The only exception is that Russia should continue to maintain its stable second-strike nuclear deterrent forces, as limited by Strategic Arms Reduction Talks (START) treaties.) Moreover, neither Russia nor Ukraine needs the weapons apportioned to them within CFE quotas (6,400 tanks and 3,450 aircraft for Russia, and 4,000 tanks and 1,000 aircraft for Ukraine). There is no outside threat to their territories in Europe, and they should not create perceptions of threat to each other. Russia could easily reduce its forces in this region to 500–800 aircraft (beside air defense) and 1,000–2,000 tanks; still less is needed (or can be maintained) by other republics.

Indeed, for the first time in Russian history there is no direct military threat to its European territory, nor should one emerge unless Russia provokes it by its own policy. It would be a great mistake for NATO to move east by accepting Eastern European countries and some republics of the former USSR if Russian military deployments and political actions do not threaten their security.

An Alternate Contingency Plan

The chief principle of the new security strategy for Russia should be to capitalize on the advantages of the present geopolitical situation and prevent its dangerous transformation. The double belt of Eastern European and former Western Soviet republics, 2,000 km wide, is the key to this strategy. Preserving this belt as a neutral territory, without foreign troops, bases, or facilities, and with a low concentration of indigenous armed forces, is the best guarantee both of the security of Russia's heartland and of Moscow's good relationships with both NATO and the Western European Union (WEU).

In turn, NATO should implement further cuts in armed forces in Europe and in the United States (foremost in tactical strike aircraft, which is the greatest concern for Russian military); refrain from expanding to the east; and persuade the nations there that their best protection is a policy of non-alignment, good relations with Russia, and a defensive (or non-offensive) military. Moscow's contribution to such an arrangement should be a deep reduction of forces in the European part of its territory and their restructuring along purely defensive guidelines. This area is to be its supply, storage, training, command-and-control, and reserve deployments area, protected by air defense units and a limited contingent of frontal aviation, as well as ground forces in defensive formations.

The main new deployment areas for Russian armed forces should be the North Caucasus, the South Urals, and the Far East. These new arms would correspond to the contingencies regarding Turkey, Iran, and China, and to the danger of the spread of Muslim fundamentalism in the North Caucasus and Central Asia. Neither the defense of Russian territory nor assistance to its allies among the former Soviet republics requires massive permanent offensive military deployments in these areas. Forward screening forces and a developed infrastructure of storage, fuel, and supplies for rapid reinforcements would suffice. Proper guarding and maintenance of this infrastructure, and air defense and protection of communications, would be sufficient and non-provocative.

The bulk of the rapid deployment force and emergency deployment force should be permanently deployed in the Ural and Volga military districts, as presently planned. But their numbers and composition may be different, and they should be provided with much better airlift and close air support. Instead of 11 planned heavy and light divisions, this force should consist of no more than 1–2 heavy and 3–4 light division equivalents. A sufficient group of forces, although much smaller than the 0.6 million troops of the 1970s and 1980s, should eventually be permanently deployed in the Transbaikal area and the Far East, due to the region's vast area and vulnerability.

To use the U.S. formulation of defense requirements, Russian conventional forces must be able to fight one and a half wars. This means that they may be called to implement large-scale theater-wide operations (comparable to Desert Storm) in one region (Central Asia or the Far East), for which mobile forces would provide rapid reinforcement from Ural or European basing areas. These forces (including frontal aviation) would be assigned the mission of reinforcing Russian-stationed forces in the Transbaikal and Far East strategic directions. They would also be able to help Russia's allied republics (first of all Kazakhstan) to repel a hypothetical aggression from across the border. These same mobile forces must also be able to implement a second, smaller-scale military action in another theater (the Transcaucasus or Central Asia), or in any region of the world as part of multilateral peace-enforcement or peace-keeping operations sponsored by the UN or CSCE (Conference on Security and Cooperation in Europe).

The Air Force should merge with the Air Defense and should have a much more prominent role. It should provide air defense in the European, Transbaikal and Far Eastern parts of the territory, long-range interdiction and ground support for Transcaucasus, Central Asian and Far Eastern contingencies, and strategic-tactical mobility for rapid deployment forces. For the European part of Russia 430 air defense interceptors would be more than adequate for the protection of the territory and control of the airspace. There is no apparent need for 1,330 frontal aviation airplanes in the European part of Russia, plus the 150 to be withdrawn from Germany, if no war is conceived against NATO or Russia's neutral neighbors to the West. Such a massive deployment consumes the scarce resources that are needed for mobility, basing, and supplies infrastructure in other regions, as well as proper storage facilities and reserve training. Besides, such a concentration (together with ground and rapid deployment forces) creates a perception of a reviving Russian threat in neighboring republics of the former USSR and in Eastern Europe.

Probably, 60–65 percent of the Air Force force in active service would suffice for Transcaucasus contingencies, training, and as a reserve to reinforce the Eastern and Southern strategic directions, or to participate in UN peacekeeping operations abroad. No frontal aviation (as opposed to air defense) is needed to cover the Northwestern or Western strategic directions. The removed aircraft may be partly redeployed to the East, or stored so that they can be used to sustain acceptable force levels in the next decade.

As for the East, 800 frontal aviation airplanes (in addition to 310 air defense interceptors) is also more than is needed at present, and may safely be reduced by 25 percent to save on maintenance, and reallocate funding to improve the basing and storage infrastructures, housing, and salaries. Saved resources could also be used to improve air-lift capabilities, tanker airplane fleets, and command-and-control systems.

Force Levels Strategy

The proposals outlined here are closely related to force levels strategy and industrial and technological policies. As discussed above, even if the AFRF can buy 20 frontal aircraft per year, which is unlikely, force levels will decrease steeply. After 2000, by when the economy may start to grow and inflation come under control, it would be necessary to produce 140–150 frontal aircraft annually to restore the 2,000 force level by 2010, or 110–120 aircraft per year to restore it by 2015. Such production rates are improbable.

But it is after 2000 that the international and strategic situation is most difficult to predict. It is then, not during the 1990s, that it might badly need some margin of security, including the decisive leverage of modern conventional forces: tactical air power and air defense. Thus, Russia should make the best of the "window of security" that provides Russia with a breathing space through the end of the 1990s. The post–Cold War world is in a period of transition and realignment; Russia, as weak as it is, does not face any tangible military threat and is surrounded by still weaker neutral or benign states. The point is to reduce active force levels much faster and much lower during the 1990s, to save resources, and improve long-neglected areas of support, maintenance, mobility, and personnel. This is the best way to preserve and enhance military and industrial potential to address unpredictable challenges to national security that might arise after 2000.

One way for the AFRF to implement this "force level maneuver" would be to withdraw from active service up to 50 percent of the relatively new airplanes (MiG-29, MiG-31, latest modifications of Su-24, Su-25, and Su-27) and put them in storage and first-line reserve training centers. If done during two years, this would draw down force levels by about 700 frontal aircraft (or 40 percent), leaving slightly more than 1,000 aircraft in service in 1996. Combined with the withdrawal of obsolete planes and the purchase of 20 planes per year, this would bring the force level to 740 aircraft by 2000 (disregarding attrition), while retaining a large reserve. From 2000 to 2015, if there are new threats to security, fourth-generation aircraft could be returned to active service.

For example, if a new military threat emerged in 2006, retrieving the aircraft would provide Russia in 2007 with 1,450 instead of the 1,300 aircraft, forecast under the presently planned gradual decline, and in 2010 with 1,370 instead of the 1,140 force level of frontal aviation. This extra 20 percent may seem quite small, but it would consist of modern and relatively unworn machines and might provide an important "margin of security," before industry gains momentum in increasing the weapons output. The margin could be larger if a larger portion of the air forces is stored in the 1990s. Finally, if during the 1990s the saved resources are used for other crucial needs a newly built-up AFRF would possess much higher combat capabilities than otherwise.

This proposal is not without problems. There are presently no satisfactory storage facilities in Russia. Its climate is harsh compared to the benign conditions of the lost Central Asian storage. Stored aircraft would consume as much as 30 percent of the maintenance costs of aircraft in active service. Maintenance of the older planes in active service would cost more: even now 60 percent of weapons and equipment procurement funds go for spare parts, 50 percent of which are consumed by older airplanes. Engines for older planes were produced in Ukraine and many former repair plants are now outside Russia. Pilots of the AFRF reserve could fly the older airplanes in storage and training centers, but would not be able to fly new models.

Most of these difficulties can be solved. First, saving 70 percent of active-duty costs is significant. The Air Force can use the funds to build and equip proper storage sites, and for many other purposes. Second, expenditures for the maintenance of older airplanes would not increase since they would not be kept in service longer than planned now. Third, because of reductions in AFRF aircraft, in many units there are now two or three crew complements for each airplane. These pilots may be transferred to first-line reserve and can continue to fly new aircraft at training centers.

Finally, the military would argue that reducing force levels to about 1,000 aircraft during the 1990s would undermine "defense sufficiency." Indeed, compared to the 5,200-aircraft force level of the Soviet Air Force in the mid-1980s, the level of 2,000 aircraft may seem barely sufficient. However, defense requirements should not be based on the past, but on present and foreseeable threats and contingencies. The contemplated force levels do not seem justified by actual security considerations during the 1990s; rather, they are the product of institutional interests acting without clear political and strategic guidance. Nor are they affordable economically, and they might undercut Russia's security in the long run: resources wasted now might be needed for defense sufficiency in a still unpredictable and conceivably much less benign future international environment.

The AFRF's planned modernization program also does not seem fully justified, in view of the limited Air Force budget and competing priorities of procurement, maintenance, and personnel, as well as the requirements of mobility, air-lift and the tanker air fleet. Continued production and upgrading of two long-range fighter systems, the Su-27 and MiG-31, is hardly affordable. Nor does the introduction of a new long-range Su-35 fighter-bomber seem justified if an advanced frontal bomber of the Su-34 type is expected around 2000. The same is true of the follow-on to the Su-25 close support aircraft; its functions might be performed by new advanced helicopters. Finally, if the Su-34 is introduced and its performance is as high as advertised, it would be worthwhile now to stop procurement of Tu-22M medium bombers, which are too expensive for conventional missions and cannot compete with ballistic missiles as a nuclear deterrent. Naval warfare missions for the Tu-22M imply war with the West, which should no longer drive Russia's operational planning and procurement. The resources saved in the AFRF modernization program could be better used for air-lift and tanker airplane production.

The long-term strategy proposed above is applicable to other armed services as well. That is, new weapons should be stored, force levels should be cut, and the personnel and force structures should be smaller than the sizes sustainable by available resources. Obviously, this runs against institutional preferences and commonly accepted practices. But the unique time Russia is living through—the post–Cold War, post-Soviet and post-communist period—would seem to warrant innovative and untraditional strategic choices.

Chapter 3

Alexander Ozhegov

The Conversion of the Russian Military Aircraft Industry

Since the early 1990s, Russia's aviation enterprises have been seeking to adjust to a sharp decline in government procurement, and the need to convert to civilian production. A series of conversion programs adopted by the USSR and then Russia have formalized these goals.[1] The State Program for Conversion, adopted in the former USSR in 1990, called for a 12 percent reduction in the production of military aircraft and a 60 percent cut in the production of military helicopters from the 1988 levels.

The government did not primarily seek to develop civil aviation; while it planned a 1990 increase in the production of engines for civil aircraft of 9 percent, it directed the aerospace enterprises to increase their production of consumer and durable goods by 60 percent; of manufacturing equipment for light industry and the food-processing industry by 30 percent; and of agricultural equipment by 220 percent.[2] In contrast, when the USSR severely curtailed production of military aircraft in the 1960s, the production capacity of the military aviation industry was used to develop civilian aviation with great success.

---

[1] Alexei Arbatov's commentary on Chapter 4 offers a complementary account of Russia's industrial conversion process. In addition to the sources cited, this article draws on material in the periodicals *Aviatsionnaya Promyshlennost (Aviation Industry)*, *Grazhdanskaya Aviatsia (Civil Aviation)*, and *Technika Vozdushnogo Flota (The Technique of the Air Fleet)*.
[2] V. Gubarev, "Conversion without illusions," *Pravda*, July 7, 1990.

Alexander Ozhegov is the head of the Economic Research Department at the Russian Bank for Reconstruction and Development.

The State Program for Conversion of the aerospace industry was changed significantly in 1990–1991 but many aviation plants were still required to devote substantial resources to manufacturing durable goods, agricultural equipment, and other products they were not experienced with.

After the disintegration of the USSR and the beginning of market reforms in Russia, government orders fell precipitously.[3] Government orders to the military industries in 1992 were cut by 62 percent from the previous year. The Ministry of Defense 1992 order to the aerospace industry was cut by two-thirds. Orders for military airplanes and helicopters in 1993 were only 15 percent of the 1991 level.[4] (See Table 3.1.)

Table 3.1. The Decline in Russian Funding for the Military Aerospace Industry

	1989	1991	1992	1993	1995	1996	2000
				Constant price funding as a share of 1989 funding			
Research & Development	1	0.53	0.46	0.41	0.46	..	0.56
Production	1	0.67	0.13	0.14	..	0.11	0.15

---

[3] Most of the enterprises in the aerospace industry were located in Russia; after the disintegration of the Soviet Union, the Aerospace Industry Department of Russia absorbed over 80 percent of the scientific and industrial resources of the former Ministry of Aerospace Industry of the USSR. While the disintegration of the USSR created difficulties for Russia's aerospace industry, the problems are much more serious in the other republics of the former USSR. For example, the aircraft plant in Tbilisi, Georgia assembled only the old types of MiG and Su fighters; many plants in Russia can replace it. The aerospace plant in Tashkent, Uzbekistan assembled civil aircraft, but all the main parts were supplied by enterprises in Russia. Only Ukraine, where the Antonov Design Bureau (Kiev), the aerospace production association (Kharkov), and the engine-building plant (Zaporozhie) are located, has significant potential in the aerospace industry. One challenge is to maintain cooperation between the Russian and Ukrainian aerospace enterprises. Several plants in Russia are preparing to manufacture aircraft designed in Kiev by the Antonov Design Bureau as part of Russia's conversion program.

[4] G. Khromov, "The defense complex: Not to destroy, but to save," *Krasnaya Zvezda*, March 3, 1993.

The Ministry of Defense canceled its order for several military aircraft, such as the MiG-29, and greatly reduced orders for many other types of aircraft and helicopters. Plants that lost entire contracts suffered because they lacked the financial resources to change their production lines. In addition, to maintain the fighting capabilities of existing aircraft, the industry must preserve the capacity to produce replacement engines and other spare parts. Plants whose orders were greatly reduced lost economies of scale. (See Table 3.2.)

Table 3.2. The Share of Military Aircraft Industry Capacity under State Control

	Government contracts as a percent of total funding	
	1989	1993
Design Bureau R&D Capacity		
Sukhoy	90	95
Mikoyan	85	10
Yakovlev	55	6
Iliushin	50	15
Beriev	60	15
Kamov	75	40
Mil	80	33
Production Capacity		
Novosibirsk	90	5
Komsomolsk	95	11
Moscow	90	3
Kazan	97	28
Nizhni Novgorod	87	12
Rostov	60	17
Arseniev	83	5

These difficulties were aggravated by political problems resulting from the incompetence of the new Russian executive and legislative bodies. For example, the 1992 budget was not approved until August 1992; military enterprises could not plan for the long term, and borrowed money from commercial banks at high interest rates. Second, the military procurement program through 2000 was not adopted until January 1993. Lacking guidance, the aerospace enterprises could not shut down production lines for obsolete aircraft and reorient those facilities for civilian products. Finally, at the end of 1991, the Ministry of Foreign Economic Relations (MFER) over-estimated the foreign market for Russian weapons, including aircraft.

MFER gave a substantial export order to the military enterprises, and especially to the aerospace enterprises, in some cases equaling or exceeding domestic orders. The majority of the enterprises implemented the order, but the sales were never made and MFER never paid for the weapons. Subsequent attempts by some military enterprises to export weapons independently from the state aggravated the situation by creating competition between different producers of the same type of weaponry and between different institutions involved in foreign trade.

Nevertheless, by 1992 many aerospace firms were operating in the new economic conditions with fewer problems than enterprises in other defense industries; above all this was due to preliminary work in civil aviation. The government has supported the aerospace industry's conversion programs. The 1992 Russian Federation budget allocated 103.9 bn rubles for basic scientific and technical research and programs; of this 10.6 bn rubles was for development of the aerospace industry. By comparison, 16.1 bn rubles were allocated for the whole Russian Academy of Sciences, and 8.7 bn for the Russian State Space Program.[5] The unconfirmed 1993 budget projections called for 684.6 bn rubles for basic scientific and technical research and programs, of which 65.6 bn rubles were allocated for developing civil aviation, 75.7 bn rubles for the Academy of Sciences, and 72.7 bn rubles for the space program.

These funds represent only half the money needed to implement the Development Program for Civil Aviation; the rest should come from low-interest, long-term "conversion" loans and the aerospace enterprises' own financial resources.

The Development Program for Civil Aviation is one of 14 parts of the 1991–1995 Federal Conversion Program, adopted by the Russian Government in July 1993. The program shapes the development of aircraft engineering, aviation engines, helicopter engineering, aggregate engineering, flight-navigation equipment, and construction materials and technologies.

The Department of Aviation Industry based its development program on two factors. First, despite Russia's economic difficulties, the number of airplane flights over the next 10 years will at least double. Second, many passenger and transport aircraft are at or near the end of their service lives, and must be replaced soon by new

---

[5] *Rossiskaya Gazeta*, August 21, 1992.

generations of planes and helicopters. For example, 20 percent of Il-62, 20 percent of Tu-134, and 5 percent of Tu-154 airplanes have passed their retirement dates.[6] It is estimated that 1,145 of the 1,400 civilian airliners in operation in Russia must be replaced by 2000.[7]

To expand production and sales of civil aircraft, they must attain a higher technical level. In particular, fuel efficiency must be increased to 15–18 grams per passenger-km from the present level of more than 50 grams per passenger-km. Improvements are also needed to meet international standards in flight safety, comfort, and environmental impact.

Under the Development Program for Civil Aviation, by 2000, the aerospace industry is expected to produce more than 6,500 aircraft and helicopters for sale in Russia, and other countries of the former USSR, and for export. In the near future, special emphasis will be placed on production of the An-38, An-74, Il-96, Il-114, Tu-204, Tu-334 and Yak-42M.

The Development Program for Civil Aviation proposed that over 60 percent of all funds be used for research and development (R&D). This figure is compatible with the world experience in this field; 40–80 percent of spending in the aerospace industry generally goes for R&D due to the need to conduct extensive tests of materials, aerodynamics, and safety.

Russia's aerospace industry was organized during the era of central management, and consists of three large organizational blocks— research institutes, which conduct basic and applied research; design bureaus, which produce prototypes; and "serial production" factories, which produce the final product.[8] These blocks are connected in the process of technological innovation, but are formally separate. The process of privatization is demonstrating the negative aspects of this separateness; it is difficult to preserve cooperation between the blocks and to provide financial support for R&D. These problems are aggra-

---

[6] S. Kolesnic, "The hasty partition of the sky is fraught with trouble," *Nezavisimaya Gazeta*, April 10, 1993.

[7] V. Baberdin and V. Rudenko, "Aviasalon in Moscow," *Krasnaya Zvezda*, September 8, 1993.

[8] The distinctions between these three blocks are by no means clear cut. For example, many research institutes can produce some aircraft components, and the design bureaus and research divisions at many factories can resolve problems that require applied engineering or basic research. However, in analyzing the aerospace industry, it is useful to consider these three types of institutions as organizationally separate.

vated by the territorial distribution of the aerospace industry. Research institutes and design bureaus are concentrated in Moscow and its satellite town Zhukovsky, while production plants are mostly located in other large cities in the central part of Russia and beyond the Urals.[9]

This chapter discusses how Russia's aerospace enterprises are faring in the process of conversion, and what steps they are taking to adjust to a market economy.

Basic and Applied Research

Many of Russia's aerospace research institutes are located in Zhukovsky, near Moscow. Zhukovsky, with a population of more than 100,000, is a city of a single culture, dominated by the aerospace industry. Its educational facilities include the Moscow Aviation Institute (MAI), the Moscow Institute of Physics and Technology (MFTI), and the aviation technical secondary school.

The Central Institute of Aerohydrodynamics (TsAGI) was founded in 1918, and is one of the oldest aviation institutes in the world. It is also one of the world's largest aerospace centers, with about 11,000 employees.[10] TsAGI performs basic and applied research, and is the main Russian center for materials and other tests of all types of civil and military aircraft. The Institute has participated in the development of all new types of Russian planes and helicopters, and has contributed to the development of the Energia-Buran space shuttle system. TsAGI's world-class technical base includes supersonic and subsonic aerodynamic wind tunnels and thermal and vacuum testing chambers.

The Institute is leading the development of the new generation of Russian civilian passenger and transport planes, including the Il-96 and Tu-204. TsAGI has been able to compensate for a reduction in military orders through its conversion efforts that focus on the

---

[9] For example, bombers and civilian aircraft designed by the Tupolev design bureau in Moscow are produced in Kazan, Samara, Ulianovsk, and Taganrog. The Su-25 attack plane, designed by Sukhoi in Moscow, was produced in Tbilisi.
[10] Here and elsewhere, unless otherwise noted, employment data is from 1992 and is cited from the 1993 Russian Defense Business Directory.

development of civil aviation and aerospace, improvements in ground transport vehicles, and design of testing systems.

In the last few years, TsAGI has increased its joint efforts with aerospace firms all over the world, including Boeing, General Dynamics, Rockwell International, and firms in France, Great Britain, Germany, India, China, and South Korea. Orders from foreign countries have been increasing. The Institute has contacts with NASA and with U.S. universities, and has established a subsidiary, TsAGI International, in the United States. Its main fields of international cooperation are basic research into flight aerodynamics; development of passenger planes; development of highly-efficient computerized and automated control systems; and aerodynamic and strength testing of aircraft at TsAGI's experimental facilities by foreign companies.[11]

Other large institutes and design bureaus in Zhukovsky include the Institute of Flight Tests (LII), whose runway is the best in Russia and the largest in Europe; the Research Institute of Aviation Equipment (NII AO), which develops flight-navigation complexes and training equipment to prepare pilots for first flights, and performs ground-based adjustment of aircraft systems; and the V. Myasishchev experimental design bureau and pilot plant, which developed the ZM tanker.

The top management of TsAGI, LII, and the other research institutes and design bureaus are planning a high-technology industrial park with an educational system with a multi-purpose regional university; high-technology aerospace enterprises that will develop new technologies and products; and industries that will adapt aerospace technologies to produce a variety of civilian products.[12]

The institutes, which represent unique national property, must be re-established as Federal Scientific Centers, and the other production capacities can be privatized.

The All-Russian Institute of Light Alloys (VILS) in Moscow develops aerospace materials such as aluminum and other light-metal alloys. It produces automated installations that control the

---

[11] "Conversion '92 Moscow," a publication of *World Trade Center Club* (Division: Trade Fairs and Exhibitions), Koln, Germany: 1992.

[12] S. Smirnov, "The International Workshop for Conversion of the Aerospace Industry," *Conversion*, No. 2 (Moscow: IZANA Publishing, 1993).

production of aluminum, titanium, molybdenum, heat-proof alloy products, and semi-finished products of various shapes.

In the late 1980s, government orders decreased by 25 percent; VILS responded by negotiating direct contracts with other customers. VILS has also reduced its research in the field of creating new alloys. Today, over 80 percent of VILS' products are designed for civilian use. Its manufacturing techniques, including stamping and production of plates and pipes, can be used in producing automobiles, drilling pipes, and other civilian products. VILS is currently producing some parts for the automobile industry, such as lightweight, durable stamped disks for truck wheels that were manufactured for Volvo (Sweden) in 1992. It has mastered light-metal manufacturing for products that can be used in agriculture, for example greenhouses, granaries, and sheds. In 1992–1993 the Institute made a handsome profit by manufacturing light kiosks for street trade; in fact, VILS has established a monopoly over the production of such kiosks in Moscow. The income from the kiosks funds basic and applied research in material science.

VILS is revamping its production facilities through cooperation with foreign firms. It is pursuing four large projects with a total value of $80 mn, to be paid for over eight to ten years. For example, VILS has bought new production lines for manufacturing pipes and sheet metal and for rolling processes.

The All-Russian Institute of Aviation Materials (VIAM) in Moscow specializes in research, development, and testing of aerospace materials, including composite materials. It produces foliated (lamellar) construction materials with more rigidity and higher performance characteristics than aluminum alloys; thermoproof fiber materials; heat-proof construction materials that are substitutes for nickel alloys; and similar products.

The State Research Institute of Aviation Systems (GosNIIAS) in Moscow, founded in 1946, has recently been developing sophisticated air-launched missiles, including air-to-air missiles with active seeking radar, and inertial guidance systems for strategic cruise missiles. GosNIIAS also works on weapons-system security and compatibility between weapons and launch vehicles, and it develops methods of defense against missile attacks.

GosNIIAS is pursuing two conversion strategies. First, it is applying new technologies developed by the military to civil aviation. With other agencies and organizations, it is developing advanced flight-control systems that use the C10 Nace and Navstar satellite navigation systems and the Horizon and Inmarsat satellite communications systems. Second, it is manufacturing credit cards and collaborating with an aviation production plant to manufacture cash registers under license with a French company. GosNIIAS also provides technical maintenance of communications channels and computer systems for commercial institutions. Unfortunately, as at other military research institutes, there are serious staffing problems; nearly 1,000 employees left GosNIIAS during 1991–1992 because of low salaries.[13]

The Central Institute of Aviation Motors (CIAM) in Moscow performs basic research and experimental projects on engines for military and civil aircraft, focusing on gas dynamics, the combustion process, and heat exchange. It has a large test complex at Lytkarino in the Moscow region. Aérospatiale (France) is planning to collaborate with CIAM on research into hypersonic jet engines for aircraft.

The Research Institute of Technology and Organization of Engines Manufacturing (NIID) is located in Moscow, and has affiliates in Kazan and Samara. NIID is the aerospace industry's leading institute for engine manufacturing technology. It develops machine tools used to make compressor blades with asymmetrical surfaces, for laser machining of heat-proof alloy and ceramic products, and for other purposes.

The research institutes located outside of the Moscow region are generally faring worse than those that are centrally located. An example is the Siberia Research Institute of Aviation (SibNIA) in Novosibirsk, which has tested 180 aircraft models developed by the Tupolev, Iliushin, Sukhoi, Mikoyan, and Yakovlev design bureaus.[14] SibNIA tests the materials of new military and passenger aircraft. It also tests planes that have been in production to determine whether their materials have degraded and whether they are still flight worthy. Such tests determine when all the aircraft of a particular model will be replaced. SibNIA is also a leader in developing technology policies and in coordinating R&D on subsonic and supersonic aircraft.

---

[13] Y. Fedosov, "One of the main people in the military-industrial complex," interview with the director of GosNIIAS, *Nezavisimaya Gazeta*, August 12, 1992.
[14] SibNIA is a smaller version of TsAGI, and is its backup center for the eastern part of the country.

However, SibNIA is now in dire financial circumstances with a debt of 194 mn rubles at the beginning of July 1993. This debt is mainly due to the insolvency of its customers: the Institute received only 50 mn rubles out of the 200 mn it was owed for contracts it fulfilled during the first half of 1993. SibNIA survives only because of funding from the government, but this is constantly delayed,[15] and in June 1993 SibNIA could not pay wages of 19 mn rubles for April and 38 mn rubles for May.

SibNIA is trying to get other contracts, and to develop new products. Some are military, such as a multi-purpose amphibious aircraft with short take-off and landing capability. Others are civilian, such as micro-hydroelectric stations for small rivers, and a wide range of automatic scales.

SibNIA's ability to conduct tests on an extremely wide range of products—from large bridge spans to durable goods—should help it become a regional certification center, but it does need additional equipment to be accredited. SibNIA is also trying to provide sponsorship for projects that would be funded from the federal budget.

Design Bureaus

As with the research institutes, almost all of the leading aerospace design bureaus are located in or near Moscow. These include the Tupolev, Iliushin, Mikoyan, Sukhoi, and Yakovlev design bureaus, which develop nearly all Russian aircraft; the Mil and Kamov design bureaus, which develop helicopters; and the Lyulka ("Saturn") design bureau, and others that develop aviation engines. Practically all of these design bureaus have their own pilot plants in Moscow or the Moscow region, but full-scale production usually takes place in other Russian cities. In the past few years, several new independent scientific and design firms were created in the aerospace industry. Some work in the field of non-traditional aviation. For example, the EKIP scientific-production firm in Moscow develops "flying wing" aircraft. The aircraft's body has aerodynamic qualities that combine the functions of the wing and fuselage. Five types of aircraft are being developed with full weights ranging from 9 to 600 tons. Prototypes of these

---

[15] "SibNIA today and tomorrow," *Sovetskaya*, July 6, 1993.

experimental aircraft are being produced at the Samara Aviation Plant.

AIRCRAFT DESIGN BUREAUS

The Tupolev Aviation Scientific Technical Complex (ANTK Tupolev) employs more than 15,000 people and specializes in strategic military aircraft. The Tupolev design bureau's military production orders declined from 85 percent of its business in early 1992 to 15 percent in 1993.[16] In the 1980s, Tupolev developed the supersonic strategic bomber Tu-160 Blackjack with a speed of 2,200 km/hour. It was added to the Air Force beginning in 1985 and, by most estimates, is the best in the world in its class.[17] Production of the Tu-95MS and Tu-160 ended in 1992, and production of the Tu-22MZ Backfire was limited.

Tupolev has been involved in civilian aviation since the 1950s and is now developing the Tu-204 passenger aircraft, which can carry 214 passengers and can be used on both mid-range (4,500 km) and long-range (up to 7,000 km) routes. The Tu-204M will be equipped with Rolls Royce engines to ensure that it can be maintained abroad. The airplane will be assembled at Aviastar Corporation in Ulianovsk, and will be sold and maintained by British Russian Aviation Corporation (BRAVIA), established in 1992 by the Tupolev Design Bureau, Aviastar Corporation, and the British investment company Flemming Russia Investment Corp. It is hoped that the Tu-204 will be certified by 1995, and that production will start in 1996.

Tupolev is trying to create a large industrial group, a joint-stock aerospace company that can be established once all the participating firms have completed the privatization process. The Tupolev Aircraft Company will include the Tupolev design bureau and pilot plant (ANTK Tupolev), the Samara aviation plant, which manufactures the Tu-154, the Ulianovsk Aggregate Plant, and the Taganrog Aviation Production Enterprise.

---

[16] N. Kalinichenko, "The first real Russian concern," *Kommersant*, No. 33 (August 16–22, 1993), pp. 21–22.
[17] "The Russian Aerospace Exhibition 'Mosaeroshow-92,'" *Bulletin of Foreign Scientific and Technical Information*, Series 1, No. 39 (September 29, 1992), and No. 41 (October 13, 1992).

The Iliushin Design Bureau, which employs 6,000 people, develops civilian and military transport and passenger aircraft, for example the Il-76 transport and the Il-78 tanker.

In the 1980s, Iliushin developed the wide-bodied airliner Il-96, which had its first flight in 1988, and its first international flight (from Moscow to New York) in July 1993. Since 1991 the Iliushin Design Bureau has worked with nearly 20 foreign firms, mostly from the United States, to modernize the Il-96. As a result, the Il-96M has Pratt & Whitney engines and avionics by Rockwell International. Its first flight was in April 1993. A future challenge is to get U.S. certification for this airplane, which is important for obtaining international sales. The main problem now is to get financial support from the Russian and U.S. governments for the aircraft's continued development. Production is scheduled to start in 1995–1996. It is estimated that the Iliushin design bureau bought $100 mn worth of equipment from Western firms, with the expectation that the Il-96M will successfully compete against the Airbus A340 for international orders.[18]

Iliushin has also developed the Il-114 aircraft, a modern short-medium range airliner. It will be produced at several aerospace plants simultaneously, beginning with the Moscow Aircraft Production Group (MAPO). Iliushin is also developing small passenger aircraft, including a business jet, the Il-126.

The Iliushin Design Bureau is trying to create a joint-stock corporation with the manufacturers of its aircraft, starting with the Voronezh Aviation Production Association, which is now in the process of privatization without Iliushin. Iliushin fears that cooperation among researchers, design bureaus, and manufacturers will suffer if individual enterprises privatize without taking their partners along.

The Mikoyan Design Bureau has always specialized in the development of combat aircraft, and after the Ministry of Defense decided to end procurement of the MiG-29, Mikoyan found itself in a difficult situation. Over the past 30 years, MiG aircraft have been the most widely-purchased fighters in the world. For example, at the

---

[18] The technical characteristics of these two airliners are almost the same, but the Il-96M has superior aerodynamics and a lower price. The estimated price for the A340 is $105–115 mn, for the Il-96M, only $70–80 mn. A. Glebova, "Russia will return to the world market of civil aviation in the year 1996," *Kommersant*, No. 23 (July 7–13, 1993).

beginning of 1992 there were over 500 MiG-29 fighters in the countries of the former USSR, and 11 other countries had been supplied with this airplane[19] including Germany, which has 24 MiG-29 fighters.

Mikoyan seems to be in the worst position of the aircraft design bureaus. Over 1,500 professionals left between January 1991 and January 1993.[20] To improve the situation, Mikoyan hopes to export more MiG-29 fighters, and has established the firm "MiGservice," a joint venture with the Znamia Truda plant, the main producer of the MiG-29.

The Sukhoi Design Bureau has been more successful than most of its counterparts. It specializes in developing combat aircraft, such as the Su-25 attack plane and the Su-27 interceptor and fighter-bomber. In 1991, the Air Force chose the Su-27 as its main fighter aircraft and decided to develop several versions, including a reconnaissance aircraft, a fighter-bomber, and an all-weather interceptor. The new Su-30 fighter was derived from the Su-27. In August 1992, China bought 24 Su-27 fighters for $35 mn each.

Sukhoi has found its place in foreign and domestic markets; in addition to its combat planes, it produces sporting aircraft. Sukhoi currently has orders for 140 Su-26 and Su-29 sporting-acrobatic airplanes from the U.S., Great Britain, Switzerland, and other countries. As a result, Sukhoi is more stable financially, and has even been able to give scholarships to 200 students at technical high schools, with the aim of attracting talented young engineers in the near future.

The Sukhoi Design Bureau was one of the first Russian military firms to collaborate with U.S. companies. In the late 1980s, it conducted design work on a supersonic business jet with Gulfstream Aerospace. If this project goes ahead, production may begin in the late 1990s. In 1993, Sukhoi developed and began pilot production of the 6-passenger S-84 airplane, using engines produced by Teledyne Continental Motors (U.S.). Managers at Sukhoi are exploring joint

[19] "The Russian Aerospace Exhibition 'Mosaeroshow-92.'"
[20] R. Beliakov, "An interview with General Constructor of Mikoyan Design Bureau R. Beliakov," *Krasnaya Zvezda*, February 6, 1993.

production of an all-terrain vehicle with Rover (Great Britain), an example of how Sukhoi might diversify.[21]

In the past, the Yakovlev Design Bureau specialized in the development of multi-role fighters with vertical takeoff and landing capabilities, such as the Yak-38 and Yak-44 carrier-based aircraft. Yakovlev is associated with the Skorost machine-building plant in Moscow and employs a total of 25,000 people in its design bureau and pilot plant. Its planes were produced at the Saratov aviation plant and the Smolensk aviation plant, with which Yakovlev has created a corporation.

By 1992, conversion at the Yakovlev Design Bureau was practically completed. During 1992–1993, Yakovlev received no money from the Ministry of Defense. It is seeking to develop small two-, four- and six-seater planes, and to continue developing and improving larger passenger airplanes. Possibilities include the production of more of its famous Yak-40 passenger jet aircraft, modernization of the Yak-42M airliner, and development of a new airliner, the Yak-46. The French companies Aérospatiale and Avions de Transport Regional (ATR) plan to co-produce their 42-seat ATR-42 passenger aircraft with the Yakovlev Design Bureau at the Yakovlev plant.[22]

The Antonov Design Bureau in Kiev, Ukraine, develops large transport aircraft and short- and medium-range airplanes, for example the An-124 Ruslan and An-225 Mriya. The first flight of the Mriya was in 1988; during its first three years it made 400 flights, including 36 flights with the space shuttle Buran. Russian aircraft plants in Omsk and Novosibirsk are now preparing to produce the An-38, a multi-purpose turboprop that carries 26 passengers, and the An-74.

Some design bureaus, research bureaus, and manufacturing facilities have united to form a scientific-production association. One example is the Beriev Aviation Complex in Taganrog, a combination of the Beriev Design Bureau and the Taganrog Aviation Production Enterprise, which specializes in the development and assembly of hydroplanes. Their best-known product is the A-40 Albatross

---

[21] M. Chernyshov, "Mikhail Simonov: On the western market it is possible to offer only super-aircraft," interview with the General Constructor of the Sukhoi Design Bureau, *Nezavisimaya Gazeta*, December 17, 1992.

[22] "East/West Aerospace Ventures on the Rise," *Aviation Week & Space Technology*, Vol. 139, No. 8 (August 23, 1993), pp. 51–59.

amphibious aircraft, which has established more than 10 world records; Beriev's hydroplanes are about five years ahead of the rest of the world for aircraft of this type. Beriev is also developing the A-200 multi-purpose amphibious aircraft for civilian use, a smaller version of the A-40.

The Beriev production plant in Taganrog has manufactured its own aircraft, and also those developed at the Tupolev Design Bureau. It has produced several modifications of the Tu-142 anti-submarine bomber, and is preparing to produce the Tu-334 passenger aircraft. It is likely that the Taganrog plant will become part of the Tupolev joint-stock aircraft company.

HELICOPTER DESIGN BUREAUS

All the former USSR's helicopters were developed at the Mil Design Bureau or the Kamov Design Bureau. These two enterprises now strongly compete for state orders, especially military orders for the Ka-50 and Mi-28.

The Mil Design Bureau in Moscow specializes in military and dual-use helicopters. Mil is developing a new helicopter, the Mi-40, based on the engine of the Mi-28. The Mi-40 is a transport aircraft for infantry troops. Mil also develops a wide range of dual-use and civil helicopters, from light to super-heavy.

The Kamov Design Bureau, with 4,000 employees, is part of the helicopter-building scientific-technical complex in Lubertsy in the Moscow region. The complex also contains the Ukhtomsky pilot plant for building helicopter prototypes. One of the best-known Kamov helicopters is the one-seat close-support Ka-50. Its distinctive feature is its armored cabin, complete with an ejection seat that allows for safe escape at any altitude.[23] It is believed that this helicopter can compete on the world market; after installation of Western electronics, the Ka-50 should be able to compete successfully for Great Britain's order for successors to 130 Lynx helicopters through

---

[23] All ejection seats for aviation and space use are developed at the Zvezda Design Bureau and machine-building plant in Tomilino, between Lubertsy and Zhukovsky in the Moscow region. Zvezda produces the best ejection seats in the world, and now has close ties to Western firms and many orders for its famous life-saving systems.

the end of the 1990s. However, Western experts criticize the Ka-50 for the excessive workload it would place upon the pilot in combat.[24]

The Kamov Design Bureau also produces naval helicopters, including those used in anti-submarine warfare, and civilian helicopters, some of which may be outfitted with foreign engines. Kamov is also developing a small unmanned agricultural helicopter with the South Korean company Daewoo.

ENGINE DESIGN BUREAUS

Russian design bureaus which develop aviation engines are more widely spread out than aircraft design bureaus, but most are in Moscow. Many others are located with production plants in other Russian cities such as Samara and Perm. The Saturn Design Bureau, which employs 4,000 workers, is part of the Central Institute of Aviation Motors in Baranov. Its principal product is Sukhoi fighter engines, including the AL-31F engine for the Su-27.[25] The Saturn Design Bureau also develops engines for other aerospace enterprises.

The Klimov Design Bureau, which employs 4,200 workers, is located in St. Petersburg along with its pilot plant. It has developed engines for the MiG-29 fighter (RD-33 engine), the Mi-24 helicopter, and the Il-114 airplane, and is currently developing advanced gas turbine engines for helicopters. Klimov signed a September 1993 agreement with a Canadian subsidiary of Pratt & Whitney, and established a joint venture to develop low- and medium-power gas turbine engines for civilian aircraft. Pratt & Whitney Canada/Klimov Ltd. (Pratt & Whitney owns 51 percent) should start producing engines for the Kamov, Beriev, and Mil design bureaus in 1994.

Production Plants

The Moscow Aircraft Production Group (MAPO) includes the Znamia Truda plant in Moscow, which was established in the 1890s, and the Lukhovitsy machine-building plant in the Moscow region. MAPO employs 30,000 people. For many years it was the main producer of

---

[24] G. Covault and B. Rybak, "Russian Helicopters Spark Controversy," *Aviation Week & Space Technology*, June 21, 1993.

[25] V. Sosunov, "Rolls-Royce is not better than ours..." *Krasnaya Zvezda*, August 28, 1993.

the MiG-29, but since the beginning of 1992 there have been no MiG-29 orders from the Ministry of Defense. In October 1992, the Russian government gave MAPO the exclusive right to export MiG-29 fighters. Not a single MiG-29 fighter was sold in 1992, and by January 1993 over 50 were sitting on the Lukhovitsy airfield.

During the past few decades, MAPO manufactured more than 3,000 MiG-21, MiG-23 and MiG-29 fighters that were exported.[26] MAPO is preparing to enter the world market for service, repair, and maintenance of these aircraft, so production of spare parts for exported MiG fighters is an important part of its development program. In addition, the Mikoyan Design Bureau and MAPO have developed proposals to install new optical equipment and other equipment on MiG-21 and MiG-23 fighters. The two enterprises have developed a program to retrofit exported MiG-29 fighters with in-flight refueling capability, a world-class navigation system of the U.S. TACAN (tactical air navigation) type, the ILS (instrument landing system), and additional fuel tanks.

MAPO managers have concluded that the only way to solve maintenance problems and assure the supply of spare parts is to create joint enterprises in countries that have imported MiG fighters. A maintenance center was established in Germany, which has 24 MiG-29s, and negotiations are underway with India and other countries. MAPO expects that these technical centers, staffed with both Russian and foreign specialists, will provide service and repair for MiG fighters from other countries in the region.

Even if some MiG-29s are sold abroad, MAPO will be unable to survive in its current form with export sales alone. MAPO's primary conversion project is to work toward assembling the turboprop Il-114 64-passenger airliner. In addition, MAPO has several other civilian projects. It has started to produce a light airplane, the T-101 Gratch ("Rook"), with the participation of Teledyne Continental Motors (U.S.), which supplies the engines. MAPO prepared for production in 1993, when the T-101 began to replace the outdated An-2 for civil use. MAPO has developed a light three-seat plane, the I-1, with engines made by Lycoming (U.S.). The Lukhovitsy plant produced approximately 150 in 1993. In conjunction with the Moscow Aviation Institute and the Institute of Flight Tests (LII), MAPO has established

---

[26] V. Rudenko, "If there is interest, there will be contracts," *Krasnaya Zvezda*, September 18, 1993.

the company Aviatica, which developed the super-light aircraft MAI-900. The consortium hopes for strong exports.

The Sokol ("Falcon") Aviation Plant in Nizhny Novgorod manufactures MiG-29 and MiG-31 fighters. After the Russian government declared in January 1992 that it would no longer purchase these aircraft, Sokol continued producing them on its own initiative. The total 1992 military order amounted to only 12 percent of Sokol's 1991 orders. Sokol had not secured the right to sell the airplanes abroad independently, and the Ministry of Foreign Economic Relations has not provided buyers. In addition, other Russian MiG producers compete for export sales. Before the 1990s, Sokol exported its fighters to the former socialist countries and some developing nations, selling about 50 aircraft in the last few years. Every airplane sold abroad made a profit for the state of four or five U.S. dollars for each ruble of expenditures.[27]

By the end of 1992, Sokol had a debt of 2.5 bn rubles, and its electricity, gas, and water were cut off. During 1992, Sokol induced nearly 2,500 employees to retire with a pension. Sokol's staff feared that Sokol would lose the government's financial support if it went private. In 1992 they decided to temporarily halt the process of incorporating as a joint-stock company to prevent the mass dismissal of employees. Staff members hoped this would allow them to save money in individual and special joint accounts so that they could purchase a controlling share of the company in the future.

Besides its attempts to secure a license to sell MiGs abroad, Sokol is gradually expanding its production of passenger aircraft and is pursuing other conversion programs. It concluded a contract with the Italian company PROCAER to assemble the 4-seat F15F Dolphin airplane, with production to start in 1993. Sokol is also preparing to produce the light-cargo passenger airplane M-101, designed at the Myasishchev Experimental Design Bureau in Zhukovsky.

Sokol is expanding its collaboration with another Nizhny Novgorod enterprise, the Alexeev Central Hydrofoil Design Bureau, which created "the Caspian Sea Monster" wing-in-ground (WIG) effect aircraft. In 1992, Alexeev signed an agreement to work together to design a heavy WIG with Aerocon (U.S.). According to the Alexeev Design Bureau, the Sokol aviation plant has begun to assemble the

---

[27] E. Kessariysky, "Will 'Sokol' fly with the one wing?" *Rossiskaya Vesti*, November 1992.

Volga-2 air-cushion amphibian, which uses the WIG effect and has a speed of 120 km per hour. Another joint project is to manufacture the Sever-4 air-cushion amphibian. Sokol has also started producing the multi-purpose Dingo amphibious airplane. Sokol continues to work on new supersonic aircraft.

The Saratov Aviation Plant, which has always worked with the Yakovlev Design Bureau, employs 13,000 workers, including 3,000 engineers and technicians. In 1991, Saratov was converted into a collective enterprise, the first in the military sector. Civil production increased by 30 percent in 1992 from the previous year. Saratov has received only 25 mn rubles for conversion purposes from the state in the past five years, including 10 mn in 1992. In current prices, this is very little compared with what many other aerospace plants received. There are more than 30 small enterprises around the Saratov Aviation Plant, at which more than 30 percent of its engineers work. Some of these small enterprises do over a bn rubles of business annually, producing products such as satellite antennas, furniture, and toys.

When Russia's conversion process began, Saratov stopped producing military aircraft and began to build only civil airplanes. The only military production now is a new type of air-launched missile for destroying radar stations.[28]

Saratov is now manufacturing a modified Yak-40. The Yakovlev Design Bureau has approved the option of installing Western engines and avionics. Saratov's emphasis is to expand production of the Yak-42, which has been in production since 1980. One of its customers is China, where this aircraft has been certified. Almost half of all Yak-42s are now exported, and the number exported has more than tripled over the last two years. The Saratov Aviation Plant is preparing to produce the modified Yak-42M aircraft, which has a capacity of around 160 passengers, 40 more than the Yak-42. One of the new projects of the Saratov Aviation Plant is the development of the "flying wing" with the Moscow design firm EKIP. It has the shape of a "flying saucer" and uses the WIG effect. The Smolensk Aviation Plant also produces Yakovlev aircraft.

The Aviastar Corporation, formerly the Ulianovsk Aviation Industrial Complex, is one of the largest aviation plants in the world, employing 36,000 workers. It was built in the 1980s on 1.5 mn square

---

[28] G. Batsanova, "Alexander Ermishin: Flying into capitalism on the 'Russian Plate,'" *Delovie Lyudi*, No. 5 (1993).

meters of land, and a new town for 150,000 inhabitants was created. All production lines at the plant were geared to build the Tu-160 strategic bomber. After three years the plant was re-engineered to produce the An-124 cargo plane, which required new equipment and the creation of some new technologies. Then in 1988, after the conversion process had begun, the Ministry of Defense sharply reduced its order for the An-124. Civil demand for this transport aircraft could not compensate for the reduction in military demand. As a result, only 15 An-124 airplanes were produced from 1986 to 1990. This average of about three a year was far less than the projected capacity of almost 30 a year.

One consequence has been a large turnover of employees; over 10 years there was a turnover of 32,000 people, or 88 percent.[29] In the late 1980s, Aviastar started retooling to assemble the Tu-204 passenger airplane; the first three Tu-204s were assembled there in 1990.

Voronezh Aviation Production Association, with 20,000 workers, is the primary manufacturer of Iliushin aircraft. It is currently starting to produce both passenger and cargo versions of the Il-96, and expects to produce more than 20 airliners annually. The enterprise hopes that the Il-96M will be certified in Russia by early 1995, and that the U.S Federal Aviation Administration (FAA) will certify the cargo version in 1996.[30] It will be harder to get FAA certification for the passenger version, because the materials used in the cabin interior do not meet safety standards; these materials are not produced in Russia. The standard Il-96 uses the Perm Motor Corporation's PS-90A turbofan engines. The Il-96-300, which is more than 10 meters longer, uses Pratt & Whitney PW 2337 engines.

The Samara Aviation Plant produces the Tu-95MS strategic bomber and the Tu-154M medium-range civilian airliner. These aircraft are powered by engines of the NK type, which are designed and produced at the Samara enterprise Trud. The Tupolev Design Bureau, Trud, and Samara have begun to develop the hydrogen-fueled Tu-155.

In recent years the Kazan Aviation Production Association has produced the Tu-160 Blackjack and the Tu-22M3 Backfire strategic bombers and the Il-62M airliner. The Backfire has been in production

---

[29] Yu. Belanov, "Winged Klondike," *Inzhenernaia Gazeta*, July 27, 1990.
[30] M. Mecham, "Il-96M Cabin Materials Halt FAA Certification," *Aviation Week & Space Technology*, June 1993.

since 1981. Kazan is in the process of halting production of the Tu-160, and is preparing to increase production of the Il-62M and to assemble the new Tu-204 airliner. The Kazan Helicopter Production Plant is one of the manufacturers of Mil Design Bureau helicopters, such as the Mi-8 and others.

Other plants that produce helicopters are the Rostov-na-Donu Helicopter Plant, which has produced the Mi-26, and the Orenburg Scientific-Production Association Strela ("Arrow"), which is starting to produce the Ka-126 helicopter.

The Polyot Production Association is located in Omsk, and has 20,000 employees. Organizationally, Polyot is part of the Department of General Machine-Building, in the rocket and missile industry, but it is undergoing conversion and returning to aircraft production. Together with the enterprises of Kharkov in the Ukraine and Arseniev in the Far East, Polyot has established the Uran Association to produce the An-74 transport aircraft, designed by Antonov. The first An-74 is due to be assembled in 1993.

The Novosibirsk Aviation Production Association, named after V. Chkalov, is one of the largest aerospace plants in Russia. It had produced only military aircraft,[31] but in 1994 it will manufacture the An-38 multi-purpose turboprop airplane.

The Irkutsk Aviation Production Association, with 14,000 employees, produced MiG fighters. Its civilian project is production of the A-200 seaplane developed by the Beriev Design Bureau. Together with the Irkutsk University, the enterprise is also developing WIG-effect aircraft with an air-cushion undercarriage. There are several variants, with takeoff mass ranging from one ton to 1,000 tons.

The Komsomolsk-na-Amure Aviation Plant produces Su fighters, and began serial production of the single-seat Su-27 in 1982. During the process of conversion, Komsomolsk-na-Amure completed the design of the S-80, a multi-purpose transport, and plans to produce 150 S-80s during 1994–1995. Under an agreement with Republic Sakha in Yakutia, the plant has started to develop and produce various types of transport equipment for the North, including air-sleighs, hydroplanes, motor deltaplanes, and micro-aircraft.

The Ulan-Ude Aviation Production Association, which employs 10,000 people, produces the Su-25T attack plane and military and

---

[31] V. Belikov, "Microliner An-38: The child of conversion," *Isvestiya*, December 10, 1991.

civilian helicopters developed by the Mil and Kamov Design Bureaus, such as the Mi-8 and Mi-17. One of its latest projects is the production of the new Ka-62 helicopter for civilian use.

The Sazykin Aviation Production Association in Arseniev produces helicopters. After it was excluded from the government order in 1989, it produced helicopters independently. Sazykin aims to continue production of helicopters, and to produce passenger airplanes for local airlines. It began to produce Mi-34 helicopters and An-74 aircraft in 1993.

The Engine Industry

One of the main directions for conversion in the aerospace industry is to improve Russian civil aviation engines. Only four countries can produce advanced aviation engines for many types of aircraft; Russia is one of them.

The Trud Science-Production Association in Samara is one of the largest in the engine industry. It develops and produces engines of the NK type, which are used in Tupolev strategic bombers and passenger airplanes and Antonov transport planes. Trud was one of the first enterprises to try to diversify its products. In the 1970s, Trud developed an aviation-type engine used for exploratory drilling for oil and gas. Trud also developed a way to pump gas with old aircraft engines that were no longer safe for flying; aircraft engines were installed along the whole length of the Urengoy-Uzhgorod pipeline, from Siberia to the western border of the former USSR, and are used at all gas pumping stations in the north of Russia. Trud recently developed a power station that produces 75,000 kilowatts of electricity using aviation engines.

The Perm Motor Corporation produces engines for 26 types of airplanes and helicopters and exports them to over 30 countries, including Germany, Japan, Korea, the Netherlands, and India. Its PS-90A engine is the first aviation engine produced in Russia to be certified as matching the international standard. Perm Motor is planning to modernize this engine in collaboration with General Electric and its French partner, Snecma.

The Perm Motor-Building Association was one of the first plants in the military sector, and later became Perm Motor Corporation, a joint-stock company. Perm Motor has compensated for cuts in military orders by producing engines for civilian airplanes, and also by diversifying its products. It manufactures multi-purpose motor-blocks called Lutch ("Ray") and Cascade. In 1992, Perm Motor produced more then 75,000 motor-blocks for agriculture, a substantial majority of the 112,000 agricultural motor-blocks produced in Russia. Perm Motor is also mastering the production of wheeled mini-tractors.

The staff of Perm Motor plans to compete to replace the gas-pumping plants used on Russian gas mains, which were produced by Rolls Royce and other Western firms. During the next 10 years, over 1,500 must be replaced. Perm Motor will base its bid on plants utilizing their PS-90 and other types of engines, and projects that its plants will be as effective as but cheaper than the Rolls Royce plants. One of Perm Motor's main competitors is likely to be Trud, which has produced such plants during the past 20 years.

The Baranov Motor-Building Production Association in Omsk employs 20,000 workers. According to its conversion program, the enterprise has started to produce TV7-117S turboprop engines developed by the Klimov Design Bureau for the Il-114 passenger airplane.

The Progress Science-Production Association in Zaporozhie, Ukraine, specializes in developing engines for subsonic airplanes. Conversion projects include gasoline saws, compressor stations, and installations equipped with gas-turbine engines that extinguish fires in mines. The main consumers of Zaporozhie's engines are the Russian aircraft enterprises; the future of this plant depends on political and economic ties between Russia and Ukraine. Other engine design bureaus and production plants are located in Rybinsk, Tyumen, Ufa, and elsewhere.

Due to the poor performance of the engines produced in Russia and Ukraine, the engine industry requires extensive investment and improvement.[32] The engine industry is an example of the need for reorganization of the entire aerospace industry, both military and civil. General Electric and Snecma estimated that 250,000 employees in Russia and Ukraine produced 15 percent of all aviation engines made in the world; the other 85 percent were made by only 100,000 employees in the U.S., France, and Great Britain.[33]

---

[32] See also J. Lenorovitz and S. Kandebo, "Reshaping Russia's Propulsion Industry," *Aviation Week & Space Technology*, March 30, 1992.
[33] A. Glebova, "Russia will return to the world market."

Military Aviation Repair

All repair work on military airplanes and helicopters is performed by the Ministry of Defense at its own facilities. One focus of conversion in which the Air Forces Aviation Repair Enterprises are involved, is the repair of civil airplanes, helicopters, and aviation engines. These enterprises are turning toward the civil sector partly because of large reductions in Russian air forces.

The decrease in the number of combat aircraft resulted in 1992 Ministry of Defense budget cuts of almost 11 percent from 1991, down to 1.2 bn rubles.[34] Civil aviation repairs performed at the aviation repair facilities increased from 100 mn rubles in 1991 to 122 mn in 1992. In addition, orders from foreign customers for repairs increased from 54 mn rubles in 1991 to 114 mn in 1992.[35]

Aircraft Exports and International Cooperation

Many military aircraft were exported by the former USSR, but exports were reduced significantly in the beginning of the 1990s. By now, deep cuts in the Russian military budget, the loss of traditional markets, and the shortage of investment for conversion are forcing managers to look for new markets for exports of military aircraft. (See also Chapter 4.)

Russian military aircraft enterprises have an excess of capacity, but need new production lines to manufacture new civilian aircraft. In many cases, the equipment on existing military production lines is new, which increases the attractiveness of obtaining orders for military aircraft. The export of military aircraft built with existing production capacity is highly profitable.[36] In addition, military aircraft is one of the few areas in which Russian technologies are competitive with Western ones. These factors have led to an intensive search for new markets. While the Russian aerospace enterprises pre-

---

[34] The data cited in this paragraph are in 1990 prices.

[35] P. Kohno and N. Kuznetsov, "Conversion of the self-financing industrial enterprises of the Ministry of Defense of the Russian Federation," *Conversion*, No. 3 (Moscow: IZANA Publishing, 1993).

[36] Some Russian experts estimate that one kilogram of an automobile is worth $20, of consumer electronics $100, and of an aircraft almost $1,000. E. Dobrovolski, "'The Black Shark' is on the guard of Russia," *Vek*, No. 37 (September 24–30, 1993), p.12.

viously sold mostly outmoded types of aircraft, now they try to sell state-of-the-art fighters and helicopters, such as the MiG-29 and the Ka-50.

Many of the aerospace enterprises now find themselves in a vicious cycle. To manufacture civilian aircraft that are desirable to developed countries with high standards, they need new production capabilities and new investment, including hard currency. But they can only get this hard currency by exporting successful aircraft to the developed countries. In any case, the process of certifying a passenger airliner and its manufacturer takes several years. To obtain hard currency, Russian military-industrial enterprises are trying to export military aircraft that have already been produced or can be produced quickly using existing capabilities.

Many managers fear that their prospects for exporting civil aviation products in the future will resemble their current difficulties in exporting military aircraft. However, they are beginning to understand that competing in the world market requires a top-notch maintenance and support service network, and that it is much easier to develop such a network with the help of foreign partners.

There are some areas in which Russian producers could compete if they had a better maintenance and support service network. For example, by some estimates,[37] the Al-31F engine for the Su-27 and the RD-33 engine for the MiG-29 are better than their foreign counterparts: they are lighter; they work with a continuous build-up of thrust and are therefore easier to control; they have a better afterburner, which also switches on continuously; and they have better gas dynamics and stability. According to these experts, the PS-90A engine has the same parameters as its foreign competitors, and is even better in fuel consumption. By other estimates, however, the PS-90A has shown trouble-free operation for only 500 hours, in comparison with 9,000 hours for Pratt & Whitney and 19,000 for Rolls Royce equivalents.[38]

The Il-96-300 is outfitted with Pratt & Whitney engines and the Tu-204 with Rolls Royce engines largely because these companies have widespread service networks, and can replace an airplane engine in a

---

[37] V. Sosunov, "Rolls-Royce is not better than ours."

[38] A. Glebova, "Russia will return to the world market."

single day anywhere in the world. Of course, Russian firms cannot do the same.[39]

There is almost no direct foreign investment in Russian aerospace plants. The only Russian aerospace enterprise that is trying to sell a large number of shares to foreign investors is the Aviastar joint-stock company in Ulianovsk. Typically joint ventures are established with a small amount of capital. An example is BRAVIA, the firm established to fund the production and marketing of the Tu-204, of which 50 percent is owned by the Flemming Russia Investment Corporation, a subsidiary of the British investment bank Robert Flemming and Company, Ltd.; 25 percent by Aviastar; and the other 25 percent by the Tupolev Design Bureau. BRAVIA is capitalized at only 1 mn rubles—less than $1,000.[40] Currently the Tu-204s are not owned by BRAVIA; their development and production, including the Rolls Royce engines, were paid for by the Russian government.

The situation with many other joint ventures is similar. The Boeing Technical Research Center in Moscow, which officially opened in September 1993, employs 20 Russian specialists who will do research in fields where Russian science and technology is advanced, including aviation metallurgy, mathematical models of fluid dynamics, and the influence of low temperature on the fuel systems of aircraft.

In the current situation, it makes sense for Russian firms to develop sporting, training, and business aircraft, and there are numerous joint projects with foreign firms in these areas. They include joint development of the Yak-130 trainer by the Yakovlev Design Bureau and Aermacchi (Italy); joint production of business jets by Yakovlev Design Bureau and Israel Aircraft Industries; development of the MiG-AT military jet trainer by Mikoyan Design Bureau and Daewoo Heavy Industries Aerospace Division (South Korea); and joint production of business jets by Mikoyan Design Bureau and Dassault Aviation (France).

In addition, during the past two years the number of serious long-term joint development and production projects in commercial transport, including high-capacity aircraft, has sharply increased.

---

[39] However, it doesn't make sense to mount foreign engines on aircraft that will be used and serviced in Russia; the PS-90A engine costs several times less than its foreign equivalents.

[40] A. Glebova, "Russia will return to the world market."

Chapter 4

Sergei Kortunov
Edited and with a
commentary by
Alexei Arbatov

Russian Aerospace Exports

Exports of military aircraft occupy an important place in security relations between Russia and other countries for a number of reasons. First, Russian military aircraft are competitive on the world arms market. The Soviet aircraft industry was long noted for its advanced technology, and the relatively low cost of producing military aircraft in the USSR—due to the low costs of energy, raw materials, and labor—made it possible to sell them at attractive prices, especially for the developing countries of Southeast Asia and Africa. Russian aircraft have been in great demand in those countries because of their high reliability, relative simplicity of handling, and other features.

Second, Russia inherited more than 60 customers in nearly all regions of the world; from 1950 to 1993, these countries received over 27,000 aircraft and helicopters of more than 152 types and models. (See Table 4.1.) The USSR supplied many of these weapons for political reasons and, more often than not, as grants or through barter deals. Recipients of Soviet military aid are dependent on Russia for the maintenance and modernization of the military aircraft supplied to them earlier.[1]

---

[1] Some countries, such as those of Eastern Europe, have tried to free themselves from this military-technical dependence and increase their cooperation with Western states,

Sergei Kortunov is the head of a Department in the Directorate on non-proliferation, disarmament, and technical cooperation in the Russian Foreign Ministry.

Alexei Arbatov is a member of the Russian Parliament (Duma), a senior fellow at the Institute of World Economics and International Relations of the Russian Academy of Sciences, and founder and Director of the Center for Geopolitical and Military Forecasts in Moscow.

Third, the Treaty on Conventional Armed Forces in Europe (CFE) created a huge surplus of Russian combat aircraft in service and in storage. This deprived Russia's enormous military aircraft industry— about 90 percent of the aerospace research institutes, design bureaus, and production plants of the former USSR—of outlets at home. Like the industries in other nations, particularly the United States and France, the Russian industry has sought outlets on the world market— a tendency that is likely to continue for the next eight to ten years.

The new Russian military doctrine's stress on airborne mobility means that the role of combat and support aircraft in the Russian armed forces will grow substantially. It is essential to preserve and enhance a technologically advanced Russian military aerospace industry, but Russia's economic and financial crisis has left this industry without contracts and brought it to the verge of collapse.[2] The aerospace industry sees military aircraft sales abroad as a way to survive during hard times, and as a way to maintain the scientific and technological potential that will be needed to equip the Russian armed forces once the economic crisis has passed.

Russia's Customers

In 1992–1993, Russia accounted for a modest share of world military aircraft exports—not more than 8 percent, compared to the Soviet share of 25-30 percent in 1989. In 1989, the USSR was the leading exporter of military aircraft as grants, and the recent decline in Russian deliveries is largely due to the fact that Russia has limited its arms exports to purely commercial deals since 1992. At present, foreign countries are equipped with about 10,000 Russian military aircraft and helicopters.

In 1992–1993, China remained the leading importer, while India was second and Iran third. As a result of UN embargoes, exports to Iraq, Libya, and Yugoslavia dropped to zero; and as a result of the disintegration of the Warsaw Treaty Organization, deliveries to Poland, Hungary, East Germany, Romania, Bulgaria, and Czech-

---

but, faced with the high prices of Western military products and the cost of re-equipping whole branches of their armed forces, they have asked Russia to restore their arms trade links.

[2] Chapter 3 examines the aviation industry's conversion process, and how individual enterprises have fared.

oslovakia also ended. In addition, deliveries to Syria, Egypt, Algeria, Angola, Yemen, North Korea, and Cuba were greatly reduced.

In the next three to five years, military-technical cooperation between Russia and former Warsaw Pact allies of the USSR—Poland, Hungary, Romania, Bulgaria, and the Czech and Slovak republics—will probably be restored. In addition, aircraft deliveries to Syria, Egypt, Algeria and Yemen are likely to increase, and if the UN sanctions are lifted, aircraft sales to Iraq, Libya, and Yugoslavia may resume. In addition, Russia will enter new markets in Asia and the Pacific (Malaysia, Philippines, Thailand, South Korea), the Middle East (Kuwait, Saudi Arabia, the United Arab Emirates), Africa (Sierra Leone, the Central African Republic, Tanzania, the Republic of South Africa), and Latin America (Brazil, Peru, Argentina, Bolivia). In the future, military aircraft may also be exported to Pakistan.

Table 4.1 Russian Exports of Aircraft and Helicopters 1950–1993

				Total number exported	
	1950-1959	1960-1969	1970-1979	1980-1989	1990-1993
Aircraft	**6,461**	**5,030**	**4,378**	**4,276**	**395**
Interceptors	3,649	3,570	3,000	2,339	219
Interceptors-Attack	0	418	784	1,121	51
Bombers	700	222	26	58	22
Fighters	0	0	0	200	0
Transport and Special	1,921	571	222	495	75
Civilian	191	249	346	63	28
Helicopters	**103**	**879**	**1,431**	**4,086**	**152**
Combat	0	0	150	576	19
Transport/Combat	93	541	640	2,241	35
Transport and Special	10	159	633	445	37
Civilian	0	179	8	824	61

Recent recipients have included NATO nations—the United States, Great Britain, Italy—and Switzerland and Japan. In the future military-technical cooperation will probably be established with France, Germany, Italy, Greece, Sweden, Turkey, and Portugal.

Russia could sell a number of products. The MiG-29, MiG-31, and Su-27 aircraft, the Il-78M tanker aircraft, and the Mi-28 and Mi-35 helicopters have proved to be highly competitive and likely to be much in demand on the world market. A new supersonic interceptor with a vertical take-off and landing capability, the Yak-141, may be much in demand in countries without a well-developed network of airfields. Among other types of aircraft under development, the most promising is a two-seat interceptor, the Su-34, which will replace the Su-24. The Su-25TK and Il-102 fighters have not yet been included in the procurement program of the Russian Ministry of Defense.

Countries that may be willing to purchase new Russian military aircraft for hard currency are:

- Argentina, the MiG-29 aircraft;
- Brazil, the MiG-29 aircraft and the Mi-28 and Mi-35 helicopters;
- Iran, the MiG-29 and Su-27 aircraft and the Mi-35 helicopter;
- Kuwait, the MiG-29 and Su-27 aircraft, the Il-78M tankers, the Mi-28 and Mi-35 helicopters;
- Peru, the Mi-35 helicopter;
- Some West European states and Turkey, the Mi-28 and Mi-35 helicopters;
- Syria, the MiG-29 aircraft and Mi-35 helicopters;
- the United Arab Emirates (UAE), the Su-27 aircraft; and
- after sanctions are lifted, Algeria for the Il-78M, MiG-31 and Su-27 aircraft, Iraq and Libya for the Su-27; and the Republic of South Africa for the MiG-29 and Su-27 aircraft and the Mi-28 and Mi-35 helicopters.

Apart from deliveries of newly-produced military aircraft, used aircraft now in service or in storage with the Russian Ministry of Defense may be supplied at low prices in modest numbers to countries with small armed forces and economic difficulties, such as Mali, Botswana, Nigeria, Cuba, and Bolivia.

Since many countries are reducing their forces and have limited budgets for purchasing new weapons, a priority for Russia is to service, repair, and modernize the military aircraft it supplied them earlier. Russia must achieve the world standard for service, organize complex repairs and modernization, and make effective use of the joint potential of design bureaus, production plants, and Ministry of Defense facilities.

In general, Russia's advantages over other arms producers are the advanced technology of its aircraft, its low prices, the possibility of barter deals, and the possibility that it will transfer arms to areas that are "sensitive" to the West—countries such as China, Iran, and possibly India.

The World Arms Market

For Russia, military aircraft represents a large export potential that has not materialized. In 1990–1993, Russia's military aircraft exports dropped sharply. Probably the most important is that since the end of the Cold War, the main military aircraft exporters have competed more fiercely than they had earlier; Russia was not prepared.

Under strong pressure from their military-industrial complexes, the governments of the main arms exporting countries have been forced to adopt protectionist policies, and actively promote their military aircraft on the world market. In the United States, Great Britain, and France, the highest state officials have become the chief promoters of arms exports.[3] This tendency was further strengthened by the CFE Treaty; signatories cut the number of aircraft in their armed forces and sharply dropped purchases of military aircraft. At the same time, with the end of the Cold War tensions increased and nationalistic ambitions re-emerged in regions that had been held in check. As a result, the Asia-Pacific region, Africa, and the Middle East wanted more weapons.

Finally, the war in the Persian Gulf heightened the demand of third world countries, including customers of the former USSR, for the most sophisticated weapons, including military aircraft. This gave the countries that manufacture military aircraft the impression that there were many new possibilities for arms exports.

All these factors stimulated intense competition between the five main exporters of military aircraft—the United States, France, Great Britain, Russia and China—to capture new and old outlets, no longer constrained by political or ideological considerations. The purely economic interests of the military-industrial complexes of these countries now dominate the politics of arms sales.

Therefore, it is not surprising that talks between the five main arms exporters were virtually halted in 1992 after only three meetings following the Gulf War. The countries simply were not interested in controlling the arms trade. As a result, the London Guiding Principles, which would have required countries to provide notification of wea-

---

[3] For example, U.S. President George Bush and Secretary of State James Baker actively promoted the sale of 150 F-16 fighters to Taiwan in 1992. President François Mitterrand of France did the same for the sale of 60 Mirage fighters.

pons sales, and worked out with much difficulty in 1991, were sacrificed to the immediate economic benefits of new arms deals.[4]

In this environment the United States has succeeded not only in finding new outlets for its equipment, but also in pushing Russia out of its traditional markets, such as Finland and Hungary.

U.S. opposition to the sale of Russian MiG-29s to Malaysia, with its use of political pressure on the Malaysian government, is a good example of an "unfair trading practice." The West's concern over the renewal of military-technical cooperation between Russia and China, and the sale to China of Su-27 aircraft and air missiles, is perceived in Russia as another example of unfair practice. Of course, all this is understandable in the world of arms trade, where no firm gives up a market without a bitter struggle, especially the Western arms companies that for years have shared markets among themselves, and are not willing to welcome a newcomer to the club.

Russia had been affected by the end of the Cold War even more painfully than the other arms-producing countries. In 1992 alone, military production fell by more than 64 percent compared to 1990. Entire production plants were closed, and the workers of the military-industrial complex, who had enjoyed a privileged position in Russia and had been a stable source of support for the regime, became a potential source of social and political instability.[5] Thus, following the example set by the governments of the principal Western countries, Russia adopted protectionist policies in support of its national arms manufacturers.

RUSSIA AS A COMPETITOR

As a state, Russia has only just made its appearance on the world market as an exporter of combat and support aircraft and helicopters, and their servicing on a commercial basis. The Soviet military-industrial complex was assured by the state of payment for the arms it produced, even though a large part of the equipment was not destined for the Soviet armed forces, but sold on favorable terms or given away to friendly regimes in return for political influence. The

---

[4] The notorious U.S. sale of 150 F-16 fighters to Taiwan served only as a long-awaited pretext for China to leave the talks.
[5] Such workers comprised a large fraction of those who voted for the radical-nationalist Liberal Democratic Party headed by Vladimir Zhirinovsky in the December 1993 parliamentary elections.

only exceptions in this respect were Iraq and Libya, which provided stable revenues, though their debt was also constantly growing.

The first attempts to place military exports on a commercial basis were made under President Mikhail Gorbachev, when the principle was proclaimed that "we shall supply anyone who pays" (except countries on which UN sanctions had been imposed or that adopted a clearly unfriendly attitude toward the USSR). The slogan "payment in the year of delivery" when the defense industry was in crisis and unprepared to compete in new markets proved unrealistic. Hard currency revenues from the sale of military aircraft fell to about $2 bn in 1991, from $7 bn in 1989. Reliance on hard-currency revenues from arms exports as a source of funds to pay for conversion, suggested at that time by the Defense Council and Military-Industrial Commission of the Council of Ministers, also proved unworkable.

The breakup of the Soviet Union was particularly harmful to the military aviation defense industry. First, the industry is not self-sufficient; for instance, it cannot produce engines for the An-24, -26, or -124 transport aircraft, nor for the Mi-8, -24 or -26 helicopters. Second, state funding for the development of aircraft and procurement dropped by 80 percent. Russia procured only 20 bombers and 5 military helicopters in 1992, compared to 50 and 100, respectively, in 1989. Third, a number of foreign policy factors aggravated the situation. As a result of the disintegration of the Warsaw Pact, arms deliveries to the countries of Eastern Europe were halted. The UN imposed arms embargoes against other long-time customers of the USSR—Iraq, Libya, and, later, Yugoslavia. On the non-traditional markets, such as the United Arab Emirates, Kuwait, Southeast Asia, and Europe, Russian salesmen met harsh competition from other manufacturers, particularly the United States, Great Britain, and France.

The prestige of Russian-made weapons, especially its military aircraft, remains as high as it had been earlier.[6] But technical quality alone cannot assure export opportunities; the modern market requires reliable after-sale servicing and supplies of spare parts, and this

---

[6] For example, in September 1992 Russia sent almost 500 officials to the Farnborough, United Kingdom, air show and exhibited 22 aircraft, including seven that had not been shown before. The President of British Aerospace was quoted as saying that the show had been "stolen by the Russians." While no agreements were signed during this event, one could be optimistic that the exhibition would bring results in time. The MiG-29 and Su-27 aircraft and the Mi-8 and Ka-25 helicopters are the most renowned.

always constituted the weak point of the Soviet arms trade.[7] The poor Soviet after-sale servicing was caused by arms companies' poor operating practices, and also by the wasteful style of the USSR's whole economy. The economy's main task was to produce; selling, repair, and provision of spare parts were considered economically insignificant. Some countries, such as Syria and India, have organized their own production of spare parts of Russian-made aircraft and helicopters because Russia cannot reliably provide parts. In some cases they bought spare parts in other CIS countries.

Purchasers also consider the political situation in a country from which they might buy military equipment, the stability of its foreign economic relations, the efficiency of its production process, and the size of its foreign debt. Many potential customers are afraid to buy Russian weapons, especially in large quantities, because they fear that in the event of a political or economic crisis, their Russian business partners may not be able to meet their obligations. Arms buyers require predictability.

Finally, an arms exporter must understand the market. While the market for complex, high-technology assets is difficult, the market for spare parts and obsolescent equipment presents a completely different picture. In many countries MiG-21s and MiG-23s are still in use and require servicing, repairs, and modernization. Russian manufacturers have clearly underestimated this large and promising market.

Administrative muddle and negligence has also hurt Russia. For example, the process for issuing an export license takes about nine months in Russia, compared to six days in the United States. This has proven to be the downfall of some arms export transactions.

Russia's lack of export expertise is a natural result of the old Soviet system. The USSR's policy of isolation from the world economy produced very few individuals or institutions familiar with the complexities of foreign trade, especially in the military sector. Producers had little idea how to market their product aggressively, and the intermediary organizations, which received no return from sales, had little incentive to do so. In a nutshell, Russian defense enterprises

---

[7] For many years developing countries that received weapons in barter deals and as grants were prepared to accept minimal after-sale servicing. Advanced weapons often went to those who were not able to handle them properly, as illustrated by past conflicts in the Middle East and the recent Persian Gulf War.

are simply not organized to seek new markets; worse, most do not understand how far they have to go.

Regulation of Russian Arms Exports

Beginning in 1991, several arms trade organizations and aerospace firms gained the right to export arms, including military aircraft, independent of the Ministry of Foreign Economic Relations.

For manufacturers and salesmen, the placing of arms exports on a commercial footing opened up the possibility of making real profits, in contrast to the past, when all the revenues went to the state. Aerospace companies' direct contact with foreign business partners was expected to increase the speed and profitability of arms sales and make the manufacturers less dependent on various middlemen; the directors of aerospace companies would market their products and conduct negotiations themselves. The arms companies were in a precarious situation. Their state contracts had been sharply reduced, but if they laid off their workers they would lose their unique aerospace technology and design capability.

At the same time, the transition to a free market led to a weakening of export controls, but the aviation industry's lack of sales skills led to the sale of combat aircraft and helicopters on unprofitable terms and the loss of potential clients. In some cases weapons were offered to customers below cost. In other cases the lack of coordination among aerospace manufacturers led to an overcrowding of the market in some countries (for instance, Malaysia), jeopardizing any exports to those countries. The arms trade organizations used their own middlemen, increasing the number of competitors, with each claiming to have credentials to negotiate for the Russian government. For example, in 1993, some 20 intermediary organizations visited Malaysia to sell Russian aircraft.

The exploration of new markets and the exposure of Russian salesmen and manufacturers to real competition should have been backed by considerable coordination of efforts, flexibility, and assistance from the state. For example, in order for some manufacturers and unique technologies to survive, urgent hard-currency loans were needed that the state simply could not provide. In addition, the old principle of "payment in hard currency in the year of delivery" remained in force, even though in the international arms trade, all deals are concluded on credit.

To rectify this situation a Presidential Decree of November 21, 1993, announced that in the future all arms deals would be concluded under the aegis of a single semi-governmental organization, Rosvooruzhenie, which would unite all of the former specialized organizations. This measure should increase the effectiveness of military-technical cooperation between Russia and foreign countries, and strengthen governmental controls over the arms trade, including exports of military aircraft.

The international transfer of conventional weapons is one of the few areas of international trade that is not governed by international regulation, nor is it subject to any mechanism for international negotiation or consultation. The main international obligations by which Russia is bound with regard to control of exports of conventional weapons flow from the "Guiding Principles for Conventional Weapons Deliveries," an agreement among the five permanent members of the UN Security Council.[8]

In addition, Russia also considers the decisions of international organizations that forbid exports to certain countries and require more openness on this subject. At present, the UN has imposed arms embargoes on Iraq, Yugoslavia, and Libya.

Russia's system of control over conventional weapons exports is based on legal and administrative measures adopted to prevent unauthorized arms deliveries. On February 22, 1992, the President of Russia signed a decree "About the forms of military production (work, services) and products waste on the territory of the Russian Federation, the sale of which is forbidden," which provides for the obligatory licensing for export of arms and military equipment and other special assets. Resolution No. 80 of the Council of Ministers of the Russian Federation, dated January 28, 1993, lists military products (work and services), whose export or import is subject to licensing, and it sets out how licenses are to be obtained. At the present

---

[8] Under the Guiding Principles, the nations undertake to avoid deliveries that could prolong or worsen an existing armed conflict, heighten tension in a region, introduce into a region a destabilizing military potential, or violate an embargo or other internationally agreed restriction; are intended for other purposes than the lawful defense of the receiving state; support international terrorism; or seriously undermine the economy of the importing nation.

time, the departments concerned have been instructed by the government to prepare for the new Parliament a law on military-technical cooperation between Russia and foreign countries that will improve the legal basis for control of arms exports.

To ensure a single, coordinated policy in the field of arms exports, an interdepartmental commission for military-technical cooperation between Russia and foreign countries was set up by a presidential decree of May 12, 1992. In addition, regulations on military-technical cooperation between Russia and foreign countries have been drafted. These govern the export and import of arms, military equipment, and services within the framework of military cooperation. A list of types of arms and military equipment that may be exported in 1992–1995 has been prepared and approved, and a list of countries to which arms exports are forbidden is reconfirmed annually.

It is important that Russia learn from Western countries how they have effectively controlled exports in a free market. A process is underway to establish contacts and hold a broad-based dialogue with Western countries on this subject, which should lead to greater coordination of the export control system for conventional weapons. The new international control and nonproliferation system which is being set up in place of Coordinating Committee for Multilateral Export Controls (COCOM) must also play an important role.

Prospects for Russian Exports

Russia has considerable arms export potential and could penetrate new, nontraditional markets. This section considers Russia's prospects for and obstacles to success in the three markets for military aircraft: new aircraft, surplus aircraft, and servicing.

In the 1990s, prospects for new aircraft exports will be shaped by the rearmament programs of some Third World countries, including South Africa, Egypt, Iran, India, Pakistan, South Korea, Taiwan, and Syria. In general, through 2000 the world market could absorb about 2,500 aircraft and 3,000 helicopters. For Russia, the most promising market remains Eastern Europe; its airfields, guidance systems, logistics and other military "infrastructure" are adjusted to Russian-made aircraft and helicopters. Under good circumstances, Russia might sell up to 100 new aircraft and helicopters per year to these countries.

Other arms sales might result from the development of links with NATO countries. The most promising countries for Russian exports are Italy, France, Portugal, and Spain. Future joint production with these countries of aircraft and helicopters for sale to third countries is not to be excluded. Russia has every right to claim its place on the world arms market, especially considering that this place is likely to be more modest than that of the United States and the former USSR.

However, Russia cannot succeed in this market with its current political instability and without effective management of its economy, including its defense industries. It is clear that Russia must attract new investments, including foreign investments, and modernize its aviation industry. It is also necessary to transfer part of the enterprises to private hands and to issue shares in the largest and most viable defense factories.

While the strong point of Russian aircraft and helicopters is their relatively low prices, this is a waning asset. The Russian cost advantage was based on artificially low prices for inputs, and as Russia moves towards a market economy, the prices of materials and labor are rising. As a result, arms producers will become increasingly non-competitive in the price of their products. In the long run, the Russian arms industry will not be competitive on the world market until the Russian economy as a whole is.

The second promising avenue of Russian arms trade is to sell off surplus aircraft and helicopters. Such models as the MiG-21bis, MiG-23ML, MiG-27K, MiG-25P, CX-22MZ, CY-24, Mi-8, Mi-24, and Mi-26, after modernization and repair, could be competitive with fourth-generation European combat aircraft. Potential buyers include former recipient countries of the USSR, such as Afghanistan, Angola, Vietnam, Congo, Mozambique, Mongolia, Syria, Cuba, Guinea, Pakistan, Laos, and Cambodia. This market could potentially absorb about 300 aircraft and 200 helicopters per year.

Russia should be prepared to encounter even more severe competition in this market than in the new armaments market. Some former allies of the USSR, including countries of Eastern Europe and even the CIS, are offering Soviet-made aircraft and helicopters themselves; this could greatly reduce the prices for these models.

Finally, there is a large market for servicing of aircraft and helicopters already supplied. Among the most promising customers for servicing are India, Syria, and Iraq. The most stable consumers of spare parts are likely to be former Warsaw Treaty Organization countries. In Latin America, relations with the former USSR's only stable client, Cuba, are now under revision.

The most promising models for service and spare parts are the MiG-21 (3,020 are located abroad), MiG-23 (1,025), Mi-8, Su-22 (520), and Mi-24 (455). The Dementiev Design Bureau is now negotiating modernization contracts for the MiG-21 and MiG-23 with several countries.

Russia's competitors in this market include China, which exports Chinese versions of the MiG-21; France, the United States, and Israel, which offered their services in modernizing Russian aircraft and helicopters in Iraq (before the Gulf War); Romania; and Hungary.

To maximize its advantages, Russia should reorganize the way it sells arms so that it is more effective and closer to international standards. Russia should also adopt a responsible attitude toward the arms trade; long experience shows that the transfer of weapons to adventurous and dictatorial regimes in exchange for political influence has cost Moscow dearly, both politically and economically.

Considering the growing competition and the saturation of the world arms market, emphasis should be on the export of sophisticated types of combat and support aircraft and helicopters. The guiding principle should probably be that everything in use by our own armed forces is for sale. (Of course military aircraft should be supplied in export versions that are inferior to versions destined for the Russian armed forces.) However, the supply or lease of advanced offensive aerospace weapons, or of weapons of mass destruction, and the technology for their production should be limited to the utmost. The proliferation of missile technology should be effected as openly as possible, with only commercial secrets being protected.

Finally, unless the arms manufacturers, the salesmen, those who place the orders—all who are involved in the selling process—receive their share of profits, export efforts will not be effective. As long as individuals' income does not depend directly on the results of their work, Russia will not be able to organize its defense industry efficiently, nor retain its leading specialists and designers and prevent the disintegration of a highly qualified labor force.

Editor's Comment: Economy and Security in Exports of Combat Aircraft

The problems and prospects of Russian combat aircraft exports lie at the intersection of two major areas: the role of military exports within the framework of defense industrial conversion, economic reforms, and Russia's participation in the world trade; and the role of arms exports in Russia's security, defense, and foreign policy. From both points of view, Sergei Kortunov's discussion of Russian arms exports, which reflects the official position of the Russian government and the dominant opinion of the political elite, raises a number of serious problems.

Military Exports as an Economic Tool

Among the numerous myths of the Cold War, one was that Soviet defense industries were an island of advanced technology, high managerial efficiency, and superb productivity in a sea of retarded, absurdly managed, low-quality civil industries. A corollary of this myth was that Soviet weapons, if given fair treatment, would successfully compete on world markets and bring large amounts of hard currency to the country. When the Cold War ended and the Soviet communist empire collapsed, both assumptions were shown to be deeply flawed. To be sure, from time to time the Soviet Union did produce high quality weapon systems and achieve breakthroughs in certain areas of science and technology. But such accomplishments required an enormous concentration of the resources of the whole nation on defense, a complete disregard for cost and neglect of the living conditions of those who worked in the defense area, and outrageous deprivation of all non-military spheres of the nation's economy, science, and culture. The whole nation was kept at a miserable standard of living compared with the nations that the USSR successfully challenged in the arms race.

Contrary to the common Western view, the problem was not confined to the distorted allocation of the major and best resources (material, human, and intellectual) to the military domain. Unlike in the United States, the problem was not just that too much of the economy was tied to military needs; rather the entire Soviet industry and economy was built to provide for defense as the only priority, to prepare for an inevitable war with "imperialist encirclement." This was the avowed goal of national strategy, starting with the first industrialization plans and collectivization of agriculture in the late 1920s, and continuing with inexorable momentum, although tacitly, until the last (twelfth) five-year plan of 1986–1990.

This priority dictated a centralized, disciplined, planned economy, which permitted the arbitrary allocation of resources, control over wages and prices, and the retention or relocation of labor, and which controlled the distribution of wealth and rewards and punishments more broadly. To ensure this degree of control, a totalitarian, repressive political and ideological system was required which permeated all levels of the economy and society. Obviously, such an economy could only provide the "labor force" with an equalized minimal survivability income to continue carrying out the directives of the ruling elite. But it was inherently unable to respond to the growing material and spiritual needs of a civilized, "post-industrialized" society. This was the fundamental source of the eventual defeat of communism.

The impoverished and primitive civilian economy was a sine-qua-non of a mammoth military-industrial complex, which had to have a measure of competitiveness in the arms race with the wealthiest and most technologically advanced states of the world. The two economies, although isolated from each other in a functional sense, were inseparable systemically, like "Siamese twins" one of which flourished by feeding on the life juices of the other.

Considering the economic and political pressure put upon the Soviet Union—one of the largest and most resource-rich industrial nations—the achievements of its military-industrial complex were quite modest. The method of achieving the goal defeated the purpose, due to the complete isolation of the defense domain from the rest of society; an unprecedentedly wasteful mode of operation; the absence of any outside control; the lack of internal competition; the full dominance of vested interests; and widespread disinformation, fraud and deception. All the evidence indicates that except for more stringent quality control and more highly skilled workers, the cost-effectiveness and management of the military-industrial complex were even more uncoordinated, short-sighted, and ill-planned than those prevailing in the rest of the Soviet economy.[9]

This became only too evident when an attempt was made in the late 1980s to convert parts of the defense industry to the production of civilian goods, capitalizing on their allegedly high efficiency, quality control and advanced technology. This attempt failed, largely, for two reasons. First, instead of converting, the military industries simply expanded civilian production, which had always been part of their planned output. In the prices for civilian products they included the enormous cost of preserving their military production capacities, for which they had no contracts because of the cuts in defense procurement in the final years of Mikhail Gorbachev's regime. The inflated prices of the civilian goods and services they produced made them unacceptable to domestic consumers; the low demand quickly discouraged this type of "conversion."

Second, the conversion was conceived as a "transition from war to peace," rather than a transition from a state-run planned economy to a private or corporate market economy. A state plan for civilian output immediately led to great cost overruns, absurd products (such as titanium spades), and demands for 60–90 bn rubles of state investment (in 1990 prices), which would have made conversion a huge additional burden for the national economy and the government budget, instead a new source of growth.

Then the 1992 program of "shock therapy," particularly the sudden price liberalization (in an highly monopolized economy), immediately led to skyrocketing costs for the labor, raw materials, energy and sub-components employed by the defense industries. Procurement contracts to defense industries were cut by 62–68 percent in 1992.[10] This was done in an economy that was 96 percent state-owned, and 70 percent based on state planning rather than market demand. The economy did not have any free channels to reallocate resources or investments from military to civilian spheres, from one branch of industry or agriculture to another, or between regions. The

---

[9] For example, by the end of the 1980s the Soviet Air Force was operating about 100 classes, types, and models of combat and support aircraft. This created insurmountable problems for maintenance, supplies, repair, and modernization.

[10] Clifford Gaddy and Melanie Allen, *Russian Arms Sales Abroad: Policy, Practice, and Prospects*, Brookings Discussion Papers, FPSP (Washington, D.C.: Brookings Institute, September 1993), p. 45.

economy did not have any market or taxation infrastructure for investments, labor, or resources, nor did it offer an environment for competition or feedback from demand to supply.

As a result, instead of moving toward market transformation, the economy—and particularly its core, the defense sector—found itself on the verge of total collapse, with all the horrible social and political implications of such a catastrophe. Since then, hard lobbying and political pressure for funding and subsidies have become the principal method of industrial survival. This is the background against which the issue of arms exports, and aircraft exports in particular, must be understood.

In February 1992, Mikhail Maley, then presidential adviser and the head of the State Committee on Conversion (and now the chairman of the inter-agency committee on defense industries in the Security Council) proposed that Russia's arms exports be increased as a way to earn hard currency for conversion.[11] Aircraft, the most technologically advanced and presumably highly competitive item of defense production, were the focus of this idea. Though subject to some criticism, the concept seemed to be largely supported in the government and remains part of Russia's official policy.

There are two major flaws in Maley's concept. One is the assumption that in a generally inefficient and uncompetitive economy, there could be an advanced sector that can meet world standards, even after its artificial state-planned economic structure is eliminated. This notion confuses competitiveness in an arms race with competitiveness in the marketplace. The other flaw was the expectation that arms export revenues could be used to implement conversion without an effective and profound general economic reform—or, alternatively, to evade conversion in the midst of a radically changing economy.

In practice, the disintegration of the centrally-planned Soviet economy has deprived the military sector of its former advantages, which could have made it marginally competitive on the world market. In particular, cheap subsidized raw materials, energy, subcomponents, and labor, along with the arbitrary allocation of resources and fixation of prices from above, have become or are fast becoming a thing of the past. With prices approaching the world level, formerly "cheap" Russian weapons are suddenly relatively expen-

---

[11] Interview with Mikhail Maley, *Rossiskaya Gazeta*, 28 February 1992, pp. 1–2.

sive.[12] The traditional inefficiency, low productivity, inflexibility, enormous overhead, and habitual cost overruns of the military-industrial complex became all too evident when Russian weapons were offered in the world marketplace.

In addition, Russian arms exporters come from a country without market experience; they lack marketing skills and must cope with bureaucratic confusion at home. They are not accustomed to the new markets, nor readily accepted. Because of Russia's economic and political instability, they cannot guarantee to fulfill orders, provide reliable servicing, and supply spare parts.

Without doubt, these are the main obstacles to the expansion of Russia's arms exports, including aircraft sales—not so-called "unfair practices." This is not to deny that the United States has applied political pressure to support its arms sales, but other arms exporters cannot be expected to welcome Russia as a new rival given the shrinking world market. This, of course, is a further obstacle to Russian aircraft exports.

As a number of Western experts have persuasively argued,[13] markets for combat aircraft in industrialized and developing countries will continue to decline, while the competition among major suppliers will intensify because of cuts in domestic defense contracts in the aftermath of the end of Cold War. The dwindling market will affect Russia's export prospects even more harshly than those of other arms producers. Some of Russia's traditional customers are subject to UN arms embargoes (Iraq, Libya, Yugoslavia, and Angola); sales to others would be counterproductive politically or economically (North Korea, Cuba, Vietnam); and others are likely to turn to new suppliers for political reasons (Eastern Europe, Egypt, and conceivably India after the failed missile deal with Russia). Finally, while barter deals are still used as an incentive, they are fast losing their attractiveness: Russia needs hard currency, not Malaysian palm oil.

This is all the more true if, as the government declares, arms exports are to facilitate conversion. However, enterprises that do manage to sell combat aircraft and other military goods will not be

---

[12] A high rate of inflation, irrational taxation, monopolization of the economy, and interrupted supplies contribute to the problem.

[13] Clifford Gaddy and Melanie Allen, *Russian Arms Sales Abroad*; and Randall Forsberg and Jonathan Cohen, "The Global Arms Market: Prospects for the Coming Decade" (Cambridge, Mass.: IDDS, January 11, 1994). See also Chapter 11.

motivated to convert to civilian production. Yet they will also be discouraged from investing all the necessary effort and money involved in arms exports if the government takes a big portion of their revenues to convert less efficient, less advanced, or less successful companies and production plants. The lucky exporters will certainly manage to conceal their profits or leave them abroad; the chaos in Russia's administrative, taxation, and accounting systems and widespread corruption will be conducive to such endeavors.

In addition, some recent arms export profits were largely based on the deeply underrated exchange ratio of ruble to dollar, a result of Russia's abnormal economic situation.[14] Improvement of the economic environment and stabilization of the ruble, which is allegedly the purpose of the arms trade, will certainly remove these unnatural profit possibilities.

All in all, the recent Russian success stories with combat aircraft exports to China, Iran, India, and Malaysia, and other arms deals should not serve as a basis for large-scale, long-term economic policy planning. Some enterprises have been using arms exports (and, even more, exports of stocks of raw materials, supplies, and equipment) to avoid or evade conversion, that is, to survive without state defense contracts or a sensible government-run conversion program, hoping for the return of the military-industrial bonanza. These moods and practices cannot last long and are no substitute for a rational, state-sponsored conversion strategy, or a promising way of gaining hard currency, improving foreign trade structure, or helping economic reforms at home. Moreover, the potential security and political implications of excessive reliance on arms exports must not be ignored.

Military Exports as a Security Matter

There is a growing view in Russia that instead of providing inadequate, inefficient, and humiliating economic aid and credits, the West should voluntarily share with Russia some of its lucrative arms exports markets. It is also argued that the West should repay Russia by letting it enter new arms markets in return for steps Russia has taken in cutting defense spending, reducing arms procurement, and cooper-

---

[14] For example, one defense manager said that selling even one fighter abroad can provide a year's wages for his entire labor force.

ating with UN sanctions against Iraq, Libya, and Yugoslavia. Otherwise, it is implied, there will be increasing political pressure to expand arms sales and revise the 1991–1993 policy of cooperation with the West. These views reflect the general conservative and nationalist shift in Russian domestic politics since the events of October–December 1993.

Such arguments are based on misconceptions, and are a matter of serious concern. The West does not owe anything to Russia. Russia's defense budget cuts and reductions of armed forces were not the reason for, but the consequence of, the alleviation of international tensions in the wake of economic and political turmoil at home. Enhancing cooperative security was in Russia's own interests: any other policy would have worsened Moscow's position in the world and the economic situation at home in the early 1990s. Expanded arms exports would have aggravated the problems, fueling tensions with the United States, overtaxing Russia's limited industrial potential, and blocking all economic cooperation with the advanced industrial nations.[15]

In fact, Russian aircraft export opportunities are likely to remain quite limited. India, Syria, Iran, and China may be the major recipients of Russian combat aircraft and other arms and military technologies in the foreseeable future. Of these four clients, the more modest recipients, India and Syria, would not create security problems for Russia, if they support regional conflict resolution and do not develop regional expansionist propensities. As a counterbalance to China and Pakistan and to Turkey and Iraq, respectively, they might even play a stabilizing role. But China and Iran, the likely principal recipients of Russian arms exports, are less congenial.

China is the only power that may present a direct military threat to Russia's security in the long run.[16] Its unprecedented economic growth, unexplained military build-up, potential domestic changes and growing nationalism, and long history of territorial border disputes with Russia and the USSR, placed against the background of

---

[15] In addition, neither appropriate behavior in world politics nor a cooperative stance in the UN is something to be specifically rewarded by other nations.

[16] For accounts of Russia's relations with other powers and regions, see Robert D. Blackwill and Sergei A. Karaganov, eds., *Damage Limitation or Crisis? Russia and the Outside World*, CSIA Studies in International Security No. 5 (Washington, D.C.: Brassey's 1994).

the military vulnerability, economic desolation, and political separatism of Russia's Siberian and Far East regions, should be a serious concern to Russian foreign policy makers and defense planners.[17]

For political and strategic reasons, the West is reluctant to supply arms to China. Russia has been quick to fill the gap even though Moscow should have been the party most concerned about Beijing's military build-up and its uncertain future propensities. Once again short-sighted enthusiasm for arms sales to China may create a grave problems for Russia's future security.

China's current military build-up is largely dependent on massive sales of Russian weapons, technologies, and licensed production, including as modern an aircraft as the Su-27, and, potentially, the MiG-29, MiG-31, and Tu-22M—exports totaling $1.8 bn in 1992.[18] The Chinese air force could have as many as 2,000 modern combat aircraft in 20 years. This could provide Beijing with the crucial edge in the overall military balance; Russia's armed forces in Siberia and the Far East are dependent on reinforcements from the European basing areas, and the communications, forward airfields, and prepositioned stocks of equipment that should facilitate such reinforcement are all vulnerable to massive air strikes.

To some extent similar concerns apply to Iran. Although in the short run Iran offers a counterbalance to Turkey—Russia's principal rival in the Transcaucasus and Central Asia—the regional situation could change. It is quite plausible that Iran may become Russia's main competitor in Central Asia and the major sponsor of Muslim fundamentalist militant movements that could destabilize Central Asia, Kazakhstan, and some parts of Russia itself. Alternatively, Iran's expansionist strategy in the Persian Gulf zone might involve Russia in a conflict with Saudi Arabia, the UAE, and their Western partners. In addition, deals with Iran may collide with potentially more profitable and strategically safer arms sales to Saudi Arabia and the UAE.

Finally, sales of state-of-the-art weapons may compromise Russia's defense capabilities if the goods are not properly adapted before delivery. For example, the Su-27, which will form the backbone of the Air Force and Air Defense of the Russian Federation for the next 10–15 years, has been technically compromised by hasty sales.

---

[17]Policy makers should also watch China's policies towards Mongolia and Kazakhstan, whose friendship and sovereignty are crucial to Russia's security.
[18] See Chapter 11.

This blunder may conceivably be more detrimental to Russian defense than the shortage of funds for Russian Air Force modernization over the next several years. In addition, Maley's concept, which stresses export-oriented military production, may distort the defense industrial base and lead to a neglect of procurement of weapons and equipment that are needed by Russian armed forces but cannot compete on the world market.

Necessary Conditions for Arms Exports

The above critique should not be construed as a rejection of all Russian arms exports. As long as international arms exports are not prohibited or severely constrained by agreements among major exporters, such exports may continue to constitute some portion of Russia's foreign trade. But this is predicated on a number of reservations and conditions.

First, Russia's short-term earnings from arms exports should not jeopardize its longer-term security interests. Arms exports can encourage the emergence of new threats; this might bring bigger contracts to Russian defense industries, but only at the cost of once again overburdening the nation's economy and finances.

Second, Russia's arms export interests should not drive its foreign policy and its positions in the UN on conflict resolution and peacekeeping problems. On the contrary, Moscow's security interests in regional stability, increased international cooperation, nuclear nonproliferation, and global restrictions on arms transfers must guide its military export policy. Obviously, to achieve these ends, there would have to be guarantees that Russian restraint in selling arms to certain countries would not be used by other suppliers as a source of expanded markets.

Third, weapons sales should not be viewed either as a way to earn money for conversion, which will never work, or as a way to avoid conversion, which will only work for a few companies for a very short time. Production for export is not a substitute for a sensible and consistent long-term state conversion program. Without such a program the entire military-industrial base is likely to collapse shortly, crushing the companies with export potential as well as those oriented mainly to production for domestic use.

Fourth, arms export earnings should not be treated as a way to sustain and retain defense industries until domestic contracts revive. Exports cannot substitute for a wise defense-industrial policy, which must thoughtfully select which enterprises should be retained in the defense sector, which should be converted to civilian production, and which should be shut down. Such a policy must be predicated on a sensible economic and financial policy in general, as well as on a rational military reform and revision of defense requirements.

Fifth, it must be recognized that in the long run, the short-term benefits of arms exports tied to passing advantages (such as low cost, barter deals, and specific customers) will not improve Russia's foreign trade structure, which is mostly based on the exports of oil and raw materials; nor will it alleviate the growing foreign debt. Rather, such deals will ultimately degrade both the state of defense industries and foreign trade.

The ability of the Russian military industry to successfully compete in the world market within reasonable political and security constraints will depend largely on the success of more general economic reforms, including reforms of the domestic defense industrial base and arms procurement system, and conversion of the major part of the military-industrial complex left behind by the Cold War. With such reforms, arms exports might constitute a valuable but quite modest part of Russian defense industry revenues, economic output, and foreign trade. Without these reforms, the arms trade—particularly sales of the most advanced and expensive aircraft—may actually damage national foreign policy and security interests.

Chapter 5

Randall Forsberg
Andrew Peach
Judith Reppy

U.S. Airpower and Aerospace Industries in Transition

Top U.S. security planners see many potential new military threats in the post–Cold War world. The Clinton administration's defense plan for fiscal years (FY) 1995–1999 calls for the United States to maintain the capability to fight two major regional wars simultaneously, in the Middle East and in East Asia, against adversaries with forces as large and well-equipped as those of pre–Gulf War Iraq—and to win each war within a few weeks, with no help from outside the region, and with minimal U.S. casualties.[1]

Developed by Secretary of Defense Les Aspin and endorsed by his successor, William J. Perry, the new U.S. strategy was first broached in February 1992, when Aspin was chairman of the House Armed Services Committee. In a paper on U.S. military options for the "post-Soviet" world, Aspin argued that the size and cost of fu-

---

[1] In the war against Iraq, which set the standard, 111 U.S. military personnel were killed and 395 injured by enemy fire. See U.S. Department of Defense, *Conduct of the Persian Gulf War: Final Report to Congress* (Washington, D.C.: U.S. Government Printing Office (GPO), April 1992), p. M-1.

Randall Forsberg is the Executive Director of the Institute for Defense and Disarmament Studies (IDDS) in Cambridge, Massachusetts, and an officer of the Center for Science and International Affairs, Kennedy School of Government, Harvard University.

Andrew Peach is a research fellow at the Institute for Defense and Disarmament Studies in Cambridge, Massachusetts, where he specializes in U.S. and West European air forces and aerospace industries.

Judith Reppy is Associate Professor of Peace Studies in the Center of International Studies at Cornell University, and Director of Cornell's Peace Studies Program.

ture U.S. forces would be shaped largely by whether the country pre-pared to fight one or two major regional wars.[2]

Around the time Aspin's paper was published, Air Force Vice Chief of Staff General Michael Carns commissioned a RAND study of the forces needed to win simultaneous major regional wars in the Middle East and East Asia.[3] The RAND study, *The New Calculus*,[4] fed into a Pentagon "Bottom-Up Review" of post–Cold War U.S. military needs, initiated by Aspin in March 1993. By late May, General Colin Powell, Chairman of the Joint Chiefs of Staff, had presented three options for consideration by the Bottom-Up Review team:

1. A "win-win" two-war strategy, with forces capable of winning two independent, widely-separated regional wars simultaneously;
2. A "win-hold-win" two-war strategy, with smaller forces that could win a major war in one region while stopping aggression in another region (the "hold"), and then shift to the second war and win it as well; and
3. A one-war strategy, with further reduced forces that could win one major regional war, but not two.[5]

Aiming to meet President Clinton's goal of a $104 bn reduction from the FY 1995–1999 Bush plan, officials selected the medium-sized "win-hold-win" forces, but argued that these forces could provide a "win-win" capability if upgraded with technological improvements along the lines recommended in the RAND study.[6] Their recommendations were adopted in the final report on the Bottom-Up

---

[2] Les Aspin, *An Approach to Sizing American Conventional Forces for the Post-Soviet Era: Four Illustrative Options* (Washington, D.C.: [House Armed Services Committee], February 25, 1992).

[3] David A. Fulghum, "RAND Study Outlines Two-War Strategy," *Aviation Week & Space Technology*, Vol. 139, No. 2 (July 12, 1993), p. 52, describes it as a "one and one-half year study."

[4] Christopher Bowie, Fred Frostic, Kevin Lewis, John Lund, David Ochmanek, and Philip Propper, *The New Calculus: Analyzing Airpower's Changing Role in Joint Theater Campaigns* (Santa Monica, Cal.: RAND, 1993).

[5] Michael R. Gordon, "Cuts Force Review of War Strategies," *New York Times*, May 30, 1993, p. 16. The force structures and objectives of the three options resemble those outlined in Aspin's 1992 paper.

[6] Fulghum, "RAND Study," cites the authors as saying that the study's "conclusions will be reflected in the soon-to-be released Bottom-Up review." See also Eric Schmitt, "Pentagon is Ready with a Plan for a Leaner, Versatile Military," *New York Times*, June 12, 1993, p. 1.

Review[7] and in the official five-year plan detailed in Aspin's January 1994 *Annual Report*.[8]

The Aspin "options" paper and the RAND *New Calculus* study, along with the *Report on the Bottom-Up Review*, clarify key assumptions behind the Clinton two-war strategy: the potential adversaries that officials believe could become involved in a major regional war with the United States; the strength of the forces that might be fielded by potential adversaries; the size and structure of the U.S. forces needed to win two such wars (and, thus, to deter them from ever starting); and the character of the campaigns the United States might wage in two theaters of war.

Close study of these factors casts doubt on the connection between regional threats and the planned U.S. forces. The proposed scale of U.S. forces and spending seems to be less a function of regional threats than of other factors: a desire to maintain a "warm" defense industrial base, an assumption that large standing forces are still needed to deter great-power war, and the inertia and vested interests associated with long-standing patterns of arms development, procurement, and deployment. After reviewing the scale of regional armaments and the timeline on which they might grow, this chapter argues that revamped U.S. military, arms production, and arms control strategies, focused on preventing rather than matching regional and great-power build-ups, would offer the United States and the world more security at less cost.

Perceived Military Threats

Outside North America, Europe, and the former Soviet Union, no potential U.S. adversary except China has military capabilities as powerful as those of Iraq before the Gulf War. In fact, only a few countries worldwide have the capability to engage in a moderately large conventional war. Even if the threshold is set very low—say, 700 tanks (about 10 percent of Iraq's 1990 tanks) and 275 combat aircraft (about 40 percent of Iraq's 1990 aircraft)—there are no countries that

---

[7] Secretary of Defense Les Aspin, *Report on the Bottom-Up Review* (Washington, D.C.: U.S. Department of Defense, October 1993).

[8] Secretary of Defense Les Aspin, *Annual Report: Report of the Secretary of Defense to the President and the Congress* (Washington, D.C.: U.S. GPO, 1994).

qualify in Latin America or sub-Saharan Africa. The few countries that match or surpass the threshold are those involved in long-standing conflicts in the Middle East and Asia: China and Taiwan, North and South Korea, and Japan in East Asia; India and Pakistan in South Asia; and Egypt, Iran, Iraq, Israel, Libya, Saudi Arabia, and Syria in the Middle East. Among this small group, even fewer countries could pose a threat which the United States might oppose with direct military intervention. India and Pakistan could not; the United States has neither security commitments nor strategic interests in South Asia. Taiwan, South Korea, Japan, Israel, Egypt, and Saudi Arabia are close U.S. allies that depend on this country for armaments and military support.

As possible future U.S. adversaries in a major regional war, that leaves just six candidates: China, North Korea, Syria, Libya, Iraq, and Iran. In East Asia, North Korea could become embroiled in a war with South Korea, or China could threaten Taiwan. In the Middle East, Iraq, if released from the current UN arms embargo, might threaten any nearby state with valuable resources.[9] Conceivably Iran might attempt to commit aggression to expand its resource base, although there is no recent evidence to suggest such a propensity. Syria and Libya could pose a threat to Israel, but this, too, seems highly unlikely. Libya cannot reach Israel except by air, and its combat aircraft lack the range and sophistication needed to attack Israel successfully. Syria has been keen to improve relations with Israel and the West, even to the extent of siding with the West in the war against Iraq.

CURRENT AND FUTURE FORCES OF POTENTIAL ADVERSARIES
Looking at capabilities rather than intentions, none of the six potential regional adversaries is nearly as threatening as pre-war Iraq. This is shown in Les Aspin's 1992 study, which sets a baseline for comparison by noting that when Iraq invaded Kuwait, it had "what was accounted at the time to be the world's fourth largest army, including some 6,000 tanks" and "a modern air force of over 700 planes"—yet the U.S.-led Desert Storm effort dealt with the Iraqi military "very handily."[10]

---

[9] That is the lesson of Saddam Hussein's previous acts of aggression aimed at seizing oil-rich territory from Iran and then, when that failed, from Kuwait.

[10] Aspin, *An Approach to Sizing American Conventional Forces*, p. 9.

According to Aspin, the current ground and air forces of Iraq, Iran, and North Korea are at best about half as strong as those of Iraq in 1990. (See Table 5.1.) Aspin's comparative assessments of ground and air force strength generally match the ratios of tanks and combat aircraft held by the potential adversaries set against those of 1990 Iraq, if archaic systems (tanks designed before 1950 and aircraft designed before 1958) are heavily discounted.[11] Iran has only 288 aircraft designed since 1958, compared with pre-war Iraq's 627, and just 265 tanks designed since 1950, as against pre-war Iraq's 3,930. The comparable figures for North Korea are 310 aircraft and 2,350 tanks. Apart from the inferior quantity and quality of its weaponry, North Korea is a "far less demanding" potential opponent for the United States than 1990 Iraq, according to the RAND study, because of the "powerful, rapidly mobilizable forces" of South Korea, the "sizable" prepositioned stocks of equipment and supplies for U.S. forces, and the command, control, intelligence, and communications structure already in place.[12]

Only China has ground and air forces which Aspin considers more powerful than pre-war Iraq's; but these forces are not germane to an attack on Taiwan. The ocean offers a natural barrier to any attempt by China to invade Taiwan, an island about 100 miles from the mainland; and China lacks the naval and air "power projection" capabilities needed to overcome this barrier. China has no aircraft carriers to provide offshore air cover for marines or paratroopers; it has no large amphibious assault ships for a massive, rapid over-the-beach landing; and its most capable aircraft are about 650 Chinese-made J-7s, a plane derived from the MiG-21, a short-range Soviet fighter designed in 1958.

U.S. Department of Defense (DoD) presentations do not actually state that the potential regional opponents are currently as powerful as pre-war Iraq. In fact, the threat claims are highly ambiguous. On the one hand, the RAND, Aspin, and DoD documents suggest that the United States must be prepared to counter two opponents with forces at least as large and well-trained as—and technologically superior to—those of Iraq in 1990. This high standard is used to

---

[11] The only exception to this general rule concerns China's ground forces, which are assessed as being 1.4 times as powerful as those of pre-war Iraq, even though about 9,000 of China's estimated 10,000 tanks are obsolete.

[12] Bowie et al., *The New Calculus*, p. 16.

Table 5.1. The Size and Growth of the World's Largest Regional Air and Ground Forces

| | Pre-war | Middle East | | | | | | | East Asia | | | | South Asia | |
| | Iraq | Iran | Iraq | Libya | Syria | S.Arabia | Israel | Egypt | China | N.Korea | S.Korea | Taiwan | India | Pakistan |
	1990	1993	1993	1993	1993	1993	1993	1993	1993	1993	1993	1993	1993	1993
Combat Aircraft														
Archaic (pre-'58)	38		14				162	56	3,345	680			37	148
Obsolete ('58-'65)	235	173	162	57	222	96	155	174	655	174	426	424	326	173
Recent (post-'65)	392	115	162	324	327	170	447	292	543	136	48	10	411	143
Total	665	288	338	381	549	266	764	522	4,543	990	474	434	774	464
Total excl archaic	627	288	324	381	549	266	602	466	1,198	310	474	434	737	316
Latter vs. Iraq '90	1.0	0.5	0.5	0.6	0.9	0.4	1.0	0.7	1.9	0.5	0.8	0.7	1.2	0.5
Aspin air rating	1.0	0.4	0.5	0.7	0.8				2.6	0.6				
Since 1972														
Acquired	594	202	594	553	474	275	612	425	3,628	757	459	361	687	416
Retired or lost	-158	-65	-485	-194	-135	-59	-195	-538	-2,704	-369	-220	-164	-534	-168
Net growth	436	137	109	359	339	216	417	-113	924	388	239	197	153	248
Acquired/yr	33	10	28	26	23	13	29	20	173	36	22	17	33	20
Net growth/yr	24	7	5	17	16	10	20	-5	44	18	11	9	7	12
Years to match Iraq '90 @33/yr		10	9	7	2				..	10				
Years to match Iraq '90 @24/yr		14	13	10	3				..	13				

Table 5.1. The Size and Growth of the World's Largest Regional Air and Ground Forces, cont'd

	Pre-war	Middle East							East Asia				South Asia	
	Iraq	Iran	Iraq	Libya	Syria	S.Arabia	Israel	Egypt	China	N.Korea	S.Korea	Taiwan	India	Pakistan
	1990	1993	1993	1993	1993	1993	1993	1993	1993	1993	1993	1993	1993	1993
Tanks														
Archaic (pre-'50)	1,600	425	1,600	1,700	2,160		1,180	1,040	8,900	1,475		905	900	1,250
Obsolete ('50-'60)	2,430	240	370	350	1,000	696	1,910	2,047	200	1,850	1,350	559		600
Recent (post-'60)	1,500	25	330	250	1,400		800	80	900	500	450		3,100	40
Total	5,530	690	2,300	2,300	4,560	696	3,890	3,167	10,000	3,825	1,800	1,464	4,000	1,890
Total excl archaic	3,930	265	700	600	2,400	696	2,710	2,127	1,100	2,350	1,800	559	3,100	640
Latter vs. Iraq '90	1.0	0.1	0.2	0.2	0.6	0.2	0.7	0.5	0.3	0.6	0.5	0.1	0.8	0.2
Aspin ground rating	1.0	0.2	0.4	0.3	0.6				1.4	0.6				
Since 1972														
Acquired	5,570	1,145	5,585	2,950	4,005	706	2,950	2,320	7,575	3,655	1,200	757	4,150	1,625
Retired or lost	-900	-1,315	-4,245	-871	-615	-95	-910	-713	-6,675	-730	-400	-1,938	-1,190	-395
Net growth	4,670	-170	1,340	2,079	3,390	611	2,040	1,607	900	2,425	840	-1,181	2,960	1,230
Acquired/yr	309	55	266	140	191	34	140	110	361	174	57	36	198	77
Net growth/yr	259	-8	64	99	161	29	97	77	43	115	40	-56	141	59
Years to match Iraq '90 @309/yr		12	10	11	5				9	5				
Years to match Iraq '90 @259/yr		14	12	13	6				11	6				

Sources: Adapted from R. Forsberg, "Wasting Billions," Boston Review XIX:2 (April-May 1994), p. 5; and "IDDS Almanac 1994."
Notes: Combat aircraft and tanks are grouped by design age, that is, the year in which the system entered production. The high rate of growth in China's combat aircraft is due to China's rapid domestic production in the 1970s of about 3,000 copies of the Soviet MiG-19, a light fighter designed in 1953.

justify future U.S. forces that are twice the size of a U.S. "Desert-Storm equivalent" force and more technologically advanced, incorporating expensive new aircraft (the F-22 for the Air Force and the F/A-18E/F for the Navy) and advanced smart weapons, surveillance systems, and command-and-control capabilities.

On the other hand, Defense Department officials have been cautious about appearing to exaggerate the capabilities of potential opponents. Thus, where the RAND *New Calculus* study of May 1993 assumes an opponent like pre-war Iraq, with 3,000–5,000 tanks and 500–1,000 combat aircraft, the October 1993 *Report on the Bottom-Up Review* downgrades the potential adversary's tank holdings to 2,000–4,000, and by January 1994, the Secretary's *Annual Report* describes the potential opponent as having 2,000–3,000 tanks, that is, as few as one-third of Iraq's 5,530 total tank holdings (or one-half of its newer holdings). In a July 1994 interview, Secretary of Defense Perry further scaled back the threat, commenting that neither Iran nor Iraq has "the capability to mount the kind of force that Iraq mounted in Desert Storm."[13]

In official DoD statements, the shrinking threat is offset by allusions to future adversary forces that could be significantly larger and more modern than those deployed today. But here too, the Pentagon greatly exaggerates plausible changes, foreshortening the time it would take for potential opponents to match, let alone surpass, the 1990 capabilities of Iraq.[14] Perry, for example, says that it will take "a couple of years."[15]

In reality, it would be likely to take Iran, North Korea, or current-day Iraq a decade or more to develop forces as strong as Iraq's 1990 forces—assuming these countries had the means to do so (they do not), and started immediately.[16] As noted in Chapter 1, when new weapons are acquired, they are rarely added to existing arsenals, equipping ever-expanding forces. Instead, new acquisitions usually replace older systems that have been lost in accidents or combat,

---

[13] William Matthews, "2 Wars Now are Too Many," *Navy Times*, July 25, 1994, p. 26.

[14] Perhaps U.S. officials mistakenly project onto Third World arms importers the U.S. capacity for arms acquisition, which is based on procurement and maintenance budgets that even today are 10- to 100-fold greater than those of any Third World nation.

[15] Matthews, "2 Wars."

[16] Iran has begun importing aircraft at a higher rate than in the past. However, most imports in 1994–2000 will be used to replace U.S. aircraft supplied to the former Shah, which Iran cannot maintain in serviceable condition.

worn out in training, or surpassed in technology. The replacement process generally produces a moderate net change in inventories.

Between 1972 and 1990, before and during its attacks on Iran and Kuwait, Iraq built up offensively-oriented ground and air forces at a rate considerably faster than ever observed in any other major Third World arms importer. (See Table 5.1.) During this period, Iraq's average annual net increases were 24 per year for aircraft (Israel and North Korea, at 20 and 18 per year, respectively, have the next highest rates) and 259 per year for tanks (Syria at 161 per year and India at 141 per year have the next highest rates).[17]

In an implausibly bad worst case, the United States' potential adversaries might suddenly begin to acquire weapons at the rate Iraq did before 1990, and might use all those acquisitions to expand their forces, without retiring or losing any of their weapons. Even then, it would take Iraq, Iran, and North Korea 10 years to match Iraq's pre–Gulf War inventory of non-obsolete aircraft and 5–10 years to match its inventory of non-obsolete tanks. Since the production process typically imposes a lead time of several years for delivery of arms import orders, it would be another 3–7 years before these countries would begin to receive weapons ordered starting in 1994. We also know that Iraq will not be able to escape from the UN arms embargo for at least two years; that neither Iran nor North Korea has the resources to buy and field weapons at Iraq's previous rate; and that neither Russia nor China will provide large quantities of arms on credit. Taking these known constraints into account, it would probably be reasonable to add five years to the estimates of each candidate's time to match prewar Iraq, starting now. Thus, it is hard to see how Iran, Iraq, or North Korea could acquire forces comparable to those of pre–Gulf War Iraq before 2010.

Planned U.S. Forces

No potential regional adversary as capable as pre-war Iraq exists today, nor could one develop within a decade. The current U.S. military plan is, nonetheless, to maintain permanent peacetime forces capable of opposing one such opponent in the Middle East and

---

[17] China acquired more aircraft (44 per year against 24), but they were very cheap, technologically obsolete systems produced domestically.

another in East Asia, undertaking simultaneous major acts of aggression.

The 1993–1994 force-planning reports provide several estimates of the ground divisions and tactical air wings that U.S. officials believe may be needed for this purpose. The *Bottom-Up Review* relies on two concepts: a "major regional conflict (MRC) building block" and the total forces estimated to be needed to win either one or two simultaneous major regional wars, more or less quickly, with or without additional forces available for smaller military actions.[18] In Table 5.2, the *Bottom-Up Review* estimates of one- and two-war forces (cols. 3–5) are compared to Aspin's 1992 estimates of a "Desert Storm–equivalent" force (col. 1) and the total force structure needed to field such a one-war force (col. 2). The current MRC building block differs from Aspin's 1992 Desert Storm–equivalent force in providing a slightly smaller contingent of active ground force divisions (6-2/3 instead of 8) and a larger number of tactical Air Force wings (10 instead of 6). These changes reflect the increased emphasis in the Clinton plan on the use of early-arriving air power to stop an invasion, destroy strategic targets, and support regional defense forces. (The roles of later-arriving ground troops and covering air power are to mount a counter-offensive that will defeat and drive back the attacker's forces, and to provide postwar stability.)

For unexplained reasons, the *Bottom Up Review*'s total one-war force (col. 3), which might be expected to add at most 3 reserve divisions to a "Desert Storm–equivalent" force, adds far more: 3 active Army divisions plus 7 reserve divisions. In contrast, for the two-war strategies (cols. 4 and 5), the proposed active and reserve ground forces are only slightly larger than two "Desert Storm–equivalents," with 2–3 extra divisions; and the proposed active and reserve air wings are about double the number of "Desert Storm–equivalent" wings (33–34 compared with 15).

---

[18] Aspin, *Report on the Bottom-Up Review*, pp. 18–30.

Table 5.2. Official U.S. "Major Regional War" Goals and Force Options

	Aspin 1992		Bottom-Up Review	
	"Desert-Storm Equivalent" [1]	One-War Force [2]	One-War Force [3]	Two-War Force [4]
Ground troop divisions				
Army active	7	8	8	10
Army reserve		2	6	6
Marine Corps active	1	2	3	3
Marine Corps reserve		1	1	1
Total active	8	10	11	13
Total reserve		3	7	7
Total divisions	8	13	18	20
Tactical air wings				
Air Force active	6	6	10	13
Air Force reserve		4	6	7
Navy carriers-in theater	4	3	4	5
Navy carriers-other active	4	3	4	5
Navy carriers reserve				1
Marine Corps active	1	2	3	3
Marine Corps reserve		1	1	1
Total active	15	14	21	26
Total reserve		5	7	9
Total wings		19	28	35

Sources: Cols. 1–2: Les Aspin, Chair, U.S. House Armed Services Committee, "Sizing US Conventional Forces for the Post-Soviet Era," February 1992, p. 15 and Chart IV; cols. 3–4: Secretary of Defense Les Aspin, "Report on the Bottom-Up Review," October 1993, p. 30.

Since it is likely to take 10–15 years for plausible regional adversaries to match Iraq's 1990 strength, there are probably other reasons for the large size of the planned U.S. peacetime forces and the proposed rate of procurement of new systems, munitions, and equipment. One reason is certainly to guard against renewed military confrontation with Russia. The *New Calculus* report argues that "should an authoritarian leadership regain power in Moscow, it might attempt to reestablish Russia's internal empire.... [S]izing U.S. forces for two regional conflicts can provide a hedge against the reemergence of a large-scale Russian military threat."[19] The *Report on the Bottom-Up Review* and the 1994 *Annual Report* of the Secretary of Defense both list the potential failure of democratic reforms in the former Soviet Union as one of the four main dangers of the post–Cold War world, and comment that "the reversal of reforms and the emergence of ultranationalist authoritarianism, particularly in Russia, would substantially alter the security situation for the United States."[20] In official U.S. Defense Department policy, this risk is not openly associated with maintaining a larger U.S. force structure than would otherwise be needed for security purposes. The only explicitly mentioned Defense Department response to the risk of democratic failure in Russia (and thus, indirectly, the risk of renewed military confrontation between Russia and the West) is a series of meetings with senior military officers from the former Soviet Union to discuss appropriate civil-military relations. Given the magnitude of the risk, this modest undertaking is probably not the only response. More likely, Defense Department documents avoid stressing the role of Russia as a potential adversary because Russian armed forces could not pose a plausible threat to the West in the near future (or prior to reclaiming parts of the former Soviet Union), and explicitly treating Russia as a potential adversary would invite a response in kind.

A second key consideration in U.S. force planning—and one that is emphasized in official statements—is the desire to maintain an active defense industrial base.

Even taking into account potential confrontation with Russia and concerns about the defense industrial base, security considerations alone do not fully account for planned future U.S. forces and procurement. The most effective way to counter future regional threats would be to establish an arms export moratorium jointly with Russia, Britain, France, and Germany. Similarly, the most effective barrier to renewed military confrontation with Russia would be global arms reductions, combined with new measures to convert the "warm" defense industries of the United States, Europe, and Russia to "cool" industrial reserve capabilities. The failure of the United States to pursue such forms of arms control suggests that other considerations lie behind planned U.S. forces and procurement—specifically, the vested

---

[19] Bowie et al., *The New Calculus*, p. 7.
[20] Aspin, *Report on the Bottom-Up Review*, p. 9, and *Annual Report*, 1994, p. 3.

interests and "old thinking" associated with long-standing patterns of arms production, deployment, and trade.

CURRENT U.S. AIR FORCES

The tactical air forces of the United States are currently the largest in the world. The U.S. Air Force (USAF) operates 3,364 fighter and attack aircraft while the U.S. Navy and Marine Corps field 1,846 such planes.[21] Navy and Marine Corps aircraft alone outnumber the combat aircraft holdings of any nation except Russia and China.[22]

The roles of the U.S. Air Force include air superiority, battlefield interdiction, close air support (CAS), tactical reconnaissance, and suppression of enemy air defenses (SEAD).[23] At the end of 1993, the Air Force was organized in 28 tactical fighter wings, 16 active and 12 Reserve and National Guard, operating six types of fixed-wing fighter and attack aircraft.[24] A standard Air Force fighter-attack wing includes 100 aircraft: 72 combat-ready aircraft plus 28 backup aircraft, maintained for pipeline, training, and testing purposes.

Since the end of the Cold War, the emphasis of U.S. naval aviation has shifted from deep-water warfare with the Soviet Navy toward coastal warfare in the Third World and support of U.S. Army and Marine Corps troops intervening in Third World conflicts.[25] Navy aircraft are currently organized in 11 active and 2 reserve air wings, deployed on 11 active and 2 reserve aircraft carriers. The typical carrier-based air wing comprises 56–60 fighter-attack aircraft, including 2 F-14 fighter squadrons with 10 aircraft each, 2 F/A-18 fighter-attack squadrons with 10 aircraft each, and 2 A-6E attack squadrons with 8–10 aircraft each. The Navy has some 780 squadron-assigned

---

[21] These figures represent only operational fighter-attack aircraft deployed at the end of 1993. They do not include 220 active bombers, 244 unarmed aircraft used by the Navy for training, or the 2,264 combat aircraft that are not formally retired but have been withdrawn from service and are maintained in storage by the U.S. Air Force and Navy.

[22] U.S. Navy aircraft operate solely from aircraft carriers; Marine Corps aircraft may be based either on land or on aircraft carriers.

[23] Secretary of Defense Dick Cheney, *Annual Report to the President and Congress* (Washington, D.C.: U.S. GPO, 1993), p. 86.

[24] The A-10, F-4, F-15, F-16, F-111, and F-117.

[25] John D. Morrocco, "U.S. Navy Reorients to Coastal Warfare," *Aviation Week & Space Technology*, Vol. 138, No. 12 (March 22, 1993), p. 56.

aircraft, plus several hundred aircraft for training, testing, and pipe-line use.

The Marine Corps maintains 4 air wings, 3 active and 1 reserve. Various aircraft units are generally paired with reinforced divisions to form "Marine Air-Ground Task Forces" (MAGTF). Current plans call for a total of up to 84 Marine Corps F/A-18s to be deployed on air-craft carriers at any given time.[26] Marine air wings vary greatly in size and composition, but at present a typical air wing comprises 130 squadron-assigned aircraft: 60 AV-8B Harrier attack aircraft, 48 single-seat F/A-18C and 12 two-seat F/A-18D fighter-attack air-craft, and 10 A-6E attack aircraft.[27] Some of the planes in the Marine Corps Reserve wing are older A-4 attack aircraft. The Marine Corps also maintains planes for training and pipeline use.

Most of the active U.S. combat aircraft are relatively new.[28] The average age of all USAF operational combat aircraft (including Reserve and National Guard planes) is about 11 years. The 1,822 F-16s, which make up nearly 60 percent of the inventory, have an average age of just 8 years. F-15s, which comprise 25 percent of the force, have an average age of 11.5 years. F-117 stealth attack aircraft, deployed in small numbers, have an average age of 8.5 years. The A-10 ground-attack planes and F-111 deep interdiction aircraft have average ages of 14 and 24 years, respectively; but attack and bomber aircraft have longer service lives than fighters, which are subjected to high-gravity stresses when they make rapid turns and loops in air superiority "dog-fights." The remainder of the active aircraft are F-4s with an average age of 25 years; they will be fully retired soon.

U.S. Navy and Marine Corps fighter and attack aircraft have an average age just over 10 years. F/A-18s, which make up nearly half the inventory, are, on average, 6.5 years old. The F-14s, the Navy's premier fighter and the second largest force segment at 414 aircraft, have an average age of 13 years. The A-6 attack aircraft and the A-4s employed in reserve units have an average age of about 20 years. Marine Corps AV-8Bs, a short take-off and vertical-landing aircraft, have an age of about 6 years.

---

[26] Aspin, *Annual Report*, 1994, p. 183.

[27] Cheney, *Annual Report*, 1992, p. 84.

[28] The 2,264 inactive combat aircraft maintained in storage are generally much older than their active counterparts.

PLANNED FUTURE U.S. AIR FORCES

The *Bottom-Up Review* calls for a reduction to 13 active and seven reserve Air Force fighter wings by the end of FY 1996. This plan represents an overall reduction of eight wings from the FY 1993 level and 6.5 wings from the Bush administration's planned "Base Force" of 26.5 fighter wings by 1997. The reductions will be accomplished by the early retirement of some older A-10s, F-15s, and F-16s. After the reductions are implemented, the Air Force should have a total inventory of about 2,000 fighter-attack aircraft.

The *Bottom-Up Review* also calls for a reduction of two Naval air wings by the end of FY 1996, resulting in a force of ten active air wings and one reserve air wing. The nation's carrier force will be reduced to 11 active and one reserve and training carrier. The Navy's requirement for fighter-attack aircraft will be further reduced by a restructuring of air wings, whereby wing strength would be reduced to 50 combat aircraft from the current strength of 56–60 aircraft, and by deploying Marine F/A-18s with carrier air wings. The combination of these changes will result in a total inventory of about 625 fighter-attack aircraft. The Navy plans to meet its reduction requirements, in part, by the early retirement of all A-6E aircraft and half of the current inventory of F-14 fighters.

The Marine Corps will still maintain three active and one reserve wing under the Clinton plan, although total inventory levels will fall due to changes in the structure of Marine air wings. By 1997, the Marines will have a force of about 525 F/A-18 and AV-8 aircraft.

Starting in FY 1996, Defense Department acquisition of fighter-attack aircraft for the U.S. armed services will fall to historically low levels. The planned reductions in force size and the relatively young age of the aircraft in service mean that procurement levels will probably remain low until 2010. FY 1994 orders for 48 new fighter-attack aircraft (36 F/A-18C/Ds for the Navy and 12 F-16s for the Air Force)[29] can be contrasted with the average of 365 planes of six or seven types ordered annually from 1980 to 1989. In FY 1995 and FY 1996, the only fixed-wing combat aircraft to be ordered are 24 F/A-18C/Ds for the Navy.

---

[29] The 16 F-16s in the FY 1994 Budget were scheduled to be the final U.S. Air Force order for this type, although there has been some recent discussion of procurement later in the decade. See Thomas E. Ricks, "Pentagon Considers Selling Overseas a Large Part of High-Tech Weaponry, *Wall Street Journal*, February 14, 1994, p. A20.

The *Bottom-Up Review* calls for new aircraft procurement to begin soon to prevent a bulge in spending after 2000.[30] The Clinton administration has canceled the Navy's A/F-X (previously scheduled to replace the A-6 starting in 2001), and the Air Force's Multi-Role Fighter (to replace the F-16 starting in 2015). The Air Force's new F-22 and the Navy's F/A-18E/F are scheduled to go forward, but the timing, the number of aircraft to be ordered, and the annual rates of procurement have not yet been decided. The Navy hopes to begin procurement of the F/A-18E/F in FY 1997 with an initial order for 12 aircraft. Senior officials have indicated that the total purchase may be as high as 600–700 units.[31] If 600 were built over 20 years, production would run around 30 per year.

The Air Force had also hoped to place the initial order for the F-22 Advanced Tactical Fighter in FY 1997, leading to a total purchase of 442 aircraft, procured at a rate as low as 24 per year.[32] Recently, however John Deutch, Deputy Secretary of Defense for Acquisition, suggested that the initial order be delayed four years (until 2001) to keep future Clinton budgets within prescribed limits.[33] Some officials argued that such a delay would kill the program.[34] The General Accounting Office (GAO) had earlier recommended starting production no sooner than 2004 on the grounds that the F-15C air superiority fighter can counter potential air-to-air threats well into the next century. Criticizing the F-22's high cost (for 442 aircraft, unit cost including pro-rated R&D is estimated at $217 mn), the GAO, in a classified

---

[30] Aspin, *Bottom-Up Review*, pp. 108–109. The ideal production curve spreads production over the life of the system to minimize boom-and-bust employment and block obsolescence of inventories.

[31] "U.S. Navy Plans Cuts in Aircraft Numbers," *Defense News*, Vol. 8, No. 36 (September 13, 1993), p. 2.

[32] An Air Force wing typically contains 100 aircraft (72 squadron-assigned and 28 backup); the 42 F-22s planned beyond the required 400 (or, in the original estimate of 648, the extra 48) would probably be assigned to dedicated training units (also called "operational conversion units"). See Bill Sweetman, "High Cost Cold Warrior?" *Jane's Defence Weekly*, Vol. 19, No. 26 (June 26, 1993), p. 19.

[33] David A. Fulghum and John D. Morrocco, "Deutch Demands Cuts, Services Scramble Anew," *Aviation Week & Space Technology*, Vol. 141, No. 9 (August 29, 1994), pp. 22–23.

[34] Ibid.

report, also argued that maintenance of the F-15C through 2015 would be more cost-effective than buying F-22s.[35]

In light of falling procurement rates, the Department of Defense has turned to aircraft upgrades, modifications, and technology demonstration programs to help maintain industrial combat aircraft design and production capacity.[36] The Navy plans to give approximately 200 F-14s a modest attack capability,[37] in part to replace 300 A-6E aircraft that are being retired early.[38] Other modification programs include a Marine Corps upgrade of AV-8 Harrier II aircraft to the Harrier II+ standard, and the modification of some Air Force F-15s and F-16s for the SEAD (suppression of enemy air defense) mission.

In another effort to preserve the industrial base, the Joint Advanced Strike Technology (JAST) program employs combat aircraft design teams affected by the cancellation of the A/F-X and MRF programs. The JAST program is expected to yield several technology demonstration aircraft that test potential common components for future Air Force and Navy aircraft.[39] Air Force and Navy planners are hoping that the JAST program may lead to one or two attack aircraft that could eventually replace the F-16, F-15E, F-111, and AV-8B.[40]

POTENTIAL FUTURE PRODUCTION REQUIREMENTS

IDDS has projected potential future production requirements for tactical combat aircraft for the U.S. Air Force, Navy, and Marine Corps through 2010. Two force levels were used: the currently planned Clinton force of 20 Air Force wings, 11 Navy wings, and 4 Marine Corps wings, and a 50 percent smaller "cooperative security"

---

[35] David A. Fulghum, "Cost, Mission Disputes Jeopardize F-22," *Aviation Week & Space Technology*, Vol. 140, No. 14 (April 4, 1994), p. 26.

[36] Aspin, *Annual Report*, p. 194.

[37] Congress provided $107 million for F-14 modifications in the 1994 defense appropriations bill, directing the Navy to assess the need for installing more powerful engines before undertaking ground-attack improvements. Robert Holzer, "U.S. Navy, Congress Spar over F-14 Improvements," *Defense News*, Vol. 8, No. 45 (November 15, 1993), p. 25.

[38] The Navy is also increasing the number of F/A-18's in a typical carrier air wing from 20 to 36 aircraft to compensate for the retirement of the A-6E. See Aspin, *Annual Report*, 1994, p. 183.

[39] Aspin, *Bottom-Up Review*, p. 38.

[40] Barbara Starr, "USN, Air Force Look at Wider Role for JAST," *Jane's Defence Weekly*, Vol. 21, No. 2 (January 15, 1994), p. 13.

force, comprised of 10 Air Force wings, 6 Navy wings, and 1 Marine Corps wing. The Clinton force would require an inventory of 3,150 combat aircraft whereas the cooperative security force would require only 1,580 aircraft. For both plans, we calculated requirements using a 22-year retirement age (the lowest current U.S. military standard) and a 25-year retirement age (a more moderate standard).[41]

The projections of U.S. combat aircraft holdings are based on the number of active aircraft at the end of 1993 and expected deliveries between 1994 and 2000 of aircraft ordered through FY 1994, plus the 72 F/A-18C/Ds which the Pentagon plans to order in FY 1995–FY 1997. Not included are possible future orders for up to 442 F-22s or 700 F/A-18E/Fs, whose timing and procurement numbers are uncertain.

To maintain the Clinton-proposed force of 20 Air Force wings, 11 carrier wings, and 4 Marine wings until 2010 with a 22-year retirement age, the United States would have to produce 1,459 aircraft by 2010—that is, 317 more than the 1,142 F/A-18E/Fs and F-22s now planned. Moreover, more than 100 aircraft per year would have to be procured every year from FY 1997 through FY 2010.

With a 25-year aircraft retirement age, U.S. production requirements to maintain the Clinton force to 2010 would drop to about 700 aircraft. (See Figure 5.1.) The Navy and Marine Corps would have to procure 168 new aircraft, a goal that lies well within reach, given current plans for the F/A-18E/F. But the Air Force would need 532 new aircraft, 90 more than the planned 442 F-22s. Moreover, with F-22 deliveries starting in 2001, maintaining the 20-wing Clinton force would require production of 50 aircraft per year at a cost of about $6.5 bn each year throughout the decade. This expense would probably be prohibitive. The implication is that the U.S. Congress is

---

[41] In estimating future production requirements, we also assumed that the Clinton cuts will be reached by 1997 (as planned) and the further cuts for the cooperative security force by 2000; typical wing strength will remain at 72 for the Air Force, 50 for the Navy, and 100 for the Marine Corps; inventory-to-squadron equipment ratios will remain at 1.4 for the Air Force and 1.45 for the Navy and Marine Corps; and peacetime aircraft attrition rates will remain at 1 percent per year for the Air Force and the Navy. (For the Marine Corps AV-8, the projections assume 2 percent per year attrition.) As discussed below, U.S. military planners could reduce production requirements by extending the service life, hastening the cuts, decreasing the inventory-to-squadron equipment ratio, or reducing the strength of the air wings.

unlikely to fund an annual rate of combat aircraft production sufficiently high to maintain the Clinton-proposed force through 2010.

In contrast, cutbacks by 2000 to a cooperative security force
inventory of 1,580 aircraft would allow the United States to suspend
all new production of combat aircraft through 2010 or, with full use of
all aircraft through the end of their service lives, much longer. With
cooperative security force levels and a 25-year retirement age, the Air
Force would have a surplus of about 470 serviceable aircraft in 2010
and the Navy and Marine Corps a joint surplus of about 400. The
period for which the cooperative security force could be maintained
without new production could be extended until as late as 2028 if all
aircraft in the inventory, including surplus aircraft retired early due to
force cuts, were cycled through a full 25 years of use.

**Figure 5.1 The Force Size and Retirement Age Sensitivity of
U.S. Fighter-Attack Aircraft**

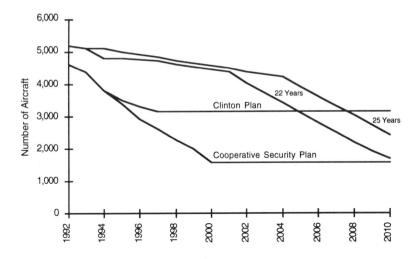

Deferring production of combat aircraft (and other major weapon
systems) as long as possible would maximize the chances for the
success of new arms control efforts. In the best case, the suspension of
production for domestic use would be accompanied by a suspension
of production for export; the U.S. production moratorium would be
matched by the other major arms producers; and the global export

ban would facilitate global and regional arms reductions. These cuts, in turn, would help build confidence and strengthen efforts for non-violent conflict resolution both regionally and globally, heading off new demands for higher force levels and new arms acquisitions. In the worst case, efforts for cooperative arms restraints would fail and new or renewed military threats would emerge. In that case, U.S. military planners would have plenty of warning time in which to reconstitute Clinton-level tactical air forces from the surplus aircraft and aircraft carriers maintained in storage.

Government Policy Toward the Aerospace Industry

The Clinton administration is committed to maintaining a sizable defense industrial base. Secretary of Defense Perry has stated that the Pentagon will maintain militarily unique production capabilities not currently needed by any branch of the armed forces for replacement production.[42] In applying this policy, the Defense Department seems to be committed to maintaining two companies, Lockheed and McDonnell Douglas, as prime contractors for combat aircraft. To keep the military divisions active without regular production orders, the Defense Department will presumably use research and development programs like the JAST program and low-rate procurement of aircraft not needed for security purposes.

While the Clinton administration's policy on combat aircraft exports and arms exports generally has not been finalized, the administration is inclined to treat exports as helpful in maintaining an active production base. During his presidential campaign, Bill Clinton advocated combat aircraft exports to Taiwan as a way to maintain jobs and preserve defense industries, even though the sale ended a 10-year U.S. embargo on such exports and prompted China to withdraw from talks on controlling the arms trade.[43] Now administration officials are proposing a loan guarantee program that will make arms exports cheaper for importers, and they are trying to persuade Congress to eliminate the extra charges on exports under the DoD's Foreign Military Sales program (which sponsors most U.S. major

---

[42] Anthony L. Velocci, Jr., "Perry Forges New Shape for Industry," *Aviation Week & Space Technology*, Vol. 139, No. 20 (November 15, 1993), p. 52.
[43] *Arms Control Reporter*, Vol. 11 (1992), p. 707.B.10.

weapon exports). Moreover, the Defense Department will soon begin a study of the links between arms exports and the defense industrial base, which will explore new forms of government support of conventional arms exports.[44]

U.S. government policy toward the shrinking of the defense industry can, with a few exceptions, best be described as one of benign neglect. Although the expansion of the industry in the 1980s and its subsequent shrinkage were clearly the result of government decisions on military spending, the Defense Department has not taken an active role in guiding the contraction, preferring instead to let the outcome be determined by the decisions of individual companies. There is rhetorical concern for the defense industrial base, but little in the way of concrete assistance. The exceptions to this general rule are illuminating: they concern jobs, foreign ownership of defense firms, and technology policy. In each of these areas, reliance solely on market solutions is seen as posing unacceptable political costs.

Job losses from cuts in defense spending have political ramifications, affecting the government's willingness to make further cuts. Thus, the stated rationale for the September 1993 decision to build an additional nuclear-powered Seawolf submarine was to maintain a critical part of the industrial base, but the decision clearly had more to do with the impact on the Connecticut economy of further layoffs from Electric Boat.[45] The early retirement of conventionally-powered aircraft carriers and their replacement with three new nuclear-powered types under construction or about to be ordered at Newport News, Virginia, was also explicitly tied to maintaining a capability for producing nuclear-powered ships. The reluctance of Congress to push for further cuts in the FY 1994 military budget, despite the urgent need to find further budget savings, can be explained by the desire to soften the impact of the defense draw-down on the economy in the absence of a well conceived and adequately funded program for economic conversion.

There are a number of government programs designed to enable laid-off defense workers to qualify for new jobs through counseling and retraining. In general, the approach has been to expand existing

---

[44] Barbara Starr, "Unique Large Orders Put U.S. Sales at $33b," *Jane's Defence Weekly*, Vol. 20, No. 25 (December 18, 1993), p. 14.
[45] Thomas E. Ricks, "Pentagon's Industrial Policy Isn't Meant to Save Jobs or Aid Firms, Official Says," *Wall Street Journal*, September 3, 1993, p. A3.

programs—such as the Labor Department's Economic Dislocation and Worker Adjustment Assistance (EDWAA)—by transferring funds from the DoD budget. Unfortunately, these programs have been plagued by slow response times and a lack of jobs for workers after retraining.[46] In California, which has experienced the largest number of defense lay-offs, most workers cannot find comparable jobs regardless of the training opportunities.[47]

Just as U.S. firms invest in foreign companies, foreign firms have sought to acquire interests in U.S.-based arms-producing firms in order to tap into the U.S. market. The U.S. government has obstructed such moves, arguing that they pose a risk of undesirable technology transfer and a threat to the defense industrial base. In the most publicized recent case, the French firm, Thomson-CSF, was forced to withdraw from a consortium that was bidding for LTV when it became obvious that the U.S. Interagency Committee on Foreign Investment would not give its approval.[48] In earlier cases, Plessey was persuaded to drop its projected purchase of the Harris Corporation by threats that Harris's important contracts with the National Security Agency would be shifted to other companies; and Fujitsu was denied permission to purchase Fairchild.[49]

About two-thirds of the Clinton administration's defense transition spending, aimed at softening the economic impact of the defense draw-down, has focused on replacing support for technology development. Under the rubric of "dual-use technology initiatives" the administration has launched programs ranging from the Technology Reinvestment Program (TRP), an interagency program that provides funds for government-industry partnerships in developing dual-use technologies, to DoD programs targeting specific technolo-

---

[46] "Displaced Defense Workers," in U.S. Congress, Office of Technology Assessment, *After the Cold War*, OTA-ITE-524 (Washington, D.C.: U.S. GPO, 1992); and Elizabeth Mueller et al., "Retraining for What? Displaced Defense Workers Come Up Against EDWAA," Project on Regional and Industrial Economics Working Paper No. 57 (New Brunswick, NJ: Rutgers University, September 1993).

[47] Anthony L. Velocci, Jr., "Aerospace Jobs Decline as Firms Seek New Efficiencies during Downturn," *Aviation Week & Space Technology*, Vol. 136, No. 3 (January 20, 1992), pp. 57–58.

[48] "Thomson-CSF Leaves Loral as Sole Buyer of LTV Unit," *Financial Times*, July 29, 1992, p. 16.

[49] "Bought-out U.S. Firms Could Lose Contracts," *Jane's Defence Weekly*, Vol. 8, No. 15 (October 17, 1987), and "Fujitsu Bid for Fairchild Semiconductor Raises Security Concerns," *Jane's Defence Weekly*, Vol. 7, No. 2 (January 17, 1987).

gies, such as high-performance computing.[50] Government investment in technology has broad political appeal, since it appears to address both defense conversion and the challenge of improving the competitiveness of U.S. civilian products in international markets. The emphasis on dual-use technology has an added advantage: it justifies DoD spending on commercial technologies on the grounds that the future defense industrial base should rely more heavily on off-the-shelf civilian technology.[51]

The effect of the technology-oriented transition programs on the aircraft industry is difficult to gauge. Most discussions of dual-use technology stress electronic and computer applications. Some programs focus on manufacturing processes, but these give priority to technology transfer to small and medium-sized firms.[52] To be successful the conversion programs require not just a supply push from the government, but a demand pull from the civilian market. Given the depressed state of commercial aircraft sales, the benefits to large military aircraft producers will be limited, despite the dual-use character of jet aircraft.

Industry Strategy for the Shrinking Market

The approach of the U.S. government, like that of the Russian government (see Chapter 4), is not surprising. U.S. arms industries have already shrunk dramatically in response to the end of the Cold War, in large part due to cuts in the U.S. military budget and in U.S. procurement orders. Aerospace companies, which have dominated the industry since 1945, are part of this transformation, although individual companies have been affected in different ways and have adopted different strategies. The outcome for the aerospace sector as

---

[50] For an analysis of the Clinton administration program, see Carol Lessure, *President Clinton's Defense Transition Program: FY 1995 Budget Request and Five-Year Funding Plan* (Washington, D.C.: Defense Budget Project, May 10, 1994).

[51] The DoD has proposed a sharp reduction in its use of military specifications in bidding procedures in order to increase the use of commercial technology. See Thomas E. Ricks, "Pentagon, in Streamlining Effort, Plans to Revamp its Purchasing Procedures," *Wall Street Journal*, June 30, 1994, p. A12.

[52] See Department of Defense, Office of the Under Secretary of Defense (Acquisition), *A Directory of Federal Reinvestment and Transition Initiatives for People, Business, and Communities* (Washington, D.C.: DoD, August 1993).

a whole is fewer companies, production lines, and employees, and a greater emphasis on inter-firm collaboration and exports. These and other business changes owe little to government policy; they are the result of individual company decisions—mostly decisions to cut back, rather than to convert excess capacity to alternative uses.

Aerospace companies dominate the Pentagon's list of the top 100 prime contractors, as they have since 1945. The major military aircraft producers—McDonnell Douglas, Lockheed, Northrop, and Grumman—have almost always been among the top 25 companies and usually among the top 10. In FY 1992, they were the top four companies on the list.[53] These companies have maintained their leading position in the industry not only because aircraft and missiles typically generate large development contracts and long production runs, but also because they have been adept at developing new technical capabilities and selling new ideas to the military. The new technology has been largely paid for by the military, either through contract research, development, test and evaluation (RDT&E), or through the independent research and development program (IR&D). This structure has created a network of close relationships between the companies and the military project offices, ensuring that established companies have had a great advantage in maintaining market position against new entrants.

Nevertheless, over time there has been considerable industry consolidation. Ever more complex weapon systems have proved too expensive to buy in large quantities (compare, for example, the planned purchase of at most 442 F-22s as against the total production run of 5,206 F-4s) and aircraft companies have been forced to merge or leave the market. As shown in Figure 5.2, the number of independent U.S. military airframe producers declined from 14 at the end of World War II to 5 in 1993.

Although most of the contraction has been through mergers and take-overs, companies have other strategies that they can use to survive in a shrinking market. There has been a remarkable increase in the number of teaming arrangements between U.S. defense contractors and between U.S. and foreign contractors, as companies join to spread development costs and improve access to foreign markets.

---

[53] Department of Defense Directorate for Information Operations and Reports, *100 Companies Receiving the Largest Dollar Volume of Prime Contract Awards, Fiscal Year 1992* (Washington, D.C.: U.S. GPO, 1993).

Figure 5.2. The Consolidation of U.S. Military Aircraft Manufacturers 1945–1994

Prime Contractors for Fixed-wing Fighter, Attack, and Bomber Aircraft Programs

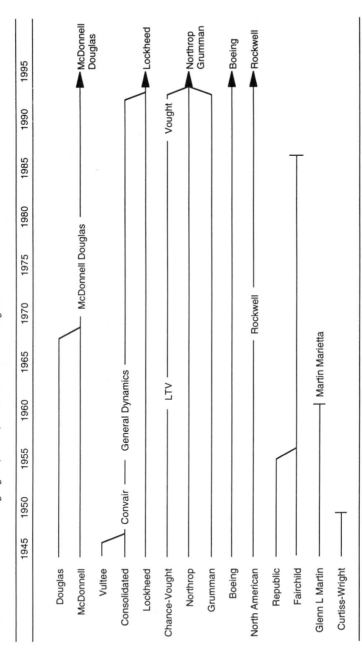

Source: Adapted from a chart prepared by Booz-Allen Analysis in Anthony L. Velocci, "Perry Forges New Shape for Industry," "Aviation Week & Space Technology," Vol. 139, No. 20 (November 15, 1993), p. 52.

Major development projects are now almost invariably undertaken by teams. For example, the competition for the Advanced Tactical Fighter (now the F-22) was between a Lockheed-Boeing-General Dynamics team (which won) and a McDonnell Douglas-Northrop team. Originally, the DoD encouraged teaming as a way of qualifying two or more sources to compete against each other in the production process; with the decline in expected procurement numbers, competition has been dropped in favor of joint production arrangements.[54]

Teaming arrangements and joint ventures between U.S. and foreign arms producers increased dramatically during the 1980s, despite U.S. government restrictions on technology transfer. Agreements within Europe increased even more as firms prepared for the advent of the Single European Market in January 1993. Most European weapons programs are now being undertaken by multinational consortia;[55] as a result, U.S. firms face stronger competition in Europe. In many cases, however, U.S. firms are involved in joint production with foreign firms, if only because of offset arrangements often connected with export sales.[56] In some ways, the globalization of arms production has undercut the ability of the U.S. government to restrict technology transfer and arms sales.[57]

The less visible part of the U.S. arms industry—the thousands of subcontractors and third-tier vendors—has also shrunk considerably, not only because the market is declining, but also because the prime contractors have altered their business strategies. Instead of spreading their purchases across a wide supplier base, the major firms are developing closer long-term relationships with a limited number of certified vendors.[58] In effect, the industry is shifting away from a

[54] United States General Accounting Office, "DoD Should Assess Cost Impact of Contractor Teaming Arrangements," GAO/NSIAD-92-15 (Washington, D.C., April 1992).

[55] Richard A. Bitzinger, *The Globalization of Arms Production: Defense Markets in Transition* (Washington, D.C.: Defense Budget Project, December 1993), Ch. 3.

[56] Frequently, arms exporters guarantee to produce components locally, or to import other locally-produced goods, as a way of offsetting (compensating for or minimizing) the large foreign exchange cost and the limits on technology transfer associated with major weapon imports.

[57] Judith Reppy, "Defense Companies' Strategies in a Declining Market: Implications for Government Policy," *Peace Economics, Peace Science, and Public Policy*, Vol. 1, No. 1 (Winter 1994), pp. 1–8.

quasi-market arrangement with competitive bidding to a network of close business alliances resembling that in Japan.

Table 5.3.   U.S. Aircraft Industry Employment 1982-1994

			Employees in thousands
	Military Aircraft	Civil Aircraft	Total
1982	285	231	516
1983	310	174	484
1984	333	184	517
1985	378	210	588
1986	*401*	238	639
1987	396	257	653
1988	386	280	666
1989	376	326	*702*
1990	346	341	687
1991	315	*345*	660
1992	275	322	597
1993	250	265	515
1994	235	249	484

Notes: 1993 preliminary; 1994 estimates. Peak years in bold italics.
Source: Aerospace Industries Association.

As noted earlier, with the termination of F-16 procurement orders in FY 1994, the McDonnell Douglas F/A-18 will be the only combat aircraft in production for the U.S. military, and the Lockheed-Boeing F-22 will be the only other plane in advanced development. While upgrades to existing aircraft will provide some added contracts, the industry is increasingly dependent on export sales. By 1996 the number of planes exported per year will exceed the number delivered to the U.S. armed services, and only foreign military sales will keep the production lines for the F-16 and F-15 open. (See Chapter 12.) To foster foreign sales in the face of competition from other suppliers, the industry has lobbied hard for government loan guarantees and has even attempted—so far unsuccessfully—to tap into the budget earmarked for conversion of defense industries to fund the guarantees. It also has offered increasingly generous offset provisions to prospective

---

[58] Anthony L. Velocci, Jr., "U.S. Shakeout Tests Suppliers' Flexibility," *Aviation Week & Space Technology*, Vol. 140, No. 7 (February 14, 1994), pp. 48–51.

buyers, ranging up to 100 percent of the value of the deal. Industry has had the strong support of the Clinton administration in these endeavors, including personal lobbying efforts by cabinet officers to help clinch particular deals.[59] In a remarkable initiative, the Defense Department has even proposed to sell off older aircraft in a kind of global yard sale in order to finance new acquisitions.[60]

Yet foreign sales will not be sufficient to compensate for the sharp decline in U.S. government procurement, and industry output and employment will continue to shrink. Employment in the U.S. aircraft industry has declined steadily since 1989 as a result of decreases first in the military and then the civil sector of the industry (see Table 5.3). Employment in the military aircraft sector of the industry peaked in 1986 and has subsequently fallen by over 40 percent. The cutbacks in military aircraft were initially cushioned by increased production in civil aircraft, but that sector, too, began shrinking in 1992. Thousands of aircraft workers laid off from military production lines have failed to find related new jobs, even when employment in other divisions of the companies was growing.

---

[59] "Weapons Merchants Go Great Guns after the Cold War," *Wall Street Journal*, January 28, 1994, pp. A1, A6–A7.

[60] David A. Fulghum, "Surplus Sales Seen Funding New Buys," *Aviation Week & Space Technology*, Vol. 140, No. 7 (February 14, 1994), pp. 20–21.

Chapter 6

Susan Willett

Michael Clarke

Philip Gummett

The British Push for the Eurofighter 2000

The uncertain prospects of the Eurofighter 2000 reflect the challenges to Western European nations as they adjust to the post–Cold War security environment during a time of economic recession. The aircraft exemplifies the dilemmas Western European governments face over the future of the defense industrial base; its checkered existence has revealed links between security and economic issues, particularly the increased economic incentive to export arms to compensate for the decline in domestic demand, and the impact of multinational decision-making on procurement decisions and industrial output.

Cancellation of the Eurofighter would intensify the contraction of the European defense industrial and technology base, and exacerbate structural unemployment. For some nations it might mean the end of combat aircraft production altogether. But should economic goals drive decisions about defense procurement? Even if defense ministries ought to support industry, arms procurement decisions should at least begin with a consideration of security needs. This chapter examines the importance of the Eurofighter program to Britain's military, aviation industry, and defense policy.

Susan Willett is a Defense Economist at the Centre for Defence Studies, University of London, where she is responsible for a research and networking program on defense procurement, defense industries, and arms trade.

Michael Clarke has been the Executive Director of the Centre for Defence Studies, University of London, since 1990.

Philip Gummett is Professor of Government and Technology Policy at the University of Manchester, UK

The RAF and the Eurofighter

BRITISH AIRPOWER DOCTRINE AND COMBAT AIRCRAFT

For many years the Royal Air Force (RAF) lacked an explicit airpower doctrine; to define its needs it relied upon the diverse roles NATO might ask it to fill. This allowed great flexibility in the RAF's interpretation of what equipment was needed to meet Britain's air power requirements, and it supported the argument that the RAF needed "balanced" forces capable of performing a range of tasks. This approach has come under severe pressure over the last several years, and on the basis of the changes in the defense environment the RAF promulgated a new doctrine, called AP 3000. The first edition of AP 3000 appeared in 1991, and a second edition in 1993 acknowledged even greater changes in the environment of airpower operations.[1]

The recent RAF doctrinal statements have decreased the traditional emphasis on strategic bombing. Instead, the present doctrine states that air strategy is composed of three elements: counter-air operations, strategic air offensive operations, and anti-surface force operations.[2] These missions do not necessarily imply specific aircraft procurement decisions; for example, strategic air operations can be performed by Tornado GR1s as well as B-2 bombers, and anti-surface operations can be conducted by GR1s or Apache helicopters. The doctrine stresses that procurement must reflect the priorities of the new missions: "Invariably, the counter-air campaign will be the primary air campaign, and the other air campaigns will be of subordinate importance. Emergency situations may occur when assets needed to achieve or maintain control of the air have to be diverted to other tasks. But such diversions must only be temporary, and they should never be used as the basis for planning."[3]

The major role and function of the RAF's combat aircraft are to destroy enemy aircraft in the air (the fighter mission) and to attack enemy aircraft and supporting installations and equipment on the ground. As of July 1993, the RAF had 554 combat aircraft. This included seven types of aircraft ranging from the robust yet aging

---

[1] *Air Power Doctrine* (Royal Air Force, 1991); and *Air Power Doctrine*, 2nd ed. (Royal Air Force, 1993).

[2] *Air Power Doctrine*, 2nd ed., p. 19.

[3] Counter-air, "the primary campaign," is the first of four major types of operation in which airpower can engage. *Air Power Doctrine*, 2nd ed., p. 41.

Buccaneer, built in the 1950s, to more sophisticated multi-role combat aircraft such as the Tornado and Harrier, some of which have only just entered service.

The RAF has three primary missions. First, it must maintain the integrity of British airspace and dependent territories in peacetime. The Tornado F3 fighter, supported by tanker aircraft, can intercept and identify enemy aircraft entering British airspace. Second, it must contribute to the NATO air reaction forces and main defense forces. For this purpose, Harriers and Jaguars are equipped and trained for mobile operations in offensive air support. Tornado GR1s provide day and night tactical reconnaissance, with the Jaguar providing a day and limited night reconnaissance capability. In addition, the Tornado GR1 has a specialist all-weather long-range interdiction role with a unique airfield attack capability. The Harrier provides a shorter-range attack capability including at night and in poor weather. Third, the RAF must be able to intervene in regional conflicts. Such operations are likely to be based on multinational responses, usually under UN auspices. They involve a significant number of Tornado F3s and GR1s, Harriers and Jaguars.

In 1993 the RAF deployed 28 squadrons, six based in Germany and the rest throughout the UK. The number of squadrons has been reduced significantly since 1987, when there were 34 combat aircraft squadrons.

The age of the RAF's combat aircraft varies widely, from the Buccaneer, which entered service in the late 1950s, to the Tornado F3s and Harrier GR5/7s, which were still entering service in 1993. By the turn of the century about a third of the RAF's holdings will have served for at least 20 years, including the Jaguars and the Tornado GR1s, which entered service in the early 1980s.

PROCUREMENT PLANS

Despite budgetary pressures, the Ministry of Defence (MoD) plans to update its front-line combat aircraft by the turn of the century. The cornerstone of the RAF's modernized capability is to be the Eurofighter 2000, a multi-role aircraft with a primary air-to-air capability and a secondary air-to-ground capability. It is designed to operate in air defense and air support roles.

In addition, the RAF's requirements include a new fleet of transport aircraft, a medium-range air defense missile, a modernization of the Tornado strike force, a replacement or upgrade for its maritime patrol aircraft, and several different kinds of helicopters. Most of these projects will be very expensive; their convergence of costs at a time of severe pressure on the defense budget suggests that some difficult choices will have to be made. Some analysts believe that the Tornado modernization could be cut or terminated, so that funds can be diverted to the Eurofighter program.

The spiraling costs to develop and produce combat aircraft have persistently influenced RAF decisions about what types and numbers of combat aircraft it procures. There was a significant difference between growth in cost of combat aircraft (around 8 percent per annum in real terms) and the size of defense budgets. The increasing cost of individual military aircraft programs relative to the defense equipment budget imposes a severe restriction on other procurement programs and creates large fluctuations in defense procurement trends. (For example, at its peak the Tornado program absorbed 18 percent of the procurement budget.)

The MoD has tried to offset the rise in unit production costs by buying fewer aircraft, funding programs less frequently, reducing the number of different types of aircraft being procured, and prolonging the lifecycle of aircraft by extending their period in service.[4] The RAF has attempted to maintain its overall capability by deploying a smaller number of aircraft with greater individual combat effectiveness, which created the need for multi-role combat aircraft such as the Tornado and latterly the Eurofighter.

From 1985–1991, the UK's defense budget decreased by 20 percent in real terms. The procurement has taken the brunt of this since the personnel budget is relatively inelastic. Costly combat aircraft programs have been stretched out, and annual orders for new combat aircraft have decreased steadily since 1989.

Since 1991, increased budgetary pressures and the changed security environment have forced a number of cuts in the RAF's inventory. On April 1, 1994, one Tornado squadron was scrapped, reducing the fighter squadrons to six. The two remaining squadrons of aging Buccaneer strike and attack aircraft will be replaced by the end of 1994 by Tornado GR1 aircraft converted to carry the Sea Eagle anti-ship missile.

---

[4] D.L. Kirkpatrick and P. Pugh, "Towards the Starship Enterprise: Are the Current Trends in Defence Units Inexorable?" *Aerospace* (May 1983), pp. 16–23.

While budgetary constraints crucially affect combat aircraft procurement, the changing nature of the air power doctrine has a comparable influence on MoD decisions. Profound changes in the global strategic environment suggest that a new air power doctrine could be emerging; if so, will the new doctrine affect decisions about the Eurofighter?

THE EUROFIGHTER

The Eurofighter 2000, originally called the European Fighter Aircraft (EFA), is intended to replace aging fighters in Britain, Germany, Italy, and Spain.[5] (France was included in preliminary negotiations, but was unable to agree with the other partners about the aircraft's basic specifications.) Its design was driven by its primary role in air-to-air combat. The aircraft is extremely agile, incorporates some stealth characteristics, and has advanced defensive aids. Another important specification is that the aircraft must be able to take off and land from a 500-meter runway, so that it would not be handicapped by extensive runway damage. This specification has limited all other capabilities of the Eurofighter. The aircraft uses advanced materials, which has made it significantly lighter. It is designed for a lifetime of 6,000 flight hours, or 25 years.

With its focus on agility, the Eurofighter is most suited to air-to-air combat with Russian aircraft. However, in view of the short range of Russian combat aircraft and the post–Cold War security environment, such an engagement is unlikely. The short take-off and landing (STOL) capability also reflects planning for a large war with the Soviet Union, rather than more likely missions.

The Eurofighter is the largest collaborative program the UK aerospace industry is involved in. The Eurofighter Consortium, the prime contractor for the airframe, is a joint venture of British Aerospace (BAe) in the UK; Messerschmitt-Bölkow-Blohm (MBB), a subsidiary of Deutsche Aerospace (DASA), in Germany; Aeritalia in

---

[5] For simplicity, we draw historical background mainly from a useful recent paper, B. Elzen et al., "Weapons Innovation: Networks and Guiding Principles," *Science and Public Policy*, Vol. 18, No. 3 (June 1990), pp. 171–193. This contains full supporting documentation. See also Bert Enserink et al., "Directing a Cacophony—Weapon Innovation and International Security," in W. Smit et al., eds., *Military Technological Innovation and Stability in a Changing World* (Amsterdam: VU University Press, 1992); and N. Frith, "The European Fighter Aircraft—Potential and Prospects," *RUSI Journal* (April 1992), pp. 21–25.

Italy; and Construcciones Aeronauticas SA (CASA) in Spain. The workshare of each participating nation reflects the number of aircraft it has ordered, and thus each country's investment in the program. (See Table 6.1.) The engine is being developed by the Eurojet Consortium, which also consists of companies from the four participating countries.

Table 6.1. Original and Revised Eurofighter 2000 Workshare Arrangements

| | Aircraft to be Produced | | |
	Original Estimate 1991	Revised Estimate 1993	Original Work Share
United Kingdom	250	250	33%
Germany	250	140	33%
Italy	165	130	21%
Spain	100	72	13%
Total	765	520	100%

Source: "Jane's All the World's Aircraft 1993-94," p. 161; and
Charles Miller and Michael J. Witt, "Eurofighter Countries Seek Broadened Sales,"
Defense News, Vol. 9, No. 18 (May 9, 1994), p. 22.

The first development aircraft was scheduled to begin flight trials in 1992 but was delayed until 1994. Production was planned to begin at the end of 1993, with the first aircraft coming off the line in 1997; this has been delayed until 2000 at the earliest. In 1988 the consortium's total cost of the project was estimated at just over £20 bn, with a total development cost of £5 bn (1988 prices), but the program has already gone far over budget. Operating and support costs are likely to add a further £18 bn to the RAF's bill.[6] The UK MoD has said that the minimum cost-effective production order is 400 aircraft. Even given the cuts in orders by participating nations, this target appears feasible.

The RAF argues that the Eurofighter is vital for its future development. While the aircraft was conceived during the Cold War to protect Western European airspace, along with the Tornado, the RAF feels that in the 1990s, air superiority will be vital wherever

[6] As a rule of thumb, 60 percent of a fighter's total cost is its operation and support over its 25-year life.

British or allied forces are operating. If the Eurofighter is canceled, the RAF will be left with its modernized Tornado GR4s, backed up by a residual Harrier GR5 and GR7 capacity as its only offensive aircraft. The Tornado F3 and the Jaguar ground attack aircraft are to be replaced by the Eurofighter rather than given another mid-life update.

Without the Eurofighter, the RAF would have an adequate-to-good ground attack capability and a rapidly diminishing air-fighting ability, assuming that F3s are kept flying and MiG-29s, Su-27s, Rafales and F-22s are eventually procured by other countries. However, more countries are upgrading their aircraft to keep them in service longer, so the RAF's air-fighting ability may not diminish as fast as senior officers expect if they are compelled to make do with the F3 for as long as possible. There is no doubt that the cancellation of the Eurofighter would eventually take the RAF out of the world-class fighter business, unless the government later bought a contemporary fighter from another country.

Failing this, the RAF would have to consolidate its capability as a force that specializes in ground attack and the other aspects of combat-support air operations, for which it has a generally good reputation. For offensive forces it would use the Tornado GR1 and GR1A and the Harrier GR5 and GR7; for airlift, the C-130, and perhaps the C-130J and C-17; and for maritime surveillance, the Nimrod.

Cancellation of the Eurofighter would force an important rethinking in the development of the RAF's new air power doctrine (though given the tenuous hold that doctrine traditionally has on British forces, this may not be regarded as a major consequence). Its future roles would be more limited, but its spectrum of activities would still be rather wide. Considering the insecurities of contemporary Europe, it may be called upon more frequently than in the past.

Industry and the Eurofighter

The British aerospace sector has evolved from dozens of fragmented companies into a highly concentrated industry dominated by one major airframe company, British Aerospace; a major aero-engine company, Rolls Royce; major subcontractors that supply avionics and equipment, GEC, Lucas Industries, Dowty and Smiths Industries; and numerous small sub-contractors. Another 48 companies are involved in contracts for development of airframe equipment, and 10 companies are involved in contracts for engine accessories. These companies perform the whole spectrum of aerospace activity: basic research, concept, design, development and manufacture, testing, and final production. Their products include airframes, space systems, guided missiles, avionics, and aviation engines.

The output of the aerospace sector accounts for roughly 2 percent of the country's gross domestic product, 5 percent of manufactured output, and 9 percent of exports of manufactured goods.[7] The sector has grown significantly in the past decade, mostly as a result of increased unit prices, rather than increased output. Its annual revenue increased from £4.6 bn in 1980 to £12.5 bn in 1990, or more than 50 percent in real terms. Despite its apparent success, pressures on the industry have been growing for almost a decade because the government is less willing to support the sector.

The first part of this section briefly describes the aircraft that are currently being produced in Britain. The parts that follow discuss the industry's weaknesses, and how the cancellation of the Eurofighter program might affect the industry and the economy in general.

SYSTEMS IN PRODUCTION

TORNADO   The Tornado, a swing-wing multi-role aircraft, is produced by the Panavia consortium, a tri-national company set up jointly by British Aerospace, MBB of Germany, and Aeritalia of Italy.[8] The Tornado program is now near completion, and forms the backbone of European air defense. More than 850 are in service and the total demand exceeds 900. The MoD had ordered 228 Tornado GR1s and 170 F3s by 1992. The last of the Tornados were delivered to the RAF in 1993. Sales of Tornados to Saudi Arabia constituted the major element of Britain's largest-ever export contract, worth more than £15 bn.

Currently there are three versions of the aircraft: The Tornado GR1 Interdictor Strike version (IDS), the Tornado Electronic Combat and

---

[7] Society of British Aerospace Companies, *Press Information* (Farnborough International, 1992), pp. 9–11.

[8] This section relies on *Jane's All the World's Aircraft 1992–93* and *British Aerospace Annual Report 1992–93*.

Reconnaissance (ECR) version, and the Tornado F3 Air Defense Variant (ADV).

The Tornado GR1 is now in its tenth year of RAF service. The first squadron is due to be withdrawn in 2006 but its service life could be extended. While much of the equipment in the Tornado was designed in the early 1970s and is now well out of date, a modernization program, the Tornado mid-life update (MLU), will begin deliveries in November 1996 and will run until 2003. Ultimately, the RAF hopes to update 161 GR1s and GR1As, although the number is still under discussion.

HARRIER   The Harrier, produced by BAe, is the only operational combat aircraft in the Western world that can take off vertically, or with a short forward run, and land vertically. This makes it eminently suitable for aircraft carriers. The Harrier is used for close support and reconnaissance roles. The Mk 4N variant was introduced into the RAF in 1969. It has been supplanted by the Mk 5 and Mk 7, which first entered service in 1988. By 1990 the RAF had ordered 109 Harriers— 2 development versions, 41 Mk 5s, 19 Mk 5As, 34 Mk 7s, and 13 Mk 10s. Deliveries of Mk 5s began in 1988 and the first Mk 7 was delivered in 1990. In addition, BAe received a contract in 1990 to upgrade 58 Mk 5 and 5As to Mk 7s.

The Sea Harrier variant developed for the Royal Navy is fitted with a "ski jump," giving it a reduced take-off run and additional payload capacity. In 1993, BAe won a contract from the MoD for 18 new Sea Harriers, and the first delivery is expected in 1995.[9] The Sea Harrier Mk 51 was developed for the Indian Navy, which has ordered 80.

The AV-8B Harrier II, developed for the U.S. Marine Corps, is the most advanced version of the Harrier, with carbon fiber composite wings and tail sections, and other aerodynamic improvements. Compared to older versions, the aircraft is more combat-capable, and can carry double the payload or fly twice as far. The U.S. Marine Corps has ordered 286 Harrier AV-8Bs, the Spanish Navy has ordered 21, and the Italian Navy has ordered 18. Total firm orders for this successful aircraft amount to 404.

In 1990, British Aerospace and McDonnell Douglas, a U.S. firm, set up a joint study group to determine the aircraft's advances in

---

[9] *Flight International*, April 7, 1993.

short take-off and landing and to improve its avionics, radar, engine, and carbon fibers. The companies hope that the Harrier III will replace current Sea Harriers around 2000–2005. It could also replace the AV-8B. BAe is now engaged in a mid-life update program for the Royal Navy's Sea Harriers, which will upgrade the avionics and weapons technology.

HAWK   The Hawk 100, produced by BAe, is a two-seat trainer and ground attack aircraft. The RAF has about 60 Hawk 100s, which started entering service in the early 1980s. Its good in-service record and proven low cost to own have made it highly successful as an export item. It has been sold to Abu Dhabi, Malaysia, and Oman, and the U.S. Navy selected a modified version, the T-45A Goshawk, for jet-pilot training.

The single-seat Hawk 200 series was developed to take advantage of new miniaturized, low-cost avionics developments and intelligent weapons. It is suitable for a variety of roles including ground attack, combat air patrol and interception, reconnaissance, and maritime strike. It can fly at night and in any weather, and can remain on combat air patrol for four hours. This variant has also been highly successful in the developing world, with sales to Brunei, the Philippines, Saudi Arabia and Indonesia. BAe and Saab of Sweden are discussing the possibility of collaboration on a follow-on variant of the Hawk.[10]

FUTURE MILITARY AIRCRAFT PROGRAMS

In 1992, BAe drew up a plan for new military aircraft ventures in addition to the Eurofighter to take the company into the 21st century.[11] The projects include a new jet trainer, which could replace the Hawk; a light combat aircraft; a next-generation fighter; and a multi-mission surveillance platform. The master plan is designed to keep British Aerospace a major military aircraft manufacturer despite the downturn in global defense spending. The firm is now seeking a partner for the jet trainer, and talks are being held over the next combat aircraft weapon system, a fighter or strike aircraft after the Eurofighter.

---

[10] *Financial Times*, June 8, 1993.

[11] *Jane's Defence Weekly*, October 5, 1992.

In addition, the company is courting the MoD to gain backing for progressive technology demonstrator programs from 1993 to 1999 that will eventually lead into new combat aircraft programs. These proposals represent follow-on strategies devised by the company to fill capacity in the future. However, the government may not be able or willing to fund all the projects that BAe wishes to undertake.

STRUCTURAL PROBLEMS IN THE INDUSTRY

The importance of the Eurofighter to the British aerospace sector cannot be overstated. With the end of the Tornado program and delays on the decision concerning the Tornado MLU, a gaping hole has emerged in British Aerospace's production orders. The lengthening of military aircraft life cycles has increased the gap between each generation of new combat aircraft; one consequence is that aerospace firms may find it increasingly difficult to maintain design teams.

In the past, the state provided the bulk of R&D funds and a secure long-term market. Often the downturns of the defense market ran counter-cyclical to upswings in civil business, so that each operation cushioned the other. Since the end of the Cold War, however, cuts in orders for military aircraft have coincided with a collapse in civil airline orders. There is little prospect of an upturn in the market in the medium term. To compound these problems, new players are competing for a share of a diminishing global market. For example, Japan, South Korea, Indonesia, Brazil, Taiwan, and Singapore have singled out aerospace as a strategic industry for investment well into the next century. There is an estimated 30 percent overcapacity in the global aerospace industry, and in some segments as much as 50 percent overcapacity.[12]

More than three decades of international collaboration with European partners has helped Britain preserve a national aerospace industry, but alliances and risk-sharing partnerships only spread the financial burden of developing new military aircraft programs; they do not reduce overcapacity. As budget cuts have reduced governments' ability to protect their national defense industries, market forces are more clearly determining the future size and shape of a global aerospace industry. The creation of a single European market has helped to intensify this process at a European level. The

---

[12] M. Bollinger, a defense aerospace analyst at Booz-Allen and Hamilton, quoted in "Recession Postponed," *Flight International*, August 19–25, 1992.

emergence of Eurocopter, Matra-Marconi-espace and other transnational joint ventures and alliances are all signs of a new dynamic. One expert predicts that by 2000 only half the current players in the aerospace industry will remain as independent companies. Possibly as many as 75–80 percent of aerospace contractors will be forced to exit the market or find themselves absorbed by more aggressive competitors, as in the oil, publishing, and consumer electronics industries. The surviving companies will be those that have solved the problems in their core businesses and accept the necessity to pare down volume.

BAe intends to concentrate on core defense and Airbus activities by selling off its space, corporate, and regional aircraft businesses, and has already sold its Rover automobile division to the German firm, Bavarian Motor Works (BMW). But this rationalization leaves a problem: BAe's core military aircraft business is for now dependent on one rather shaky international program; maintaining this program becomes synonymous with the survival of the industry. It forces the question, "Can a country retain a strong position in aircraft production unless it has a strong military aircraft program?" This concern increasingly informs government policy and public debate toward the industry.

EMPLOYMENT

The UK economy is enduring the worst recession since the 1930s, so industrial and employment consequences of the possible cancellation of the Eurofighter program are uppermost in people's minds. Indeed, the cancellation of the Eurofighter would be catastrophic for an industry that has already lost 60,000 jobs in the past decade.

The MoD estimates that the development phase of the Eurofighter created 3,000 to 4,000 jobs directly, and perhaps another 5,000 indirectly. Industry estimates, that at the peak of production, the program will employ 20,000 workers in the aerospace industry and 20,000 at firms that supply goods and services to the aerospace industry.[13] The loss of 20,000 to 40,000 jobs would affect the national rate of unemployment, but would be most devastating at the local and regional level.

[13] House of Commons Defence Committee, *European Fighter Aircraft, 6th Report, Session 1991–92*, HC299 (London: Her Majesty's Stationery Office [HMSO], 1992), p. xxix.

According to the Society of British Aerospace Companies (SBAC), in 1990 the industry had 180,000 employees, including 30,000 in the electronics industry.[14] (See Table 6.2.) A further 250,000 people were indirectly employed by the industry.

Table 6.2. UK Aerospace Industry Employment 1980–1990

	Employees in thousands
	Employees
1980	230
1981	250
1982	231
1983	218
1984	200
1985	204
1986	201
1987	207
1988	187
1989	194
1990	180

Source: SBAC 1992

During the 1980s, many jobs were eliminated due to investments in areas such as computer-aided design and manufacturing systems, which helped increase the industry's productivity (and also contributed to overcapacity). More recently labor has been displaced as a result of cutbacks and delays in orders. In the past, mostly office and craft workers and middle management were laid off, while the number of scientists, technicians, and professionals increased.[15] In fact, the aerospace industry employs over three times the proportion of professional scientists, engineers, and technologists as the rest of the engineering industry.[16] But as the recession deepens, defense companies have been forced to release skilled labor, whom they have

---

[14] *Press Information*, p. 11.

[15] J. Lovering. "The British Defence Industry in the 1990s: A Labour Market Perspective," *Industrial Relations Journal* (February 22, 1991), pp. 103–116.

[16] J. Lovering, "Restructuring the British Defence Industrial Base after the Cold War: Institutional and Geographical Perspectives," *Defence Economics*, Vol. 4, No. 2 (1993), pp. 123–140.

been accused of hoarding in the past.[17] There is little evidence that these workers have been able to find alternative employment.

The cancellation of the Eurofighter would make it even harder for companies such as British Aerospace to retain their core of skilled aero-engineers, designers, and technicians; this could threaten the very future of the industry. If these workers cannot find new jobs—which is not unlikely, given the virtual collapse of the UK's engineering industry—then valuable skills and technical knowledge would be lost to the UK economy for good.

THE UK TECHNOLOGY BASE

In the past, technological advance was sometimes stimulated by governmental investment in large, long-term, mission-oriented projects with exacting technical standards. The Manhattan Project and the Apollo Moon Program are two examples. In addition to achieving their program goals, such projects have created "spin-offs," technologies for use in civilian pursuits. Sometimes they also create a demand for new technologies.

Within the environment of these projects, the normal commercial criterion of return on investment is to some extent suspended; thus it is not surprising that these projects require resources of a magnitude that only a government or alliance can provide. Following the "large projects" view, cancellation of the Eurofighter would be detrimental to the United Kingdom's technology base.

Recently, however, some have argued that the technological benefits that in the past flowed from major military projects no longer necessarily do so. Now, civil demands in some fields are at least as great as those of the military, especially in electronics. In this view, the technological leading edge is shifting to the civil sector. Moreover, evidence suggests that spin-off from military projects is not actually very common. Based on this view, cancellation of the Eurofighter might not devastate the United Kingdom's capacity for technological innovation.

Unfortunately, neither model takes account of the degree to which defense funds dominate a sector of technology within a country. When the prime source of research funding is the defense ministry,

---

[17] C. Freeman, "R&D Technical Change and Investment in the UK," *The Restructuring of the UK Economy*, F. Green, ed. (Hemel Hempstead: Harvester Wheatsheaf, 1989), pp. 199–244.

then the loss of the funding could be serious to the civil sector. This is likely to be an especially important consideration in countries such as the United Kingdom, where the general manufacturing base is weak by international standards, so there is a considerable premium on retaining the technological strengths that remain. These considerations apply with some force to the aerospace sector, the only industry for which the state provides more than 50 percent of research and development expenditure.

The European Commission has proposed that it might be useful for the sector as a whole if the European Union supported increased research in those areas common to both the military and the civil sectors.[18] One such field might be new materials research. It is notoriously time-consuming, and therefore requires the time and funding characteristic of defense projects. Aerospace is one of the field's main "technology drivers." In many respects new materials technologies, especially those involving polymer composites, are still something of a "black art," where continuous practice in the application of the technologies is necessary for their maintenance. Some aspects of avionics (including flight control systems) and other aspects of electronics, as well as technologies associated with engine and turbine design and manufacture, would also be good areas for European Union sponsorship.

It is also important to note that aircraft firms are able to recruit and retain staff on military programs who then become available for civil programs, and that the combination of the two can help with the problem of maintaining "critical mass" in design teams. Finally, cancellation of the Eurofighter project could mean the loss of design capabilities, with implications for maintaining a "critical mass" of staff and facilities in aircraft and aero-engine design.

THE ABILITY OF UK FIRMS TO ADJUST
Uncertainty about the future of the Eurofighter comes at a time when the global aerospace industry is facing the worst cyclical downturn since the end of the Second World War. Britain's particular difficulty is that its industrial and technological abilities are firmly geared toward the military sector, with only very limited engineering strength

---

[18] Commission of the European Communities, *A Competitive European Aeronautical Industry* (Brussels: Commission of the European Communities, *Communication from the Commission*, 1990), para. 5.2 and Annex 6.

in other sectors. Its ability to move toward civil leadership may be unusually limited.

In response to defense market changes, aerospace companies have adopted a number of strategic responses in a bid for survival. First, mergers and acquisition have led to the emergence of larger national companies, while the growth in cross-border activities has resulted in the internationalization of what was once a highly protected national industry.[19] Second, there have been some attempts to reduce defense dependency through diversification strategies. There have been fewer efforts to transform military technology for civil use.

But diversification has only marginally compensated for the loss of defense orders.[20] Most UK aerospace companies have tended to consolidate around their core defense programs, which they feel are still their main source of expertise and strength. Most UK defense contractors are wary of attempting to diversify during a recession. The norm for companies has been to seek to increase their shares in defense market niches, through mergers and acquisitions, and to shed defense divisions that are no longer lucrative.

The recession is hardly the only difficulty facing the industry. There are also considerable barriers to exit from the military sector.[21] These include inexperience in commercial marketing; an emphasis on product rather than process innovations; a hierarchy of skills and a technological orientation geared to the weapon systems acquisition process; management that is isolated from commercial practices; a production structure defined by large-scale systems integration; protected markets (because of government procurement); and risk aversion (created by government subsidies in R&D and capital investment).

In contrast, Britain's partners in the Eurofighter might not be so severely affected by cancellation. Germany is very strong in engineering, and its aircraft industry is already much less defense-dependent than that of Britain. Cancellation of the Eurofighter would have greater consequences in the UK than in Germany for techno-

[19] See Walker and Gummett, "Britain and the European Armaments Market," *International Affairs*, Vol. 65, No. 3 (1989), pp. 419–442.

[20] See Schofield, Dando, and Ridge, *Conversion of the British Defence Industries*, Peace Research Report No. 30 (Department of Peace Studies, University of Bradford, 1992).

[21] A.J. Alexander, *National Experiences: A Comparative Analysis, in Conversion Economic Adjustment in an Era of Arms Reduction*, Disarmament Topical Papers (New York: United Nations, Vol. 11, 1991), pp. 3–61.

logical development. For Spain, participation in the Eurofighter represents a deliberate effort to raise national technological standards. The program has reached 65 percent of Spain's total defense R&D investment in some recent years. Thus its cancellation would raise important political questions about the wisdom of such a heavy commitment, particularly since Spanish firms generally play a junior role. However, Spanish expectations of benefit from the Eurofighter have always focused more on the R&D stage than on production; according to one specialist, cancellation would be serious for many firms and devastating for some, but would not be overwhelming.[22]

The cancellation of the Eurofighter would, for a while at least, weaken the scope for international collaboration in defense. In particular, if Germany were seen as the prime culprit, then, given the high proportion of German military programs that are being developed collaboratively, the consequences of mistrust could be grave. Moreover, progress on the construction of a new European security architecture in general, and a new defense procurement system in particular, would also be set back.

Government Policy Toward the Aircraft Industry

In terms of technological advance, Britain's aviation industry has benefited hugely from military expenditures.[23] Most of the industry's basic research from before 1945 until at least the late 1970s was supported by work done at what were primarily defense research establishments. In 1960, military R&D amounted to eight times civil R&D; by 1967 it was still three times greater.[24] Moreover, for several decades after World War II, government R&D spending was dominated by aviation R&D (along with atomic energy), so that military aircraft programs received the lion's share of state R&D funding.

Within the government, responsibility for aircraft policy has been concentrated since 1973, with the Procurement Executive of the Min-

---

[22] J. Molas-Gallart, "Spanish Participation in the Development and Production of Arms Systems," *Defense Analysis*, Vol. 6, No. 4 (1990), pp. 351–365.

[23] This section draws on P. Gummett, "Civil and Military Aircraft in the UK," *History and Technology*, Vol. 9 (1992), pp. 203–222.

[24] K. Hayward, *Government and British Civil Aerospace* (Manchester: Manchester University Press, 1983), p. 2.

istry of Defence.[25] However, the government maintains a common R&D base for military and civil aircraft, organized around the Royal Aircraft Establishment, now the Aerospace Division of the Defense Research Agency (Farnborough), other government establishments such as the Royal Signals and Radar Establishment, and key firms.

There has been considerable instability in government policy at the level of individual projects, with a string of cancellations. David Edgerton has remarked that "so much of the history of the post-war [British] aircraft industry is the history of R&D programs rather than the history of the production of aircraft."[26]

Since the 1970s, both the government and the firms have pursued international collaboration for military and civil projects. At this point, there is no possibility of either military or civil fixed-wing aircraft being developed in Britain on a purely national basis.

In the 1980s, reforms in defense procurement altered the close relationship between government and the aerospace industry, increased the competitive element in defense procurement, and increased the scope for foreign firms to enter the UK market. Still, the aircraft industry continued to enjoy a privileged position. Nor was Britain alone in regarding the aircraft industry as special; since the late 1980s the European Commission has sought to assist the European aircraft industry to compete with the United States and, increasingly, Japan.

Several themes characterize the British government's attitude toward the aviation industry. One is the long-standing and widespread belief that Britain is a major player in the international aerospace stakes. Although now weaker than ever before, this belief is still strong. It is reinforced by arguments that, against a background of general decline in the UK manufacturing base, relatively successful areas of high technology industry must be sustained.[27] A second

---

[25] Responsibility had previously lain variously with the Ministries of Supply, Aviation, and Technology, all of which had substantial (and often dominant) defense responsibilities, but usually mixed with civil. Only with the implementation, completed in 1973, of the Rayner Report, Government Organisation for Defence Procurement and Civil Aerospace, CMND 4641 (London, HMSO, 1971), was a sharp separation made between defense procurement (including military aircraft) and civil aerospace.

[26] David Edgerton, *England and the Aeroplane* (London: Macmillan, 1991), p. 92.

[27] Anecdotally, but revealingly, a piece of gossip in political circles after the announcement in late 1992 of massive closures of coal mines, with severe unemployment consequences, was that "at least that means that EFA is safe!"

theme is the importance of maintaining a strategic manufacturing capability for military purposes. Increasingly, this belief is expressed in terms of a European rather than a British capability. Third is the traditional rivalry with France, which would make any British government reluctant to abandon the military aircraft field in Europe to France. None of these themes guarantees continued support for any particular project, especially under a government that shares many of the values of the Thatcher era. It does, however, suggest that letting go of a military aircraft capability, albeit one conceived now in terms of partnership with other European countries, would be a very difficult political decision.

Public statements by the government reflect the difficult choices it faces. Thus, the UK MoD is adamant about its "hands off" role toward industry, even though official statements continually refer to the Eurofighter's economic importance. The 1992 Defence Select Committee Report on the aircraft stressed that "the significance of EFA to the UK high technology industrial base must feature in MoD's analysis of desirability of EFA proceeding to production."[28]

In fact, the problem of defining a post–Cold War defense policy for Britain has not been the subject of any substantial debate among the political parties. While the opposition parties have criticized the government's work on defense policy, none of the parties has outlined any alternatives, still less tried to make political capital out of a different vision of British defense.[29] On questions of procurement—especially of the Eurofighter—they have criticized the government for jobs lost to cutbacks, and have demanded that government adopt a more coherent approach to procurement so that British defense industries have a better basis for planning. All the parties support the Eurofighter, though there is some disquiet at how it has been handled.[30]

AN EXPORT SOLUTION?
During the 1992–1993 review of the future of the Eurofighter, then-Defence Secretary Malcolm Rifkind had announced that even if all

---

[28] House of Commons Defence Committee, *European Fighter Aircraft, 6th Report, Session 1991–92*, HC299 (London: HMSO, 1992), p. xxix.

[29] See M. Clarke, *The British Labour Party and Defence* (Washington, D.C.: Institute for Defense Analysis, 1992).

[30] See, for example, *House of Commons Debates* (January 20, 1992), cols. 30–36.

other partners withdraw from the program, the UK would produce the Eurofighter, and would make up the shortfall with export orders.[31] And certainly on the basis of the recent success of the Tornado and Hawk, the government has cause to be optimistic about the possibility of substituting export orders for declining domestic procurement.

The UK military aerospace sector has been a relatively successful exporter. In the 1960s, the UK aerospace industry supplied 10 percent of the world aerospace market (not including the socialist countries), 14 percent in the mid-1970s, and 17 percent in 1990. With the active support of the government, aerospace exports increased from £1.7 bn in 1980 to £7.9 bn in 1991. In 1980, 40 percent of revenue was from exports; by 1990, 65 percent. The aerospace industry is one of the few manufacturing sectors to consistently produce a substantial contribution to Britain's trade balance. In 1990 aerospace exports exceeded aerospace imports by £1.6 bn. From 1980–1990, the aerospace industry's contribution to Britain's balance of trade was some £16 bn.[32]

However, export opportunities are being eroded by many factors. First, continual inflation in defense equipment costs will undermine manufacturers' attempts to maintain at least stable output. Second, the selling of used equipment among allies, permitted under the Treaty on Conventional Armed Forces in Europe (CFE), has depressed demand for new equipment. Third, developing countries' demand for arms imports is declining, and political efforts to curtail exports of conventional weapon systems to unstable regions are likely to affect future arms sales. For example, international lending institutions such as the World Bank and the International Monetary Fund (IMF) hope to link economic assistance to defense spending reductions in Third World nations. Fourth, competition in the defense markets is likely to increase. Russia is seeking to penetrate formerly Western-dominated markets by selling MiG-29s and other front-line aircraft at cut-rate prices to virtually any buyer. U.S. companies have been aggressively marketing and selling their combat aircraft in markets that have been traditional sources of demand for UK products. At the same time, the

ability of the UK government to provide financial as sales is also eroding with budgetary difficulties. require credit to purchase costly fighter aircraft.

Even the Middle East, an important source of der systems, has seen a decline of about 75 percent in Traditional UK customers such as oil-rich Saudi Ar have been less able to purchase arms. At least in the is unlikely that the Eurofighter could be as successfi in these markets.

Increasingly, aerospace manufacturers are look Pacific rim for new markets. In the past, British Ae well with sales of the Hawk in this region, but int from the United States and increasingly Russia su such an easy market to penetrate for more soph aircraft. In addition, many countries in the region are own defense industrial capabilities and increasi technology transfer in the form of licensed productic the long-term benefits for exporters and ultimat petitors.[33]

Finally, a major partner's withdrawal from the E would likely have an adverse effect on sales pote prefer equipment with a seal of approval by the dor producing countries. The squabbles about the appr aircraft in the contemporary strategic environment, of its life-cycle costs, will not have been missed by p

---

[31] For more information on the history of the Eurofighter program, see *IDDS Almanac 1994: World Combat Aircraft Holdings, Production, and Trade* (Cambridge, Mass.: IDDS, forthcoming).

[32] *Press Information*, 1992, p. 12.

[33] For an excellent discussion of the long-term implications of the Pacific Rim, see U.S. Congress, Office of Technology Ass *Trade: Commerce in Advanced Military Technology and We* (Washington, D.C.: U.S. Government Printing Office, June 1991).

Chapter 7

Marco De Andreis
Giulio Perani

Italy's Aerospace Industry and the Eurofighter 2000

With few foreign orders for their products, Italian aerospace firms have been hit especially hard by a shrinking domestic market. No concrete defense procurement plan has been established since the end of the Cold War, but the firms are hoping that the Italian Air Force will purchase the Eurofighter 2000 and make further orders for the AM-X in order to replace its aging F-104s.

The first part of this chapter examines the composition of the Italian Air Force and its procurement plans. The second part details Italy's domestic production of combat aircraft and the development of the AM-X and the Eurofighter 2000, and discusses the industry's recent difficulties. The last part assesses Italy's ability to export combat aircraft.

Italy's Fighter-Attack Forces

CURRENT FORCES

The main missions of the Italian Air Force are the defense of the Italian airspace; the support of land operations for the defense of Italian

Marco De Andreis is a Senior Researcher and the Director of International Security Studies at the Centro Studi di Politica Internazionale (CeSPI, Center for the Study of International Politics) in Rome.

Giulio Perani is Research Director of the Military Spending and Arms Production Project at Achivio Disarmo in Rome.

Research by Marco de Andreis and Giulio Perani was funded by the Center for the Study of International Politics in Rome.

territory; and the support of maritime operations for the defense of territorial waters and of sea lines of communications in the Mediterranean.[1]

As in most other countries in the northern hemisphere, the end of the Cold War has meant an identity crisis for the Italian military: there is no longer a clearly identified enemy to help sustain budgets and force levels. In Italy's case the situation is compounded by the disastrous state of the public finances (public debt was 116 percent of the gross domestic product in 1993), so that avoiding savings in the defense sector is all but impossible. The Army will bear the blunt of the coming cuts. The Navy and the Air Force will be less affected for two reasons: a shift in emphasis from the defense of continental Europe toward the Mediterranean, and a shift toward peacekeeping and peacemaking operations.[2]

From 1988 to 1992, total defense procurement has hovered around lire 4,500 bn per year (about $3 bn). The Air Force has absorbed about 37 percent of this.

With almost 80,000 men of all ranks in 1990, the Air Force accounted for roughly one-fifth of total uniformed personnel. Italy's Air Force is more manpower-intensive than the other air forces of NATO Europe. In October 1992 Salvo Andò, then Minister of Defense, announced that the workforce would be cut by about 20 percent, down to 60,000, over the next ten years.[3]

The Italian Air Force currently deploys six close air support (CAS) squadrons (two with a primary role as training-conversion units, and four with a secondary reconnaissance role); two reconnaissance squadrons; eight air defense squadrons (one with a primary role as a training-conversion unit); four fighter-bomber squadrons; and two training and one aerobatics squadrons (with a secondary CAS role).

---

[1] See *La Difesa: Libro Bianco 1985* (Rome: Ministero della Difesa, 1985); and *Modello di Difesa* (Rome: Ministero della Difesa, 1991).

[2] Both the Navy (with several escort vessels in the Persian Gulf) and the Air Force (with 10 Tornados) took part in the war for the liberation of Kuwait in early 1991. The Air Force air transport branch is bearing the burden of carrying troops and equipment for the Italian armed forces peacekeeping missions in Albania, Somalia and Mozambique. The acquisition of four Boeing 707s converted into tankers for aerial refueling will give Italian Air Force fighters a capability for longer-range missions.

[3] See Statement of the Italian Minister of Defense Salvo Andò before the Defense Committee of the Italian Chamber of Deputies: Camera dei Deputati, *Atti Parlamentari*, Commissione IV Difesa, October 14, 1992.

Air Force wings regroup one or two squadrons. There are 13 fighter wings in the Italian Air Force. A liaison unit (often also with search and rescue duties) is normally attached to a wing. These units may have helicopters (AB-212s), light planes (S-208ms, P-166ms), or old jet trainers (MB-326s).

As all-weather fighter-interceptors, the Italian Air Force employs primarily F-104ASAs. Air defense squadrons commonly have 15 aircraft, three of which are for training. Two aircraft at each air defense squadron are kept in high alert status. The F-104ASAs of the 18th squadron at Trapani have a secondary role as fighter-bombers.

As all-weather fighter-bombers, the Italian Air Force employs both F-104ASAs and Tornados. Two squadrons are nuclear-certified.[4] The Tornados are all of the interdiction-strike (IDS) version. The aircraft of the 156th squadron at Gioia del Colle, equipped with Kormoran anti-ship missiles, are also assigned naval interdiction missions. Four Tornados, based in Cottesmore, Britain, form the Italian component of a trinational (Britain, Germany, and Italy) training squadron.

The AM-X, a subsonic fighter for CAS, short-range attack, and reconnaissance, is in the process of replacing G-91Ts, G-91Ys, and RF-104Gs. As of mid-1993, 72 AM-Xs (3 of which are two-seat trainers) had been delivered, out of a total order of 136. CAS and fighter-bomber squadrons commonly have at least 18 aircraft.

A bitter dispute between the Air Force and the Navy, which had lasted several decades, came to an end in 1989 when the Parliament voted to allow the Navy to manage and deploy carrier-based, fixed-wing aircraft. Shortly thereafter, the Navy chose the McDonnell Douglas/British Aerospace AV-8B as its fighter for the "defense of the fleet," to be based on the 13,000-ton carrier *Giuseppe Garibaldi*. Eighteen AV-8Bs have been ordered; two two-seat training TAV-8Bs have already been delivered. Eight more aircraft could be ordered if there is a decision to build a second aircraft carrier. The *Garibaldi*, which is operational about six months a year, has a maximum capacity of 18 aircraft, some of which will be anti-submarine warfare (ASW) helicopters. In all likelihood, it will never accommodate more than 10 AV-8Bs. Given these constraints, the investment of around

---

[4] In 1992, some 150 nuclear bombs were deployed in Italy. See "Where the Bombs Are," *Bulletin of the Atomic Scientists* (September 1992). It is realistic to assume that at least two-thirds of these weapons are assigned to U.S. Air Force F-16s based in Aviano.

lire 1,500 bn ($1 bn), the cost of the ship plus the cost of the aircraft, in carrier-based naval aviation has been heavily criticized.

PROCUREMENT

The Italian Air Force procurement budget has been constantly reduced over the past few years. This downsizing has notably modified the pattern of air force procurement in terms of dependence on domestic suppliers, relations between research and development (R&D) and procurement spending, and priority equipment.

Out of a Ministry of Defense 1994 proposed budget of lire 26,250 bn, about lire 5,575 bn (21.2 percent) was specifically devoted to the Italian Air Force.[5] According to the Ministry of Defense, more than 40 percent of the Air Force budget should be allocated for paying wages to military personnel. Training and operational activities account for another 32 percent. Thus, a very limited share remains for investments in weapon systems and R&D activities. According to this Ministry of Defense proposal, only lire 1,269 bn can be spent in 1994 for developing and purchasing new military equipment. In 1993, procurement spending was reduced by 14.3 percent; this will cause a reduction of 120 bn lire (22.4 percent) in military aerospace R&D spending.

From 1988 to 1994, the largest procurement programs of the Italian Air Force are the development and production of the Eurofighter 2000, the production of the AM-X, the last purchases of the multi-role Tornado fighter, the development and acquisition of long-range air defense radars, the acquisition of 20 Spada-type surface-to-air missile (SAM) systems for air defense of Italian Air Force bases, and the upgrading of the remaining F-104 fighters that are still in service. Recent Air Force procurement has supported domestic aerospace production, mainly through the acquisition of a large number of AM-X fighters. A challenge for the Air Force will be to find a wise trade-off between preserving current production capacities, by purchasing AM-Xs, and improving future technological capabilities, through funding Eurofighter 2000 research and development activities.

The Eurofighter 2000, AM-X, and Tornado accounted for at least 65 percent of the total procurement budget from 1988–1994. Outlays for the Eurofighter and AM-X reached 70 percent of the total procurement budget in 1991–1992 and decreased to about 64 percent in

---

[5] The 1994 Italian Ministry of Defense budget, as approved by the Parliament in December 1993, came to lire 26,167 bn.

1993–1994. The AM-X order has been reduced to 136 aircraft, down from the original order of 238 aircraft. By December 1992, all but 52 aircraft had been delivered; 70 percent will probably be completed in 1995. In the coming years, the Eurofighter will probably lock up a very large share of the Air Force procurement budget.

In mid-1991, the Air Force still planned to purchase 165 Eurofighters—enough to modernize all eight current air defense squadrons. In November 1991, the order was reduced to 130, or six squadrons, and finally to 90–110, or four or five squadrons in October 1992. At that time, further development of the Eurofighter was in question, and Defense Minister Andò insisted that the aircraft unit cost be no more than lire 75 bn (some $50 mn).[6]

The cost of the aircraft has been a moving target, and due to the currency exchange crisis, Italian cost estimates are hardly credible. In mid-1991, the unit cost was projected at lire 65 bn, the same as the AM-X.[7] By July 1992, the cost jumped to lire 100 bn; less than three months later it was lire 150 bn.[8] Then in December 1992, the defense ministers of Britain, Germany, Italy, and Spain decided to go ahead with the Eurofighter project, which implies that Andò's limit of lire 75 bn per unit had been met.[9] The aircraft that came out of the December meeting was considerably less ambitious in its avionics and armaments. To further complicate the matter, the 1994 defense budget,

---

[6] Statement of Minister of Defense Salvo Andò before the Defense Committee of the Italian Chamber of Deputies, 1992.

[7] See Senato della Repubblica, *Stato di previsione del Ministero della Difesa per l'anno finanziario 1992*, July 29, 1991, p. 316. All estimates herein of Eurofighter 2000 and AM-X unit costs include pro-rated costs for R&D, industrialization, and logistical support.

[8] The source of the former figure is the 1993 defense budget; the source of the latter is the Corte dei Conti (roughly the equivalent of the U.S. Comptroller General). Part of the increase may be attributable to the currency exchange crisis: between July and September the lira declined almost 10 per cent against the Deutche Mark (DM) and the dollar. See Camera dei Deputati, *Stato di previsione del Ministero della Difesa per l'anno finanziario 1993*, July 31, 1992, p. 325; and Camera dei Deputati, Commissione IV Difesa, *Audizione della Corte dei Conti ai fini dell'esame preliminare del bilancio a legislazione vigente*, September 30, 1992, p. 22.

[9] The aircraft unit cost quoted after the Brussels meeting was DM 90 million, or $57 million. See R. Cohen, "Nodding to Times, Europe Opts for a Downsized Jet Fighter," *International Herald Tribune*, December 11, 1992. Both figures correspond roughly to lire 80 bn at the exchange rate of the time.

which was introduced to the Parliament on July 31, 1993, confirms the previous year's order for 130 Eurofighters at a unit cost of lire 113 bn.

Italy has found it difficult to decide on procurement funding for the next few years. The end of the Cold War, Italy's September 1992 financial crisis that brought it out of the European Monetary System, and cost overruns for the Eurofighter and the AM-X prompted two successive Defense Ministers, Andò, and his predecessor, Virgilio Rognoni, to outline varying plans to reduce the armed forces. In November 1991, Rognoni suggested that the Air Force maintain a total of 19 fighter squadrons compared to the 23 squadrons currently maintained. Then, in October 1992, following the September crisis, Andò suggested that the Air Force operate only 15 to 16 fighter squadrons. While both documents were supposed to be reviewed by the Parliament, neither was, and neither plan is legally binding. While not official, these plans offer a blueprint for future Defense ministers to follow in order to keep costs low while maintaining a viable Air Force.

According to the current schedule, the Air Force will begin to receive the Eurofighter in 2000, and the aircraft will become operational in 2005. This delay from the original schedule has raised the question of whether Italy needs a "gap filler" between the F-104, which is being retired, and the Eurofighter. (See Table 7.1.) In November 1993, Italy and Britain agreed that the Italian Air Force would lease 24 Tornado ADVs for 10 years. These will be surplus aircraft of the Royal Air Force. They will complement 60 F-104S/ASAs (to be modified and updated yet again) in the air-defense role.

There will be a decrease in the number of attack airplanes, but the Air Force plans to maintain all its squadrons for the near future. The F-104ASAs of the 102nd squadron will not be replaced by new aircraft, but by Tornados now in training units or in storage. They will be reconfigured as electronic combat and reconnaissance (ECR) variants.[10]

---

[10] Though based on a 40-year-old design, Italian F-104Ss are, on average, less than 20 years old and should still be structurally sound. Moreover, in addition to the 1986–1991 ASA updating program, the Air Force has just launched an added refurbishing program involving 100 F-104S/ASAs. The stated goal of this program, costing lire 910 bn ($600 mn), is to allow the fleet of F-104Ss to serve until after 2000, when the Eurofighter 2000 is expected to enter service. Following the November 1993 decision to lease 24 Tornado ADVs, the number of F-104S/ASAs involved in this updating may be reduced.

The AM-X will replace both the RF-104G and the G-91. The original order of 238 (including 51 AM-XTs) was cut down to 136 (including 26 AM-XTs) in mid-1991; this was considered sufficient for six CAS/Recce squadrons, including one dedicated to training. In October 1992, Mr. Andò proposed that the Air Force would forego the last 52 aircraft, which would reduce the order to 84 aircraft, or four squadrons. The 1994 defense budget, however, confirms the order for 136 AM-X. There are currently no plans to change the three MB-339 training and aerobatics squadrons.

Table 7.1 Italian "Gap Filler" Aircraft Options before the Eurofighter 2000 Enters Service

	Billions of Lire	
	10-Year Cost	Added Cost*
Maintain 80–90 upgraded F-104s	1,876	..
Purchase substantial number (probably 70) of F-16s	2,072	196
Lease 24 British ADV Tornadoes; maintain 60 F-104s	2,176	300
Purchase limited number of F-16s; maintain 60–80 F-104s	2,366	490
Purchase limited number of F-15s; maintain 60–80 F-104s	2,834	958
Purchase substantial number (probably 50) of F-15s	3,159	1,283

Source: Statement of Italian Minister of Defense Fabio Fabbri before the Defense Committee of the Italian Senate, reported in "Le ragioni di una scelta," Rivista Aeronautica, January 1994.
Note: * Added cost over least expensive option.

Air Force planners consider the proposed reductions as temporary measures to ride out short-term fiscal problems. Once these are overcome, they believe, programs will be reintroduced more or less in their original form: the last 52 AM-Xs will be produced, 130 Eurofighters will be procured, and so on.[11] Obviously, if Italy's economy and public finances deteriorate further, aircraft procurement will be closer to the recommendations of former Defense Minister Andò. In any case, at least four squadrons will be disbanded, and over the next 20 years Italy will order between 138 fighter aircraft (90 Eurofighters, 32 AM-Xs, and 16 AV-8Bs) and 238 fighter aircraft (130 Eurofighters, 84 AM-Xs, and 24 AV-8Bs). These are modest figures compared to recent orders for fighters by countries such as Saudi Arabia and Taiwan.

---

[11] Actually, cancellation of the final 52 AM-Xs appeared very unlikely; all parts except the airframes had already been ordered and paid for.

Aside from the highly questionable investment in naval aviation, the current procurement plans of the Italian Air Force would replace outdated aircraft on a less than one-to-one basis, through the purchase of the short-range AM-X and the Eurofighter. On the other hand, the aircraft with the best offensive capability, the Tornados, were acquired recently; the question of their replacement will not be raised until the late 1990s. This creates an opportunity for Italy to participate in some future cooperative security agreement that would reduce or eliminate long-range attack fighters.

Italy's Fighter Aircraft Industry

Postwar reconstruction of Italy's fighter aircraft industry centered around licensed production. After 1949, 150 De Havilland Vampires were produced, and 221 North American F-86Ks were produced between 1956 and 1958. Since then, Italy's aircraft industry has continued to produce U.S. combat aircraft under license; used its experience to begin to indigenously produce combat aircraft such as the AM-X and the G-91; and produced or developed more advanced aircraft, such as the Tornado and the Eurofighter, as a member of international consortia. Italy's aerospace industry has indigenously designed only helicopters, jet trainers, and other light aircraft.

DOMESTIC PRODUCTION

THE G-91 Between 1958 and 1966, FIAT Aviazione produced 522 G-91s: 128 for the Italian Air Force and 394 for the Luftwaffe; another 294 G-91s were produced under license in the Federal Republic of Germany (FRG). Some 50 aircraft were given to the Portuguese Air Force by the Luftwaffe. FIAT Aviazione also produced 120 G-91T two-seat trainers: 76 for Italy and 44 for the FRG.

In the mid-1960s FIAT Aviazione developed a two-engine derivative, the G-91Y, which was adopted by the Italian Air Force only. Sixty-three were produced between 1966 and 1977. The G-91Y is currently being replaced by the AM-X.

LICENSED PRODUCTION OF THE F-104 In March 1961, Italy joined the majority of its NATO partners in adopting the Lockheed F-104 Starfighter as its front-line fighter. A consortium of Italian aeronautics firms led by FIAT Aviazione and Aerfer built 229 F-104Gs from 1962 to 1966. Of these aircraft, 154 went to Italy, 50 to the FRG, and 25 to the Netherlands.

In 1965, the Italian Air Force called for an air-defense variant of the F-104G, the F-104S. Between 1969 and 1979, Aeritalia (a public-owned firm resulting from the merger of FIAT Aviazione and Aerfer) produced 246 F-104Ss, including 40 for Turkey. Between 1986 and 1991, Aeritalia has been updating Italy's F-104Ss to the ASA (Ammodernamento Sistemi d'Arma, Weapon Systems Update) standard. The program improved the aircraft's air-to-air self-defense and interception capability through a new lookdown-shootdown radar, advanced electronic counter measures (ECM), and weapon delivery systems.

THE TORNADO Toward the end of the 1960s, NATO (except for France) began considering a successor to the F-104G. Italy joined Britain and the FRG in opting for what was supposed to be a multi-role fighter, but ended up a relatively heavy all-weather fighter-bomber, the Tornado.

In 1969, the Panavia consortium was formed by British Aerospace (BAe), Messerschmitt-Bölkow-Blohm of Germany, and Aeritalia, to develop and produce the Tornado. The program as a whole was managed by a NATO agency. Work on the aircraft was distributed according to the number of aircraft each country ordered and its financial participation in the program: 42.5 percent each to the FRG and Great Britain, and 15 percent to Italy. Each industrial partner was responsible for the final assembly of the aircraft ordered by its own country. This cumbersome agreement helps explain the manifold increase in the project cost over the years, which triggered inquiries in the Parliaments of all three countries.

The first Tornado prototype flew in 1974, and the first operational aircraft entered service in 1982. Nearly 1,000 Tornados have been produced: 100, all of the interdictor-strike (IDS) variant, for the Italian Air Force; 324 IDS and 35 ECR for the Luftwaffe; 255 IDS and 212 Air Defense Variant (ADV) for the Royal Air Force; and 48 IDS and 24 ADV for Saudi Arabia.

Italian production of the Tornado airframe is mainly limited to the wings. FIAT Avio, with Rolls Royce and MTU, is part of the consortium that produces the engine. The Tornado program involved practically all the Italian aeronautics industry, playing a considerable role in its recent growth. When the end of this program was in sight, the

industry tried to grow even further by focusing on follow-on programs. British Aerospace is responsible for all the commercial and
production activity for export orders of the Tornado.

THE AM-X The AM-X was launched by the Italian Air Force and
Aeritalia at the end of the 1970s. Two other partners joined later:
Aermacchi, and the Brazilian firm Embraer, making the AM-X the first
international joint venture in military aeronautics between a developed country and a developing country. Aeritalia has a 46.3 percent
share of the work, Aermacchi has 24 percent, and Embraer has 29.7
percent. The Italian order has recently been reduced from 266 aircraft
to 136, and further cuts are possible (see above). Brazil has ordered
79 aircraft.

The original intention was to build a cheap, light fighter for close
air support, but in development it became apparent that the AM-X
would be rather expensive and complex for the mission it was
assigned. In fact, Italy sought the international partnership to soften
the cost increases, but unfortunately, this partnership has repeated
the mistakes made by the Panavia consortium: uneconomical division
of labor, duplication of assembly lines, etc.

The first AM-X prototype flew in May 1984 and was destroyed
soon after in an accident. The first production AM-Xs were delivered
to the Italian Air Force in 1989. In the spring of 1992, all Italian
AM-Xs were grounded after a series of accidents caused by mal-
functioning Rolls Royce Spey engines. They resumed flights that
autumn.

THE EUROFIGHTER The Eurofighter 2000 is described in Chapter 6.
Suffice here to recall that the organizational structure of the consortium in charge of building the Eurofighter appears to have been mod-
eled on the Panavia consortium—which goes a long way to explain
why costs have exploded to the point that the project is in jeopardy.

Workshares were assigned in 1988 proportionally to the number
of aircraft originally ordered: 21 percent to Italy, which ordered 165
aircraft; 33 percent each to Britain and Germany (250 aircraft each),
and 13 percent to Spain (100 aircraft). Workshares have been
adjusted twice, and in December 1993 the shares were: Britain, 41.5
percent (250 aircraft); Germany 23.3 percent (140 aircraft); Italy 21.6
percent (130 aircraft); and Spain 13.6 percent (82 aircraft).

The Italian prime contractor for the Eurofighter is Finmeccanica-Alenia. One hundred nineteen Italian firms are involved in this program, 23 as major contractors; practically all the aerospace industry is working on the Eurofighter. The development phase of the Eurofighter program involves about 2,000 Italian technicians; a total workforce of 15,000 will be probably involved in the production phase.

The first flight of an Italian-built prototype is scheduled for the last months of 1994.

THE MB-326 AND MB-339 The Aermacchi jet trainer MB-326 made its first flight in 1957. Over the next 20 years, some 800 aircraft were sold, more than half produced under license in countries such as Australia, Brazil, and South Africa. The MB-326 is versatile; it is an advanced trainer, and, with its 1,800 kilograms of payload, a simple, light fighter for ground attack, close air support, and counter-insurgency missions. A single-seat variant was developed to better fulfill the latter role; this was also produced in South Africa as the Impala II. The MB-326 is still in service in the Italian Air Force, largely in liaison roles.

During the 1970s, Aermacchi developed a successor to the MB-326, the MB-339, which made its first flight in 1976. It is basically the same aircraft as the MB-326, with some aerodynamics and avionics improvements and a more powerful engine. The Italian Air Force bought 101 MB-339s for training and for the Aerobatics Squadron. Other buyers of the aircraft include Peru, Malaysia, Nigeria, Dubai, New Zealand, and Argentina—which employed its MB-339s against the British fleet during the Falklands War. A single-seat variant, the MB-339K, has found no buyers.

OTHER AIRCRAFT SIAI Marchetti has designed the S-211, another jet trainer. Cheaper, lighter, and simpler than the MB-339, the S-211 made its first flight in 1981. So far only 64 planes have been sold, to Singapore and the Philippines. The aircraft was not adopted by the Italian Air Force.

Following an agreement with McDonnell Douglas in spring 1994, Finmeccanica-Alenia will begin to assemble 13 AV-8Bs in Italy. The aircraft will be fitted with the Hughes APG-65 radar. Italy's share of the cost of the program is estimated at 15 percent, or $750 mn.

ORGANIZATION OF THE INDUSTRY

The Associazione Industrie Aerospaziali (Aerospace Industries Association, AIA) groups 52 Italian firms that produce airframes, aviation engines, navigation systems, electronic countermeasures, missiles, rockets, and satellites.[12] In 1992, AIA members employed 42,000 workers, and had a combined output of lire 8,000 bn ($6.5 bn at the 1992 exchange rate), of which lire 2,900 bn, or 36 percent, is from exports. Exports have steadily declined through the 1980s: they accounted for 70 percent of total output in 1981, 64 percent in 1984, and 43 percent in 1987. The fall in foreign orders was more than compensated for by a rise in domestic demand. There has been a recent modest growth of output, despite a significant reduction in employment.

Italy's aerospace industry is small compared to those of its NATO partners and France. In 1988, France's industry was two and a half times as large in terms of employment and five times as large in terms of output; Germany's twice and three times as large respectively; and Britain's four times as large on both counts.[13]

Finmeccanica-Alenia, founded in 1990 through the merger of Aeritalia and Selenia, and currently a branch of Finmeccanica, is the largest and most important aerospace and electronics firm in Italy. In 1992 it had an output of lire 3,800 bn, and almost 18,500 employees. A number of companies in the Italian aerospace sector are subsidiaries of Finmeccanica: Elmer, FIAR, Alfa Romeo Avio, and Officine Aeronavali Venezia. The activities of the Finmeccanica group range from the production of large airframe structures for passenger aircraft, to the production of airborne radars and communication devices, to the transformation of large civilian and military aircraft.

The bulk of the Italian aerospace industry is owned by the state. Finmeccanica-Alenia is owned by the public holding company, Istituto per la Riconversione Industriale (IRI). Agusta, the major helicopter producer and the second largest aerospace firm, was controlled until 1992 by another public holding company, EFIM. In 1992 EFIM went bankrupt and its aerospace and defense firms were acquired by Finmeccanica. Finmeccanica also owns substantial minority stakes in

---

[12] This section relies on *Relazione Esercizio 1992* (Rome: Associazione Industrie Aerospaziali, 1993).

[13] See Commission of the European Community, *The European Aerospace Industry: Trading Position and Figures 1990* (Brussels, February 1990).

a number of private firms, including Elettronica, Aermacchi, and Rinaldo Piaggio. As a consequence, Finmeccanica can be considered a semi-monopolist in the Italian aerospace sector.

FIAT is the largest privately-owned group in the Italian aerospace field. It includes FIAT Aviazione (engines), FIAT CIEI (electrical equipment), and BPD (rocket and missile propulsion, ammunitions).

Multinational groups with activities in Italian aerospace are: Oerlikon-Buhrle of Switzerland (Contraves Italiana produces radars for SAM systems); GEC Marconi (Marconi produces telecommunication equipment, United Technologies (Microtecnica is a mechanical specialized firm); and Litton Industries (Litton Italia produces inertial navigation systems).

THE INDUSTRY'S DIFFICULTIES
In Italy, public ownership has regularly translated into political patronage, mismanagement, and waste. The current fiscal crisis, though, has made these practices more difficult, as shown by the EFIM bankruptcy. So far, the Italian government has not included aerospace industries among those that will be privatized, but recent changes in the Italian political system suggest that a firmer attitude toward privatizations could lead IRI to sell some or all of its majority stake in Finmeccanica.

The slump in foreign demand was caused not only by the financial difficulties of Italy's Middle Eastern customers, but also by the structural weaknesses of Italian aerospace production. For example, Italy still imports, or produces under license, all its gas turbine aviation engines. Its airframe design and production capability is clearly limited to light fighters, light military transports, and trainers. Thus, Italian aerospace firms are exposed to increasing competition from Third World and East European producers with the advantage of cheap labor.

Since about 57 percent of the value of total AIA sales go to the military sector, and military exports have declined, it is clear that the industry has grown dependent on Italian Air Force orders, which will be very limited over the next two decades. Unfortunately, shifting from military to civilian production is neither easy nor promising, at least in the short term. This is especially true for the Italian aerospace industry, which pursues very different military and civilian strategies. While Italy consistently pursues European ventures for its combat aircraft, it opted not to join the Airbus air transport consortium and to work instead as a sub-contractor for both Boeing and McDonnell Douglas.

Through the Eurofighter program, Britain, Germany, and Spain indirectly subsidize their national aerospace industries, which are members of the Airbus consortium. Thus, the Eurofighter can be seen as a means to support Airbus in its competition against its U.S. rivals in the commercial aircraft market. France does the same through the Rafale program. But it is hard to see how Italy's involvement in the Eurofighter can benefit its civilian aircraft industry.

Until two years ago, a primary aim for Italian aerospace firms was to preserve existing employment levels and production capacities. Since the early 1990s, reduced orders have forced aviation firms to focus on their core business, limiting both the development of new products and conversion to civilian production. (A number of conversion studies and blueprints have been carried out, but no consistent strategies emerged.) In the past few years, increasing reductions in demand have forced almost all Italian aerospace firms to reduce their workforces substantially. For example, between 1990 and 1992 Finmeccanica-Alenia reduced its workforce by 16 percent, and Agusta reduced its workforce by 30 percent. This lagging restructuring poses substantial problems for Italy's ability to maintain adequate technological capabilities in a period of dramatic downsizing and financial set-backs.

In the short term, the aerospace industry is stressing its competitive advantages in niches of production. Finmeccanica-Alenia is strongly marketing its more competitive products: air traffic control systems, the G-222 light transport aircraft, and the ATR commuter plane family. FIAR is selling Singapore 40 kits for upgrading the radars of its fighter aircraft and Elettronica is selling its electronic warfare equipment to several countries. But a major emphasis is the Eurofighter 2000 as the only way to avoid more cuts or shutdowns.

In the long term, a need for a basic restructuring will emerge. Some firms are considering measures that will make them more flexible and "market oriented," such as strengthening R&D and design capacity, strengthening (or creating) marketing capacity, and streamlining the production process, as well as such managerial efforts as improving workforce efficiency, creating multifaceted skills, simplifying hierarchical structures, widening the use of information technology, and introducing new production models.

Italy's Third World Markets

From 1982 to 1986, 98 percent of Italy's exports of military aircraft, helicopters, ships, armored vehicles, large-caliber artillery, radars, and guidance systems went to developing countries. During this period, the value of such exports declined from $1,357 mn in 1982 to $327 mn in 1986 (constant 1985 dollars).[14] From 1987 to 1991, the Third World accounted for 74 percent of Italian exports of major weapon systems. Their value further declined from $599 mn in 1987 to $172 mn in 1991 (constant 1990 dollars).[15] In 1992, according to Stockholm International Peace Research Institute (SIPRI) estimates, Italian exports of major conventional weapons rose to $335 mn (1990 prices),[16] but largely consisted of helicopters and light aircraft. According to the United Nations Register of conventional arms, Italy's military aerospace exports consisted of only seven MB-339 trainer aircraft (six to New Zealand and one to the United Arab Emirates), and 10 A-109 attack helicopters to Belgium.[17] In addition, Italian arms exports increasingly consist of spare parts, components, and upgrade kits, rather than weapon system platforms. In 1993, 75.6 percent of arms export deals approved by the Italian government were worth less than 500 mn lire. Only 63 deliveries have been worth more than 3 bn lire (roughly $2 mn).

This contraction can be explained by the poor competitiveness of Italy's products, and the financial difficulties of Italy's traditional customers. In addition, in July 1990, a new law (No. 185) made the transfer of arms much more difficult than in the past. Arms exports are now forbidden to countries that are subject to a UN arms embargo, involved in armed conflicts, or violating international human rights agreements. By these criteria, Italy could not transfer arms to such countries as South Africa, Iraq, Iran, and Libya, as it did until the end of the 1980s.

The share of aircraft exports within the overall transfer of arms has been substantial, but little of this has been fixed-wing combat air-

---

[14] *SIPRI Yearbook 1987* (New York: Oxford University Press, 1987), p. 183.
[15] *SIPRI Yearbook 1992* (New York: Oxford University Press, 1992), p. 272.
[16] *SIPRI Yearbook 1993* (New York: Oxford University Press, 1993), p. 444.
[17] For a comparison of SIPRI and UN data, see E. Laurance, S. Wezeman, and H. Wulf, *Arms Watch: SIPRI Report on the First Year of the UN Register of Conventional Arms* (Oxford: Oxford University Press, 1993).

craft. Instead, Italy has exported Bell, Boeing, and Sikorsky helicopter models built by Agusta under license, Aeritalia G-222 transport aircraft, and Siai-Marchetti SF-260 light, propeller-driven trainers. Aermacchi trainers account for the lion's share of Italian-built jet aircraft exports that are or can be used as fighters. There are very few exports of heavier fighters, even counting the Saudi order for Tornados as a partly Italian export. The market for Aermacchi's MB-339 and Augusta's S-211 is drying up as East European countries such as the Czech Republic and Romania offer a very large number of aircraft at very low prices. One opportunity in this market is the search by the U.S. Navy and Air Force for a new jet trainer.[18]

At present, the industry's hopes hang on the AM-X. Despite the best efforts of the aggressive exporters Finmeccanica-Alenia, Aermacchi, and Embraer, the AM-X has yet to win a single foreign order. If the AM-X is marketed at a cost close to that borne by the Italian taxpayer, it has little chance of beating a host of U.S., French, and Russian fighters with a comparable price but far better performance. In the longer term, the Eurofighter is the only other possibility, even with its limited Italian workshare. But betting on a commercial success of Eurofighter 2000 seems hard; it has no especially advanced features and will make a very late entry into a market already characterized by abundant supply and limited demand.

---

[18] Aermacchi is offering its MB-339 in collaboration with Lockheed and Hughes, and Agusta is promoting its SIAI Marchetti S-211 with Grumman.

Chapter 8

Ulrich Albrecht
Peter Lock
Jonathan Cohen

Germany—The Reluctant Eurofighter Partner

By August 1994, Germany's parliament had not committed itself to procure the Eurofighter 2000 for its Air Force, though it had already invested 5 billion Deutsche Marks (DM 5 bn) in the project. Despite the political and economic changes since the end of the Cold War, Germany is the only producer of combat aircraft that is considering the cancellation of a large fighter aircraft program begun before Russia and the West declared that they were no longer enemies.

This chapter examines Germany's attitude toward the Eurofighter. The first section provides an overview of Germany's current and planned forces, including the Eurofighter, and assesses whether Germany considers the aircraft a military necessity. The second section argues that the aerospace industry's continued interest in the project must be understood in the context of competition with the United States. The third section considers the aircraft's function in Germany's military industrial policy.

Ulrich Albrecht is Professor of Peace and Conflict Studies in the Political Science Department of the Free University of Berlin, and acting director of the University's Institute for International Politics and Regional Studies.

Peter Lock is a Senior Researcher at the Free University of Berlin.

Jonathan Cohen is a research fellow at the Institute for Defense and Disarmament Studies in Cambridge, Massachusetts, where he specializes in the conventional arms trade.

Germany's Air Force

Germany has 721 fighter-attack aircraft, 617 in the Air Force and 104 in the Navy. Most of Germany's aircraft are modern, with only its F-4s produced before 1975. Aside from 24 MiG-29s, Germany's entire inventory consists of Western-produced aircraft (Alpha Jets, Tornados, and F-4s) held by West Germany prior to reunification. By the end of 1993, the Air Force consisted of 33 fighter-attack aircraft squadrons: approximately 5.5 close air support, 10 ground attack, 7 fighter, 2 reconnaissance, 2 electronic combat, and 6.5 training squadrons. The Navy had 5 squadrons: 3 attack, 1 reconnaissance, and 1 training squadron.

The Tornado IDS is the mainstay of both the Air Force and the Navy. The Air Force uses 277 Tornados for a variety of roles including ground attack, reconnaissance, electronic combat, and training. The Navy uses its Tornados in attack, reconnaissance, and training roles. The Navy plans to convert 40 Tornado attack aircraft to the reconnaissance role and transfer them to the Air Force. These aircraft will replace Germany's inventory of 43 RF-4E reconnaissance aircraft, which are now being retired.[1] The Tornados will be maintained through 2000, and will be upgraded periodically as funds are available. These upgrades will enhance the aircraft's computer systems and electronic warfare capabilities, but may not extend their service lives.[2]

Germany is one of the few countries that possesses the combat-capable version of the Alpha Jet. The Air Force formerly used approximately 100 Alpha Jets for close air support, but they have all been withdrawn from front-line duty and will be kept as trainers.

The Air Force maintains 193 F-4F fighters, reconnaissance aircraft, and trainers; 107 of them make up six of the Air Force's seven fighter squadrons. Of these, five squadrons, or approximately 92 aircraft, will likely remain in service until at least 2000 and are scheduled to be replaced by the Eurofighter 2000. The 36 F-4F ground attack aircraft will most likely be retired by 2000 and will not be replaced.

---

[1] Mark Lambert, ed., *Jane's All the World's Aircraft 1993–94* (Surrey, UK: Jane's Information Group, 1993), p. 171.
[2] Nick Cook, "Tornado Upgrades Set to Narrow Work Gap," *Jane's Defence Weekly*, Vol. 21, No. 13 (April 2, 1994), p. 5.

The Air Force does not operate any of the German Democratic Republic's Russian-built MiG-21, MiG-23, and Su-22 fighter-attack aircraft. However, 20 MiG-29 fighters and 4 MiG-29 trainers will be maintained through 2010.

By 2000, Germany will probably have reduced its fighter-attack aircraft inventory by approximately five squadrons and almost 100 aircraft. In 2002, the Air Force expects to receive the first of its current order of 140 Eurofighters. These aircraft are to first replace Germany's F-4s, and then its Tornados as they are retired toward the end of the next decade.

However, the Eurofighter program has faced considerable opposition. First, it was designed during the Cold War for confrontation with the Soviet Union. Its designers assumed it would operate in an environment with many destroyed airfields, and would take off close to enemy territory. The Eurofighter's short take-off and landing (STOL) ability restricts all other aspects of its performance; in addition, the need to limit costs has reduced some of the extreme agility and STOL capability of the original design.

Second, it has fallen behind schedule. As late as December 1989, the Eurofighter was to make its first flight in December 1991; this deadline was missed by more than three years. The first flight took place in March 1994, near Munich. (The German defense minister did not attend, an obvious attempt to evade any commitment and pressures concerning Germany's outstanding decision on participation in the production phase.) Ten days later, the second development aircraft made its first flight in Britain (at a martial ceremony with high-level political presence). Delays are typical of cooperative projects in Western Europe. In the past, such delays were not penalized; weapon systems and aircraft were simply procured later, often while research and development continued in order to achieve a fully operational status only after years of service.[3] In order to tailor a politically acceptable price tag, particularly lean and hardly operational versions were conceived and ordered. Expensive add-ons were billed later.

Without the Eurofighter 2000, Germany will have no replacement for its aging fighter, attack, and air defense aircraft during the next

---

[3] The findings of a recent confidential report of the Federal Accounting Office in Germany, leaked to the public, revealed that the armed forces regularly procured major weapon systems that were not operational; some are not operational even now. *Wehrdienst*, No. 8 (1994), p. 2.

decade. There have been recent discussions about the possibility of purchasing up to 200 MiG-29s from Russia at reduced rates if Germany does not procure the Eurofighter 2000.[4]

DOES GERMANY NEED THE EUROFIGHTER?

There are a number of indications that Germany may not wish to procure the Eurofighter. In 1993, Stiftung Politik und Wissenschaft, a government-supported think tank, published a study commissioned by the Air Force on the future missions and requirements of the Air Force. This study is expected to have some influence on procurement decisions.[5] As the largest procurement project, which will absorb the bulk of the Air Force's sharply reduced investment funds, the Eurofighter might be expected to occupy a prominent place in this report; however, it is mentioned once.

The study listed six missions that could be assigned to the Air Force, with their likely frequency:
1. Humanitarian actions—very frequent
2. UN peacekeeping missions—very frequent
3. Peace enforcement missions (military intervention for peace-making)—frequent
4. Opposing limited aggression (as in the Gulf War)—rare
5. Higher-intensity conventional war—unlikely
6. Large-scale aggression involving the danger of nuclear escalation—very unlikely.

For each mission, the study identified what capabilities the Air Force would need; the capabilities of the Eurofighter are useful for the three most unlikely missions.[6]

The study focuses on "crisis-reaction forces," leaving surprisingly little room for neo–Cold War rhetoric. The need to pursue military integration with Germany's eastern neighbors is emphasized.[7] It is

---

[4] "More on Russian Offer to Sell 200 MiGs," *Foreign Broadcast Information Service,* FBIS-WEU-94-086 (May 4, 1994), p. 9.

[5] Stiftung Wissenschaft und Politik, *Einsatzaufgaben und strukturelle Konsequenzen für die Luftwaffe unter zukünftigen sicherheitspolitischen Rahmen bedingugen* (Ebenhausen, September 1993) (SWP. 390), pp. 1–3.

[6] *Einsatzaufgaben*, Vol. 2, pp. 26ff. It should be noted that the U.S. Air Force did not employ an aircraft in the Gulf War with as limited a combat range as the Eurofighter. Even the carrier-based aircraft had longer ranges. See: Elliot A. Cohen, "The Air War in the Persian Gulf," *Armed Forces Journal International* (June 1993), pp. 10–14.

[7] *Einsatzaufgaben*, Vol. 2, pp. 43ff.

even suggested that Germany might advance its own interests by financing the integration of the command, control, communication, and intelligence (C3I) systems to expand the geographical reach of threat detection. The study also suggests involving the Russian military in crisis-reaction missions to help prevent Russia from falling back into a confrontational and isolationist stance, and to considerably enlarge the potential scope of action of German crisis-reaction forces.[8]

Speeches by top military officers at the 1994 meeting of the German Society for Defense Technology also indicated ambivalence toward the Eurofighter.[9] The highest ranking officer of the German armed forces, Inspector General Klaus Naumann, identified air defense, precision-guided munitions, and air transport as areas that need urgent change to adapt to the new strategic environment. Naumann did not state his position on the forthcoming Eurofighter procurement decision, but his assessment of Germany's security situation does not seem to give any priority to the Eurofighter in air defense. He sees three major sources of insecurity: the dissolution of the former Soviet Union, situations emanating from the many unresolved national and ethnic issues, and conflicts on the peripheries of Asia and Africa that tend to spill over to Europe. In none of these scenarios would the specific properties of the Eurofighter be particularly valuable. Range and stealth are needed for such scenarios; the Eurofighter has neither.

At the same meeting, the Inspector of the Air Force ranked the acquisition of the Eurofighter as the number one procurement priority, and a new tactical air defense system as number two; he somewhat reluctantly added that the air transport capacity should at least be maintained at the present level.

Schönbohm, the Ministry of Defense (MoD) official responsible for procurement, asserted that Germany's capability to defend its territory can be maintained in the foreseeable future without any large new procurement programs if the situation does not change radically. For this reason, he says, the crisis-reaction forces can receive unrestricted priority. Schönbohm sees an urgent need for appropriate equipment and training and for improvements in logistical and medical support. He also cites strategic intelligence, strategic air transport, defense

---

[8] Ibid., p. 48.
[9] The meeting was reported in *Wertechnik*, No. 5 (1994), pp. 16–19.

capability against ballistic missiles, and support for German troops stationed abroad as areas that should be improved. He did not mention the Eurofighter.

Finally, the chapter on the Air Force in the recently published *White Book on the Security Situation of the Federal Republic of Germany and on the Situation and Future of the Armed Forces* does not discuss the Eurofighter.[10] For air defense, the Patriot, Hawk, and Roland missile systems, together with two wings of Phantom fighters and four wings of Tornado fighter bombers, will serve in NATO crisis reaction forces. *The White Book* also gives priority to deep strike interdiction, a major task the Eurofighter 2000 cannot handle.[11]

In sum, there is no pressing demand for the Eurofighter by the MoD or the Armed Forces. There seems to be an implicit consensus to treat the DM 6.4 bn development price as a sunk cost rather than to procure the aircraft for far more than DM 100 mn per plane. Only the Air Force seems to hesitate to abandon the plane before it knows what it will get instead.

The Eurofighter in Corporate Strategy

The aerospace sector has long been a major transatlantic political battleground. The Eurofighter 2000 must be understood in terms of the aspirations of the remaining aerospace corporations in this highly politicized market.[12]

Virtually uncontrolled mergers, particularly in the United States, are the corporate response to eliminate the large overcapacity built up during the Reagan rearmament. Civil aerospace is not an alternative; that sector is also in the middle of a deep recession. The U.S. government seems to accept the resultant monopolistic and oligopolistic pattern in many subsectors of aerospace procurement as the lesser of two evils and shows no intent to submit this unprecedented re-

---

[10] Bundesministerium der Verteidigung, *Weißbuch 1994: Weißbuch der Bundesrepublik Deutschland und zur Lage und Zukunft der Bundeswehr* (April 5, 1994).

[11] *Weißbuch*, p. 119.

[12] As one example of the political nature of the industry, Airbus reproached Europe's political leaders for not having vigorously intervened, as President Clinton reportedly did, to encourage a large sale of civil aircraft to Saudi Arabia.

structuring to an examination under the existing antitrust legislation.[13] Through these mergers, the U.S. military aerospace industry is becoming more like those of the European arms-producing countries, which have one principal supplier. In the war over subsidies in the aerospace sector between the United States and Europe, it might become easier to negotiate the real issues as structural differences diminish. For all the countries, the aerospace sector is important for its size, its potential to develop the technologies needed to stay ahead in the global race for competitiveness, and as a way to provide for an efficient national defense.

In 1992, the combined revenue of the U.S. and European Community (EC) aerospace industries amounted to European Currency Unit (ECU) 150,000 mn (in 1985 prices), of which one-fifth was European.[14] Roughly 50 percent of European aerospace revenue was from military items, down from 70 percent at the beginning of the 1980s. In 1991, civil aerospace sales were higher than military sales for the first time. U.S. 1991 military sales were slightly higher than those of Europe, lower than the 1987 peak of 75 percent. A rough calculation from this data puts the military market of the U.S. aerospace industry in the early 1990s at 250 percent of the total revenue—civil plus military—of its European counterpart. Although the United States' volume of procurement has shrunk rapidly, the ratios in the mid-1990s should remain similar. This enormous difference in military procurement and exports provokes European claims that the military sector serves its U.S. rivals as a hidden subsidy for civil aerospace production, which must be balanced by additional European government support.

An EC regulation limits indirect government product research and development support of a single company to 25 percent of the cost of basic R&D. Since the European aerospace industries have consolidated at national levels to just one corporation, the regulation is likely to limit government support in spite of the flexibility of account-

---

[13] The exemption of the aerospace sector from antitrust legislation is pervasive. The formation of Deutsche Aerospace (DASA) as part of Daimler-Benz was ruled unacceptable by the Antitrust Commission; the government used its prerogative and gave its permission for the formation of what became the dominant player in defense and aerospace.

[14] Unless otherwise stated, the figures used in this section are taken from the European Commission (DG III), *The European Aerospace Industry: Trading Position and Figures 1994* (Brussels: April 1, 1994) (III/4001/94 EN).

ing. Hence the big corporations are tempted to seek indirect support; they resort to expensive military projects as a means to succeed in the fierce competition with U.S. manufacturers. Deutsche Aerospace's (DASA) battle to continue German participation in the Eurofighter project could be interpreted from this angle. DASA's R&D outlays amount to 30 percent of its revenue, well above Aérospatiale's 24 percent and British Aerospace's 5 percent, and may be dangerously close to regulatory limits.[15]

The Eurofighter is also valued because of the number of people it employs. The whole aerospace sector employed fewer than 400,000 workers (estimated) in 1993, 100,000 less than the all-time peak in 1981. However, if the presently assumed program costs, including development, are spread over 25 years, the program would account for about 4 percent of the aerospace sector's revenue if the industry does not grow. This would support about 5,000-6,000 jobs in Germany, and likely fewer if the sector's productivity increases.[16] If the sector maintains its ten-year growth average, the share of the program would fall to a mere 3 percent of aerospace turnover by the time the production starts.[17] Thus, the Eurofighter 2000 is actually a marginal project for the aerospace sector, though it is an important element of public support for the sector.

Cancellation of the project would not cost more than 5 bn DM, or 2.5 bn ECU, according to medium-term finance planning of the German government. Annual outlays for the Eurofighter would absorb an average of about 20 percent of all procurement—Navy and Army included—leaving the Air Force with a limited ability to acquire modern and efficient ground-based air defense systems or platforms for airborne intelligence, or large transport aircraft, or other needed equipment. It is quite likely that if the Eurofighter is canceled, the Air Force will be able to make a more rational choice of which systems to procure. This would orient production toward diversified systems

---

[15] *Wehrdienst*, No. 8, p. 5.

[16] On the basis of this statistic, about 5,000–6,000 jobs depend on the German share in the program. Jürgen Schrempp, the head of DASA, however, threatens that 8,000–10,000 jobs would have to go in his company and approximately the same number at suppliers if the program were to be canceled. *Frankfurter Rundschau*, June 3, 1992, p. 12.

[17] These rough calculations are based on the assumption that total program costs will amount to £32 billion.

better adapted to the military tasks ahead; it is therefore unlikely that the aerospace corporations would be the losers.

Then why do DASA, the aircraft, defense, and space propulsion systems arm of Daimler-Benz, and British Aerospace (BAe), the main partners of the Eurofighter consortium, wish to stick with the Eurofighter? For example, alternative projects would certainly supply a similar volume of contracts for DASA.

In the British case, the answer seems obvious. Over the past five years, BAe has concentrated on its core business as a military supplier and producer of short- and medium-haul civil transport aircraft, despite its 20 percent participation in the Airbus consortium. BAe has consolidated under its roof an impressive array of military production lines, including some acquisitions and joint ventures on the Continent.[18] Hence, the Eurofighter program constitutes the very core of BAe's business strategy: to present itself as a diversified first-class arms producer that can satisfy the most demanding customer of sophisticated systems. This is why Britain has repeatedly stated that it would go ahead with production, even without German participation.

In contrast, Daimler-Benz is clearly oriented toward global high-tech markets. It forms international joint ventures to adjust its capacity to market, particularly in military production, and continuously expands into foreign networks of subsidiaries and enters global alliances.

It is not clear that the Eurofighter would be a successful venture for its manufacturers. Export sales are assumed in the Eurofighter's cost calculations, but the market segment for such an expensive fighter aircraft with limited capabilities is extremely small. The only prospective customers are some rapidly industrializing East Asian countries and three or four oil-rich Arab countries. Industrializing countries would certainly want a large share of the production and technological know-how for themselves, which would considerably reduce the benefit to the European aerospace sector. In addition, the market for military aircraft will be characterized by the availability of new and refurbished second-hand aircraft. The Eurofighter will also compete with the French Rafale. Finally, the United States has not yet

---

[18] Heckler & Koch, the leading German small arms manufacturer, was at the brink of bankruptcy when British Aerospace took it over.

canceled the F-22, which would compete for the same sales as the Eurofighter.

Since the beginning of the 1980s, the driving force behind the European aerospace industry is clearly civil production for commercial markets. While civil revenue almost quadrupled between 1981 and 1991 (in current prices), military revenue rose only 50 percent (in current prices). This trend is likely to continue in spite of the current slump. The industrial culture of civil units is distinct from that of military organizations, which must work hard to overcome the disabling effects of the maximalist design demand in the cost-conscious culture of civil production.[19]

DASA seems stronger than the French Aerospatiale or BAe in civil production and internationalization.[20] In the 1980s, Daimler-Benz, under the direction of Edzard Reuter, intensely diversified and became increasingly oriented toward global markets. Under the direction of the German government, the corporation also began to consolidate the German aerospace industry and became the foremost "global player" in Germany, supplying as much as 40 percent of German military national and global procurement.

While Daimler-Benz accepted that Germany would not finally decide whether to procure the Eurofighter before the federal elections, its threats to announce even deeper cuts in employment and to transfer R&D activities to foreign joint ventures led the federal government to underwrite half of a DM 1.2 bn research program for aeronautical research.[21]

Thus the Eurofighter consortium is an alien element, outside the evolving corporate dynamics of the European defense industrial base. For the time being it links the divergent corporate identities of British Aerospace and Daimler-Benz, each pursuing its own aims with the project.

---

19 Even the civil Airbus consortium has only recently restructured its bureaucratic procedures in order to meet the challenge of Boeing's much leaner production. See Paul Betts, "Penalties for Excess Baggage," *Financial Times*, December 1, 1993, p. 13.

20 A decade ago, among the three countries, Germany's aerospace industry was growing fastest, France's second-fastest and Britain trailed far behind Germany. However, in 1992 the order was France, Britain, and then Germany. DASA still remains the largest aerospace corporation in Europe, but other corporations are closing the gap.

21 "Ein Milliardenprogram für die Luftfahrtforschung," *Frankfurter Allgemeine Zeitung*, July 2, 1994.

The Eurofighter in Europe's Military Industrial Policy

The Eurofighter project should also be understood in the context of military industrial policy. Military industrial policy seeks to strengthen a nation's autonomy in procuring the sophisticated equipment it needs to support its military doctrine. Traditionally the United States, with its extraordinary volume of procurement and exports, has set the pace of military high-tech, while other nations try to follow. But as the United States has found, sophisticated technology is increasingly the result of an integrated global economy; the military research laboratories and segregated military-industrial branches have decreased in importance.[22] This change of paradigm threatens the bureaucratic organization and hierarchies of military high-tech.

The new frugality of defense budgets is speeding the trend toward using civil components, which are often qualitatively superior in sophisticated defense systems. It is safe to project that the integration of civil modules will eventually assimilate the military design architecture to the logic of civil high-tech. A design in civil engineering must be as flexible as possible so that it can be adapted for different markets without losing the cost advantages of mass production. This principle leads to the design of versatile modular components, at all levels of the design architecture.

The Eurofighter, however, is still a typical product of the traditional military design philosophy: it conceives of a system customized for narrowly defined military tasks and supposedly ahead of existing technology. The demand for innovation, a major sales argument for the initiation of the project, does not allow the design compromises that would lead to increased modularization. The basic parameters were fixed during the initial R&D phase and cannot be changed as important innovations generated by the civil economy become available.[23]

---

[22] United States Congress, Office of Technology Assessment, *Redesigning Defense: Planning the Transition to the Future U.S. Defense Industrial Base* (Washington, D.C.: Government Printing Office, July 1991), Chap. 4.

[23] The mechanical gyroscope of the Eurofighter is an example. The system configuration was defined in the late 1980s. By now, it is evident that laser-based gyroscopes are better and weigh much less, but the gyroscope cannot be changed; the system integration would have to start all over again. See Peter Müller-Reich, "Der Faserkreisel: Ein Beispiel für Dual-Use," Berlin, 1991, mimeo.

Clearly, military design philosophy has not yet visibly reacted to the new realities, but there are a number of indications that it eventually will.[24] The chairman of Martin Marietta can imagine that the next generation of battle tank will use truck engines instead of the current Abrams tank gas turbine.[25] The use of computer-aided design/computer-aided modeling (CAD/CAM) technologies, which directly link the designer and production, and testing by simulation are further manifestations of change.[26]

These innovations are expensive to introduce. There are indications that some U.S. defense contractors were able to use the lavish support of their defense contracts to pay the learning costs while they introduced CAD and CAM and then moved into the manufacture of high-quality components for civil aerospace, among other applications.

There would be some logic to the continuation of the Eurofighter from the corporate perspective if the project merely served as a cover-up for subsidized innovation of process technology, particularly in the development of an application of composites.[27] Too little is known about the inside of the consortium to suggest that this is an implicit corporate strategy.

The Eurofighter lobby argues that the project serves military industrial policy because the project sustains a strategic capability: the Eurofighter allows Europe to avoid total dependency on fighter aircraft design from the United States. The strongest argument of this type is that experienced R&D teams cannot be mothballed, awaiting some future project. Therefore, Europe must continuously employ its R&D capacity. In fact, the first exploratory talks about the fighter aircraft to follow the Eurofighter have already been conducted. The increasing amalgamation of civil and military technology, and equally

---

[24] For example, pressure to overhaul military specifications and standards, which are considered the chief impediment to utilizing efficient civil technologies and process technologies, is mounting. See John D. Morrocco, "Uncertain U.S. Military Needs Hamper Industry Restructuring," *Aviation Week & Space Technology*, Vol. 134, No. 26 (June 17, 1991), pp. 62–66.

[25] David White, "Survival of the Slimmest," *Financial Times*, June 6, 1992, p. 13.

[26] See special section in *Aviation Week & Space Technology*, Vol. 140, No. 1 (January 3, 1994), pp. 55–58.

[27] Craig Covault, "Europe Faces Shake-up in Materials Industry," *Aviation Week & Space Technology*, Vol. 140, No. 4 (January 24, 1994), pp. 53.

important, process technology, may have changed the parameters needed for Europe to re-enter military aircraft design if interrupted.[28]

BAe and DASA have very different strategies for preserving their capabilities should the Eurofighter fail to enter production, with differing implications for future military industrial capabilities. As mentioned above, Britain intends to produce the aircraft, even without German participation. How BAe and the British government will absorb the increased financial burden if Germany drops out is difficult to see, but not altogether impossible. The aircraft's capabilities have been drastically reduced, so it is not clear whether the foreign customers BAe envisions will find the aircraft attractive. Even the British Air Force might opt to procure a U.S. aircraft off the shelf, which would deprive BAe of its role as a prime contractor, leaving it with the production of components.

Alternatively, BAe has ventured a revival of the Concorde project and proposed the development of a new supersonic passenger aircraft that would certainly be built with extensive public support. This scenario would convert BAe into the European partner of an U.S. producer of military aircraft, similar to the role Westland plays in the European helicopter market.

In contrast, DASA relies on its expanding position as Europe's largest manufacturer of civil aircraft. It is also playing an active role in the consortium, proposing a "future large aircraft" along with France and other continental nations. In its quest to expand its markets, DASA is particularly oriented toward Eastern Europe and Russia. Since barter-type arrangements are needed to finance this important market, Russia's aerospace industry is already being integrated as a subcontractor of DASA. DASA would certainly not hesitate to strike a deal with Antonov, the producer of the world's largest transport aircraft, when the "future large aircraft" issue matures. Enlightened politicians should welcome an irreversible integration of the Russian aerospace industry into the European compound, not least in order to

---

[28] In the case of the United States it is asserted: "Sustaining America's capability to make warplanes should be comparatively easy. The business of producing commercial aircraft and space vehicles will keep most of the necessary skills current." Lee Smith, "Can Defense Pain Be Turned to Gain?" *Fortune*, February 8, 1993, p. 94. The opposite view is expressed in Kenneth R. Mayer, "Combat Aircraft Production in the United States 1950–2000: Maintaining Industry Capability in an Era of Shrinking Budgets," *Defense Analysis*, Vol. 9, No. 2, pp. 159–169.

counter U.S. dominance. The only certainty is that DASA would not design and produce a fighter on its own.

Supporters of the Eurofighter often claim that the project is an important element in the construction of transnational cohesiveness in Europe. The opposite is true. The Eurofighter scheme will expand Europe's production capacity, which by all economic logic should be drastically cut. There will be six production sites for rather similar fighter aircraft, four of the Eurofighter consortium, and one each for the Rafale and the Gripen (Russia not being counted as European). There is hardly a more uneconomical way to organize Europe's defense. These military projects, with all their illogical dimensions and inefficiencies, are rooted in their countries' national militaristic traditions, of which, compared to other European countries', Germany's is considerably weaker than in the past. As a pan-European militaristic tradition does not yet exist and probably never will, there is no force that can consolidate the Byzantine inefficiency of Europe's military defense in the sky.

In 1992, the German defense minister was ready to end the project, but Chancellor Helmut Kohl rushed to reassure the British prime minister that the Eurofighter would continue. Kohl probably sensed, correctly, that a German withdrawal would inflict an unacceptable wound to the British self-esteem. It would have left Britain unprepared for an alternative military posture and a new military industrial policy. Two years later, the odds are still against German participation in the production, though Britain still has not moved toward alternatives. Pressing problems in Eastern Europe loom on the German agenda. Germany must reconsider the weight of Britain in its political equation.

Conclusion

The political environment in which defense contractors operate has changed profoundly. European Parliaments are finally beginning to scrutinize the procurement process, which the executive branch has always considered its preserve. Given the danger that the Eurofighter might be canceled, one would expect that the consortium would leap forward to reach the point of no return—the beginning of production—even at the expense of putting its own money into an acceleration of the development. Either the diseconomies and organizational difficulties facing the consortium are vast, or possibly one or some consortium members may be withholding some of their know-how and technology in anticipation of a break-up, which would create fierce competition in a global race for survival. The firms' common interest seems to be the enhanced access to R&D money that the project has facilitated, which will supposedly prepare them for competition in the future. This conjecture immediately invites a bold hypothesis: the industrial parties are actually not committed to build this militarily outdated aircraft under all circumstances. Instead, they are using it to prepare themselves to participate in the next generation of military aircraft. This leads to the intriguing question of whether the consortium members will seek to produce the next aircraft in their present configuration, possibly adding the French producer Dassault, or whether different, competitive global alliances will emerge.

For the time being, however, the industry forecasts a military-industrial desert in Europe, surrounded by dominant U.S. manufacturers and a dangerous, still-powerful Russian military-industrial complex, if production does not go ahead. Playing to the geo-strategic fears, the consortium believes that Germany's parliament will eventually favor production.

Chapter 9

François Chesnais
Claude Serfati
Andrew Peach

The Rafale and French Military-Industrial Autonomy

France is investing heavily in the development of the Rafale, a new multi-role combat aircraft that is currently scheduled to enter service at the end of this decade. Part I of this chapter looks at France's tactical air forces today and explores the Rafale's place in maintaining France's force levels. Part II focuses on the Rafale's role in France's defense industry.

Planned French Air Forces and Aircraft Production

The tactical aviation forces of France consist of the land-based French Air Force (FAF) and the carrier-based *Aéronavale* (naval aviation). Their missions are to deter attacks on the territory of the French Republic (both France itself and overseas possessions); to defend the Republic in the event of attack; and to provide the capability to inter-

François Chesnais is a professor of economics at the University of Paris-Nord.

Claude Serfati is a Maître de Conférences at the University of Versailles-Saint-Quentin and a member of the research laboratory ORINTE.

Andrew Peach is a research fellow at the Institute for Defense and Disarmament Studies in Cambridge, Massachusetts, where he specializes in U.S. and West European air forces and aerospace industries.

vene in conflicts outside of France or Europe, either unilaterally or as part of a multilateral force.[1]

The French Air Force has recently gone through a major restructuring to allow it greater flexibility in force planning and crisis response. All FAF missions are now performed by two primary operational commands: *le Commandant des Forces aériennes stratégique* (FAS, the Strategic Air Force Command), and *le Commandant de la Défense aérienne et des opérations aériennes* (CDAOA, the Air Defense and Air Operations Command). In addition to these two operational commands, there are five "organic" commands that group all FAF equipment and personnel by major function. Aircraft maintained by the organic commands are drawn on by the operational commands as needed. *Le Commandement de la Force aérienne de combat* (CFAC, the Combat Air Force Command) is the organic command that serves as the repository for all fighter-attack aircraft of the FAF.[2] In 1993, the FAF deployed 23 fighter-attack squadrons with approximately 370 combat-ready tactical aircraft, and 5 strategic bomber squadrons with about 60 bomber aircraft. The typical FAF tactical squadron has 15 combat-ready aircraft as well as several pipeline aircraft and is capable of performing air-to-air and air-to-ground missions.[3]

The Strategic Air Forces serve as the airborne leg of France's nuclear triad. These forces consist of two squadrons with a total of 15 Mirage IV-P bombers, which have been modified to carry the ASMP (Air-Sol Moyenne Portée) medium-range nuclear missile, and three squadrons of Mirage 2000N attack aircraft.

The Air Defense and Air Operations Command (CDAOA) is responsible for all defensive and offensive air missions, including tactical strike. Attack units consist of one squadron of Mirage III, one squadron of Mirage 5, two squadrons of Mirage F1-CT, one squadron of Mirage 2000N, and five squadrons of Jaguar aircraft. In addition, two squadrons of Mirage F1-CRs perform reconnaissance missions

---

[1] Assemblée Nationale, Commission de la Défense Nationale et des Forces Armées, *Rapport sur le Projet de Loi de Programmation (No. 733) Relatif à l'Équipement Militaire pour les Années 1990–1993*, No. 897, October 2, 1989, pp. 293–294.

[2] "Nouvelles Structures de Commandement de l'Armée de l'Air," *SIRPA Actualité*, No. 18, May 2, 1994, pp. 65–69.

[3] The FAF is increasing its typical squadron strength to 18–20 aircraft over the next several years. See Assemblée Nationale, Commission de la Défense Nationale et des Forces Armées, *Rapport sur le Projet de Loi de Programmation pour les Années 1992–1994*, Vol. 1, No. 2935, October 7, 1992, p. 462.

and have a secondary attack role. Air defense is provided by seven squadrons of Mirage 2000B/Cs (also known as the Mirage 2000DA) plus four squadrons of Mirage F1-Cs. There are also four operational conversion unit (OCU) squadrons attached to the CFAC as training units. These units consist of one squadron each of the Jaguar A/E, Mirage III-B/E, Mirage 2000B/C and Mirage F1-B/C.

The front-line force of the *Aéronavale* consists of three squadrons of the Super Étendard single-seat strike fighter and one squadron of the F-8E Crusader interceptor. The Super Étendards are presently being modified to carry the ASMP (Air-Sol Moyenne-Portée) tactical nuclear missile to provide the *Aéronavale* with an offensive strategic capability. In addition, one squadron of eight Étendard IV-P aircraft is tasked to reconnaissance and one squadron of ten Étendard IV-Ms is used for training. *Aéronavale* squadrons are smaller than their FAF counterparts, with 8 to 12 combat-ready aircraft each, as well as several pipeline aircraft. The French navy maintains two aircraft carriers, and keeps one at sea at all times with the *Aéronavale* force.

The age of the combat aircraft in the FAF inventory varies widely. By 2000, about half of the aircraft will have been in service for at least 20 years, the current standard retirement age for FAF aircraft. These older aircraft include the Mirage types III, IV, and 5, which are among the oldest aircraft currently in service with the French Air Force; the Mirage F1-B/C, which first entered service in 1974; and the Jaguar A/E, which were delivered between 1973 and 1981.

The newest aircraft in the French inventory are of the Mirage 2000 series. The first squadron of Mirage 2000B/Cs entered service in 1984 in an interceptor and air superiority role. The nuclear strike Mirage 2000N entered service in 1988. Deliveries of this type are expected to be completed in 1994. The Mirage 2000D (the conventional attack version of the 2000N) began deliveries in 1993.

All *Aéronavale* aircraft but the Super Étendards, which entered service between 1978 and 1982, will have reached the end of their planned service lives by 1998 or 1999. The U.S.-built F-8 Crusader, which was designed nearly 40 years ago, was originally due to retire in 1993 but will be kept in service until the end of the decade with the help of a service life extension program.[4]

---

[4] Simon Michell, ed., *Jane's Civil and Military Aircraft Upgrades 1993–94* (Surrey, UK: Jane's Information Group, 1992), p. 51.

Planned Reductions in Combat Aircraft

The *Armées 2000* plan, which went into effect in July 1991, called for a reduction of the French armed forces as a result of the end of the Cold War and the subsequent relaxation in tensions in Europe. Budgetary pressures, brought on in part by the global recession, also had much to do with France's decision to reduce military expenditures. Under *Armées 2000*, the FAF will reduce its active force level to 20 squadrons (17 fighter-attack and 3 strategic bomber) by 1996 from 28 squadrons in 1993, while increasing squadron strength from 15 to 18–20 aircraft. This is a reduction from 430 combat-ready aircraft to 380.[5] A force reduction for the *Aéronavale* is also possible by the end of the decade.[6] (See Table 9.1.)

Planned Combat Aircraft Procurement

A new military program law covering the years 1995–2000 was issued in May 1994 by the conservative government of Prime Minister Edouard Balladur. The program sets yearly spending levels and attempts to halt the recent decline in defense spending. A priority of the government is to maintain all of France's major weapon programs, including the Mirage 2000 and the Rafale. To this end, the program projects yearly increases of 0.5–1.5 percent in procurement spending through 2000 at the expense of research and development spending.[7] France's defense budget had been decreasing in real terms since 1991, while the costs to develop major weapons such as the Rafale were increasing. The procurement budget took the brunt of these cutbacks, resulting in the curtailment or stretching-out of most combat aircraft

---

[5] The FAF had a total inventory of 622 combat aircraft in 1992, including pipeline equipment and inactive aircraft maintained in storage. The *Aéronavale* had a total inventory of 101 combat aircraft in 1992, also including pipeline and stored aircraft.

[6] There have been reports that the *Aéronavale* will trim its orders for the Rafale M from 86 units to 78, effectively reducing naval air power by one squadron. See Mark Lambert, ed., *Jane's All the World's Aircraft 1992–93* (Surrey, UK: Jane's Information Group, 1992), p. 61.

[7] J.A.C. Lewis, "France to Cut R&D to Fund Equipment Buys," *Jane's Defence Weekly*, May 28, 1994, p. 6.

programs. In 1989, 28 new combat aircraft were ordered, 18 in 1991, none in 1992, and 2 (the first production Rafales) in 1993.[8]

Table 9.1. France's Tactical Aviation Forces in 1993 and 2000

Combat-coded squadrons and aircraft

Type	Role	1993 Squadrons	1993 Aircraft	2000 Squadrons	2000 Aircraft
Air Force		28	430	20	380
Mirage 2000N	Bomber	3	45	2	40
Mirage 2000D	Bomber			1	18
Mirage IV-P	Bomber	2	15		
Mirage 2000B/C/-5	Air Defense	7	115	6	108
Mirage F1-B/C	Air Defense	4	65	1	20
Mirage F1-CR	Reconnaissance	2	40	2	40
Mirage 2000D	Ground Attack			3	54
Mirage F1-CT	Ground Attack	2	30	2	40
Jaguar A	Ground Attack	5	75	2	40
Mirage 2000N	Ground Attack	1	15	1	20
Mirage 5-F	Ground Attack	1	15		
Mirage III-E	Ground Attack	1	15		
Aéronavale		5	58	5	60
Rafale	Multi-role			1	12
Super Étendard	Attack	3	38	4	48
F-8E Crusader	Air Defense	1	12		
Étendard IV-P	Reconnaissance	1	8		
Total		33	488	25	440

Source: Assemblée Nationale, "Avis sur le Projet de Loi de Finances pour 1994," No. 583, October 7, 1993; "Projet de Loi de Programmation Militaire pour les Années 1995–2000," No. 1153, April 20, 1994; and Military Balance 1993–94.

At 199.3 bn francs ($35 bn), the 1994 military budget shows a real increase of 1.3 percent compared to the 1993 budget; for procurement funds, the increase is 3.4 percent. A total of 19 new combat aircraft are authorized for the FAF and the *Aéronavale*, including 3 Rafales. However, development of the Rafale and construction of the *Charles*

---

[8] French military planners have calculated that they would need to procure an average of 33 aircraft per year in order to maintain a force level of 450 combat-ready aircraft. See Assemblée Nationale, Commission de la Défense Nationale et des Forces Armées, *Avis sur le Projet de Loi de Finance pour 1992 (No. 2240)*, Vol. X, *Défense: Air*, No. 2258, October 9, 1991, p. 19.

de Gaulle nuclear aircraft carrier were stretched out by six months to fund the aircraft orders.[9]

The program for 1995–2000 includes provisions for ordering up to 59 Rafales for the FAF and *Aéronavale*. Eleven of these aircraft are scheduled to be ordered in 1996 and 1997, followed by 16 per year in 1998–2000. However, only 13 Rafales will be delivered by the end of 2000.[10]

Both the FAF and *Aéronavale* intend to rely heavily on the Rafale after the turn of the century. In all, 320 Rafales are currently planned, 234 for the FAF and 86 for the *Aéronavale*. Firm production orders as of the 1994 defense budget stand at five production aircraft (one for the FAF and four for the *Aéronavale*), with initial, low-rate deliveries to begin in early 1998.

Delivery schedules for the Rafale have slipped two to three years due to cost increases, budget shortfalls, and technical problems. Due to the pressing need to replace its aging Crusaders, the *Aéronavale* is now scheduled to receive 12 of the first 13 production Rafales between 1998 and 2000. The FAF will receive its first Rafale in 1998 with deliveries to resume after the *Aéronavale* has filled its first squadron in 2000. The Rafale is expected to achieve initial operating capability in the FAF in 2002.

The Mirage 2000 series represents the largest single ongoing combat aircraft production program in France. Between 1993 and 1998, 111 Mirage 2000s of various types are scheduled to be delivered to the FAF. The Mirage 2000D is the latest aircraft in this series, with 90 aircraft ordered by the FAF. This conventional attack variant of the Mirage 2000N tactical nuclear-strike aircraft will replace the Jaguar in the conventional ground-attack role. In 1993–1994, in addition to initial deliveries of the Mirage 2000D, the FAF is scheduled to receive the final 18 Mirage 2000B/Cs of an order of 153, and the final 3 Mirage 2000Ns of an order of 75. The 2000B/Cs will replace the Mirage F1-C in the air superiority role.

---

[9] The Rafale is now expected to enter service with the *Aéronavale* in 1998, rather than in 1997, and with the FAF in 2002. The *Charles de Gaulle*, which was originally scheduled to enter service in late 1998, is now expected to enter service on July 1, 1999. See Giovanni de Briganti, "French Spending Jumps," *Defense News*, October 11, 1993, p. 1; and J.A.C. Lewis, "French Spending Rise Secures Major Items," *Jane's Defence Weekly*, October 16, 1993, p. 15.

[10] "France to Buy More Rafale Fighters," *Military and Arms Transfers News*, July 1, 1994, p. 5.

Both the FAF and the *Aéronavale* have turned to upgrading older aircraft as an interim measure to maintain force levels until the Rafale enters service. Fifty-five Mirage F1-Cs, which were made surplus by the conversion of FAF air defense squadrons to the Mirage 2000B/C, are being modified for the ground-attack role. Forty-one such conversions, designated the Mirage F1-CT, were funded through 1994. Deliveries of the Mirage F1-CT began in 1992 and are scheduled to be completed in 1995, replacing Mirage III and Mirage 5 aircraft as the latter retire from service. In addition, 37 of the oldest Mirage 2000B/Cs are being upgraded to the Mirage 2000-5 standard, with a more advanced radar and greater weapons load. These aircraft, which will augment the FAF's air defense capability, are scheduled to be delivered between 1994 and 1997.

The *Aéronavale* is extending the life of 72 aircraft between 1990 and 2000. Sixteen Crusaders, which were originally due to retire in 1993, will be overhauled by the end of 1994 in order to keep them flying until 1998–1999, when the Rafale attains initial operating capability. Fifty-six Super Étendards are being modernized between 1992 and 1997 so that they may remain in service until 2005, when they will also be replaced by the Rafale.

Production Requirements

IDDS has projected potential future combat aircraft production for the French Air Force and *Aéronavale* through 2010 using two aircraft retirement ages: 20 years, the current military standard in France, and 25 years.[11] We assumed that France will maintain the planned 1996 force level of 20 active Air Force squadrons and 5 active *Aéronavale* squadrons to 2010, and that both services will maintain an inventory-to-squadron equipment ratio of about 1.25.[12] In reality, French planners could decide to further reduce force levels, or to decrease the

---

[11] See *IDDS Almanac 1994: World Combat Aircraft Holdings, Production, and Trade* (Cambridge, Mass.: IDDS, forthcoming) for a more detailed discussion of production requirements.

[12] In addition to squadron-assigned equipment, the services maintain "pipeline" and reserve aircraft. The former are earmarked for maintenance replacements; the latter are wartime spares (or to cover peacetime attrition losses).

inventory-to-squadron equipment ratio, or both, thereby reducing new production requirements below the ceilings reviewed here.[13]

The projections of French combat aircraft holdings for the two retirement ages are based on France's current inventory of combat aircraft and firm orders placed through 1994 for domestic deployment by 2000. For aircraft on firm order but not delivered by the end of 1993, IDDS has projected the likely service entry dates based on past patterns.

Even if the Rafale program is fully funded at 320 aircraft and 16–18 aircraft are delivered each year starting in 2001 as currently projected,[14] the French Air Force and *Aéronavale* will not be able to maintain their planned lower force levels through 2010 with a 20-year retirement age. To do so, the two services would need 337 new aircraft; Rafale deliveries by 2010 are expected to total only 187. To avoid a shortfall of 150 aircraft, France would have to produce 26 aircraft per year from 1998 to 2010. This is not impossible—French aircraft manufacturers produced an average of 29 aircraft per year for domestic deployment in 1981–1990—but it is a significantly higher rate than in recent years, and is unlikely to be financed given the fiscal situation in France.

A 25-year aircraft retirement age would result in a lower production requirement of 216 aircraft for the FAF and *Aéronavale* by 2010. Under this scenario, the FAF would operate with a surplus of aircraft until 2002. The *Aéronavale* would have an inventory shortfall beginning in 1999, but its decline would be less steep than with a 20-year retirement age. This scenario is more closely in line with currently planned deliveries of the Rafale. However, an additional 29 aircraft beyond the 187 currently planned by 2010 would have to be produced in order to avoid a shortfall.

Exports

The French aerospace industry has received only one firm export order for combat aircraft to be produced this decade. This order,

---

[13] Current French plans call for a force of about 550 combat aircraft overall when pipeline needs are taken into account, comprising 475 aircraft for the FAF and 75 aircraft for the *Aéronavale*.

[14] After initial, low-rate deliveries of 12 Rafales to the *Aéronavale* in 1998–2000.

placed by Taiwan in 1992 for 60 Mirage 2000-5 aircraft, represents the first export order for new-production French combat aircraft since 1985.[15] Deliveries are scheduled to begin in 1995 and are projected to be completed by 1999.

Several potential export orders for French combat aircraft this decade have been mentioned in the trade press. One is a potential order for 44 Mirage 2000E aircraft for Pakistan, for which a provisional agreement was signed in January 1992.[16] Another is a potential order from the United Arab Emirates for 50 Mirage 2000-5 aircraft.[17] Austria is also expected to make a decision within the next couple of years on a replacement for its 24 Saab Draken aircraft. And Qatar has been mentioned as a candidate to purchase new Mirage 2000s. Many analysts think that other aircraft producers will win the bulk of these contests.

The French Military Aerospace Industry and the Rafale

France's aerospace industry is largely organized around the production of military goods and the General Directorate for Armament (DGA). The DGA funds two-thirds of the industry's research and development expenses, and also helps open export markets and assures a tightly interwoven network of relations among the companies in this sector. The production of combat aircraft is an essential part of France's military-industrial complex and has profoundly influenced its configuration.[18] Since the late 1950s, the Dassault group has dominated the industry; thanks to the support of various defense ministers and public consensus, it is now the only French producer of combat aircraft.

The needs of Dassault and of other aircraft manufacturers largely determine French combat aircraft production. In fact, it was largely

---

[15] The previous order, placed by Greece, was for 40 Mirage 2000s delivered between 1988 and 1992. See Mark Lambert, ed., *Jane's All the World's Aircraft 1993–94* (Surrey, UK: Jane's Information Group, 1993), p. 77.

[16] *Jane's All the World's Aircraft 1993–94*, p. 77.

[17] Philip Finnegan, "United Arab Emirates' Arms Buys Stir World Concern," *Defense News*, Vol. 8, No. 14 (April 12, 1993), p. 10.

[18] F. Chesnais and C. Serfati, *L'Armement en France: Genèse, Ampleur, et Coût d'une Industrie* (Paris: Éditions Nathan, 1992).

the needs of the manufacturers that led to the decision to launch the Rafale program, despite its enormous costs, strong opposition from the Navy Chief of Staff, and criticism regarding its lack of "stealthiness." Thanks to the Rafale, France can challenge the United States in its status as the sole Western producer of next-generation combat aircraft. The Rafale program reflects France's drive for national autonomy and its focus on ensuring the "durability" of its defense industry.

This aim is reinforced by the recent behavior of the United States. For example, the manner in which the U.S. administration declared and prosecuted the war against Iraq, combined with the collapse of the Soviet bloc, allowed the United States to guide international diplomacy solely according to its own interests. U.S. companies, faced with declining contracts from the Pentagon, have supplanted the other arms-selling countries in a number of their traditional client states. The Pentagon vetoed the sale of the missile division of LTV, a U.S. defense contractor, to the French conglomerate Thomson, which led French leaders to conclude that the U.S. Department of Defense will do everything in its power to prevent foreign competitors from encroaching on its territory. To French leaders, these actions reveal the true meaning of U.S. declarations on "industrial cooperation with Europe in arms production."

The French defense industry has negatively affected France's foreign policy. For example, after France sold Mirage fighters to Taiwan, China no longer allowed French firms to bid on contracts in mainland China. The large French industrial concerns and other multinational corporations that are counting on the promising markets in mainland China protested that export policy should no longer be decided by the Minister of Defense, nor be determined by the needs of the Dassault firm. This incident highlights the difficulty for French officials to reconcile their desire that France appear as a global power independent from the United States, the need to sell arms at any price, and the needs of the rest of the French industrial base.[19]

---

[19] See also François Chesnais, "The French National System of Innovation," in Richard R. Nelson, ed., *National Innovation Systems* (New York: Oxford University Press, 1993).

Overview of the Industry

During the past decade, net aerospace foreign earnings have exceeded 25 bn francs ($4.4 bn) each year. The industry has contributed more to the trade balance than the agricultural and foodstuffs sectors in recent years. In spending on research and technological innovation, aerospace firms are just behind electronics manufacturers, but if we relate R&D expenditures to the value created in each industry, the aerospace industry comes out far ahead. As a percentage of total domestic R&D, France spends less on aerospace R&D than the United States, but more than the United Kingdom, and far more than Japan or Germany. The French aerospace industry produces a wide and growing range of civil and military products. In the civilian sphere, the company Aérospatiale controls (jointly with Eurocopter) 30 percent of the world helicopter market and has very strong exports of certain types of helicopters. In conjunction with the Airbus consortium (of which 37.9 percent of the capital is French), Aérospatiale's world market share in passenger transport aircraft rose to 30 percent in 1992. In the area of commercial motors, Snecma (Société Nationale d'Étude et de Construction de Moteurs d'Aviation) possesses 36 percent of the world market, including its business within the CFM consortium (a joint venture with General Electric, of which Snecma owns 50 percent of the capital).

In the military sphere, French industry also maintains a strong presence in helicopters (with GIE Eurocopter, of which 60 percent of the capital is held by Aérospatiale) and in combat aircraft.[20] In the area of missiles, French industry is also well represented with several major corporations (Aérospatiale, Thomson-CSF, and Matra), and over half of some types of missiles are exported. In space, French corporations have gained strong positions in the launcher area within the European Space Agency (ESA), and in the field of satellites through consortia and international joint ventures. Finally, decisions made since the beginning of the 1990s by the Minister of Defense reveal a strong desire to attain uncontested leadership in Europe in the area of military space.

The French aerospace industry was built around military objectives after World War II and took on its present structure in the 1960s. Intense development of combat aircraft was soon followed by

---

[20] In the 1980s, Dassault sold 12 percent of all combat aircraft globally.

production of nuclear-armed missiles. The DGA has shaped the aerospace industry through its orders of studies and equipment. Its objective has always been to avoid competition among French companies. Most of the large firms are sole suppliers to the French armed forces for specific systems, and the top three firms account for 80 percent of the market. Aérospatiale has this position in the production of ballistic missiles, commercial aircraft (except for a small number of business jets produced by Dassault), and commercial and military helicopters. Dassault is the sole supplier of combat aircraft. Engines for fixed-wing civil and military aircraft are produced exclusively by Snecma, and helicopter engines are produced solely by Labinal (which took over Turboméca). Three large enterprises produce missiles (Aérospatiale, Thomson-CSF, and Matra), but the DGA rotates contracts among them according to types of missiles to reduce competition.

The National Office for Aerospace Research and Studies (ONERA), created in 1946 and placed under the direction of the Defense Ministry, is responsible for basic R&D in the aerospace industry, and it also plays an important role in coordinating the research of all firms in the field, as well as conducting tests and simulations on their behalf. In 1993 its budget was 1.717 bn francs, of which 78 percent came from the DGA, while only 6 percent came from the General Department for Civil Aviation (DGAC). It employs 2,400 people, of whom 1,130 are engineers and managers. The ONERA distributes the results of its advanced aerospace research freely to businesses, and encourages them to undertake joint research projects. It is the principal institution for the transfer of technology between the military and civil aircraft development.

The industry is characterized by a strong integration of the means of production, and by the necessity of collaboration among the different contractors participating in a combat aircraft program. Aircraft production requires the integration of many different technologies and skills. The airframe manufacturer is typically the prime contractor, since the airframe determines the plane's essential characteristics, such as aerodynamics, loading capacity, and weight.

Within the defense industry, aerospace sales are roughly equaled by those of the electronics industry as avionics have become an ever more central component of aircraft. Still, it is the firms that specialize exclusively or primarily in the aerospace industry that form the skeleton of the defense industry.

Starting the 1960s, the governments led by Charles De Gaulle tried to extend the various skills acquired by the military to the civil sector, organizing large technological projects in civil aerospace, including the Concorde supersonic transport, the Airbus consortium, and the Ariane space launch vehicles. The result has been a continuous increase in activity in the civil sphere.

The only large civil technological agency in the country is the National Center for Space Studies (CNES), which is overseen by the Ministry of Research and which spearheads many of the European space programs. The Defense Ministry's drive for increased activity in space has led to a closer relationship in recent years between the CNES and the DGA. In 1991, the Delta Committee brought the two agencies together to harmonize military and civil R&D in space.[21] This changing institutional relationship between military and commercial research is described by the directors of the CNES as "very original in comparison with what is done elsewhere, notably in the United States,...very well-adapted to the special needs of the French context, and of great importance for the future."[22] This agreement will reinforce the role of the Defense Ministry (through the DGA), which remains the backbone of the aerospace industry as a whole. The DGAC (under the authority of the transportation ministry) has only a secondary role in the field of aircraft development.

The split between Dassault as a producer of military aircraft and Aérospatiale as a producer of civil aircraft is atypical: in most countries, aircraft manufacturers produce both civil and military aircraft. Nonetheless, the ties between the two large French aircraft manufacturers are significant. First, Aérospatiale is an important subcontractor for Dassault. Second, under the authority and with the financing of the DGA, the two companies organized a joint research program in the late 1970s to produce composite wings for the Falcon 100 executive transport. The Falcon 100 is the only major civil aircraft produced by Dassault. According to Dassault executives, it is the major link between Dassault and Aérospatiale.[23]

---

[21] R. Pellat and J.D. Lévi, *Rapport d'activité 1992, CNES*, p. 57.
[22] Ibid., p. 5.
[23] Personal communication.

Dassault

Within France's high-technology industry, Dassault is one of the last firms that remains under the control of one family. This is especially remarkable since the state holds 36 percent of Dassault's capital, and, in principle, has maintained a majority in its administrative council since 1977 through its double voting rights. However, the state has never exercised its full prerogatives as a majority shareholder. In particular, it has never forced a merger on Dassault, as it has with other firms in the military area.

Today the firm consists of two holding companies. The first, called Dassault Industries, is 100 percent held and managed by Serge Dassault, the head of the firm. It brings together the industrial holdings: Dassault Aviation (49.7 percent), Dassault Electronique (59.7 percent), Dassault Falcon Service (100 percent), and Dassault Belgique Aviation (100 percent). Its administrative board is composed of family members, close associates, and the presidents of the businesses. The second holding company is overseen by René Massaing but 100 percent held by Claude Dassault. It brings together personal property and real estate: the Château Dassault vineyards (100 percent), Productions Dassault (100 percent), Intertechnique (34 percent), Europe 1 (20 percent), the Institut Mérieux (15 percent), Gaumont (7.5 percent), and Gaz et Eaux (5 percent). It also manages the grounds and buildings rented to Dassault Aviation. Altogether, Dassault was worth more than 6 bn francs at the start of the 1990s, making the Dassault family one of the nine wealthiest in France. According to government sources, the amount paid by Dassault Aviation to the Dassault family was 207,400,000 francs in 1990, about 1.2 percent of the firm's income.[24] Serge Dassault takes great pride in the fact that the firm has no structural financing costs.[25]

Dassault is often thought of as a company of engineers that subcontracts whatever it can. It presents itself as a company whose strength is its capacity to conceive, design, and construct prototypes, and which relies principally upon component-suppliers for large-scale orders, but maintains absolute control of assembly. The firm has always refused to act as a component-supplier to other firms, even when it needs work.

---

[24] A. Schwarzbrod, *Dassault, le Dernier Round* (Paris: Olivier Orban, 1992), p. 130.
[25] Ibid., p. 226.

Table 9.2 First Flights of Dassault Combat Aircraft 1951–1991

Year	Aircraft		
1951	MD 450 Ouragan (Tay)	MD 452 Mystère II (Nene)	MD 450 Ouragan (Atar)
1952	MD 450 Ouragan (side inlets)	MD 452 Mystère II (Tay)	MD 453 Mystère de nuit
	MD 452 Mystère II (Atar 101C)	Mystère IV (Tay)	
1953	MD 452 (Atar PC)	Mystère IV-B (Avon PC)	
1954	MD 452 Mystère II (Atar PC)	Mystère IV-N (Avon)	
1955	MD 550 Mirage I (BI Viper)	Super Mystère B1	
1956	Super Mystère B2 (Atar)	Etendard II (Gabizo)	Etendard IV
	Mirage III (Atar 101 G)		
1957	Etendard VI (Orpheus)		
1958	Super Mystère B4 (Atar 9 PC)	Etendard IV M (Atar 8)	Mirage III-A
1959	Mirage IV	Mirage III-B	
1960	Mirage III-C		
1961	Mirage III-O (Avon)	Mirage III-E	Mirage III-R
1962	Mirage Balzac		
1963			
1964	Mirage III-T (TF 406)		
1965	Mirage III-V	Mirage III C2 (Atar 9K)	
1966	Mirage F2	Mirage F1	
1967	Mirage 5	Mirage G	
1968			
1969	Mirage Milan		
1970			
1971	Mirage G8 two-seat		
1972	Mirage G8 single-seat		
1973	Alphajet		
1974	Super Etendard	Mirage F1-E (M53)	
1975			
1976	Mirage F1-B		
1977			
1978	Mirage 2000		
1979	Mirage 4000	Mirage 50	
1980	Mirage 2000B		
1981	Mirage F1-CR		
1982	Mirage III-NG		
1983			
1984	Mirage 2000N		
1985			
1986			
1987	Rafale A		
1988			
1989			
1990	Mirage 2000-5 two-seat		
1991	Mirage 2000-5 single-seat	Mirage 2000D	Rafale CO1
	Rafale MO1		

Source: P. Goudou, "L'industrie mondiale des avions de combat," L'Armement, 1991.

Observers often say that Dassault's R&D capacity has grown too large. At the end of the 1970s, the Dassault Aviation research division would have needed to produce a new prototype every three years, and a new plane no less than every ten years if it worked at full capacity. In fact, in 40 years, the firm produced 56 combat aircraft prototypes, many of which never proceeded much beyond first flight, let alone to production. (See Table 9.2.) However, the growing cost to design and build prototypes has caused a gradual reduction in the number of such "first flight" aircraft.

This R&D overcapacity has led Dassault to build prototypes of aircraft which compete with each other. A typical case was the twin-engine Mirage 4000, which the French Air Force, already over-equipped, was unwilling to purchase. Lacking the FAF's "seal of approval" the Mirage 4000 was a complete failure on the export market. The need to keep the research division busy also explains the launching of the Rafale only a decade after the Mirage 2000, a program that was premised on sales through the year 2000 without competition from another Dassault aircraft. Despite the fact that the French market will be saturated later this decade by the extremely expensive Rafale, Dassault has developed numerous versions of the Mirage 2000.

Experts feel that the Mirage 2000-5, which was designed for the export market, arrived much too late—only a few years before the new generation of aircraft planned for 2000, yet too late for countries that need aircraft equivalent or superior to U.S. aircraft. In addition, the Air Force had refused to buy the new model so that it could afford the Rafale.[26] An Air Force official explained "We already have Mirage 2000s with RDM radar, Mirage 2000s with dual-standard RDI radar, and twin-seat Mirage 2000s. If we added a fifth type, we would never be able to work things out logistically, because when you place an order, you're already spending a billion francs just on logistics."[27] Since then, in the face of strong pressure from the DGA and Dassault, former Defense Minister Pierre Joxe decided to equip the Air Force with Mirage 2000-5s in order to facilitate export sales of the aircraft.

The excessive growth of Dassault's R&D capacity was facilitated by the multiplication of projects in the 1970s financed jointly by Das-

---

[26] D. Fortin, "Plusiers officiers de l'air contestent l'utilité de commander des Mirage 2000-5," *Tribune de l'Expansion*, November 26, 1992.
[27] Schwarzbrod, *Dassault*, p. 256.

sault (using its export profits) and the DGA under the rubric of "the combat aircraft of the future" (ACF).

The only collaborative production programs of Dassault, the Atlantique and Jaguar aircraft, were projects begun by Brequet, which Dassault acquired in 1972. According to Serge Dassault, "Cooperation ruins the competitiveness of a firm: when you do it alone, you do everything, conception, calculations, the trials...you know how to make a plane. When four of you do it, you just do parts, a quarter...and after a while, you don't know how to do the whole thing anymore.... And when you export the plane, you're only exporting a part of it.... I prefer to make three hundred complete planes instead of eight hundred wings."[28]

Not surprisingly, the firm has extreme difficulty in accepting the principle of modern aircraft as "weapon systems" in the full sense of the term, calling for complimentary skills and cooperation with other firms. While the Mirage 2000-5 and the Rafale were initially "built by Dassault," these aircraft are now weapon systems whose performance depends on the quality and proper functioning of diverse components. Other aerospace firms are no longer just parts suppliers but equal partners. Dassault's partners in the Rafale program are reportedly worried about its "lack of resoluteness and attention" in overseeing the project.[29]

It is even more difficult for Dassault to collaborate with foreign firms, however powerful and eager to cooperate they may be. This refusal to move beyond France's borders is evident in the refusal to purchase the U.S. business jet producer Learjet, which would have allowed Dassault to penetrate the North American market.[30] Dassault's preference to work alone and the state's commitment to supporting the research capacity of its defense industry help explain why French negotiations to take part in the European combat aircraft program were not successful.

In late 1992, Dassault signed a contract with Taiwan to supply 60 Mirage 2000-5 fighters during the second half of this decade. This was the firm's first export contract since 1985. Dassault was able to survive this hiatus for several reasons. First, until the beginning of the 1990s, Dassault was still fulfilling export contracts with Jordan and

---

[28] Ibid., p. 144.
[29] Ibid., p. 150.
[30] Ibid., pp. 225–226.

India signed at the beginning of the 1980s. Second, maintenance and spare parts are important sources of revenue. Dassault supplies spare parts for 7,300 aircraft in service around the world. The maintenance alone of 700 aircraft sold between 1978 and 1990 provides more than 1 bn francs per year. Third, since the restructuring and "voluntary departures" of 1988–1989, profits from sales of military aircraft to the Defense Ministry, along with modest commercial production, ensure the survival of Dassault. Following the 1988–1989 restructuring, the company expected revenues of 10 bn francs, 6 bn from French government orders and 4 bn from commercial sales. Serge Dassault describes exports as "cherries on the cake"; the firm relies on the French military market, no matter what the cost for the rest of the economy.

The Rafale

The Rafale program has enjoyed remarkable political consensus. In 1986, during debate on the military program for 1987–1991, not a single parliamentarian voiced the slightest criticism of the program. Since then, despite significant changes in the global political context, increases in the program's cost, and a severe economic crisis, the consensus has remained intact.[31]

The only certain cost to date is that at the end of 1992, nearly 20 bn francs had been spent.[32] Cost estimates for the program vary greatly, and have continued to grow, from 180 bn francs in 1988 to 300 bn francs in 1993.[33]

As with the Mirage 2000 and other programs before it, a considerable rise in both development costs and projected production costs has resulted in a decrease in the Rafale's overall production run. The initial requirements for the Rafale program called for 336 aircraft to be built, 250 for the Air Force and 86 for the Navy. The Air Force sub-

---

[31] Criticisms by some officials have been dismissed as pressure from the "atlanticist lobby" in a report by the Defense Commission of the National Assembly. See *Rapport sur le Projet de Loi de Programmation (No. 2877) pour les Années 1992–1994*, Vol. 1, No. 2935, October 7, 1992, p. 477.

[32] Assemblée Nationale, Commission des Finances, *Rapport sur le Projet de Loi de Finance pour 1994 (No. 536)*, No. 2935, Annex 39, October 7, 1993, pp. 73–75.

[33] All cost estimates are given in constant francs and are within a 10 percent margin of error.

sequently decided to procure more two-seat versions than single-seat-ers; since these are about 3 percent more expensive than single-seaters, the Air Force's requirement was cut to 234 aircraft (139 two-seaters and 95 single-seat aircraft).

Significant cost overruns have already been acknowledged, while the program has only just completed its development phase. Forty bn francs (1992 prices) were budgeted for the Rafale's development. Five prototypes were to be built: three for the Air Force, including one two-seater, and two for the Navy.[34] This has since been reduced to four; the second single-seater for the Air Force was canceled. According to some estimates, by June 1993, two-thirds of the funds budgeted had already been spent, while the third prototype had only just been completed.

Another indication of the rise in costs is the Air Force's decision to order fewer Mirage 2000B/Cs. Since 1982, this aircraft has progressively replaced the Mirage F1. The Air Force had planned to order 192 Mirage 2000B/Cs, but reduced its order in 1991 to 168 to preserve funds for the Rafale program.[35]

AN ESSENTIAL PROGRAM FOR THE DEFENSE INDUSTRY

The Rafale program is essential for Dassault and the other large defense contractors: it provides a two-decade production plan; it allows for research and military technological innovation in essential domains (and it certainly ensures the "durability" of these corporations' R&D capacities); and it maintains the cohesion of the arms industry, since all contracts were awarded to French firms. Dassault Aviation has a 35 percent share of the program, Snecma 30 percent, Thomson-CSF 13 percent, and Dassault Electronique 8 percent; 150 mid-size companies also participate on a much more modest scale.

Some parliamentarians believe that once production begins, 15 percent of France's total equipment outlays will be devoted to the production and maintenance of the Rafale. According to a summary of studies issued by the parliamentary Defense Commission, the Ra-

---

[34] Michel Bernard, Assemblée National, Commission de la Défense Nationale et des Forces Armées, *Projet de Rapport d'Information sur l'Avion de Combat Tactique*, September 22, 1988, p. 71.

[35] The FAF will actually receive 153 Mirage 2000B/Cs as the final 15 were converted to the Mirage 2000D standard. See *Rapport sur le Projet de Loi de Programmation pour les Années 1992–1994*, Vol. 1, No. 2935, p. 464.

fale will consume one-third of the Air Force's equipment budget.[36] By the beginning of 1993, 19.5 bn francs had been spent on the program; this was only 12 percent of the program's total cost.

According to the parliamentary report on the military program law for 1990–1993, "the future of AMDBA [Dassault] essentially rests upon the Rafale program which will equip the Air Force and *Aéronavale* beginning in 1996. This program represents by itself an important part of the future of the French aircraft industry."[37] While this is a crucial program for many French firms, it is absolutely vital for the Dassault group, which manages 47 percent of the program. The company has remained almost entirely dependent upon its combat aircraft sales, and it is likely that military orders will represent a greater share of Dassault's business in the near future; the company's primary strengths are the production of airframes and its experience as a systems integrator. The Rafale program has limited the decline in the firm's revenue, which began in the mid-1980s when the number of military aircraft produced was cut in half.

The Rafale program is also crucial for Snecma. While its commercial activity accounts for most of its income, this activity is conducted by the CFM International consortium, a joint venture with General Electric. The Rafale program will give Snecma the opportunity to improve its competence in certain technologies so that it does not become overwhelmed by General Electric.

The defense industry spends a large part of its resources in racing for technological innovation. Since the birth of the Fifth Republic in 1958, French officials have undertaken large programs designed to function as technological catalysts in order to maintain the country's strategic independence. These programs are in fact an essential mechanism to ensure the survival of firms specialized in military production. In fact, "incremental" innovations are insufficient to assure the employment of the research facilities and laboratories of these businesses and of the DGA.

Thus, a proposal to modernize the Mirage 2000 instead of pursuing the Rafale program was unacceptable for Dassault. In fact, to underline the irreversibility of the Rafale program and to implement

---

[36] Bernard, *Rapport d'Information sur l'Avion de Combat Tactique.*

[37] Assemblée Nationale, Commission de la Défense Nationale et des Forces Armées, *Rapport sur le Projet de Loi de Programmation (No. 733) Relatif à l'Équipement Militaire pour les Années 1990–1993*, No. 897, October 2, 1989, p. 464.

its industrialization more rapidly, the French government reduced its order for the Mirage 2000B/C from 192 aircraft to 168 and then to 153. Still, Dassault and its partners were largely compensated for the loss from this reduction through an FAF program to upgrade 37 older Mirage 2000B/Cs to the Mirage 2000-5 standard, and the decision to order 15 additional Mirage 2000Ds.

In order to justify the Rafale program's astronomical cost, the DGA and the defense industry claim that it represents a significant improvement in performance. The same rationale is given for the army's Leclerc tank and the Navy's *Charles de Gaulle* nuclear aircraft carrier. However, the Rafale's cost is five times greater than that of the Leclerc tank and more than ten times that of the *Charles de Gaulle*, while its expected performance has been vigorously debated.

THE RAFALE'S DESIGN

The tremendous increase in the cost of new-generation combat aircraft led the government to decide to procure a single aircraft that could be used for air-to-air and air-to-ground missions by both the Air Force and the Navy; rather than have Dassault design different aircraft for each service. The Navy considers that a "generic" combat aircraft will not fill its needs. The Rafale will replace as many as seven different aircraft types currently in service with the FAF and *Aéronavale*,[38] and there will be 95 percent commonality in systems between the Air Force and Naval versions of the aircraft.[39]

The Chief of Staff of the Navy strongly resisted the decision to procure a common aircraft and refused to fund the Rafale M, which will not be operational until at least 1998, because he judged that the program did not suit the *Aéronavale's* needs. Rather than wait for the Rafale M, the Navy hoped to purchase 15 F/A-18 aircraft from the United States to replace its aging Crusaders, which were scheduled to be retired in 1993.[40] In the end, the Navy was persuaded to modernize the Crusaders to maintain them in service until at least 1998.

---

[38] The Rafale will replace the Crusader, Étendard IV, and Super Étendard in the *Aéronavale* and the Mirage III, Mirage 5, Jaguar, and Mirage F1 in the Air Force. See Turbé and Beal, "Rafale's Split Personality."

[39] J.P. Philippe, "Rafale on Course," *Military Technology*, September 8, 1992.

[40] Numerous parliamentary reports relate the Navy's discomfort in not having a viable interceptor before the delivery of the Rafale. See Assemblée Nationale, Commission de la Défense Nationale et des Forces Armées, *Rapport sur le projet de loi de finances pour 1990*, No. 920, October 12, 1993, p. 78.

Yielding to the demands of the Navy would have opened a discussion on the necessity of the Rafale in a world that had been changed by the fall of the Soviet Bloc and a deepening economic crisis.

This common design necessitated certain technical compromises. Folding wings, which would have been useful in the naval version, were abandoned in the face of the significant development costs they would have entailed. The Rafale's wings and forward fuselage were designed to meet the requirements of carrier operations. Because of this, the Air Force version will have a greater empty weight and be less aerodynamically efficient than if it had been designed solely according to Air Force specifications.[41]

Other difficulties arose from the desire that the Rafale be a multi-role aircraft. This objective required sophisticated avionics, which in turn necessitated significant modifications in the aircraft's configuration; the Air Force decided to make most of its aircraft two-seaters to reduce pilot workload. The installation of a second position in the cockpit in turn led to numerous modifications that increased the aircraft's weight by about 3 percent, or 300 kilograms, for a total of about 9.6 tons, and reduced its fuel capacity by 10 percent, thereby shortening its range. The Rafale has continued to gain weight, going from an initial weight of 8.5 tons in 1988 (empty weight) for the single-seat version, to 9.06 in 1989, to 9.35 in 1993, to 9.7 for the two-seater.[42] The two-seat version costs approximately 3 percent more than the single-seat version.

Despite these limitations, the aircraft incorporates several technical advances. The Rafale uses a significant amount of composite materials. The Mirage 2000, which first flew in 1978, contained 7 percent composite materials in its total structural mass. The use of composites by Dassault has increased, and the company reports that composites will make up 30 percent of the Rafale's structural mass. The aircraft's information management system, developed by Dassault Electronique, has been substantially improved in comparison with the system equipping the Mirage 2000. The older system contains 300,000 lines of code; the Rafale's has 1 million. Dassault also sought to introduce an advanced "fly-by-wire" flight control system, and improved the ergonomics of the cockpit.

---

[41] Turbé and Beal, "Rafale's Split Personality."

[42] J.P. Casamayou, "Le Rafale domine le salon," *Air et Cosmos*, June 14, 1993, pp. 60–61.

Technological innovation, however, has been more limited in other areas of the Rafale's design. The aircraft's RBE2 radar system, a passive electronically-scanned unit with look-down/shoot-down capabilities being developed by Thomson-CSF with Dassault Electronique, has encountered technical problems that have delayed the Rafale program by at least six months.[43] And the Delta wing employed on the Rafale, a typical characteristic of Dassault aircraft, is not capable of achieving high angles of attack, which provide a significant tactical advantage in combat. Prototype testing indicates that the Rafale can reach a 40° angle of attack, which is significantly inferior to the 70° angles of attack achieved by the U.S.-designed X-29 and X-31 experimental aircraft.[44]

It also appears that the Rafale was not subject to significant research in the field of stealth in its initial design phases. When this failure was recognized in the late 1980s, several changes were made to reduce the aircraft's radar signature. However, those responsible for the program prefer to speak of the Rafale's "unobtrusiveness," since they admit that it will not be a truly stealthy aircraft.[45]

---

[43] Thomson-CSF accounts for 75 percent and Dassault Electronique for 25 percent of the design, development, and production of the radar.

[44] Other sources maintain that the Rafale can achieve only a 32° angle of attack. See Gérard Turbé and Clifford Beal, "Rafale's Split Personality," *International Defense Review*, Vol. 24 (October 1991), pp. 1079–1081.

[45] G. Chambost, "Rafale, le premier chasseur polyvalent," *Défense*, June 1993, p. 25.

Chapter 10

Elisabeth Sköns
Fredrik Wetterqvist

The Gripen and Sweden's Evolving Defense Industrial Policy

Sweden's policies on its future holdings, production, and exports of fighter-attack aircraft are a function of its overall security and arms control policy. This policy is now under revision as a consequence of the major changes in the international security environment over the past three or four years and the 1991 change of government from a nine-year rule by the Social Democratic government, to a coalition government of conservative, liberal, center and Christian Democratic parties.

For decades, the heart of Swedish security policy was its neutrality, defined as non-alignment in time of peace aiming at neutrality in case of war.[1] Sweden's policy rested on two essential foundations: an active foreign policy promoting détente, international disarmament, and peaceful development; and a firm and consistent defense policy that demonstrated Sweden's will and ability to defend itself.

---

[1] For an official and elementary description of Sweden's traditional security policy, see *Sweden's Security Policy: Entering the '90s*, Statens Offentliga Utredningar (The Government's Official Reports) No. 23, 1985 [*SOU 1985:23*], report by the 1984 Defense Commission (Stockholm: Gotab, 1985). A more recent official report is *Svensk säkerhetspolitik i en föränderlig värld* (*Swedish security policy in a changing world*), *SOU 1990:5* (Stockholm: Gotab, 1990).

Elisabeth Sköns is a Research Fellow with the Project on Arms Production and Arms Transfers at the Stockholm International Peace Research Institute (SIPRI), and a regular contributor to the SIPRI Yearbook.

Fredrik Wetterqvist is First Secretary at the Swedish Ministry for Foreign Affairs.

The current government has declared that Sweden will now pursue a foreign and security policy with a clear European identity.[2]

During a major parliamentary debate on security issues in May 1992, most of the parties agreed on two basic propositions.[3] First, there is no change in the policy of military non-alignment aiming at neutrality in case of a war near Sweden. This presupposes the maintenance of an adequate defense capability. Second, military non-alignment does not preclude Sweden's participation in the evolving and multifaceted cooperation in Europe. Rather, Swedish security policy is now characterized by full participation in the goals shared by all European states. In keeping with its new policy, Sweden applied for membership in the European Union in July 1991, and decided to participate in the NATO Partnership for Peace in April 1994.

Despite the changes in Sweden's security environment and security policy, the government has concluded that Sweden is not released "from its responsibility for independent defense of its large air space and extensive land and sea territory strategically located between the North Atlantic and Northwestern Russia." The defense plan for 1992–1997 increases defense expenditures by SEK 7.3 bn (about U.S. $1.2 bn) in 1992/93 prices.[4] Sweden's policy on arms control and disarmament has also been affected by the end of the Cold War: "The focus is increasingly shifting from disarmament as a method of managing or influencing a given conflict between two sides to arms control as one process among several on the road toward a security architecture."[5] In fact, the government has expressed skepticism about the

---

[2] Minister of Foreign Affairs, Margareta af Ugglas, in her introduction to the budget, *Regeringens proposition 1991/92:100 Bilaga 4: Utrikesdepartementet* [*Prop. 1991/92: 100:4*] (*Government Bill Fiscal Year 1991/92 No. 100, Appendix 4: Ministry for Foreign Affairs*) (Stockholm: Norstedts Tryckeri AB, 1992), p. 10.

[3] Documented in *Säkerhet och nedrustning* [*1991/92:UU19*] (Parliamentary Foreign Policy Committee report on security and disarmament), and the debate protocols to this, *Prot. 1991/92:117*, May 21, 1992. See also G. Herolf and R. Lindahl, "Sweden: Reevaluating security in a changing European setting," Stiftung Wissenschaft und Politik, SWP-IP (Ebenhausen, November 1993).

[4] *Försvarsutskottets betänkande 1991/92:FöU12, Totalförsvarets fortsätta utveckling 1992/93–1996/97* [*1991/92:FöU12*] (*Report of the Standing Defense Committee, Fiscal Year 1991/92, No. 12: The future development of the total defense in 1992/93–1996/97*) (Stockholm: Allmänna Förlaget, 1992), p. 144.

[5] *Nedrustningspolitik och nedrustningskontroll i en ny tid* (Disarmament policy and arms control in a new era), Ministry for Foreign Affairs, Stockholm, January 1992, p.

value of formal multilateral arms control negotiations, and suggests that informal arms control can be faster and more effective.[6]

While Sweden recognizes that the risk of a great-power war has decreased to a very low level, and that the military-strategic importance of Northern Europe has been reduced in keeping with its defense policy, Sweden will continue to protect itself from unlikely but potentially dire threats. In the event of a conflict between great powers, Swedish territory could be valued as a short-cut for flight operations, a transit route, a forward basing area (mainly for combat aircraft), or a base for forward air surveillance. In guarding against such uses of Swedish territory, fighter-attack aircraft play a major role. The government feels that Sweden must maintain an Air Force of 16 squadrons, a number established in 1992.[7]

This position is largely motivated by uncertainties about the future security situation in Europe, and thus constitutes a resort to a worst-case scenario. Once the situation in Europe stabilizes, an alternative view may become possible. In 1997, when the next decision about the Gripen must be made, it may be easier to assess the requirements of the Swedish Air Force.

Thus, while Sweden has a positive attitude toward negotiations on reductions in conventional forces in Europe, it is not prepared to enter negotiations on reductions in fighter-attack aircraft, at least not in the short term.[8] The government is deeply committed to completing production of the latest combat aircraft designed in Sweden, the JAS 39 Gripen. If negotiations would affect only the older fighter-attack aircraft, the Draken and Viggen, the Swedish government might be more open.

---

48 (author's translation). This report documents the basic principles of the new disarmament and arms control policy.

[6] *Nedrustningspolitik*, p. 49.

[7] *Regeringens proposition 1991/92:102, Totalförsvarets utveckling till och med budgetåret 1996/97 samt anslag for budgetåret 1992/93* [*Prop. 1991/92:102*] (*Government Bill Fiscal Year 1991/92 No. 102: The development of the total defense through fiscal year 1996/97 and appropriations for fiscal year 1992/93*) (Stockholm: Allmänna Förlaget, 1992), p. 36.

[8] Interview with M. Sahlin, Under-Secretary of Defense, May 22, 1992.

The Swedish Air Force and the Gripen Program

The size and quality of the Air Force and the ground-based air defense are among the highest priorities of the Swedish "Total Defense."[9] In particular, the fighter-attack units are considered vital to air defense. Compared with the air forces of other European countries, the Swedish Air Force has many combat aircraft per capita, but is small per unit of territory. Since 1945 the Air Force has had an "extended defense" strategy, which essentially means it patrols Swedish air space and the Baltic Sea. The Air Force has a limited offensive capability; it lacks bombers, long-range attack aircraft, or air refueling tankers. The attack squadrons have a substantial air-to-ground and anti-ship capability.

Since World War II, Sweden has produced all of its fighter-attack aircraft, which is exceptional for a country with a population of just 8 million. The rationale for independent production of such advanced weaponry has been the policy of non-alignment.

There are 330 fighter-attack aircraft in the Swedish Air Force, all various models of the Draken (Dragon) and the Viggen (Thunderbolt). Developed in the 1950s, the Draken was originally designed to intercept transonic bombers but was later produced in eight different versions including several interceptor types, a two-seat tandem trainer, a reconnaissance plane, and a long-range attack and reconnaissance version designed for export. The Drakens now in service were delivered to the Air Force between 1963 and 1972 and were all modified in 1991.

The Viggens are an average of ten years younger than the Drakens. The last production unit was delivered in 1990. The Viggen is a multi-mission single-engine plane designed for the Swedish Air Force's basing and air defense control systems. The aircraft has an advanced aerodynamic configuration, using a foreplane fitted with flaps in combination with a main delta wing to provide short take-off and landing

---

[9] Total Defense is the Swedish concept for the combined Military and Civil Defense. The Military Defense consists of army units, naval units, air force units, operational command, and joint authorities. The Civil Defense includes vital supply and maintenance functions, civil command and coordination, civil defense and rescue services, psychological defense, and other functions. The total defense budget also includes funding for the Ministry of Defense (administration) and for emergency and UN units. See *Fakta om Totalförsvaret 1992–93* (*Facts about the total defense*) (Stockholm: Office of the Swedish Chiefs of Staff, 1993), p. 23.

(STOL) capability. The Viggen was produced in five versions: interceptor, interceptor with attack capability, attack with interceptor capability, land and sea reconnaissance, and tandem two-seat trainer.

The JAS 39 Gripen, a new indigenously-designed fighter, is currently making the transition from development to production.[10] The Gripen is to succeed the J 35 Draken and the JA 37 Viggen aircraft in one of the largest industrial efforts ever undertaken in Sweden. It accounts for about half of the Air Force equipment budget and about 10 percent of the total defense budget.[11]

The basic specifications for the Gripen were established during the 1970s. The Swedish Air Force needed an aircraft that could perform fighter, interceptor, attack, and reconnaissance missions. It seemed likely that Sweden would not be able to keep up with the international trend toward larger, twin-engined, sophisticated, and increasingly costly combat aircraft. The Air Force required that its new fighter-attack aircraft be lightweight so it would use less fuel than earlier fighters (particularly the Viggen); have some stealth capability; and allow a single pilot to carry out all missions. In addition, it required that one professional technician aided by four conscript soldiers be able to provide turnaround service and maintenance of the aircraft. Finally, because Sweden will use regular roads and highways throughout the country as runways and taxiways for military aircraft in time of war, the aircraft had to be able to take off and land in less than 800 meters.

In 1982, the Riksdag approved indigenous development and procurement of the JAS 39 Gripen. It decided to develop and produce 30 aircraft, and approved a general plan to purchase 110 more by 2000. The government's commitment to the Gripen program has never been subject to reconsideration.

The Air Force has nine combat aircraft wings, each with two or three squadrons. The total number of squadrons after full mobilization is 26.5, of which 19.5 are active in peacetime (11 fighter, 5.5 medium attack, and 3 reconnaissance). Three squadrons are made up of inactive S 37 Viggen reconnaissance aircraft, and the remainder are

---

[10] JAS is the acronym for "Jakt, Attack, Spaning" (fighter, attack, and reconnaissance). "Gripen" means griffin, a mythical cross between a lion and an eagle.
[11] Interview with B. Reinholdsson, an expert on the JAS 39 in the Swedish Ministry of Defense, June 9, 1992.

light attack squadrons used for training in peacetime.[12] Neither the Army nor the Navy has any advanced combat aircraft.[13]

The five-year defense plan for fiscal years 1992/93 through 1996/97 calls for a reduction from 19.5 squadrons to 16. This reduction began in 1992 and should be completed during the beginning of the next decade. In addition, a program is underway to modernize all combat aircraft and the Sk 60 trainer.[14] Modifications focus on improvements to the Viggen's weapon systems. In fact, some of the Viggens (those being modernized to the AJS configuration[15]) should be able to perform the same missions as the Gripen; the first such aircraft should be ready by fall 1994.[16]

During the current period, the backbone of the Air Defense will be the eight Viggen fighter squadrons and two Draken fighter squadrons. Thirty JAS 39 Gripens will enter service and 18 AJ 37 Viggens will be retired, leading to a temporary increase in the number of fighter-attack aircraft.[17] Eventually, all Viggens and Drakens will be replaced by the Gripen. At a typical strength of 12 operational and 6 reserve aircraft per squadron, the Air Force would need 288 Gripens. To date it has ordered 140: 30 in 1982, and 110 in 1992 for delivery between 1996 and 2002 at a rate of 20 aircraft per year.[18] An additional order could be placed in 1997, when the next five-year defense plan is scheduled to be determined.[19]

Over the next 10–15 years all of the AJ 37 and S 37 and about 50 of the JA 37 Viggens will be taken out of service and will be replaced with the JAS 39 Gripen. All eight fighter squadrons of JA 37 will be phased out between 2002 and 2012 unless the government decides to order fewer JAS 39 and instead further modernize the JA 37.[20] In addition to the indigenous production of new types of aircraft, there are

---

[12] Interview with H. Högstadius, Information Department, Swedish Air Force General Staff Planning Section, June 17, 1992, and *Prop. 1991/92: 102*, p. 54.

[13] The Army has 17 Sk 61C (BAe Bulldogs) for observation missions.

[14] Private communication, Å. Engman, J 35 and Sk 60 expert at Försvarets Matérielverk (FMV), May 8, 1992; and Saab-Scania, *Verksamheten 1990* (annual report), p. 22.

[15] The AJS configuration (attack, fighter, reconnaissance) emphasizes the attack role.

[16] *Prop. 1991/92:102*, pp. 60–61; *Svenska Dagbladet*, June 3, 1991, p. 8; and Engman, personal communication.

[17] *1991/92:FöU12*; and *Prop. 1991/92:102*.

[18] Sahlin interview.

[19] Sahlin interview; and *Prop. 1991/92:102*, pp. 54, 64–65.

[20] Reinholdsson interview.

three ways the Air Force can affect the future size of its fighter-attack aircraft fleet: it can extend the service life of some aircraft; it can order additional production of existing types of aircraft; or it can purchase foreign aircraft. Currently, there are no plans to extend the service life of any of the Viggens, apart from conversion to the AJS configuration, and no new orders of the Viggen or foreign aircraft are being discussed.[21]

CURRENT STATUS OF THE JAS 39 GRIPEN PROGRAM
Five prototypes of the JAS 39 Gripen have been manufactured and two series-produced aircraft were completed by April 1994. The first prototype crashed in February 1989. The second series-produced aircraft was delivered to the Air Force in June 1993 and crashed in August. After the accident, the delivery of the third series-produced aircraft, planned for September 1993, was delayed until May 1994.[22] As of April 1994, a total of ten aircraft were to be delivered by the end of 1994.

In December 1993, development and production were two years behind schedule.[23] Yet in September 1993, the office of the Supreme Commander expressed the expectation that two squadrons of JAS 39 would be operational as of June 30, 1997, that is, according to plan.[24]

The major remaining government decision on the Gripen program is the selection of beyond-visual-range air-to-air missiles, a potential deal for 500–1000 missiles, worth around SEK 4–6 bn (U.S. $500–800 mn). The contenders are: MICA, produced by Matra (France); Active Sky Flash, produced by British Aerospace; and AIM-120 AMRAAM, produced by Hughes Missiles Systems and Raytheon (U.S.).[25]

---

[21] B. Andersson, FMV, personal communication.

[22] "Flygvapnet får otestat Jasplan" (The Air Force receives untested JAS plane), Dagens Nyheter, April 22, 1994, p. A5.

[23] JAS-39 Gripen: En granskning av JAS-projektet [SOU 1993:119](A review of the JAS Project), Report by the parliamentary JAS Commission (Stockholm, December 1993), p. 128.

[24] Försvarsmakten (Office of the Supreme Commander of the Swedish Armed Forces), Konsekvenser av en eventuell försening av JAS-projektet (Consequences of a possible delay in the JAS project), Stockholm, September 27, 1993, Appendix 1, p. 5.

[25] On July 28, 1994, the government announced that it would buy the AIM-120 AMRAAM. An interim order of 100 missiles will allow a later evaluation of advanced missile systems. (Jane's Defence Weekly, August 6, 1994; Svenska Dagbladet, July 29, 1994, p. 12.) AMRAAM had not previously been considered a feasible option because of U.S. restrictions on re-exports. However, in early 1994, the U.S. Secretary of De-

As of mid-1993, the government budget for the two JAS orders had an estimated value of SEK 60.2 bn ($7.5 bn) at February 1992 prices.[26] Of this, SEK 17 bn were for the development and production of 30 Series I aircraft; SEK 21 bn for the production of 110 Series II aircraft, and the development of the JAS 39B trainer version and support systems; and SEK 22 bn for armaments, countermeasures and other costs. Per unit, the average budgeted cost is about SEK 430 mn per aircraft, or about $80 mn.

At least until early 1994 the budget for the JAS program was not affected by the restrictive budget policy the government adopted to reduce the large budget deficit. Not even the austerity packages introduced during the winter of 1992–93 affected the Gripen program.

Until 1994 there was also broad consensus on the economic resource allocation for the Gripen program. A parliamentary commission appointed after the Gripen accident in August 1993 to assess whether the Gripen program could reach its goal within the adopted economic limits by and large felt that it could, but the commission did criticize how the program allocates and spends money. In particular, it found that it is difficult to determine the size of cost overruns of the project. For example, the JAS budget shows ten years' payments at then-current prices, while the government reports use constant February 1992 prices. A rough recalculation to February 1992 prices increases the JAS budget by SEK 4–5 bn.[27]

The commission also found it difficult to assess the impact of changing exchange rates. About half of future payments are to foreign suppliers, mainly U.S. companies. The substantial depreciation of the Swedish currency since November 1992 means a cost increase of about SEK 5–6 bn for these payments until the end of 1993. However, since payments will be made over ten years it is difficult to assess the final impact.[28]

In spite of these accounting problems, the overall assessment of the JAS commission was that the economically most risky period has

---

fense declared that the United States would agree to re-exports of the Gripen armed with AMRAAM to "a number of suitable countries," but this would not waive the U.S. requirement for congressional approval of each re-export case. Also see "Robotköp skapar problem" (Missile purchase creates problems), *Svenska Dagbladet*, April 25, 1994, p. 9.

[26] *JAS-39 Gripen*, pp. 119, 121.

[27] Ibid., p. 123.

[28] Ibid.

now passed, so that the government is unlikely to suffer from future overruns.[29]

However, in April 1994 it was made public that the Air Force ran a deficit of almost SEK 700 mn (nearly $100 mn) due to cost overruns in the JAS program amounting to SEK 5–6 bn because of the deteriorated exchange rate between the dollar and the Swedish krona. This had forced the postponement of matériel acquisitions, primarily within the JAS program, but would not affect the planned procurement of air-to-air missiles later in the year.[30]

The effects of potential budget constraints on the JAS program beyond the first 140 aircraft are difficult to assess. This is more a matter of government policy than economics. Owe Wiktorin, the Swedish Supreme Commander since July 1, 1994 and a former fighter pilot, has committed himself to a third order of JAS aircraft.[31]

Domestic Production Capacity and Industry Strategy

Fighter-attack aircraft production in Sweden has proceeded without time lags between generations. Sweden has sought to avoid dependence on other countries for its arms procurement, which could make it susceptible to pressure in wartime. A domestic arms industry that can develop and produce weapons has been regarded as a condition for Sweden's military independence. Thus, Sweden has had an unusually large arms industry in relation to its size, and is unusually self-sufficient, producing 70 percent of its military equipment.[32]

The government also thinks that the arms industry makes a substantial contribution to the Swedish economy.[33] The industry employs 25,000 people; another 8,000 work for sub-contractors. These 33,000 people represent 10 percent of total employment in the Swedish machinery and metal-working industry. Sweden's great competence in

---

[29] Ibid., p. 129.
[30] "Akut ekonomisk kris i flygvapnet" (Acute economic crisis in the Air Force), *Svenska Dagbladet*, May 4, 1994, p. 11.
[31] "Nye ÖB vill köpa fler Jas-plan" (New Supreme Commander wants to buy more JAS planes), *Dagens Nyheter*, December 3, 1993, p. A5.
[32] S. Hirdman, *Sweden's Policy on Arms Exports*, Ministry for Foreign Affairs Information (Stockholm: Norstedts, 1993), p. 1.
[33] *Prop. 1991/92:102*, pp. 78–79.

the arms industry also allows it to take part in the international exchange of knowledge and in international arms projects.[34]

These security and economic considerations play a part in Sweden's procurement decisions. For example, in the 1970s, when the Riksdag was considering a new combat aircraft, the government stressed that the purchase of a foreign aircraft would mean the end of the development capacity of Sweden's aircraft industry. The life cycle of military aircraft was lengthening, so the Swedish Armed Forces would not have a continuous need for development of new aircraft, but some level of research, development, and production was considered necessary to ensure the maintenance of the current fighter-attack force. Another consequence of the reduced need for domestic fighter-attack aircraft production was judged to be the need to cut the fighter-attack workforce by 50 percent. The government had already begun to provide state loans to the domestic aircraft industry. It was also thought that the development of a Swedish fighter would guarantee a base for continued investment in civilian aircraft programs, while civilian production was seen as a precondition for developing and producing a multi-role fighter at an acceptable cost. There was also broad consensus in the Riksdag that the Air Force was a vital part of the Armed Forces, and that the country's capacity to develop and produce military aircraft was of great importance for Sweden's security and defense policies.[35]

The government recognizes that it cannot maintain the current range and degree of independence of the arms industry. The increasing technical complexity and development costs of weapon systems, combined with reduced orders for each system, will lead to restructuring and some reduction of the industry as well as increased international cooperation. Thus, priorities must be set among different arms production sectors. The criteria that have been set up for making such priorities are, first, that Sweden must be able to use and maintain its equipment in wartime and in war-threatening crises without any foreign support, and second, that Swedish know-how must be guaranteed for technologies that other countries guard with special secrecy and whose delivery would be blocked during a crisis.[36] In other

---

[34] Ibid., p. 77.

[35] *Faktaboken om JAS 39 Gripen* (Linköping: IG JAS, 1991), pp. 11–12; and *Regeringens proposition 1979/80:117 (Government Bill Fiscal Year 1979/80 No. 117).*

[36] *Prop. 1991/92:102,* pp. 10 and 77–85; and *1991/92:FöU12,* pp. 6, 98–100.

types of crisis the requirement for an independent arms industry could be relaxed as a consequence of Sweden's possible future membership of the European Union.[37]

It is the government view that cancellation of the JAS project would have serious and far-reaching negative consequences for Swedish industry and for general high technology competence. For example, "some fields in engineering at the universities would have to be reduced or disappear altogether, and the civilian part of the aircraft industry would encounter difficulties even in completing its [current] aircraft projects, the Saab 340 and Saab 2000."[38]

The government's position on the further development of fighter-attack aircraft is that "the development potential for the JAS shall be used to its fullest extent so that domestic as well as future foreign customers' demands of the system can be met."[39] Further development of the original 1982 JAS 39 version is expected. It is believed that Sweden's competence in military aircraft would be facilitated through the transfer of knowledge to the Swedish industry that would result from increasing international cooperation in the field of aero-tech.[40]

In January 1994, the government announced a joint government-industry support program for the maintenance and development of the Swedish aerospace industry. A total of SEK 180 mn was devoted to a national research and development (R&D) program in aerospace technology; a new institution that will promote R&D in this sector; and increased resources for university education in aerospace technology.[41]

The industry's current orders include the modernization of the Air Force's Viggens, and 140 Gripens. No new type of fighter-attack aircraft is under development, but the Gripen is undergoing continuous development. In addition to domestic production, the industry has some modernization work on previously exported fighter-attack aircraft. Sweden is bound by an agreement with Finland and Austria to provide service for their Drakens until 1995.[42] (Denmark deploys

---

[37] Prime Minister Carl Bildt in his introduction to *Prop. 1991/92:102*, p. 10.

[38] *Prop. 1991/92:102*, p. 68 (author's translation).

[39] Ibid., p. 68.

[40] Ibid., p. 81.

[41] "Möjligt med nytt stridsflyg efter JAS" (Possibility of a new combat aircraft after JAS), *Svenska Dagbladet*, January 30, 1994.

[42] Engman, personal communication.

Draken aircraft as well, but is said to look for an F-16 upgrade rather than upgrading its Drakens.)

SAAB AND IG JAS

Saab-Scania is the only aircraft producer in Sweden. In 1993, its military aircraft activities were organized in the Saab Military Aircraft Division, part of Saab Aircraft along with Saab Aircraft AB (commercial aircraft) and Saab Service Partner. Resources were shared between the military and commercial operations and some production was carried out jointly. In early 1994 the company decided to merge Saab Military Aircraft with Saab-Scania's other arms-producing operations as Saab Defense.[43]

Sales by Saab Aircraft have declined since 1991. A rationalization program is being carried out to adjust its capacity to the downturn of the market within the commercial and military operations. Its workforce has fallen from 7,200 at the end of 1990 to about 6,000 at the end of 1993. There are plans to cut it to 5,350.

Sales by Saab Military Aircraft accounted for 37 percent of total sales in the Saab Aircraft business area in 1993. The main program is the JAS 39 Gripen; other operations include advanced development, modification, and maintenance of earlier aircraft systems, such as the Viggen and Sk 60. These programs accounted for 27 percent of total sales in 1993.[44]

Saab produces one commercial aircraft, the Saab 340 regional airliner; 351 had been delivered by the end of 1993. Another regional airliner, the Saab 2000, is in the development and testing stage.

The prime contractor for the Gripen program is an industrial consortium formed for this purpose, Industrigruppen JAS (IG JAS). It includes the main producers in the Swedish aerospace sector: Saab-Scania, FFV Aerotech (Celsius), Ericsson Radar Electronics, LM Ericsson Telecommunications, and Volvo Flygmotor AB. Saab-Scania is the airframe contractor of the program, and most of the development, assembly, and testing takes place at its facilities.

---

[43] Saab Defense also includes Saab Missiles (autonomous weapons), Saab Instruments (defense electronics and optronics) and Saab Training Systems (military training matériel).

[44] Saab-Scania Holdings Group, *Annual Report 1993*, pp. 22–24.

IG JAS employed about 3,300 people in 1991 (mostly within Saab Aircraft), about half of them university-educated engineers.[45] By 1993, IG JAS employed 4,000 people at Saab Aircraft, Volvo Flygmotor, and Ericsson Radar Electronics.[46] (See Table 10.1.) The 1982 agreement between IG JAS and the government included an employment goal for the Gripen program: 800 jobs would be created within ten years in regions with high unemployment; at least 100 of these would be in the Norrbotten region in northern Sweden. By 1987 the Gripen program had created 1,200 jobs.

Table 10.1. Swedish Military Aircraft Industry Employment 1990–1993

	1990	1991	1992	1993
Saab Aircraft Division	4,000	3,500	3,000	2,855
Ericsson Radar Electronics	2,475	2,250	2,188	2,194
FFV Aerotech	2,350	1,435	1,500	1,400
Volvo Flygmotor AB	1,300	2,050	2,083	1,873
Total	**10,125**	**9,235**	**8,771**	**8,322**

Sources: "Svensk försvarsindustri" (Swedish defense industry), Sveriges Försvarsindustriförening (FIF, Swedish Defense Industry Association), March 4, 1992, pp.1-5; and "Nya bilagor till Fakta om försvarsindustrin," FIF, March 11, 1994.
Notes: The figures refer to employees in war matériel operations only. Saab Aircraft Division was replaced by a new unit, Saab Military Aircraft, on April 1, 1994. Engine maintenance activities for the Air Force by FFV Aerotech and Volvo Flygmotor were merged in 1991 into a joint venture, Volvo Aerosupport.

IG JAS produces about 60 percent of the overall program. The rest is weapons, electronic countermeasures, ground equipment etc., that are being procured directly by Försvarets Matérielverk (FMV).[47] An estimated 40 percent of the share of the total value of a complete Gripen is foreign components.[48] It was understood in the contract between IG JAS and FMV that foreign collaboration would be needed in order to keep development costs down, but the effects of this lower indigenous production were to be reduced through other industrial in-

---

[45] S. Fölster, "JAS ger en samhällsekonomisk vinst" (The JAS program is profitable for the national economy), *Svenska Dagbladet*, December 19, 1991, p. 3; Minister of Defense Anders Björck, speech in Linköping, April 1,1992; and *Prop. 1991/92:102*, p. 67.
[46] *SOU 1993:119*, p. 125.
[47] *Faktaboken*, p. 20.
[48] *Prop. 1991/92:102*, p. 66.

vestments, governmental support, and development and production of civilian air and space products.[49]

The industry is convinced there will be no cutbacks in the JAS 39 Gripen program, and it also expects an order for a third series of 150–180 aircraft from the Swedish government.[50] IG JAS is considering development of the JAS-39C, a version with a more powerful engine and improved radar and weapon systems.[51]

Exports

In 1993, the value of Swedish arms exports was SEK 2,863 mn (around U.S. $350 mn), of which SEK 1,216 mn was military equipment for combat (MEC) and SEK 1,647 mn was other military equipment (OME).[52] These exports account for 1 to 2 percent of total Swedish exports, and 40 percent of the value of arms production.[53] Sweden's share in total global exports of major weapon systems is about 1 percent.

Swedish arms exports peaked in 1988/89 with volumes twice as high as in 1993, reflecting a single large order to India, and have since returned to roughly the same level as ten years earlier. However, since Sweden has expanded its definition of war matériel, the 1993 figure includes items that are not included in the figures for previous years. Recalculated data show a significantly lower level for 1993.

Sweden has delivered military equipment to about 35–40 countries each year during the past decade, and roughly 65 countries have received Swedish war matériel. Roughly half of Swedish arms exports have gone to Western Europe (half of these to the other Nordic countries), 30 percent or more to Asia, and about 10 percent to North America. There have been few recipient countries in Africa, Latin

---

[49] *Faktaboken*, pp. 7, 19.

[50] Personal communication, J. Ahlgren, Director of public relations at Saab-Scania; and "North European countries to bolster air power," *Defense News*, January 24, 1994, p. 16.

[51] Ibid.

[52]*Regeringens skrivelse 1993/94:237 med redogörelse för den svenska krigsmaterielexporten år 1993* (Government report to Parliament on Swedish war matériel exports during 1993) (Stockholm: Allmänna Förlaget, 1994), p. 6.

[53] In the past, the export share was around 50 per cent. *1991/92:FöU12*, p. 99.

America and Oceania, and exports to the Middle East and East Europe have been negligible.[54]

Major recipients in the developing world, ranked by imports from 1990 to 1992, were India, Singapore, Malaysia, Brazil, Tunisia, Uruguay, Pakistan and Indonesia.[55]

Since 1991 Asian imports of Swedish military equipment have declined substantially to a level of 6–14 percent. This is primarily the result of the completion of a large order by India, signed in 1986, for Swedish howitzers. Since 1992, Australia has taken a significant share of Swedish exports of military equipment because of a large order for submarine systems, including licensed production of a Swedish design as a long-term industrial contract. The volume of deliveries of military equipment to Western Europe (at constant prices) was lower from 1990 to 1993 than from 1986 to 1989.

Sweden exports all types of military equipment. Its most lucrative military exports annually include munitions and pieces of ordnance. Aircraft and aircraft components account for 5–10 percent of the value of total arms exports.

Foreign sales of the JAS 39 Gripen are being strongly promoted. The decision to approve development of its trainer version, the JAS 39B, is considered an important condition for a successful export strategy.[56] However, no export deals have been concluded. The only firm competition in which the JAS 39 entered was for the Finnish Air Force, but in May 1992, Finland chose the U.S. F/A-18 Hornet.

Exports would lower costs for both IG JAS and the government. According to Saab, the volume of orders must at least double, and preferably triple or quadruple, to make the price of the JAS 39 Gripen competitive on the international market.[57] Official unit cost prices for the Gripen, however, are much lower than those of its competitors. Estimated average unit fly-away prices for the Gripen range from

---

[54] Hirdman, *Sweden's Policy*, p. 15.

[55] *Regeringens skrivelse 1992/93 med redogörelse for den svenska krigsmaterielexporten år 1992* (Government report to Parliament on Swedish war matériel exports during 1992) (Stockholm: Allmänna Förlaget, 1993).

[56] See for example the analysis of the Supreme Commander of the Swedish Armed Forces in his background report to the 1992 Defense Decision, ÖB 92 (Stockholm, June 14, 1991).

[57] *Svenska Dagbladet*, August 10, 1993, p. 1.

about SEK 150 mn ($19 mn)[58] to SEK 130–160 mn.[59] However, the unit program cost is SEK 430 mn.

Until 1993, the Gripen was only promoted in Western Europe, with markets most likely seen in Austria, Hungary, and Norway.[60] Although some Asian countries were believed to have an interest in the Gripen, IG JAS thought that the political situation in those countries did not permit sales.[61] By early 1993 both the perceptions and the marketing activities of IG JAS had changed substantially. A list of potential buyers of the Gripens presented by Saab Military Aircraft in March 1993 included Argentina, Brazil, Chile, Ecuador, Malaysia, New Zealand, Singapore, and Thailand. Saab estimated that these countries and Western Europe would replace 1,500 aircraft in the next 17 years, and that it could capture about one-third of this market; that is, it could export 500 planes through 2010.[62] The Gripen has since been marketed in several countries outside Western Europe, including Chile and Malaysia.

Industry and the government cooperate closely in export promotion. In March 1993, Koordinations-och Referensgruppen (KRG, or the Coordination and Reference Group) was established, with representatives from the Ministry of Defense Krigsmatérielinspektionen (War Matériel Inspectorate), the Foreign Trade Department of the Ministry for Foreign Affairs, the unit for company development in the Ministry of Industry and Commerce (Näringsdepartementet), the arms procurement agency (FMV), and Saab Military Aircraft. This group was created because fighter aircraft deals are largely a matter of politics, government export guarantees, and offsets,[63] which had been illustrated by the failure to sell the Gripen to Finland.

It is unclear how the 1993 accident will affect potential export customers. Saab has repeatedly argued that it will have no impact on export sales, since accidents are common for prototypes of new gen-

---

[58] *Konsekvenser*, Appendix 1, p. 7.

[59] Personal communication with Nils Gullberg, who is responsible for the JAS project at the Ministry of Defense, January 14, 1994.

[60] *Svenska Dagbladet*, June 14, 1993, p. 6.

[61] Interview with E. L. Asplund, Assistant Director of Information at Saab Military Aircraft, May 1992; and Sahlin interview.

[62] "Saab satsar på export av JAS" (Saab counts on exports of JAS), *Dagens Nyheter*, March 19, 1993, p. A5.

[63] "Exportgrupp för JAS utsedd" (Export group for JAS appointed), *Svenska Dagbladet*, March 31, 1993, p. 10.

eration aircraft. Indeed, shortly after the accident, the president of Austria confirmed that it would include the JAS in its 1996 review.[64] Hungary also declared its continued interest in September 1993, but has since procured second-hand Russian MiG-29s. In addition, an opinion poll taken one month after the accident showed that 93 percent of the respondents—74 defense politicians and key military people from 23 countries—did not find the accident remarkable.[65]

GOVERNMENT POLICY ON EXPORTS

The major theme in current government arms export policy is that although arms exports help maintain Sweden's indigenous arms production capacity, their role is limited and will further decline in importance. Therefore, the government sees international cooperation in armaments development and production as essential to the future survival of the Swedish arms industry. This implies a major reorientation of Sweden's arms trade and production policy.

A recent study on the economic role of arms export for Swedish arms procurement and for the Swedish arms industry made a number of conclusions that support the government's view.[66] First, a viable arms industry must have a capacity greater than what can be filled with orders from Sweden alone. While exports help cover the costs of maintaining the industry, their contribution varies significantly among firms. The income from exports is less important than their ability to help maintain the industry.

Second, civil production can at most constitute a marginal alternative to exports in this respect, though there are differences from firm to firm here too; in the aviation and to some extent the electronics field, military-industrial resources and capacities have sometimes been used for civil production.

Third, if all arms exports were stopped, some firms would not survive, and Sweden would be forced to purchase a substantial portion of its required weapon systems from abroad. How that would affect the Swedish arms procurement bill cannot be assessed. Finally,

---

[64] *Dagens Nyheter*, August 25, 1993, p. A8.

[65] *Svenska Dagbladet*, October 31, 1993, p. 8.

[66] P. Jennergren, "Företagsekonomiska effekter av svensk vapenexport" (Business economic effects of Swedish arms exports), App. 2 in *Utlandssamverkan på krigsmaterielområdet* [SOU 1989:102] (*Foreign Cooperation in War Matériel*), Swedish Official Reports Series (Stockholm: Allmänna Förlaget, 1990).

arms exports will probably be reduced in the future. It may no longer be financially feasible to develop certain types of systems within the country. This could reduce exports; it is difficult to sell arms abroad without being able to point to purchases of the same system by the Swedish defense forces. In addition, arms exports are gradually changing in character, increasingly becoming a question of technology transfer.

Government policy is based on two propositions. First, the possibilities of using exports to increase production and better recuperate costs are limited, both because the world market demand is declining and due to foreign policy reasons to favor a restrictive arms export policy. Second, exports and other forms of collaboration with other countries are increasingly tied together in a variety of common projects, facilitated by the fact that the borders between civil and military technologies are becoming increasingly unclear. Therefore, great importance should be attached to the possibilities of foreign armaments collaboration.[67]

The government is positive toward international agreements on further restrictions on the export of conventional weapons, but also feels that all countries have a legitimate right to self-defense and to procure the equipment required for that purpose.[68]

The current national policy on the export of military equipment and international collaboration on armaments came into force on January 1, 1993.[69] As with the preceding policy, the government must specifically permit export of military equipment. Applications for export licenses are reviewed by the Military Equipment Inspectorate (Krigsmatérielinspektionen, KMI) in the Foreign Trade Department of the Ministry for Foreign Affairs and are evaluated according to a number of guidelines.[70] Permits for exports may only be granted if the export is considered necessary to fulfill the Swedish defense forces' requirements for war matériel or know-how, or is otherwise desirable

---

[67] *Prop. 1991/92:102*, p. 84.

[68] Hirdman interview; Sahlin interview.

[69] Act 1992:1300 and Ordinance 1992:1303. This legislation also regulates production of and international collaboration on armaments.

[70] *Regeringens proposition 1991/92:174 Lag om krigsmateriel* (*Government Bill Fiscal Year 1991/92, No. 174: Law on War Matériel*) (Stockholm: Gotab, 1992); *Report No. 1 by the Parliamentary Committee on foreign affairs* (Stockholm: Gotab, 1992), which contains the formulations of the decision by Parliament; and *SOU 1989:102*, the government study on which the decision is based.

for reasons of national security, and the deal does not conflict with the principles and aims of Swedish foreign policy. In addition, there are unconditional and conditional obstacles to exports or collaboration. According to the unconditional obstacles, such permits may not be granted if the export would contravene an international agreement signed by Sweden, a resolution adopted by the UN Security Council, or a rule of international law concerning exports from neutral states in times of armed conflict. The conditional obstacles include violations of human rights, international conflict, and internal armed disturbances in the recipient country.[71]

The new legislation and guidelines have broadened the definition of military equipment so that more products are subject to export control. They have also introduced two broad categories of military equipment: "military equipment for combat purposes" (MEC), and "other military equipment" (OME). OME consists of items previously contained under the single category "military equipment" and items that were not previously controlled. The conditional guidelines for OME are less restrictive. For example, if a potential recipient country is "involved in an international conflict which may lead to an armed conflict," it should receive an export permit for OME, but not for MEC.[72] Another difference is a positive presumption for exports of OME, but not for MEC.

Finally, the export rules for international collaboration in armaments have been changed fundamentally. Under specified conditions, a country cooperating with Sweden may freely export equipment that includes Swedish components.[73]

In practice, changes in the arms export policy are usually slow in Sweden, since the opposition parties in the Riksdag are involved in deciding which countries are eligible for exports. Although formally the opposition only has an advisory role, the practice has always been to have consensus in decisions on arms exports. In 1992, KMI determined that the application of the rules had not changed in any significant ways during recent years.[74] While the circle of eligible recipi-

---

[71] Hirdman, *Sweden's Policy*, pp. 37–39, which contains an unofficial translation of "guidelines for the exportation of military equipment and other forms of collaboration abroad."

[72] Ibid., p. 38.

[73] Ibid., p. 39.

[74] Hirdman interview.

ents of Swedish arms was being widened, the KMI felt that this was a result of changes in their political and security situation, rather than in Sweden's export policy. According to the KMI, potential new recipients primarily include countries in Central Europe; the Middle East was the only region for which liberalization of Swedish arms exports was not being considered.[75]

By early 1994 these assessments were already outdated. Export permits had been granted to Bahrain, Kuwait, Oman, Qatar, Saudi Arabia, Thailand, and the United Arab Emirates.[76] All permits to the Gulf countries and most to Thailand were for OME, the less restrictive category, and some were for types of military equipment that had not previously been regulated. The government argues that Sweden's arms export policy has not become less restrictive, but critics argue that acceptance of these countries as recipients of OME will facilitate their future acceptance as recipients of MEC. The government has also approved marketing of submarines to Pakistan and Thailand. The decision on Pakistan reportedly includes far-reaching commitments on export credit guarantees and on continued deliveries during future conflict.[77]

PAST AND FUTURE COMBAT AIRCRAFT EXPORTS

During the past two decades Sweden has exported 51 Draken to Denmark, 45 to Finland, and 25 to Austria.[78] There have been no exports of the Viggen, despite strong marketing efforts in the 1970s.[79] The Viggen was marketed in Europe and in developing countries.[80]

In the future, Sweden could sell Drakens and Viggens retired from Swedish service, and the new JAS 39 Gripen. The sale of retired fighters is currently not being discussed at all, but Sweden does not preclude this as a possibility. However, the rather long service life planned for these aircraft according to current defense planning

[75] Hirdman interview.
[76] "Svenska vapenaffärer granskade" (Swedish arms export deals investigated), *Svenska Dagbladet*, February 27, 1994, p. 8.
[77] "Pakistan garanteras ubåtar även under krig" (Pakistan is also guaranteed submarines during war), *Dagens Nyheter*, February 19, 1994, p. A4.
[78] Interviews with Karl Lundholm, Saab Military Aircraft Division, June 17, 1992, and Kari Kokkonen, General Defense Staff, Helsinki, June 17, 1992.
[79] Hirdman interview.
[80] The United States once blocked a sale of the Viggen to India. This was possible because Viggen had a U.S.-produced engine (Pratt & Whitney); Hirdman interview.

means that they would not be a very attractive offer.[81] The Viggen fighters are also considered very expensive to operate and maintain.

It is often repeated that the JAS 39 Gripen is not economically dependent on exports; that is, the calculations that formed the basis for the 1982 decision to go ahead with the program were not based on any exports. Still, the interest in exporting the JAS 39 is very strong, both in the industry and in the government—many feel that the sale of the JAS 39 abroad would benefit Sweden's security policy, defense economy, and industrial relations.

In particular, there is an interest in finding an international partner for the further development of the JAS 39 Gripen design in the late 1990s. Sweden, like most other countries, will have resource constraints in carrying out future modifications of JAS 39. Therefore, Sweden probably needs a future partner in order to maintain its combat aircraft industry, one of the strengths on which its policy of neutrality rests.

---

[81] Sahlin interview.

Chapter 11

Jonathan Cohen
Andrew Peach

The Spread of Advanced Combat Aircraft

As domestic orders for combat aircraft have declined, the major arms-producing nations have turned increasingly to exports as a way to maintain production lines, design capability, and jobs. Many producers are hoping for increased exports to East and Southeast Asia, South Asia, and the Middle East. While these regions have had sizable recent imports, their current firm and potential orders for 1994–2000 cannot begin to offset the global drop in imports since the end of the Cold War, much less the global decline in domestic orders in the arms-producing countries.

IDDS estimates indicate that worldwide transfers of combat aircraft averaged about 740 per year in the 1970s and 615 per year in the 1980s.[1] In contrast, for the rest of the 1990s, international transfers will average between 195 and 280 planes per year.[2] Moreover, no region's average annual import figure for the rest of the decade will be as high as that in the 1970s or 1980s. Rather than offset the slump in domestic orders, export orders will decline as well.

---

[1] *IDDS Almanac 1994: World Combat Aircraft Holdings, Production, and Trade* (Cambridge, MA: Institute for Defense and Disarmament Studies, forthcoming).
[2] Firm orders already placed will result in deliveries in 1994–2000 averaging 195 per year; IDDS estimates of maximum potential additional orders come to an average of 85 per year.

Jonathan Cohen is a research fellow at the Institute for Defense and Disarmament Studies in Cambridge, Massachusetts, where he specializes in the conventional arms trade.

Andrew Peach is a research fellow at the Institute for Defense and Disarmament Studies in Cambridge, Massachusetts, where he specializes in U.S. and West European air forces and aerospace industries.

Table 11.1. Importers' Combat Aircraft Acquisitions and Holdings 1994–2000

| Country | Combat Aircraft Acquisition 1994-2000 | | | | | | Combat Aircraft Holdings | | | |
| | All | | Dom | Imports | | | 1993 | | 2000 Projected | |
	Firm	Total	Firm	Firm	Potential	Total	Old	Total	Old	Total
China	636	696	490	146	60	206	4,000	4,543	2,037	2,790
Taiwan	335	335	125	210		210	424	434	85	425
South Korea	102	102		102		102	426	474	310	460
Malaysia	44	59		44	15	59	54	54	40	84
Japan	46	46	24	22		22	137	375	104	344
Thailand	12	27		12	15	27	59	83	30	112
North Korea	0	25			25	25	834	990	630	765
Indonesia	5	20		5	15	20	42	59	22	59
Singapore	0	18			18	18	146	151	127	151
Australia	0	15			15	15	0	92	0	92
Total E&SEA	**1,180**	**1,343**	**639**	**541**	**163**	**704**	**6,122**	**7,255**	**3,385**	**5,282**
Iran	98	173		98	75	173	173	288	129	344
Saudi Arabia	132	157		132	25	157	96	266		315
Syria	0	60			60	60	222	549	162	549
Egypt	46	46		46		46	230	522	90	398
Israel	21	45		21	24	45	317	764	95	570
UAE	0	25			25	25	0	45		70
Oman	8	18		8	10	18	13	45		42
Kuwait	0	15			15	15	22	77	20	75
Total ME&NAfr	**305**	**539**	**0**	**305**	**234**	**539**	**1,073**	**2,556**	**496**	**2,363**
Turkey	100	100		100		100	565	683	395	610
Italy	77	85	64	13	8	21	272	438	53	320
Greece	40	65		40	25	65	235	452	115	372
Finland	64	64		64		64	65	65		64
Switzerland	34	34		34		34	241	241	116	150
Austria	0	25			25	25	24	24		24
Spain	8	23		8	15	23	30	171		158
Portugal	20	20		20		20	22	74		70
Total Eur&Can	**343**	**416**	**64**	**279**	**73**	**352**	**1,454**	**2,148**	**679**	**1,768**
Pakistan	138	178		138	40	178	321	464	219	450
India	101	151		101	50	151	363	774	250	722
Total SA	**239**	**329**	**0**	**239**	**90**	**329**	**684**	**1,238**	**469**	**1,172**
Brazil	30	42	30		12	12	75	100	50	106
Chile	0	15			15	15	50	65	16	68
Total LA	**30**	**57**	**30**	**0**	**27**	**27**	**125**	**165**	**66**	**174**
South Africa	0	15			15	15	0	69	0	75
Total Afr	**0**	**15**	**0**	**0**	**15**	**15**	**0**	**69**	**0**	**75**
Global Total	**2,097**	**2,699 0**	**733**	**1,364**	**602**	**1,966**	**9,458**	**13,431**	**5,095**	**10,834**

Source: "IDDS Almanac 1994."

Notes: The table covers only countries with firm or potential combat aircraft import orders for delivery between 1994–2000 and annual military spending over $1 bn. IDDS estimates that the rest of the world may import up to 50 combat aircraft by 2000. "Old" indicates aircraft designed before 1966. The 12 aircraft shown in the potential import column for Brazil refer to possible domestic production of the AM-X.

Most of the leading importers have already placed orders for combat aircraft to be delivered by 2000. Presently, there are firm import orders for 1,364 combat aircraft. (See Table 11.1.) IDDS estimates that through 2000, no more than about 650 additional aircraft will be ordered for import worldwide. Out of the 21 countries that have placed firm orders for combat aircraft to be delivered from 1994 through 2000, IDDS estimates that only six may place further orders for 25 or more combat aircraft by 2000.[3] Among all remaining countries worldwide (those that have not placed import orders for delivery in 1994–2000), IDDS estimates that at most nine countries which had 1992 military spending over $1 bn (Australia, Austria, Chile, Kuwait, North Korea, Singapore, South Africa, Syria, and the United Arab Emirates) may place orders for aircraft to be delivered by 2000.[4] Import and spending trends from 1972 to 1992 show that countries that spend less than $1 bn a year on defense rarely import combat aircraft, and import few planes when they do.[5] (See Table 11.2.)

Table 11.2. Firm Import Orders by Level of Military Spending

						Deliveries of firm orders for new combat aircraft			
	Countries						Imports		
1992		Of which:			No. with	Importers		Average order	
Military		Pro-	Embar-	Candi-	imports	as share of	Total	Per	Per
Spending	Total	ducers	goed	dates	94–00	candidates	94–00	candidate	importer
> $35 bn	5	5	0	0	0	..	0	0	0
$4-32 bn	23	1	1	21	12	57%	999	48	83
$2-4 bn	17	0	1	16	7	44%	352	22	50
$1-2 bn	16	0	1	15	2	13%	13	1	7
< $1 bn	50	0	3	47	0	0%	0	0	0
Total	**111**	**6**	**6**	**99**	**21**	**21%**	**1,364**	**14**	**65**

Source: "IDDS Almanac 1994."
Note: All countries with combat aircraft are included.

---

[3] IDDS estimates of potential additional orders by country, shown in Table 11.1, are based on reports of planned procurement and holdings, trends in military spending, and the size, age, and sophistication of current aircraft holdings.
[4] IDDS estimates that countries with military spending under $1 bn may import a combined total of up to 50 combat aircraft by 2000.
[5] Randall Forsberg and Jonathan Cohen, "The Global Arms Market: Prospects for the Coming Decade," Cambridge, Mass.: IDDS, February 9, 1994.

There are several reasons for the decline in international transfers of combat aircraft and other major weapon systems. First, the end of the East-West confrontation has removed a major impetus for arming. Many countries—particularly in Europe—are reducing force levels rather than replace aging aircraft on a one-for-one basis.

Second, the enormous costs of procuring new combat aircraft, coupled with fiscal constraints, have prompted many importers to upgrade older aircraft rather than buy new aircraft from the major producers. For example, many countries with large inventories of U.S.-made F-5s or Soviet-made MiG-21s (Canada, Greece, Turkey, India, Hungary, Romania, and the Czech Republic) are upgrading those aircraft or contemplating doing so.[6] Others are likely to follow suit.

Third, some countries are importing used aircraft with which to modernize their air forces at little or no cost. More than 300 used aircraft are already promised for delivery between 1993 and 1997. Further transfers of used aircraft are likely later this decade as both the United States and Russia implement deep force cuts, creating large surpluses of front-line combat aircraft.[7] Many European states will also have surplus aircraft as former Warsaw Pact countries reduce their forces in compliance with the Treaty on Conventional Armed Forces in Europe (CFE), and NATO countries respond to the new security environment with cuts of their own.

Fourth, secondary arms producers are procuring more weapons at home. Five countries that formerly imported most of their combat aircraft—China, Taiwan, Japan, India, and Brazil—have developed indigenous aerospace industries that are currently producing combat aircraft for domestic use (and, in the case of China, export). A number of other countries, including South Africa, Israel, Romania, the Czech Republic, Slovakia, Poland, and Argentina, have some production expertise and facilities as a result of earlier work on combat aircraft or current production of armed jet trainer aircraft. As the cost of advanced combat aircraft keeps rising, the secondary producers may encroach further on the primary producers' markets through produc-

---

[6] *IDDS Almanac 1994.*

[7] The United States may sell up to 400 out of 700 F-16A/Bs retired from the U.S. Air Force, and transfer the remainder at no charge to close allies. See Thomas E. Ricks, "Pentagon Considers Selling Overseas a Large Part of High-Tech Weaponry," *Wall Street Journal,* February 14, 1994, p. A20.

tion of less capable and cheaper aircraft for domestic use and possibly export.[8]

The following sections look at trends among major importers of combat aircraft in East and Southeast Asia; Middle East and North Africa; Europe and Canada; South Asia; Latin America; and sub-Saharan Africa. We clarify where imports are declining and where they are holding steady, and assess the impact of secondary producers of combat aircraft on the world market for international transfers.

East and Southeast Asia

The primary arms producers have put great effort into selling combat aircraft to countries in East and Southeast Asia.[9] Today, this region accounts for nearly 20 percent of the world's holdings of combat aircraft. Of 7,591 combat aircraft in the area, about 85 percent were designed before 1966 and have obsolete technology. To replace the obsolete systems, countries in the region have placed import orders for 541 combat aircraft to be delivered by 2000; including domestically-produced planes, they will acquire at least 1,180 combat aircraft. This will replace about 20 percent of the region's older aircraft.

Imports in East and Southeast Asia account for about 40 percent of global firm orders for combat aircraft. Several factors are driving arms procurement in the region. First, the United States has reduced its military presence in East and Southeast Asia since the end of the Cold War; despite pledges by the Clinton administration that there

---

[8] The current fly-away cost of the F-16C/D (Block 50) is about $23 mn ("Lockheed is Offering Air Force F-16 Jets at a Reduced Cost," *Wall Street Journal*, July 7, 1994, p. B2), while the MiG-29 is priced at $25 mn and the MiG-31 at $45–50 mn (Mark Galeotti, "The Russian Arms Bazaar," *Jane's Intelligence Review*, November 1992, pp. 490–91). Cost estimates found in Chapter 2 are comparable for the MiG-29 and $35–40 mn for the MiG-31. Next-generation aircraft are likely to cost far more. Some estimates put the unit cost of the French Rafale at about $56 mn ("France Boosts its Rafale Order to Five," *Jane's Defence Weekly*, Vol. 21, No. 9 (March 5, 1994), p. 30), while an unofficial U.S. government estimate puts the unit price of the F-22 at $130 mn, excluding some development costs, or $217 mn if those costs are included. (Jeff Cole, "New F-22 Funding Cuts May Increase Jet Fighter's Final Tab by $700 Million," *Wall Street Journal*, January 4, 1994, p. A3).
[9] Countries in East and Southeast Asia that spend more than $1 bn annually on defense are Australia, China, Indonesia, Japan, Malaysia, North Korea, Singapore, South Korea, Taiwan, Thailand, and Vietnam.

will be no further cuts, many nations fear that the United States will further reduce its commitments and cease to play a stabilizing role in the region after 2000. As a result, regional rivalries that were long suppressed by the threat of a major East-West war may again rise to the surface. While many countries in the region would like to cooperate on security matters within a regional organization such as the Association of Southeast Asian Nations (ASEAN), there is no common threat for a substantial group to focus on; instead, each country is attempting to allay its own security concerns with force modernization.

Second, China's expanding economy, massive military, territorial claims in the South China Sea, and recent moves to acquire advanced air and sea armaments and technology have created concern in many East and Southeast Asian nations. Under its 1992 Territorial Waters Act, China claims sovereignty over the entire South China Sea, and reserves the right to use force to maintain control over the shipping lanes and the Paracel and Spratley Island groups—to which China, Vietnam, Malaysia, Brunei, Taiwan, and the Philippines all have ancestral claims.[10] These islands would give China control over international shipping routes from the Persian Gulf to Japan, and over the major gas and oil deposits that the area may hold. Beijing has also refused to renounce the use of force to reunite Taiwan with mainland China. Many East and Southeast Asian countries view Chinese military and diplomatic moves as hegemonic and are modernizing their air forces to counter potential future Chinese threats.

Third, the continued division of the Korean Peninsula and deployment of large military forces along both sides of the demilitarized zone separating North and South Korea remain prominent security concerns in East Asia. North Korea's nuclear weapon program and its development of medium-range ballistic missiles have heightened military tension throughout Northeast Asia.

Finally, many of these countries have quickly growing economies, allowing them to increase procurement funds. In fact, military spending in East and Southeast Asia has increased steadily since 1983, growing at a real average annual rate of 4 percent.

Because of this spending increase, the primary arms producers have hoped that the countries in East and Southeast Asia would import enough combat aircraft to offset the drop in domestic and export

---

[10] Richard C. Bernard and Barbara Opall, "U.S. Prods Military Dialogue with China," *Defense News*, Vol. 9, No. 10 (March 14–20, 1994), p. 1.

orders elsewhere. IDDS estimates show that this is improbable: beyond the 541 firm import orders already placed, East and Southeast Asian countries are unlikely to order more than 160–165 combat aircraft for delivery by 2000. The resulting range of average annual imports, from a low of 77 for firm orders to a high of 101 for firm plus potential additional orders, lies well below the annual averages for the 1970s and 1980s of 156 and 125, respectively.

Projected Chinese combat aircraft acquisition through domestic production (490) and import (146) accounts for over half of the regional acquisition and almost one-quarter of global acquisition of new aircraft in 1994–2000. China is currently modernizing its force of some 4,500 combat aircraft through a combination of means: purchasing Russian aircraft, producing more advanced versions of its J-7 and J-8 aircraft, developing new aircraft such as the HJ-7, F-9, and XJ-10, and retiring some of the oldest systems without replacement. IDDS estimates indicate that by 2000, China will have retired or replaced over half of its 4,000 aircraft of pre-1960 designs and reduced its total holdings to about 2,800 aircraft. This smaller force, with up to 700 new aircraft, will be much more capable than the present one.

China merits special attention as a secondary arms producer. From 1994 to 2000, China will produce more aircraft for domestic use than any other country in the world, and it will be second only to the United States in overall aircraft production (for domestic use and export). Yet China is not a primary producer of advanced combat aircraft; 80 percent of its domestically produced aircraft are based on older Soviet aircraft, mainly the MiG-19, designed in 1955, and the MiG-21, designed in 1958. The remaining, Chinese-designed aircraft, which resemble their Soviet predecessors, are not technologically advanced by current international standards.

After producing an average of 340 aircraft (mainly MiG-19 copies) per year in the 1970s, China cut its domestic production to 110 aircraft (mainly MiG-21 copies) per year in the 1980s and then 70 aircraft per year in the early 1990s. In 1989, China began producing the J-7III, an improved version of the J-7/MiG-21, at the rate of 50 aircraft per year.[11] It has also begun producing upgraded versions of the same plane, the J-7M and J-7P, for export to Iran and Pakistan. Compared with the J-7III, the export aircraft have more powerful

---

[11] Kenneth W. Allen, *People's Republic of China People's Liberation Army Air Force* (Washington, D.C.: Defense Intelligence Agency, May 1991), p. C-6.

engines and better avionics, supplied by General Electric (GEC) Avionics of Britain.[12] Some developing countries import the Chinese J-7M even though it is technologically inferior to current Western and Russian combat aircraft because it is also far cheaper. With Western avionics, the J-7M sells for only $3.7 mn,[13] compared with the F-16 which sells for $23 mn. China plans to market the J-7 abroad and produce it for the People's Liberation Army Air Force (PLAAF) well into the next century.[14]

Serial production of the J-8II began in 1992. This aircraft is an upgraded, all-weather dual-role version of the Chinese-designed J-8 with Western avionics.[15] In 1986, China and the United States created the "Peace Pearl" program to upgrade the J-8 into the J-8II under the terms of a United States Air Force-sponsored Foreign Military Sale.[16] After the Tiananmen Square incident in 1989, the United States canceled the program but China continued to move ahead without U.S. involvement. Production for the Chinese Navy is currently underway at a rate of about 20 aircraft per year. China is trying to develop and market an export version of the J-8II, the F-8II, but no foreign orders for this plane have been placed to date.

Production of the A-5 Fantan, the most frequently flown aircraft in the PLAAF, continues only for export. The newest export version, the A-5M, contains avionics developed by the Italian company Alenia.[17] Recently, Pakistan placed an order for 98 A-5Ms to be delivered during 1994–1998.

Chinese engineers continue to study Soviet- and Russian-designed aircraft in an effort to integrate new technology into current production lines and perhaps reverse-engineer newly-designed aircraft, as China has done in the past. In January 1993, China reportedly made an agreement with Iran to receive several of the Soviet-designed Iraqi aircraft that were flown to Iran during the Gulf War. Chinese experts have since studied these aircraft and identified several components and sub-systems they can use. For example, China will attempt to

---

[12] Mark Lambert, ed., *Jane's All the World's Aircraft 1993–94* (Surrey, UK: Jane's Information Group, 1993), p. 45.

[13] Kenneth W. Allen, interview with Jonathan Cohen, April 28, 1994.

[14] Ibid.

[15] *Jane's All the World's Aircraft 1993–94*, p. 56.

[16] Richard A. Bitzinger, *Chinese Arms Production and Sales to the Third World* (Santa Monica: RAND, 1991), p. 21.

[17] *Jane's All the World's Aircraft 1993–94*, p. 53.

adapt the MiG-29's R-33 engine for use in the J-7Ms and J-7Ps being built for Iran and Pakistan.[18] It may also try to reverse-engineer the MiG-29 as the basis for a more advanced indigenously produced fighter.

China is also developing four new or modified aircraft: the JH-7, J-9, Super-7, and XJ-10. First flown in 1988, the JH-7 is an all-weather fighter-bomber designed for strike and maritime attack missions. The aircraft was expected to enter service with the PLAAF in 1993 but production has apparently been delayed.[19] Development of the JH-7 is probably continuing, however, as China has begun to market it abroad. The JH-7 will probably not be produced in large quantities unless export orders reduce the high cost of production.[20]

The Super-7, an upgraded version of the J-7M to be produced for export only, entered development in 1988 after the China National Aero-Technology Import and Export Corporation signed an agreement with the U.S. Grumman Corporation. U.S. participation was suspended after the Tiananmen Square incident, but China seems to be trying to develop and produce the aircraft by 2000.[21]

The J-9, first flown in 1989, is a single-seat fighter that is expected to enter service with the PLAAF by 2000.[22] The J-9 will probably use Western avionics and may be too expensive for the PLAAF to procure in large quantities. The XJ-10 is an indigenously designed fighter that China claims will belong in the same class as the F-16 and MiG-29. The aircraft will incorporate Israeli technology and is expected to make its initial test flight in 1997.[23]

China did not import any combat aircraft from the time of the Sino-Soviet split (1960) until 1990–1991, when China ordered 12 Su-24s and 72 Su-27s from Russia. China will probably order 70–80 MiG-31s, MiG-29s, Su-27Ms, or Su-30s in the next few years.[24] By

---

[18] "Chinese Air Force Modernization Drive," *BBC Summary of the World*, August 7, 1993.

[19] *Jane's All the World's Aircraft 1993–94*, p. 58.

[20] Allen interview.

[21] *Jane's All the World's Aircraft 1993–94*, p. 44.

[22] Ibid.

[23] "Russia and China Dispute Barter Terms," *Arms Transfers News*, Vol. 94, No. 7 (May 6, 1994), p. 3.

[24] IDDS estimated 146 "firm" import orders for China to be delivered in 1994–2000, as shown in Table 11.1. Fifty-eight of these have been confirmed. The remaining 88 are unconfirmed orders that IDDS believes China has made or will soon do so.

2000, China may import 60 additional combat aircraft, over and above the 160–170 aircraft now on order or likely to be ordered, if independent Chinese development of more advanced aircraft proves unfeasible.

Published reports suggest that ideally, China would like to produce the Russian MiG-31, MiG-29, Su-27M, or Su-30 under license, and also import technology from Russia that will allow it to indigenously design and produce more modern combat aircraft in the future.[25] To close a pending deal for 120 Su-27Ms, officials from Sukhoi, the company building the Su-27M, have proposed to include substantial technology transfer and to establish an Su-27M assembly line in China. China has argued it cannot afford 120 aircraft, and a final agreement remains to be worked out.[26]

Taiwan and Japan are secondary combat aircraft producers. Faced with growing Chinese military capabilities, Taiwan spent $10.46 bn on the military in 1992—a 67 percent real increase over 1984 spending. Taiwan is planning to allocate $30 bn over 1994–2000 for arms procurement, much of it for combat aircraft.[27] Planned procurement includes a domestically-designed fighter, the Ching-Kuo or Indigenous Defense Fighter (IDF), which Taiwan began developing in 1982 after the U.S. government blocked exports of F-16 and F-20 fighters. The Taiwanese Air Force received 10 pre-production IDFs in 1992–1993 and the first production unit in early 1994. The first squadron of 27 IDFs is expected to be operational by the end of 1994.[28] A total production run of 130 aircraft is expected, with the final deliveries scheduled for 1998.[29]

In addition to the IDF, Taiwan has ordered 210 combat aircraft imports for delivery by 2000—the largest number on order in any country. In 1992, the United States agreed to sell 150 F-16A/Bs to

---

[25] Julia A. Ackerman and Michael Collins Dunn, "Chinese Airpower Revs Up," *Air Force Magazine*, Vol. 76, No. 7 (July 1993), pp. 56–59; and David Boey, "Chinese May Choose Su-35 [Su-27M] Over MiG-29," *Defense News*, Vol. 9, No. 12 (March 28–April 3, 1994), p. 14.

[26] Boey, "Chinese May Choose."

[27] "Building up the Island Nation," *Jane's Defence Weekly*, Vol. 21, No. 3 (January 22, 1994), p. 24.

[28] Reuters, "Taiwan: First Home-built Fighter Enters Air Force," February 17, 1994, in *Arms Transfers News*, Vol. 94, No. 3 (February 25, 1994), p. 5.

[29] The initial requirement for 256 IDFs has been reduced due to Taiwan's recent orders for F-16s and Mirage 2000s. See *Jane's All the World's Aircraft 1993–94*, p. 363.

Taiwan for $5.95 bn, with deliveries starting in 1996 or 1997 and continuing until 2000. The same year, Taiwan ordered 60 Mirage 2000-5s for a reported $6.6 bn, with deliveries expected between 1995 or 1996 and 1999. It is very unlikely that Taiwan will import any more combat aircraft by 2000; in that year, its air force will have 335 new combat aircraft and 85 F-5E/Fs, compared with the 434 aging planes in its inventory today.

In Japan, Mitsubishi Heavy Industries is co-developing with Lockheed the FS-X fighter, an upgraded version of the F-16. The Japanese Air Self Defense Force (JASDF) currently plans to produce 72 FS-Xs to replace the Japanese-designed F-1 aircraft in the close air support-fighter role. The total order may eventually reach 130 aircraft if additional versions are developed. The first flight of the FS-X is planned for June 1995, and orders of 12 aircraft per year are expected to be placed in 1996–2001 for delivery in 1999–2004. Since Japan's constitution forbids arms export, the FS-X will not be exported.

Mitsubishi is also currently producing the F-15J air superiority fighter under license from the United States. Production of this aircraft for the JASDF, which began in 1981, is likely to continue through 1996 or 1997. The JASDF ordered 4 F-15s in 1994 and plans to place a final order for 6 in 1995, bringing the total number ordered to 210 aircraft. The final 28 aircraft are scheduled to be delivered in 1994–1997. Japan is unlikely to import any additional combat aircraft for some time following completion of this order because its air force is expected to decrease to about 340 aircraft, consisting mainly or exclusively of new F-15s and F-SXs.

South Korea also has a large number of combat aircraft on order. To compensate for potential U.S. force reductions, South Korea is spending about 30 percent of its $11.4 bn defense budget on weapons procurement.[30] In 1991, South Korea placed a follow-on order for 120 U.S. F-16C/D fighter-bomber aircraft (of which it will produce 72 under license) for $5 bn. In 2001, the South Korean air force will have 168 F-16s and a total combat aircraft inventory around the present size of 460. South Korea might then order more license-built F-16s to replace F-4s and F-5s that will be reaching the end of their planned service lives.

---

[30] Republic of Korea Ministry of National Defense, *Defense White Paper 1993–1994* (Seoul, 1994), pp. 185–187.

To defend its claims in the South China Sea and deter expansionary moves by China, Malaysia is creating a rapid-deployment force that will include newly imported combat aircraft.[31] Malaysia has ordered a total of 44 combat aircraft from the United Kingdom, Russia, and the United States, to replace its current inventory of 33 A-4 and 21 F-5 aircraft. Air force modernization began in 1988 when Malaysia ordered 18 British Hawk 200s. These aircraft will probably be delivered in 1994–1995. In 1993, Malaysia ordered 8 U.S. F/A-18s and announced that it also planned to purchase 18 Russian MiG-29s, a deal that was finalized in mid-1994. The MiG-29s will be delivered by the end of 1995, and the F/A-18s in 1997. Malaysia may import another 15 Hawk 200s to strengthen its air defense.[32]

Thailand and Indonesia have also placed firm orders for combat aircraft to be delivered over the next few years. In 1991, Thailand ordered 18 U.S. F-16s to be delivered in 1993–1995. Thailand has also ordered many used aircraft, including 38 U.S. A-7Es to be delivered in 1995–1997, and 10 U.S. F-5A/B fighters from South Korea, which it will probably receive in 1995–1996. Since November 1993, Thailand has been negotiating with Spain to import 8 used U.S.-UK Harrier attack aircraft.[33] Because of Thailand's modernization program and strong economy, IDDS estimates that it may import another 15 new or used aircraft by 2000.

Indonesia purchased 10 British Hawk 200s in 1992 as part of a plan to buy 100 warplanes over 25 years to replace its aging U.S. A-4s and F-5s. These aircraft are being built under license in Indonesia.[34] Five are presently in service, and the other five are to enter service by the end of 1994. Indonesia has been unable to purchase more Western aircraft due to its human rights violations in East Timor and reported use of the Hawk 200s to attack civilians in that region.[35] Indonesian officials have expressed interest in purchasing another 15 Hawk 200s,

---

[31] Philip Finnegan, "Malaysia Plans to Boost Rapid Deployment," *Defense News*, Vol. 9, No. 25 (June 27–July 3, 1994), p. 6.

[32] Voice of Malaysia (February 25, 1994) in *Foreign Broadcast Information Service* (FBIS), FBIS-EAS-94-038 (February 25, 1994), p. 47.

[33] "Spain: Sale of Harriers to Thailand Under Negotiation," *Arms Transfers News*, Vol. 93, No. 21 (December 10, 1993), p. 4.

[34] *International Security Digest*, Vol. 1, No. 2 (December 1993), p. 2.

[35] "US Bans Small Arms Sales to Indonesia," *Arms Trade News* (May 1994), p. 1; and "British Hawk Aircraft in East Timor," *Arms Transfers News*, Vol. 94, No. 3 (February 25, 1994), p. 7.

plus used U.S. F-16s and U.S.-made F-5s from Jordan, but the United States and Britain may not permit these orders to be filled.[36]

Australian Defence Minister Robert Ray has expressed concern over the diminishing U.S. presence in the Pacific. He believes that Australia should become more involved in Southeast Asia and develop its maritime strength.[37] This is one of the main reasons for Australia's purchase of 15 used F-111Gs from the United States in 1992. These aircraft, which will be delivered by the end of 1994, will help extend the lives of Australia's current inventory of 22 F-111Cs beyond 2015.[38] With a relatively large military budget ($6.9 bn in 1992), Australia could afford to purchase some new combat aircraft, and IDDS estimates that it may order up to 15 new U.S. combat aircraft by 2000.

At the end of the 1980s, North Korea concluded a contract with the former Soviet Union to buy 100 MiG-29s, after having received 14–20 MiG-29s in the mid-1980s. Although none of the 100 planes was delivered, North Korea succeeded in assembling two MiG-29s in 1992.[39] In the future, North Korea may be able to produce more MiG-29s, possibly under license, which would give Russia much-needed export income. North Korea could conceivably purchase or produce under license up to 25 MiG-29s by 2000 in an effort to begin replacing the obsolete J-5s, J-6s, and MiG-21s which make up 890 of its 990 combat aircraft.

Singapore recently placed a firm order for 18 F-16 fighters.[40] The imports will be used to strengthen Singapore's air defense over coastal waters in the South China Sea. These aircraft will probably be delivered toward the latter part of the decade, making it unlikely that Singapore will import any more new combat aircraft by 2000.

---

[36] *International Security Digest*, Vol. 1, No. 2 (December 1993), p. 2; and "US Bans Small Arms Sales to Indonesia," p. 1.

[37] Frank Cranston, "Australia Should 'Firm up Asian Alignment,'" *Jane's Defence Weekly*, Vol. 21, No. 9 (March 5, 1994), p. 14.

[38] Gregor Ferguson, "Australia Debates Buy of F-111Gs," *Defense News*, Vol. 8, No. 26 (July 5-11, 1993), p. 8.

[39] Yu Yong-won, *Choson Ilbo* (February 7, 1994), p. 2, in *FBIS*, FBIS-EAS-94-025 (February 7, 1994), p. 45.

[40] This order was placed after our database was finalized for this book. As a result, tables and statistics appearing in Chapters 11 and 12 list Singapore as having a potential, rather than firm, order for 18 aircraft.

Vietnam, the only other potentially significant arms importer in East and Southeast Asia, probably will not order any combat aircraft in the near future. Long a recipient of Soviet arms on generous aid terms, Vietnam cannot afford to spend the hard currency required to buy new Russian aircraft.

The Middle East and North Africa

Many combat aircraft producers expect growth in exports to the Middle East and North Africa. Certain figures might appear to warrant this hope: the countries of the region have 3,795 fighter, attack, and bomber aircraft, of which 1,600 (42 percent) were designed before 1966; in addition, Saudi Arabia, Iran, and Israel have recently placed orders for combat aircraft.

A closer look at the region, however, indicates that a substantial decline in imports, which began in the 1980s, is likely to continue. There are currently firm orders for 305 combat aircraft to be delivered in 1994–2000. IDDS estimates that countries in the region could order as many as 234 more aircraft for delivery by 2000, the greatest number of potential new orders for any region. Together, firm and potential orders produce a range for average annual combat aircraft imports of 44 to 77. This is but a fraction of earlier imports into the region, which averaged 227 per year in the 1970s and 146 per year in the 1980s.

Until the end of the Cold War, many countries in the region, including Israel, Egypt, and Syria, imported large numbers of combat aircraft on generous credit terms or as outright military grants from the United States and the former Soviet Union. The end of East-West competition in the region and recent moves towards a comprehensive peace between Israel and its neighbors have greatly diminished the reasons for competitive arming. And while the United States continues to provide significant military assistance to Israel and Egypt, Russia can no longer offer generous terms to the former allies of the Soviet Union.[41]

---

[41] These changes are also reflected in defense budget trends. Military spending in the Middle East and North Africa declined by 41 percent from 1983 to 1990, before the Persian Gulf War caused a brief upsurge. The downward trend is believed to have resumed in 1993–1994.

Rather than procure new aircraft, some countries in the region are importing used aircraft, upgrading their current planes, or both. The U.S. Air Force is retiring nearly 700 F-16A/Bs by FY 1996, some of which will be sold at bargain rates while others will be given away to U.S. allies, including, potentially, Israel, Egypt, Bahrain, Jordan, Morocco, and Tunisia.[42] Bahrain is likely to upgrade its F-5s, and Egypt may upgrade its MiG-21s.

The instability of the Persian Gulf area has replaced the risk of war between Israel and its Arab neighbors as the dominant security concern in the region. Iran, which is importing Chinese and Russian weaponry, is stirring fears among other Gulf states that it may seek some form of hegemony in the region. Iran and the United Arab Emirates (UAE) both claim three islands in the Persian Gulf whose location offers control over the entrance to the Gulf. Relations between Iraq and Iran are tense, and the disputed border regions at issue in their 1980s war remain in contention. Iraq remains a significant military power in the region, and both Kuwait and Saudi Arabia worry that if the UN trade and arms embargo is lifted while Saddam Hussein is still in power, Iraq may launch another armed attack. These various sources of instability around the Persian Gulf have motivated most of the recent orders for combat aircraft in the Middle East.

Saudi Arabia, seeking to deter expansionary moves by Iran or Iraq with annual military spending over $30 bn, has ordered 132 aircraft to be delivered by 2000. These include 72 U.S. F-15S strike fighters, a slightly downgraded version of the U.S. Air Force F-15E Strike Eagle, to be delivered in 1995–1999. The Royal Saudi Air Force (RSAF) also ordered Tornado and Hawk aircraft from Britain in a series of contracts under the 1985 Al Yamamah sales agreement. The Saudis will receive the remaining 45 of 48 Tornado IDS (Interdictor Strike) aircraft by 1997, supplementing an earlier purchase of 72 Tornados delivered in the late 1980s and early 1990s. The final 15 of 20 Hawk light fighter-ground attack aircraft will be delivered by 1996. Beyond a potential added order for up to 25 Hawk 200s, IDDS estimates that Saudi Arabia is unlikely to order more combat aircraft by 2000. Upon delivery of current orders, the RSAF will have an unusually modern inventory of more than 300 fighter and attack aircraft, all delivered after 1985. Furthermore, because of declining oil prices, the Saudi

---

[42] Ricks, "Pentagon Considers Selling."

government has been forced to stretch out payments for and delivery of the arms it has already ordered.[43]

Iran has recently placed import orders comparable in size to those of Saudi Arabia. Under a five-year, $10 bn defense development plan,[44] the Iranian air force has ordered 144 Russian and Chinese combat aircraft: 60 MiG-29s and 12 Su-24s from Russia, and 72 J-7s from China. IDDS estimates that 46 of these aircraft were delivered by the end of 1993, and that the remainder will be in service by the end of 1997. These aircraft will replace most of Iran's inventory of 198 U.S.-built F-14s, F-4s, and F-5s, for which it lacks adequate spare parts and maintenance. Iran is also trying to employ some of the 120 aircraft that it acquired from Iraq during the 1991 Gulf War, including 12 MiG-23s, 4 MiG-29s, 24 Mirage F1s, 4 Su-20s, 40 Su-22s, 24 Su-24s, and 7 Su-25s.[45] There are reports that Iran may also be interested in purchasing 48–120 bombers. China has recently demonstrated its new JH-7 bomber to the Iranian air force,[46] and there are unsubstantiated reports that Iran has ordered 12 Tu-22M bombers and an unspecified numbers of MiG-31s and Su-27s from Russia.[47] In addition to the confirmed orders for 144 aircraft, IDDS estimates that Iran may order and take delivery of up to 75 additional Russian or Chinese aircraft by 2000, that is, 25 per year in 1998–2000. The type and amount may depend, in part, on the willingness of Russia and China to establish aircraft manufacturing or component assembly plants in Iran.[48]

Oman has ordered 12 Hawk 200 light multi-role aircraft. Four of these were delivered by the end of 1993 and the remaining eight are expected by the end of 1995. Oman may order another 10 Hawks for delivery by 2000.

---

[43] John D. Morrocco, "Saudi Restructures Arms Deals with U.S.," *Aviation Week & Space Technology*, Vol. 140, No. 6 (February 7, 1994), p. 22.

[44] Anoushiravan Ehteshami, "Iran's National Strategy," *International Defense Review*, Vol. 27, No. 4 (April 1994), p. 29.

[45] *The Military Balance 1993–1994* (London: Brassey's, 1993), p. 116; and Ehteshami, "Iran's National Strategy," p. 33.

[46] David Boey, "Chinese Firm Seeks Bomber Sale in Iran," *Defense News*, Vol. 9, No. 12 (March 28, 1994), p. 38.

[47] Ehteshami, "Iran's National Strategy," p. 34; and James Kraska, "Iran Flexes Maritime Muscles in Gulf," *Defense News*, Vol. 8, No. 39 (October 4, 1993), pp. 25–26.

[48] Boey, "Chinese Firm Seeks Bomber Sale."

Both Egypt and Israel are modernizing their air forces with combat aircraft and financial support from the United States.[49] Egypt, which aims to replace old Soviet-designed aircraft with newer U.S. aircraft, has ordered 46 F-16s under the Peace Vector IV program, to be produced under license in Turkey. Deliveries began in the first half of 1994 and are expected to be completed in 1997, supplementing three prior orders for a total of 110 F-16s that were delivered beginning in 1982. IDDS estimates that Egypt will not order more newly produced combat aircraft before 2000, but it may receive as many as 48 used F-16A/Bs from the USAF.[50]

Israel has ordered 21 US F-15I strike fighters to be delivered in 1997–1999, with an option to purchase four more. The F-15I, which will be almost identical to the USAF's long-range F-15E and marginally better than the Saudi F-15S, will be the most advanced aircraft ever exported by the United States.[51] The purchase represents a shift in emphasis from short-range offensive and defensive air operations against Israel's immediate neighbors to the capability to strike more distant targets in countries such as Iran, Iraq, and Libya.[52] The Israeli Air Force also plans to order some shorter-range multi-role aircraft to fill out its traditional force structure. This requirement may be met by the transfer of 50 or more used F-16A/Bs from the U.S. Air Force. Alternatively, Israel may order up to 20 new F-16s or F/A-18s aircraft or exercise its option for more F-15Is.[53]

Israel Aircraft Industries, Ltd. (IAI) produced about 50 copies of the French Mirage III aircraft in the early 1970s under the name Nesher (Dagger), following France's 1967 decision to terminate deliveries of Mirage IIIs to the Israeli Air Force.[54] Israel later developed a modified version of the Nesher called the Kfir (Lion Cub), and produced 212 of

---

[49] Israel and Egypt, which have long been the two largest recipients of U.S. foreign assistance funds, will receive $5 bn of the $13 bn FY 1995 aid package.

[50] Egypt's latest defense white paper lists equipment support, maintenance, and training as its highest priorities. Philip Finnegan, "Egypt to Focus on Upgrades, Support Equipment," *Defense News*, Vol. 9, No. 18 (May 9, 1994), p. 8.

[51] Barbara Starr, "Israel's F-15I Will Have Edge over Saudi 'S'," *Jane's Defence Weekly*, Vol. 21, No. 5 (February 5, 1994), p. 3.

[52] Jeff Cole, "McDonnell Gets Israeli Jet Order for $2 Billion," *Wall Street Journal*, January 28, 1994, p. A3.

[53] Richard C. Barnard and Barbara Opall, "Israelis Focus on Quantity in Buy of Fighter," *Defense News*, Vol. 9, No. 27 (July 11, 1994), p. 3.

[54] Bill Gunston, ed., *The Encyclopedia of World Air Power* (New York: Crescent Books, 1980), p. 216.

these aircraft from 1975 to 1989. Thirteen were delivered to Colombia and several others were leased to the U.S. Navy and Marine Corps as aggressor training aircraft.[55] With US assistance, IAI also developed the Lavi (Young Lion), a close air support aircraft. This program was terminated by the government in 1987 for political and financial reasons.[56] Israel's recent orders for U.S. aircraft indicate that it has abandoned efforts to build indigenously-designed fighter-attack aircraft. IAI is presently concentrating on aircraft upgrade programs and electronics.

Several traditional importers in the Middle East and North Africa, including Kuwait, Syria, and the UAE, have not yet placed any orders for combat aircraft to be delivered by 2000, but may still do so. Russia has reportedly written off 80–90 percent of Syria's $10 bn debt for Soviet military equipment—on condition that Syria purchase some $500 mn in additional arms with hard currency.[57] The prior debt has been the major impediment to new procurement in Syria, which is now considering the purchase of 14 Su-27s, 30 Su-24s, and 50 MiG-29s to replace the oldest of its 549 Soviet-built combat aircraft.[58] IDDS estimates that Syria may receive as many as 60 new aircraft from Russia by 2000.

In the wake of the Gulf War, the UAE is expected to place an order for new aircraft in 1994 or 1995 to expand its current force of 45 French Mirage 2000s. Preferring a U.S. aircraft, the UAE is considering the F-15, F16, and F/A-18. IDDS estimates that the UAE may order and receive up to 25 new combat aircraft by 2000.

Kuwait is also expanding its air force and may import additional F/A-18s from the United States to supplement an earlier order for 40 delivered in 1992–1993. Falling oil prices and the cost of rebuilding after the Gulf War have limited the funds available for Kuwait to modernize its armed forces. However, it may try to sell its recently

---

[55] John W. R. Taylor, ed., *Jane's All the World's Aircraft 1988–89* (Surrey, UK: Jane's Information Group, 1988), pp. 137–138.

[56] Simon Mitchell, ed., *Jane's Civil and Military Aircraft Upgrades 1993–94* (Surrey, UK: Jane's Information Group, 1992), p. 77.

[57] James Bruce, "Russia/Syria Sign to Smooth Arms Trade," *Jane's Defence Weekly*, Vol. 21, No. 19 (May 14, 1994), p. 3.

[58] Ibid.; and *International Security Digest*, Vol. 1, No. 6 (May 1994), p. 5.

retired A-4 attack aircraft to finance additional F/A-18s.[59] IDDS estimates that Kuwait may receive up to 15 new aircraft by 2000.

Four other countries in the region with annual military spending over $1 bn have not placed orders for new combat aircraft and are, under present circumstances, unlikely to do so before 2000. Two of these countries, Iraq and Libya, are currently under a UN arms embargo. Algeria, a former Soviet client, is battling a domestic insurgency, against which advanced combat aircraft are of little use. Finally, Morocco appears unable to afford a new aircraft purchase. In 1992 it ordered 20 used US F-16A/Bs, but then canceled the deal for lack of adequate funding.

One country with military spending under $1 bn, Qatar, has been rumored to be interested in buying 8–12 Mirage 2000s or F/A-18s. Qatar would finance such a purchase through the sale of older aircraft, and has reportedly reached an agreement in principle to sell its Mirage F1s to Spain.[60]

Europe and Canada

Historically, the non-arms producing countries in Europe, as well as Canada, have been among the largest importers of combat aircraft.[61] On average, these nations imported 190 combat aircraft per year in the 1970s, and 215 per year in the 1980s. Not surprisingly orders in this region have dropped off steeply since the end of the Cold War. Seven European countries have current firm orders for 215 aircraft imports to be delivered by 2000.[62] We estimate that an additional 70 or so combat aircraft could also be imported in this region by 2000, yielding average annual imports of 30–40 per year.

---

[59] "Kuwaiti Skyhawk Sale to Pave Way for Acquisitions," *International Defense Review*, Vol. 27, No. 6 (June 1994), p. 21.

[60] Ibid.; and "Javier R. Ventosa, "Initial Agreement on Purchase of 13 Mirage F1s From Emirate of Qatar," *Madrid YA* (May 27, 1994), p. 10, in *FBIS*, FBIS-WEU-94-114 (June 14, 1994), p. 33.

[61] Apart from the primary arms producers, the countries in Europe with annual military spending over $1 bn are Austria, Azerbaijan, Belarus, Belgium, the Czech Republic, Denmark, Finland, Georgia, Greece, Hungary, Moldova, the Netherlands, Norway, Poland, Portugal, Serbia-Montenegro, Spain, Switzerland, Turkey, and Ukraine.

[62] All but a handful of these are U.S.-designed F-16s or F/A-18s; the rest are U.S.-British AV-8s. In addition, Italy plans to produce 64 AM-Xs domestically. (See Chapter 8.)

Most combat aircraft imports will replace aged aircraft retiring from service. Nearly half of the 7,148 combat aircraft in the region were designed before 1966. The older aircraft in the inventories of former Warsaw Pact nations will generally not be replaced, while those in Western inventories will be replaced on a less than one-for-one basis. Only Greece and Turkey, the largest industrial arms importers in 1988–1992,[63] are still building up their arms inventories in a competitive way. They will receive half of the European imports, both supplied and partly financed by U.S. aid.

Turkey has orders for 100 F-16C/Ds to be delivered by 1999. Turkish Aerospace Industries has been producing F-16s under license at a plant near Ankara since 1987. The latest order represents the last of three Turkish Air Force orders totaling 240 aircraft, all but eight of which will have been produced in Turkey. The final installment of 80 F-16s, estimated at $1.8 bn, will be financed largely through a post–Gulf War defense fund established by Saudi Arabia, Kuwait, the United Arab Emirates, and the United States.[64] In addition to acquiring new production aircraft, Turkey is receiving used aircraft through CFE cascades,[65] and is upgrading some older aircraft. The air force will receive the last 23 of 46 used RF-4s from Germany in 1994. Turkey also plans to upgrade 60 F-5E fighters and 54 F-4 fighters by 2000.[66] IDDS estimates that Turkey will not order any more new aircraft this decade. By 2000, well over half of Turkey's combat aircraft will be new or recently modernized.

Greece is also modernizing its air force with new F-16s and used aircraft, purportedly to counter Turkish modernization.[67] Forty F-16C/Ds are scheduled to be delivered in 1997–1998, supplementing a like number delivered in 1988–1990. In 1993, the Greek Air Force re-

---

[63] *IDDS Almanac 1994.*

[64] Lale Sariibrahimoglu, "Projects Making Progress," *Jane's Defence Weekly*, Vol. 21, No. 23 (June 11, 1994), p. 28.

[65] In the "cascading" process permitted under the terms of the CFE Treaty, countries can transfer relatively new systems that they must retire to another country, which must eliminate a like number of its own holdings. See Jonathan Dean and Randall Forsberg, "The CFE Treaty and Beyond: The Future of Conventional Arms Control," *International Security*, Vol. 17, No. 1 (Summer 1992).

[66] Theresa Hitchens, "Aging Fighters Worldwide Create Fierce Competition," *Defense News*, Vol. 9, No. 22 (July 4, 1994), p. 10.

[67] "Air Force to Buy New F-16's to Counter Turkey," in *FBIS*, FBIS-WEU-92-170, September 1, 1992, p. 54.

ceived 28 used F-4s from the United Kingdom and 62 used A-7s from the United States. It will receive another 8 used British F-4s in 1994. Since Greek combat aircraft are fewer and older than their Turkish counterparts and Greek orders are lower, IDDS estimates that Greece may order as many as 25 additional new aircraft for delivery by 2000.

Several other European countries are ordering U.S. aircraft to replace old aircraft that are being retired. Finland has ordered 64 F/A-18s for delivery in 1996–1999 to replace its entire inventory of old MiG-21s and J-35 Drakens. Switzerland has ordered 34 F/A-18s to be delivered in 1995–1996 to replace its old Hunter aircraft in the fighter-ground attack role. Portugal ordered 20 F-16s to be delivered in 1994 to replace its Italian-built G-91 aircraft. IDDS estimates that these countries will not order any additional combat aircraft this decade.

Italy and Spain have ordered the U.S.-British AV-8B Harrier II Plus vertical and short take-off and landing (V/STOL) aircraft. Italy has ordered 13 AV-8Bs with delivery projected for 1995–1996, with an option for another 8. These planes, to be assembled from U.S.- and British-made components, will bring Italian holdings of AV-8s to 16.

The Spanish Navy has ordered 8 AV-8Bs for delivery in 1995–1996, and it may convert 11 old Harriers to the Harrier II Plus standard. As a member of the Eurofighter 2000 consortium, along with the United Kingdom, Germany, and Italy, Spain is planning to procure 87 Eurofighters after 2000. Due to the advanced age of many aircraft in the Spanish Air Force, IDDS estimates that Spain could order up to 15 new combat aircraft by 2000 if the Eurofighter is canceled or further delayed. But Spain may purchase or lease used aircraft instead. In fact, it was recently reported that Spain had reached an agreement to purchase 13 used Mirage F1s from Qatar; these would serve as attrition replacements for Spain's current inventory.[68]

Among the countries in Europe that have not already ordered new combat aircraft, only one is likely to do so: Austria will probably order 25 aircraft to replace its J-35 Drakens. The candidates being reviewed by the Austrian Air Force include the F-16, F/A-18, Mirage 2000, JAS-39 Gripen, and MiG-29.[69]

---

[68] Ventosa, "Initial Agreement on Purchase of 13 Mirage F1s."
[69] "Firms Line Up to Supply New Austrian Fighter," *Jane's Defense Weekly*, Vol. 21, No. 23 (June 11, 1994), p. 16.

Eleven countries in Europe, as well as Canada, had 1992 military spending over $1 bn but are not expected to place orders for new combat aircraft to be delivered by 2000. The European countries are Belgium, Bulgaria, the Czech Republic, Denmark, Hungary, the Netherlands, Norway, Poland, Romania, Serbia-Montenegro, and Slovakia.

None of the former Warsaw Pact countries is likely to be an importer. Between 1987 and 1992, the combined military spending of the Czech Republic, Slovakia, Poland, Hungary, Bulgaria, and Romania dropped by half, and their combined arms imports fell nearly to zero. Rather than use scarce defense funds to purchase new weapons, the former Warsaw Pact countries are upgrading old ones. All are upgrading at least some of their MiG-21s, and Slovakia and Hungary are also upgrading MiG-29s.[70] In addition, all of these countries are dismantling equipment under the CFE Treaty.

Several former Warsaw Pact countries have active aircraft industries. Aero Czech and Slovak Aerospace are collaborating to produce the L-59 trainer-light attack aircraft and L-159 subsonic light-attack aircraft, modified versions of the L-39 trainer. The Czech Republic plans to use these aircraft in all but front-line combat roles.[71] Poland is producing the Iryda I-22 armed jet trainer for domestic use in training, reconnaissance, and close air support roles.[72] Romania's Avione, in a joint program with the Yugoslav firm Soko, recently produced the IAR-93 light combat plane.[73] Romanian production of this aircraft may have ended in 1993,[74] or the program may continue since Avione had delivered only 39 out of Romania's recent order for 165 IAR-93Bs.[75]

---

[70] Russia transferred 28 MiG-29s to Hungary and 6 to Slovakia in return for cancellation of its trade debt. See Brigitte Sauerwein, "In Transition: The Army of the Czech Republic," *International Defense Review*, Vol. 27 (April 1994), pp. 69-71; Brooks Tigner, "Poland to Tap Units for Allied Training," *Defense News*, Vol. 9, No. 17 (May 2–8, 1994), pp. 4, 29; Ryan Tutak, "Hungarians to Appoint Single Defence Chief," *Jane's Defence Weekly*, Vol. 21, No. 9 (March 5, 1994), p. 18; and "Bulgaria Poised For Reform," *Jane's Defence Weekly*, Vol. 20, No. 14 (October 2, 1993), p. 21.

[71] Paul Beaver and George Mader, *Jane's Defence Weekly*, Vol. 21, No. 22 (June 4, 1994), p. 14.

[72] Theresa Hitchens, "Aging Fighters," p. 12; *Jane's All the World's Aircraft 1993–94*, pp. 228–229.

[73] *Jane's All the World's Aircraft 1993–94*, pp. 228–229.

[74] Yugoslavia's production ended in 1992 when Soko's Mostar factory was damaged in fighting and subsequently dismantled. Ibid., p. 179.

[75] Ibid., p. 250.

The Netherlands, Belgium, Norway, and Denmark are all participating in an F-16A/B mid-life upgrade program instead of purchasing new combat aircraft. The Netherlands and Belgium are also cutting
their force levels. The Netherlands is planning to upgrade 136 of its
185 F-16s and sell the remainder (or place them in storage).[76] Of the
135 F-16s in Belgium's air force, 48 will be upgraded, 24 will remain in
service without being upgraded, and 45 will be put up for sale.[77]
Norway is upgrading 56 of its 60 F-16s and all of its 22 F-5s. Denmark is upgrading all but two of its 63 F-16s.

Canada, which will reduce military spending by 12 percent over
the next five years,[78] will upgrade at least 50 of its 117 F-5s rather
than buy new aircraft.

The countries that emerged from the former Yugoslavia are under a
UN arms embargo, and will be unable to import combat aircraft for
some time.

Five former Soviet republics located in Europe—Ukraine, Belarus,
Georgia, Moldova, and Azerbaijan—each spend over $1 bn annually
on defense, but IDDS does not project that any of these republics will
purchase new combat aircraft. Ukraine and Belarus must both reduce
their holdings of combat aircraft under the CFE Treaty and will have
smaller but still modern forces by 2000. Moldova and Azerbaijan also
have relatively modern forces. Georgia has only two combat aircraft
and has shown no interest in acquiring more.

South Asia

Like East Asia and the Middle East, South Asia is considered a potentially lucrative market by combat aircraft producers. The countries
in the region[79] have ordered a total of 239 combat aircraft to be deliv-

---

[76] Giovanni de Briganti, "North European Countries to Bolster Air Power," *Defense
News*, Vol. 9, No. 3 (January 24–30, 1994), p. 16.

[77] Giovanni de Briganti, "Belgians, Dutch OK F-16 Upgrade," *Defense News*, Vol. 8,
No. 26 (July 5–11, 1994), p. 1.

[78] "More Cuts in Canada," *International Defense Review*, Vol. 27 (April 1994), p. 6;
and "Canada Cuts Defense as Policy Review Continues," *Aviation Week & Space
Technology*, Vol. 140, No. 10 (March 7, 1994), p. 41.

[79] Four former Soviet Republics—Kazakhstan, Kirgizstan, Tajikistan, and Turkmeni-
stan—are now considered part of the South Asia region which until 1992 comprised

ered by 2000. IDDS estimates that the region could potentially import another additional 90 combat aircraft, for an average of 34–47 imported aircraft per year in 1994–2000. The region imported 56 aircraft per year on average in the 1970s and 86 per year in the 1980s.

Arms procurement in South Asia is driven largely by conflicts between India and Pakistan and between India and China. The situation remains explosive along the 1,100-mile Indo-Pakistani border, particularly in the contested, strategically located Kashmir region. India's primary security concerns regarding China stem from that country's occupation of Tibet.[80] Relations have further deteriorated due to China's military ties and arms sales to Pakistan.[81] These two factors, along with China's military modernization program and increased naval activity in the Indian Ocean, have heightened Indian fears and play a significant role in India's continued arms procurement.

India's Finance Minister Manmohan Singh recently presented a draft defense budget for fiscal year 1994–1995 that would increase India's defense spending by 8 percent over the previous year in constant dollars.[82] Much of the increased spending is earmarked for India's Light Combat Aircraft (LCA). This aircraft, an all-weather air superiority fighter and light close air support plane, is being developed by Hindustan Aeronautics Limited (HAL) with the assistance of foreign partners at an estimated total cost of $4.3 bn. Various U.S. and Israeli companies have worked closely in the plane's development, and UK, French, and German companies were engaged in various ways during the initial stages.[83]

The Indian government approved the development of the LCA in 1983 as a replacement for India's MiG-21s and domestically designed Ajeets and as a naval aircraft. The initial prototype flight is sched-

---

only eight countries: Afghanistan, Bangladesh, Burma, India, Nepal, Pakistan, and Sri Lanka.

[80] Chris Smith, *India's Ad Hoc Arsenal: Direction or Drift in Defense Policy?* (Oxford: Oxford University Press, 1994), p. 33.

[81] Vivek Raghuvanshi, "India Fears Pakistani Defense Cooperation with China," *Defense News*, Vol. 9, No. 12 (March 28–April 3, 1994), p. 42; "Sino-Indian Border Talks," *Jane's Defence Weekly*, Vol. 21, No. 6 (February 5, 1994), p. 8.

[82] Rahul Bedi, "India Stems the Fall in its Defence Spending," *Jane's Defence Weekly*, Vol. 21, No. 12 (March 12, 1994), p. 3.

[83] Rahul Bedi, "Collaboration Invited for LCA Programme," *Jane's Defence Weekly*, Vol. 21, No. 4 (January 29, 1994), p. 4.

uled for December 1996 and India hopes to acquire 300 LCAs over 15 years, beginning in 2002.[84] India has not succeeded in bringing in additional foreign partners to assist in development, however. As a result, the LCA, which is already behind schedule and over budget, may face further delays. India believes that further foreign involvement could reduce the production cost of each aircraft from $22 mn to $17 mn, enhancing its marketability.[85]

Since 1983, HAL has been producing the MiG-27 under license from Russia. Of a total of 200 MiG-27s ordered, 112 had been delivered by the end of 1993. The rest will be delivered in 1994–1999. India also ordered 30 Russian MiG-29s to be delivered from 1994 to 1996. The MiG-27s and MiG-29s will replace all but 100 MiG-21s, which are to be upgraded by Russia. In February 1994, India announced that it would also purchase 66 Hawk 200 attack/trainer aircraft from the UK, but the deal has since been delayed and may be canceled.[86] Recently, India has expressed interest in purchasing additional MiG-29s and 20 Su-30s or Mirage 2000s, should Pakistan acquire 28 F-16s.[87] IDDS estimates that India may import up to 60 combat aircraft by 2000 to supplement those already on firm order.

Pakistan is modernizing its inventory through aircraft upgrades and imports from China. Pakistan had previously ordered 111 U.S. F-16s in four installments, of which about 40 had been delivered by 1990. The U.S. administration then halted further deliveries because it could no longer certify that Pakistan was not developing weapons of mass destruction, as required under the 1985 Pressler Amendment. Recently, the Clinton administration proposed to deliver the F-16s that Pakistan has already paid for if Pakistan agrees to stop and

---

[84] *Jane's All the World's Aircraft 1993–94*, p. 106; "India Considers Partners for LCA," *International Defense Review*, Vol. 27 (April 1994), p. 14; "Martin Tapped to Provide Flight Controls for Indian LCA," *Defense Marketing International*, Vol. 5, No. 25 (December 10, 1993); "India Resource Crunch May Delay Aircraft Project," *Arms Transfers News*, Vol. 94, No. 8 (May 20, 1994), p. 5.

[85] Vivek Raghuvanshi, "India Reverses, Seeks Light Combat Aircraft Partner Abroad," *Defense News*, Vol. 9, No. 1 (January 10, 1994), p. 10.

[86] It is not known how many of these Hawks will be of the Hawk 200 attack variety. Annika Saville, "Rao Delays Awarding Hawk Deal to Britain," *The Independent* (March 16, 1994), p. 14, in *FBIS*, FBIS-WEU-94-052-A (March 17, 1994), p. 3.

[87] "India Proposes Purchase of MiG-29 Fighters," *Arms Transfers News*, Vol. 94, No. 7 (May 6, 1994), p. 4; and Vivek Raghuvanshi, "Russia Offers India Su-30 Fighter," *Defense News*, Vol. 9, No. 25 (June 27–July 3, 1994), p. 28.

eventually eliminate its nuclear and ballistic missile programs.[88] So far, Pakistan has appeared unwilling to make such a commitment due to India's ongoing nuclear and missile programs. Therefore, Pakistan has turned to China for combat aircraft, recently placing orders for 98 A-5s, 40 J-7Ms, and 40 J-7Ps. Forty of the 80 J-7s had been delivered by the end of 1993; the remaining 40 are expected to be delivered at 20 per year in 1994 and 1995. The 98 A-5s will be delivered by China at 20 per year in 1994–1998. IDDS estimates that Pakistan may procure up to 40 additional aircraft from China or Russia to replace older aircraft or increase the size of its air force.

No other country in South Asia has placed an order for combat aircraft, nor are such orders likely before 2000. Only Kazakhstan may have annual military spending over $1 bn, and its combat aircraft holdings, inherited from the former Soviet Union, are relatively modern.

Latin America

Prospects for combat aircraft sales to Latin American countries, historically a small market, have all but vanished in recent years. Between 1988 and 1992, the region's military spending decreased by almost 20 percent, from $18 bn to $14.6 bn. The six countries that account for three-quarters of the region's military spending—Brazil, Venezuela, Argentina, Colombia, Cuba, and Chile—are the only countries that might import a sizable number of combat aircraft. Of these, only Brazil (a secondary combat aircraft producer) and Chile show any signs of interest in new aircraft.

Brazil is unlikely to import any combat aircraft for years, due to its weak economy and growing international debt. The Brazilian Air Force is small, with only about 100 combat aircraft, and the air force budget has reportedly shrunk to 20 percent of its 1987 level.[89] Moreover, Brazil is producing a light ground attack and reconnaissance aircraft, the AM-X, jointly with Aeritalia and Aermacchi of Italy. The Brazilian Air Force plans to buy new AM-Xs and upgrade its F-5s

---

[88] Barbara Starr, "USA Puts Proliferation Price on F-16 Delivery," *Jane's Defense Weekly*, Vol. 21, No. 12 (March 26, 1994), p. 4.

[89] Philip Finnegan, "Brazil AF Battles Budget Flak," *Defense News*, Vol. 9, No. 13 (April 4, 1994), p. 3.

and Mirage IIIs. Out of 56 AM-Xs ordered to date, 25 had been delivered through 1993 and the remaining 31 should be in service by 1998. IDDS estimates that Brazil may order up to 12 additional AM-Xs for delivery by 2000.

Chile may replace its aging Hunter ground attack aircraft, and British Aerospace has proposed the Hawk 200 for this purpose.[90] But Chile is more likely to acquire 20 used aircraft. It will probably purchase the used Mirage 5s being offered for sale by Belgium, but may also look at British Jaguars, South African Cheetahs, and Israeli Kfirs.[91] IDDS estimates that Chile could import up to 15 new combat aircraft by 2000 if it does not purchase used aircraft.

Like Brazil, Argentina has a small air force (about 100 combat aircraft) but has managed to develop a modest indigenous aircraft industry. Fábrica Militar de Aviones produces the IA-63 Pampa, an armed jet trainer unsuitable for front-line combat roles. Argentina is currently purchasing 40 used U.S. A-4 Skyhawks and it may receive used F-16s as well. IDDS estimates that Argentina will not place any orders for new combat aircraft imports by 2000.

No other Latin American countries are likely to import new combat aircraft this decade. Venezuela recently purchased 18 used Mirage 50 fighters from France and has no requirement for additional aircraft. Colombia has 28 relatively new Kfirs and Mirage 5s. Cuba, which is undergoing a severe financial crisis, does not have the means to purchase combat aircraft.

Sub-Saharan Africa

Prospects for combat aircraft sales in sub-Saharan Africa are, like those for Latin America, almost non-existent. No country in sub-Saharan Africa has placed an order for combat aircraft since 1986, when Angola ordered 48 MiG-23 fighters from the Soviet Union.[92]

South Africa, the only country in the region with annual military spending over \$1 bn, is included in IDDS estimates as the only candi-

---

[90] "Bids Line Up For Fighter Replacement," *Jane's Defence Weekly*, Vol. 21, No. 13 (April 2, 1994), p. 10.
[91] Ibid.
[92] Stockholm International Peace Research Institute (SIPRI), *SIPRI Yearbook*, 1990–1993 (Oxford: Oxford University Press, 1990–1993).

date for new combat aircraft imports by 2000. Since 1977, when the United Nations placed South Africa under an international arms embargo, the South African company Atlas Aviation has developed aircraft upgrades for the South African Air Force. The Cheetah, a highly modified Mirage III, was undertaken first, with Israeli assistance. Then in 1990, Atlas proposed to develop a new multi-role fighter based on the Cheetah to enter service after 2000.[93] Now, however, with the lifting of the UN embargo, South Africa is likely to produce a more advanced French or British aircraft under license.[94] Toward the end of 1993, in anticipation of the end of the embargo, the United Kingdom and France began discussions with South Africa concerning the sale of combat aircraft and setting up joint ventures between their arms industries.[95] The UK has suggested the Hawk 200 aircraft as a replacement for South Africa's Cheetahs and possibly its Mirage F1s.[96] France, which has a long-standing relationship with the South African government and military, has proposed the Mirage 2000 as a replacement for the Mirage F1s and eventually the Cheetahs. IDDS estimates that South Africa will place an order for 15 new aircraft to be delivered by 2000.

Conclusion

The export market for advanced combat aircraft has shrunk substantially in recent years and shows no sign of expanding again. Although many low-intensity conflicts persist, the need for major weapon systems such as advanced combat aircraft has greatly diminished. The latest combat aircraft have also become too expensive for many countries. Some air forces are extending the service lives of their older aircraft or retiring them without replacement. Others are buying used aircraft to modernize their forces. Secondary producers are filling more

---

[93] Helmoed-Römer Heitman, "Next Fighter To Be New Build," *Jane's Defence Weekly*, Vol. 13, No. 8 (February 24, 1994), p. 321.

[94] "France to Announce S. African Contracts Soon," *Defense Marketing International*, Vol. 5, No. 24 (November 26, 1993), p. 2.

[95] Charles Miller, "UK Intends to Sell Arms to S. Africa," *Defense News*, Vol. 8, No. 35 (September 6, 1993), p. 1; "France To Announce S. African Contracts Soon"; and Barbara Opall, "S. Africa Boosts Global Military Ties," *Defense News*, Vol. 9, No. 7 (February 21, 1994), p. 1.

[96] Miller, "UK Intends to Sell Arms to South Africa," p. 1.

of their own needs, reducing their demand for imported aircraft. For all these reasons, exports will not offset the decline in domestic orders in the primary producers (the United States, Russia, the United Kingdom, France, Germany, Sweden, and Italy) to the extent that it will preserve all the current advanced aircraft-producing firms.

The trends cast doubt on the viability of the secondary producers' combat aircraft industries. Will they become more competitive with primary producers, or be undercut by the primary producers? The developments reported in this chapter support both outcomes, but suggest that deterioration of these industries is the more likely.

The technological expertise needed to produce combat aircraft has spread around the world in recent years, allowing secondary producers to emerge. China, India, and Japan have the industrial bases, many of the requisite technologies, and the gross domestic products to produce combat aircraft in large quantities. Even smaller countries, such as Taiwan and Israel, have proven their ability to produce combat aircraft. Other countries can design and produce armed jet trainers and light attack aircraft. But only China competes with the primary producers in the export market—due to the low cost of its lower performance aircraft.

The key to future global production and trade is the tremendous cost of indigenous design and development of systems on the cutting edge of technology. When combined with the shrinking demand for such systems, the high entry cost is likely to prevent secondary producers from competing for exports on the world market for the indefinite future. The only possible exception might be aircraft designed by Russia and produced by China—if Russia were to permit such competition.

Some secondary producers may, however, compete in exporting armed jet trainers and light combat aircraft. For countries that wish to upgrade their forces without incurring large debts, these low-cost aircraft may offer an attractive alternative to high-priced, front-line aircraft. Choices of this kind are already evident in many of the orders for the Hawk 200 and in the Czech Republic's decision to replace many old front-line aircraft with the L-159 light-attack aircraft and L-59 armed jet trainer.

In the future, secondary arms producers will face the problem of ever-increasing development costs that the primary producers now find nearly insupportable. Early secondary producers, such as Israel and South Africa, abandoned efforts to develop indigenously-designed combat aircraft for cost reasons. Taiwan reduced the number of IDFs it planned to produce as soon as it was permitted to import more capable and cost-effective U.S. and French combat aircraft. India may ultimately drop the LCA project as its cost continues to rise. These trends indicate that in the future there will be fewer, rather than more, secondary combat aircraft producers.

Chapter 12

Randall Forsberg
Jonathan Cohen

Issues and Choices in Arms Production and Trade

Not surprisingly, the former Cold War adversaries still account for most of the world's military spending and arms production. In 1992, Latin America, Africa, the Middle East, and Asia absorbed just one-quarter of world military spending, while the United States and Canada, the countries of Europe, and the republics of the former Soviet Union accounted for three-quarters. Seven of these countries—the United States, Russia, France, Britain, Germany, Italy, and Sweden—develop and export *all* technologically-advanced major weapon systems. Together, the seven primary arms producers and China produced 99 percent of the 38,622 combat aircraft in service worldwide in 1993 and 99.7 percent of the 14,295 imported aircraft.[1]

Because of their unique role in developing, producing, and exporting ever-more sophisticated weaponry, the seven primary arms

---

[1] Although it produces and exports large numbers of weapons, China is not a primary arms producer because it cannot produce weapons that are technologically competitive with systems in production in the West. Nearly all Chinese-built weapons are derived from Soviet systems designed before 1960; even today the most advanced combat aircraft in production in China are the J-7III, a Chinese derivative of the Soviet MiG-21 (designed in 1958), and the J-8II, an aircraft originally derived from the J-7. Most of the 6,075 Chinese-produced aircraft in service in 1993 were in China; some 1,560 were exports, held mainly by poorer Third World countries.

Randall Forsberg is the Executive Director of the Institute for Defense and Disarmament Studies (IDDS) in Cambridge, Massachusetts, and an officer of the Center for Science and International Affairs, Kennedy School of Government, Harvard University.

Jonathan Cohen is a research fellow at the Institute for Defense and Disarmament Studies in Cambridge, Massachusetts, where he specializes in the conventional arms trade.

producers play a unique role in shaping the post–Cold War security environment. These nations are continuing traditional patterns of arms deployment, production, and export—ignoring the new risks posed by perpetuating old practices. The case for continuing past patterns of arming rests on three false assumptions: first, that many unidentified countries might pose serious future threats of major war; second, that the main arms producers have little influence over when and how new capabilities for major war may develop; and third, that such capabilities might emerge relatively soon.

In reality, the opposite is true:

- Only a few countries have the military capability to engage in a major war, and these countries are well known.
- Countries can acquire a "major-war" capability only by importing advanced weapon systems and military technological know-how from the primary arms producers.
- Because of the long lead time needed to develop large modern military forces, new or greatly improved capabilities for major war are unlikely to develop before 2010, if then. When they do appear, their growth will be apparent for at least a decade before they are fully developed.

Only Russia and the United States have armed forces capable of conducting a worldwide conventional war, with combat in Asia and the Pacific as well as Europe and the Atlantic. Although such a war is unthinkable today, many fear that it could once again become a significant risk. Russian security analysts fear an eastward expansion of NATO, incorporating first Poland, the Czech and Slovak republics, and Hungary, and later, conceivably, Ukraine and the Baltic states. This would put a potential adversary on Russia's doorstep, within easy military range of its political and industrial heartland. Russian political and military leaders would view such a development with great alarm.[2] Similarly, leaders in central Europe and the Baltics fear a

---

[2] See Chapter 2. At a conference in Berlin, German Defense Minister Volker Rühe recently suggested that Russia's former East European allies might become full members of NATO within a few years while Russia would never be a full member. According to the *New York Times*, Rühe said "If Russia were to become a member of NATO, it would blow NATO apart. NATO would become like a United Nations of Europe. This isn't going to work, and why should we lie about it or be ambiguous about it?" In addition, the article says, "Mr. Rühe asserted that Poland, Hungary, the Czech Republic and Slovakia deserved to become members of NATO and the European Union because unlike Russia, 'they belong to the European system and they were artificially separate

revival of Russian nationalism and imperialism. They argue that this could lead to Russian military occupation of the former Soviet republics and later, perhaps, a pre-emptive military drive aimed at establishing Russian control over the territory of former Warsaw Pact allies.[3] The continued large size of the standing armed forces of Russia and the West and ongoing innovation in their armaments reflect caution about the possibility that East-West relations might deteriorate. Concern about this risk is certainly warranted—but large military forces and a "warm" defense industrial base (which perpetuate fear and suspicion because they permit rapid mobilization for war) and technological advances in weaponry (which create uncertainty about the adequacy of preparations for defense) may do more to hasten than prevent a return to East-West military confrontation.

The next largest war that would be possible with existing military forces is a regional war between Russia and China. China's acquisition of modern armaments with longer range and greater sophistication is a concern for Russia, even though Russia is supplying the weapons. The modernization of China's armed forces also worries the United States, Japan, and other nations in East Asia and around the Pacific rim. The future of Japanese military power is less clear, but could also be a concern in parts of East Asia.

Apart from China and Japan, the countries that are currently or potentially capable of engaging in major regional wars are other past and potential future major arms importers: the two Koreas, Taiwan, India, Pakistan, Israel, Egypt, Syria, Libya, Iraq, Iran, Saudi Arabia, Greece, and Turkey. The primary arms producers have substantial control over the rate at which these importers can strengthen their existing military capabilities. In the case of China and Iran, Russia is the only source of advanced weaponry. For Japan and South Korea

---

from it.'" According to the article, U.S. Defense Secretary William Perry took issue with this view, refusing "to rule out the possibility that Russia might eventually join the alliance. 'I'm not at this time prepared to close the door on that issue as my colleague Volker has,' Mr. Perry said." "NATO Membership for Russia Doubted," *New York Times*, September 10, 1994, p. 3.

[3] Few informed observers in the West fear near-term Russian military aggression, but the comments of right-wing extremists like Vladimir Zhirinovsky make it hard to dismiss the scenario, and Zhirinovsky has had extensive press coverage in the West as well as in Russia. For example, the cover of a July 1994 issue of *Time* magazine featured the following words: "From Russia with Venom: The Inside Story of Vladimir Zhirinovsky, the Zealot Who Would Make Russia Dangerous Again." *Time*, Vol. 144, No. 2 (July 11, 1994), pp. 38-44.

(or, in the long term, a potentially unified Korea), the United States plays the same role. If the United States and Russia agreed to ban major arms transfers and persuaded the members of the European Union to join them, the development of new military capabilities among the top arms importers would be delayed for 20–30 years. It would take a very large financial investment and a period of at least two decades for a major importer to build up an indigenous arms industry capable of independently designing advanced weaponry, and then begin producing such weapons for domestic use (and, possibly, export).

In sum, the unique position of the primary arms producers as the world's sole exporters of advanced weaponry gives them exceptional knowledge of and control over new threats of major war. This has been true since 1945, but the Cold War precluded efforts by the primary producers to cooperate in heading off new threats. Cooperation to achieve these goals is now politically possible for the first time.

Forms of arms control that seemed unthinkable in the past—reducing forces globally, "mothballing" arms production lines, delaying or suspending the introduction of new weaponry, and limiting arms exports—could head off new regional threats and reduce the risk of renewed East-West confrontation. Not surprisingly, these far-reaching forms of arms control would tend to enhance and complement one another—just as policies favoring larger forces, an active industrial base, rapid introduction of new technology, and extensive exports tend to complement and reinforce one another.

Neither arms control nor arming alone is likely to be the best way to address possible future military threats. As with other dangers such as illness or crime, a combination of prevention and readiness for intervention is likely to be more effective than either approach taken alone. Before considering the mix of arming and arms control that would do most to enhance security, it is useful to consider the economic factors that will constrain the range of feasible options.

The Future Global Arms Market

In the United States and Europe, and to some extent in Russia, policies regarding weapon innovation, exports, and even force levels are being driven by the desire to maintain an active defense industrial base in a period when worldwide demand for newly-produced weapons has collapsed. Among the seven primary arms producers, there is little demand for production of new weaponry for domestic use. In the United States, the standing armed forces are being reduced by about half, and due to a high rate of arms production in the 1980s, the inventories of existing weaponry will not need replacement for many years. In Russia, funding for arms procurement has fallen by 90 percent in the last few years and shows no sign of a significant increase before 2000 (if then). Britain and Germany, setting a new priority on peacekeeping and peacemaking, find themselves without a plausible domestic need for new weapons intended mainly to deter an East–West war. Even in France, Sweden, and Italy, force levels and domestic production requirements are declining, and they may decline further if and when these countries develop substantially revamped post–Cold War security policies.

The decline in the main arms producers' domestic markets for new weaponry, illustrated by combat aircraft, is far more dramatic than generally realized. Russia and the United States are reducing their production of combat aircraft for domestic use from 614 and 344 per year, respectively, in 1973–1982 to 20–40 per year each in 1997–2000. (See Table 12.1.) These huge cuts bring annual U.S. and Russian domestic procurement down to the scale that has long been the rule in Europe. Average annual production for domestic use by the five European producers totaled 122 per year in 1973–1982, but will drop to 36 per year in the late 1990s. Together, the seven primary producers will produce an average of just 98 combat aircraft per year for domestic use in 1997–2000—a reduction of 90 percent from their combined average annual production of 998 for 1973–1992.

China, replacing a large combat aircraft inventory based mainly on MiG-19s with a smaller one based mainly on J-7 derivatives of the MiG-21 and their J-8 successors, has cut domestic production by 80 percent, from 340 aircraft per year in 1973–1982 to about 70 per year at present and projected for the indefinite future. Even at this far lower rate, China will still account for over one-third of world combat aircraft production for domestic use in the late 1990s.[4] Counting

---

[4] The main reason for the surprisingly large Chinese share is the very low cost of the relatively simple aircraft produced in China for domestic use: at about $2 mn each, the price of these planes is less than 10 percent of the cost of current-generation aircraft made by the primary producers, such as the U.S. F-16, which costs $23 mn, or the Russian Su-27 (being imported by China), which has an estimated price of $30-40 mn.

Table 12.1. Combat Aircraft Production by Producer 1973-2000

		Annual Avg		1993	1994	1995	1996	1997	1998	1999	2000	Annual deliveries of firm orders for new combat aircraft 94–00 Total
	Customer	73–82	83–92	1993	1994	1995	1996	1997	1998	1999	2000	Total
France	Domestic	42	35	28	30	18	18	18	18	11	6	119
France	Export	63	53	0	0	12	12	12	12	12	0	60
France	Total	105	88	28	30	30	30	30	30	23	6	179
Germany	Domestic	20	41	0	0	0	0	0	0	0	0	0
Germany	Export	0	3	1	5	5	5	4	0	0	0	19
Germany	Total	21	43	1	5	5	5	4	0	0	0	19
Great Britain	Domestic	33	47	0	5	10	8	8	0	0	0	31
Great Britain	Export	19	17	15	28	23	10	4	0	0	0	65
Great Britain	Total	52	63	15	33	33	18	12	0	0	0	96
Italy	Domestic	4	19	20	20	20	20	4	0	0	0	64
Italy	Export	3	0	1	2	2	2	1	0	0	0	7
Italy	Total	7	19	21	22	22	22	5	0	0	0	71
Sweden	Domestic	23	10	2	8	10	10	20	20	20	20	108
Sweden	Export	2	6	0	0	0	0	0	0	0	0	0
Sweden	Total	25	16	2	8	10	10	20	20	20	20	108
Eur Subtotal	Domestic	122	152	50	63	58	56	50	38	31	26	322
Eur Subtotal	Export	87	78	17	35	42	29	21	12	12	0	151
Eur Subtotal	Total	209	229	67	98	100	85	71	50	43	26	473
Russia	Domestic	614	430	44	20	30	30	30	40	40	40	230
Russia	Export	330	223	22	85	101	46	36	24	23	12	327
Russia	Total	944	653	66	105	131	76	66	64	63	52	557
USA	Domestic	344	333	169	144	101	47	24	24	24	24	388
USA	Export	259	229	70	75	87	132	150	133	87	48	712
USA	Total	603	562	239	219	188	179	174	157	111	72	1,100
Primary Prod	Domestic	1,080	915	263	227	189	133	104	102	95	90	940
Primary Prod	Export	676	530	109	195	230	207	207	169	122	60	1,190
Primary Prod	Total	1,756	1,445	372	422	419	340	311	271	217	150	2,130
China	Domestic	339	109	70	70	70	70	70	70	70	70	490
China	Export	58	81	59	58	58	20	20	18	0	0	174
China	Total	397	191	129	128	128	90	90	88	70	70	664
Oth Secondary	Domestic	34	25	18	12	29	54	54	6	12	12	179
Oth Secondary	Export	2	3	0	0	0	0	0	0	0	0	0
Oth Secondary	Total	35	28	18	12	29	54	54	6	12	12	179
World Total	**Domestic**	1,453	1,050	351	309	288	257	228	178	177	172	1,609
World Total	**Export**	735	614	168	253	288	227	227	187	122	60	1,364
Grand Total	**Total**	2,188	1,664	519	562	576	484	455	365	299	232	2,973

Source: "IDDS Almanac 1994." For 1994-2000, other secondary producers are Brazil, Taiwan, and Japan.

secondary as well as primary producers, worldwide production of combat aircraft for domestic use is expected to fall from at least 1,453 per year in the 1970s to about 180 per year in the late 1990s.

The global market for arms exports is not contracting to the same extent, but has shrunk dramatically and will probably continue to decline. In the 1970s and 1980s, world combat aircraft exports totaled about one-half of combat aircraft production for domestic use, or about one-third of all production. (See Table 12.1) In the mid- to late 1990s, due to the precipitous drop in domestic demand, production for export in the United States and Russia will surpass that for domestic use for the first time. As a result, production for export by the seven primary arms producers as a group will surpass production for domestic use beginning in 1995. From 1994 to 2000, the producers' domestic procurement of combat aircraft will average 134 per year, while their production for export will lie in the range of 170 (firm orders placed to date) to 253 (firm orders plus potential additional orders) per year.

These figures signal a dramatic change in the role of arms exports in defense industrial policy. Until quite recently, exports have been an adjunct to domestic procurement, adding profits to a production process that would have continued largely unchanged if there had been no exports. Now exports are becoming vital to the survival of major weapon industries, keeping production lines open when they would otherwise shut down. If continued unchecked, reliance on exports to maintain a defense industrial base will undoubtedly compromise the security policies of the main arms producers. It will lead them to promote rather than restrain exports even when their own exports or those of other producers undermine their security, exacerbate regional conflicts, and divert resources to a futile competition for technological advantages in weaponry.

The increased weight of exports in overall arms production is relative: it does not reflect a rise in exports, but an export decline that is more modest than the decline in domestic demand. Exports dropped from at least 735 per year in 1973–1982 to 615 per year in 1983–1992, and they are projected to fall to the range of 195 (firm orders) to 285 (firm plus potential additional orders), on average, in 1994–2000. That range represents a decrease of 60–75 percent compared with the level in the 1970s.

Despite this drastic contraction in export orders, many industry and government officials in the primary arms-producing countries are forecasting substantial exports for the period from 1997–1998 to 2010. In Russia, exports are still considered vital to the maintenance of the defense industrial base. In Sweden, Britain, and France, officials hope that export orders for the Gripen, the Eurofighter 2000, and the Rafale will help reduce the unit cost of domestic procurement; Britain and France count on them to keep the domestic industry viable.

To provide a context for evaluating the prospects for exports—and the potential for new threats of major war—after 2000, it is helpful to look at the reasons for recent cutbacks in imports among major and minor importers. The projected decline in exports through 2000 involves a combination of simultaneous but disparate contractions in four groups of importers (see Table 12.2): 15 major importers—countries that, according to IDDS estimates, will have had average annual imports over 1973–2000 of at least 12 aircraft per year; China; the smaller industrial importers in Europe; and the smaller Third World importers (in Table 12.2, "Rest of World").

In the 1980s, the average annual imports in the 15 major importers and the smaller Third World importers fell by 10 percent and 40 percent, respectively, from 350 to 330 (the major importers combined) and from 220 to 124 (the smaller Third World importers combined). The decline among the major importers was due to a massive one-time build-up in Libya, whose imports of combat aircraft shot up to 53 per year in the 1970s and then fell to 3 per year in the 1980s.[5] Other major importers showed offsetting increases and decreases between the 1970s and the 1980s. In contrast, most smaller importers reduced acquisitions in the 1980s. Many Third World nations imported small quantities of arms for the first time in the 1960s or 1970s, as a symbol of newly-acquired independence or with U.S. or Soviet military aid; the global recession of the 1980s led to a decline in both types of imports.

Unlike the developing countries, the industrial countries in Europe increased imports in the 1980s compared with the 1970s by about 20

---

[5] The growth in Libya's combat aircraft from 22 in 1972 to 528 in 1982 represents the fastest 10-year increase by any importer. But because this build-up was followed by a decade with virtually no imports (a total of 25 aircraft in 1983-1992), Libya's *sustained* average annual acquisition and net growth (26 and 16, respectively) are well below those of pre-Gulf War Iraq (33 and 26).

Table 12.2. World Combat Aircraft Acquisition Through Domestic Production and Import 1973–2000

	Domestic Production				Import				Total Acquired			
	73–82	83–92	93	94–00	73–82	83–92	93	94–00	73–82	83–92	93	94–00
Primary Producers	1,080	915	263	134	26	9		2	1,106	924	253	136
China	339	109	70	70		3		29	339	112	70	99
Major Importers	34	3	6	21	350	330	112	191	383	332	118	191
Other NA/Eu		18	2		140	150		25	140	168	2	25
Rest of World		5	10	6	220	124	56	38	222	129	66	44
World Total	1,453	1,050	351	230	735	615	168	285	2,188	1,665	519	515
Of which:												
Russia	614	430	44	33					614	430	34	33
USA	344	333	169	55					344	333	169	55
France	42	35	28	17					42	36	28	17
Great Britain	33	47		4					33	47		4
Sweden	23	10	2	15					23	10	2	15
Germany	20	41			22	7			42	47		
Italy	4	19	20	9	4	2		2	8	22	20	11
Primary Producers	1,080	915	263	134	26	9		2	1,106	924	253	136
Taiwan		0	6	18	28	8		30	28	8	6	48
Pakistan					16	24	20	25	16	24	20	25
Iran					11	6	28	25	11	6	28	25
Saudi Arabia					11	16	8	22	11	16	8	22
India	4				28	37	12	22	31	37	12	22
South Korea					32	14		15	32	14		15
Turkey					22	42	18	14	22	42	18	14
Greece					21	16		9	21	16		9
Syria					25	22		9	25	22		9
Egypt					16	23	20	7	16	23	20	7
Israel	23				24	16		6	47	16		6
North Korea					27	48		4	27	48		4
Japan	7	2		3	15	16	6	3	22	19	6	7
Libya					53	3			53	3		
Iraq					21	**39**			21	39		
Major Importers	34	3	6	21	350	330	112	191	383	332	118	212

Average annual combat aircraft acquisition

Source: "IDDS Almanac 1994."

Notes: Projected 1994–2000 acquisitions include potential as well as firm orders. Potential orders account for 2 of the 222 domestically-produced aircraft, and 90 of the 285 imports—in all, 92 of the 507 aircraft projected to be acquired. For a breakout of 1994–2000 firm and potential combat aircraft imports by country, see Table 11.1. Parts may not add to totals due to rounding.

percent. This reflected arms build-ups in both Eastern and Western Europe during the Reagan era.

For 1994–2000 combat aircraft imports by the 15 major importers dropped sharply compared with their level in 1983–1992. Firm orders indicate a decline of 50 percent; firm plus potential additional orders show a drop of 40 percent. The decline among the major importers—from 350 per year in the 1970s to 330 in the 1980s and then to the range of 144 (firm orders) to 191 (firm plus potential orders) in the 1990s—is likely to continue in 2001–2010. Japan is developing a do-mestically-designed variant of the U.S. F-16 for production after 2000. Taiwan, Turkey, and Egypt will have completed major acqui-sitions by 2000. Syria, Egypt, and Israel are reducing their combat air-craft inventories, and Egypt and Israel are expected to import some used rather than new U.S. aircraft to replace older planes. Greece is now importing mainly used U.S. aircraft, and may continue to do so. North Korea cannot afford substantial imports. Iraq and Libya may or may not remain under UN arms embargoes into the next century.

This leaves just 5 out of 15 major importers that may sustain or increase their 1994–2000 rates of import in 2001–2010. South Korea, which has been building up steadily, may continue to do so; India, which is developing a domestically designed plane, may turn to im-ports if the domestic project is too costly; Pakistan, which is expand-ing its forces to match those of India, is likely to continue importing at the current rate; Iran, which is currently replacing some 200 U.S.-made aircraft, may use imports after 2000 to expand the size of its air force; and Saudi Arabia is likely to try to match any growth in the forces of Iraq or Iran.

Among smaller Third World importers, the steep decline in im-ports that began in the 1980s is continuing. By 1993 annual imports had dropped another 50 percent (to 56), and in 1994–2000, they are projected to decline by at least one-third more (to an annual average of no more than 38 firm plus potential orders). The reasons for this decline—particularly the end of grant aid from the United States and Russia and dire domestic economic conditions—are unlikely to change in the next decade.

Smaller industrial importers in Europe, who imports rose to an an-nual average of 150 in the 1980s, have shown a precipitous drop in the 1990s, comparable to that in U.S. and Russian domestic produc-tion. Average annual imports in 1994–2000 are expected to fall to the range of 18 (firm orders) to 25 (firm plus potential additional orders) and to stay in that range through the next decade.

In 1992 China began importing major weapons for the first time since the Sino-Soviet split in 1960. With expected 1994–2000 imports for 21 (firm) to 29 (firm plus potential) aircraft per year, China can now be counted not only as a secondary producer and exporter but also as a major importer.

Despite recent spurts of growth in imports in China, Taiwan, Pakistan, India, Iran, Saudi Arabia, and South Korea, trends elsewhere indicate a continuing decline or sustained low level of global arms transfers and domestic demand for 2001–2010. The projected decline in the export market for 1994–2000 is a product of declining force sizes and low rates of acquisition of new weapons among most of the 15 major importers as well as the smaller industrial importers in Europe and in the Third World. At present, there is no reason to expect these factors to change substantially after 2000.

In the reduced global market, Russia's only major arms export customers are China, India, Iran, Syria, and, for the longer term, possibly Iraq (see Table 12.3). Three of these clients—China, Iran, and Iraq—are the countries whose potential future military growth is of greatest concern to nations in East Asia and the Middle East, the United States, and Russia itself. There is, thus, a direct relationship between unrestrained arms exports by the major producers and the potential growth of major new regional threats which the main producers' armed forces are intended to guard against. Because they are the only source of new regional threats, exports undertaken for commercial gain and to keep arms industries alive require an enormous offsetting investment, paid by taxpayers, in armed forces and military budgets that are far larger than would be likely in a world without exports.

The ongoing decline in the export market means, however, that even with increased reliance on exports, global arms production capacity will continue to shrink. In Russia the survival of the Sukhoi and Mikoyan firms is at issue. In Britain, the lack of an export market for the Eurofighter 2000 may result in prohibitively high unit costs, leading to the curtailment or even cancellation of the project. In any event, shrinking exports, poor economies of scale for domestic

Table 12.3. Deliveries of Firm and Potential Combat Aircraft Orders by Producer 1994–2000

New aircraft to be delivered between 1994 and 2000

Producer Customer	Orders Firm	Orders Potential	Total	Producer Customer	Orders Firm	Orders Potential	Total
USA				**Great Britain**			
Taiwan	150		150	Saudi Arabia	60	25	85
South Korea	102		102	Malaysia	18	15	33
Turkey	100		100	Indonesia	5	15	20
Saudi Arabia	72		72	Oman	8	10	18
Greece	40	25	65	Exports	91	65	156
Finland	64		64	Domestic	31		31
Egypt	46		46	Total	122	65	187
Switzerland	34		34				
Thailand	12	15	27				
Israel	21	24	45	**France**			
Spain	8	15	23	Taiwan	60		60
Japan	22		22	Domestic	119		119
Portugal	20		20	Total	179	0	179
Singapore		18	18				
Australia		15	15				
Kuwait		15	15	**Mixed Producers**			
Italy	13		13	Austria		25	25
Malaysia	8		8	North Korea		25	25
Exports	712	127	839	UAE		25	25
Domestic	388		388	Chile		15	15
Total	1,100	127	1,227	South Africa		15	15
				Italy		8	8
				Rest of World		50	50
Russia				Total	0	163	163
China	146	60	206				
India	101	50	151				
Iran	62	50	112	**Other Producers: Domestic Production**			
Syria		60	60	Taiwan	125		125
Malaysia	18		18	Sweden	108		108
Exports	327	220	547	Italy	64		64
Domestic	230		230	Brazil	30	12	42
Total	557	220	777	Japan	24		24
China							
Pakistan	138	40	178				
Iran	36	25	61	**World Total by Producer**			
Exports	174	65	239	**Export**	**1,364**	**640**	**2,004**
Domestic	490		490	**Domestic**	**1,609**	**12**	**1,621**
Total	664	65	729	**Grand Total**	**2,973**	**652**	**3,625**

Source: "IDDS Almanac 1994."
Note: "Mixed Producers" applies to countries that may import from more than one primary producer.

production, and ever-growing development costs are likely to make the current round of major weapon projects in Europe the last to be conducted independently. Starting after 2000 if not before, Britain, France, Germany, Italy, and Sweden will almost certainly attempt to form a Europe-wide defense industry with a Europe-wide market.[6] But in the post–Cold War environment, even a sweeping consolidation of this kind may not lead to a viable defense industry. If Russian arms production remains at its current low level and Russian armed forces remain largely inactive, it will be even more difficult than it has been in the past to develop a Europe-wide consensus on security threats, military funding, defense industrial needs, and design and performance parameters for new weapons.

In sum, the shrinking global arms export market, the rising unit costs of major weapon systems, and the radically improved relations among the primary arms producers have combined to create conditions that are optimal for new forms of arms control.

Issues and Choices for the Main Arms Producers

The end of the Cold War opens up new choices and poses new problems for security. Currently, the armed forces of the former Cold War adversaries are being reduced slowly, haphazardly, and unilaterally. The priority in these nations is to maintain readiness for unforeseen crises and avoid mobilization lead times of months or years. In the post–Cold War environment, however, maintaining large standing forces has a new price: it invites renewed East-West confrontation by fueling fear and suspicion and facilitating rapid rearmament.

Similarly, with respect to the defense industrial base, the primary arms producers are putting the highest priority on reaction time. In the United States, Britain, Germany, and even Russia, production lines are being kept open primarily because closed factories could take several years to reopen. But active production lines engender fear and

---

[6] Dassault Aviation of France and British Aerospace announced in early 1992 that they wanted to cooperate in developing a joint successor to the Rafale and the Eurofighter 2000 for service beginning around 2020. Officials said that if the proposal were approved by their governments, they would invite the German and Italian firms working on the Eurofighter 2000 to participate. J.A.C. Lewis, "UK, France plan EFA successor," *Jane's Defence Weekly*, Vol. 17, No. 9 (February 29, 1992), p. 337.

suspicion because, like standing armies, they facilitate rapid pre-war and wartime build-ups.

The end of the Cold War also calls into question the continuing technological competition in weaponry—a race that is a function of the size of the standing forces and the regular replacement of equipment reaching retirement age with new systems. This unabated technological competition is manifest in tactical combat aircraft, where the costs of developing and producing the U.S. F-22, the French Rafale, the Swedish Gripen, and the British-German-Italian Eurofighter 2000 are justified on the grounds that these new planes are needed to counter new Russian aircraft (either deployed by Russia or exported to regional powers), such as the planned Su-34 fighter-attack plane, the Su-27M air superiority fighter, and a possible new MiG fighter (the 1.42). At the same time, the costs of developing and producing these new aircraft in Russia are justified on the grounds that the new planes are needed to counter Western advances. The problem with this circular argument is two-fold: the new systems cost billions more to develop and produce than it would cost to maintain forces with existing technology; and exports undertaken to offset these costs (and keep production lines open) multiply potential future threats and decrease security.

Even if exported weapons do not incorporate the latest technological advances, they can pose problems for regional security and for the security of the exporters. For example, even though the combat aircraft that Russia is now exporting to China (the Su-24 and the Su-27) were designed in the 1970s, these aircraft incorporate military technology 20 years newer than that previously available in China. Observers in Russia, East Asia, and even the United States consider the acquisition of systems with more modern technology—even in small numbers and with limited technological advances—a significant and potentially threatening first step toward a substantial qualitative improvement in China's air force.

For each of these issues—the size of standing forces, the maintenance of a defense industrial base, the rate of introduction of new weaponry, and arms exports—the post–Cold war environment challenges the notion that more is better. In each case, the challenge involves cost as well as the impact on security. Large standing armed forces and active production lines for advanced weaponry cost billions or tens of billions of dollars per year to maintain, and the price rises if new technology is introduced. In the case of exports, local economic benefits are more than offset by the costs of maintaining larger armed forces than would otherwise be needed. The opportunity costs of old patterns of arming weigh particularly heavily when their purpose is to insure against very small risks, most of which are extremely unlikely to arise for 10–15 years, if then. The opportunity costs are doubly painful when there is reason to believe that old patterns of arming may do more to exacerbate than to deter future risks of war.

The change in relations among the major arms producers from hostile to cooperative has made it possible to explore opportunities to enhance security and save resources through new forms of arms control. This means investigating the possibility of deeper, negotiated or reciprocal global reductions in forces, combined with steps to mothball most defense industries, suspend the introduction of new weaponry, and limit or halt exports of major weapon systems. Such changes would have vast repercussions that make many observers reluctant even to consider them. But while the world's militarily most powerful nations are on good terms with each other and none perceives any near-term risk of major war with another, there is no reason not to explore cooperative or coordinated steps that might provide greater security at lower cost for all concerned.

Combat aircraft offer a useful illustration of the linked choices that now face the primary arms producers concerning force size, defense industrial base, innovation in weaponry, and arms exports. With forces of varying size and age and different rates of procurement of replacement aircraft, the primary producers' combat aircraft holdings and production exemplify the range of options and consequences for unilateral military planning. Overall, the planned procurement programs of these seven nations will lead to the production of about 700 new aircraft for domestic use between 1995 and 2000. With this rate of procurement and with a retirement age of 25 years, the combat aircraft holdings of the primary producers will decline by about one-third, from about 12,800 in 1993 to about 8,900 in 2000.[7] (See Table 12.4.) Most of the reductions will be made in the large inventories of the United States and Russia, which will decline by 30–40 percent, from about 5,000 active combat aircraft in 1993 to around 3,300 in

---

[7] Bigger cuts are likely to be made in some countries as some weapon systems are retired before the end of their useful service lives. The potential future holdings shown in Table 12.4, cols. 4-5, represent ceilings, assuming a 25-year retirement age.

Table 12.4. The Primary Arms Producers' Combat Aircraft Holdings and Production 1993–2010

Total Active Aircraft

	Current holdings 1993 [1]	Planned procurement		Average an. procurement		Future holdings with planned procurement	
		1995 –2000 [2]	2001 –2010 [3]	1995 –2000 [4]	2001 –2010 [5]	2000 [6]	2010 [7]
France	**701**	**89**	**174**	**15**	**17**	**582**	**498**
Air Force	633	77	126	13	13	532	438
Navy	68	12	48	2	5	50	60
Germany	**718**	**0**	**140**	**0**	**14**	**627**	**364**
Air Force	617	0	140	0	14	523	301
Navy	101	0		0	0	104	63
Great Britain	**520**	**26**	**162**	**4**	**16**	**479**	**489**
Air Force	466	8	162	1	16	419	464
Navy	54	18		3	0	60	25
Italy	**326**	**44**	**120**	**7**	**12**	**309**	**315**
Air Force	324	44	120	7	12	294	300
Navy	2			0	0	15	15
Russia	**4,754**	**210**	**500**	**35**	**50**	**3,316**	**1,922**
Air Defense	1,380	60	60	10	6	1,032	380
Air Force	2,060	90	340	15	34	1,270	930
Navy	752	60	100	10	10	635	452
Strategic	562			0	0	379	160
Sweden	**338**	**100**	**178**	**17**	**18**	**296**	**288**
USA	**5,430**	**244**	**480**	**41**	**48**	**3,286**	**3,058**
USAF	3,584	95	240	16	24	2,119	1,848
USN&MC	1,846	149	240	25	24	1,167	1,210
Grand Total	**12,787**	**713**	**1,754**	**119**	**175**	**8,895**	**6,934**

Source: The Appendix. Assumes 25-year retirement age for aircraft in service in 1993.

2000. At the same time, France, Germany, Italy and Sweden will cut about 15 percent of their smaller inventories, which in 1993 ranged from 325 to 720 active aircraft.

Over the following decade, diverse rates of procurement and different initial ages of equipment will lead to disparate changes in the primary producers' holdings. Because the United States' 1993 holdings are relatively new, U.S. forces need not change much by 2010. Between 2001 and 2010, about 700 aircraft will be retired and 480 new planes (F-22s and F/A-18E/Fs) will be delivered, leading to a net reduction of about 200 aircraft. This will leave the United States with 3,058 aircraft, of which about 25 percent will have been produced after 1994. Russia's 1993 inventory, unlike that of the United States, is moderately old. Initially, average annual production of about 35 aircraft per year in 1995–2000 will suffice to keep Russia's inventory on a par with that of the United States; but after 2000, even with production rising to 50 aircraft per year for 2001–2010, Russia's inventory will fall to 1,922 by 2010—a decline of 40 percent.

In France and Italy, new production will represent over half of the 2010 inventories of about 500 and 315 aircraft, respectively. In Germany and Great Britain, newly produced aircraft will constitute about 40 percent of the 2010 inventory. But because British holdings in 1993 are relatively young while those of Germany are much older, the British force will not decline much (from 520 in 1993 to 489 in 2010) whereas the German force will decline by nearly half (from 718 in 1993 to 364 in 2010). In Sweden the entire inventory of 288 Gripens will have entered service after 1993.

Given current unilaterally developed policies, the likely future disparity between the armed forces of Russia and those of Western nations could easily lead to more insistent calls in Russia for increased military spending and higher rates of arms procurement. This would strengthen the hand of those who want Russia to adopt a more assertive or even expansionistic foreign policy. In the West, such a development would be viewed as confirming the fears of the skeptics who believe that renewed military competition and confrontation among the great powers is inevitable.

Even without smoldering dissatisfaction in Russia, one feature of projected developments after 2000 makes self-fulfilling threat inflation likely in all of the primary arms producers. In order to keep current procurement schedules and meet projected force needs, all of the primary arms producers will have to increase the scale of combat aircraft production for domestic use in 2001–2010—in many cases quite substantially. (See Table 12.4, cols. 4 and 5.) Because increases in procurement orders for combat aircraft will be very costly, descriptions of potential future military threats will abound. In these future threat assessments only two groups of countries will be mentioned: other arms producers, whose standing forces and growing arms production will be viewed with alarm; and major Third World arms importers, whose imports will have made them more threatening than they are today.

The alternative to this self-defeating, unilateral approach to security is for the primary producers to agree to reduce their forces, and curtail arms production and export. Suppose, for example, that the leaders of the major arms producing countries spent the next few years negotiating a conventional arms control regime for the decade after 2000, with two main goals: a 50 percent cut in the inventories now projected for 2000 (with a preliminary lower bound of 300), and a moratorium on production and export of most major weapon systems for the period from 2001 to 2010. These mutually reinforcing goals would create an exceptionally stable military environment in which to continue to strengthen East-West relations. They would also provide a stable environment in which major regional arms races would be suspended and regional arms reductions would be encouraged and facilitated. At the same time, they would foster efforts to develop integrated, effective multilateral peacekeeping and peacemaking forces and agreed guidelines for their use. This would reduce the burden on the United States and Russia to maintain forces capable of unilaterally dominating any major regional war (or, worse, any two major regional wars).

The reduced force to be fielded in 2000 (see Table 12.5, col. 4) would largely if not entirely eliminate the need for new production of combat aircraft between 2001 and 2010.[8] This would create an opportunity for each producer to suspend production and export of

---

[8] This is true for the United States, Britain, and France, and probably for Russia if aircraft withdrawn before the end of their useful service lives (in the reduction process) were reintroduced into active service later. Germany and Italy, which would not have enough serviceable aircraft to meet the 50 percent cut force goal for 2010 could bridge the gap with surplus U.S. aircraft. Only for Sweden might it make sense to complete the planned replacement of Viggens with Gripens over the period to 2010. This might minimize Swedish military costs by confining maintenance and operations to the two types of Swedish-produced aircraft.

weapons without concern about the risk that other producers would reap an advantage in exports or in technological advances. It would, at least temporarily, end the costly, needless, and potentially destabilizing technological competition in weaponry; it would also create a situation in which restraints on exports would be far less discriminatory than at present, since the same arms acquisition limits would apply to arms producers and arms importers.[9]

Limits on force levels and arms production for the period after 2010 would be subject to negotiation in 2001–2010. During this period, the goal of international discussions would be to develop a security system oriented to non-offensive defense and multilateral peacekeeping.

Apart from vested interests in the status quo and entrenched habits of thinking and acting, there are three main obstacles to this ambitious arms control agenda. The first obstacle is a dated image of security and danger. The idea of shutting down active arms production lines—though studied and even implemented for some systems—has lain beyond the realm of serious public discussion since 1945. As a result, the concept evokes a sense of insecurity: "What if a threat arises that we have not foreseen and we are not able to respond quickly because it will take years to rebuild the industries?" "Would we even be able to rebuild the industries in a matter of years, or might certain capabilities be lost for good?" These are appropriate questions, which need and deserve serious study. But from the viewpoints of both cost and security, it does not make sense to treat an active industrial base as a given, without seriously investigating the alternatives.

A second obstacle is that many people cannot conceive of a fundamental transformation of the present military system. Some observers might argue, for example, that even it were feasible to shift to a "cool" industrial base, a change of this kind would be at best temporary. What is at issue, they might claim, is not whether to end production altogether, but whether to suspend it temporarily or keep it going at a low level—and the relative economic and human costs and security risk of each approach. But there are good reasons to

---

[9] This sketch of a global conventional arms control regime linking force levels, production, and trade is preliminary and illustrative. The suggested force reductions, the scope and duration of a moratorium on production and trade, and the statement of goals for the longer-term future are meant to be suggestive, not definitive.

Table 12.5. The Primary Arms Producers' Combat Aircraft Holdings with a 50-Percent Cut and a Production Moratorium

Total Active Aircraft

| | Holdings in 1993 [1] | Projected holdings in 2000 w/planned 1995-2000 procure. [2] | Serviceable aircraft in 2010 with no procure. after 2000 [3] | Reduced forces for 2000-2010 | |
				Goal: ~ 50% of projected holdings in 2000 [4] = [2] / 2	Surplus or deficit of serviceable aircraft in 2010 [5] = [3] - [4]
France	**701**	**582**	**324**	**330**	**-6**
Air Force	633	532	312	300	12
Navy	68	50	12	30	-18
Germany	**718**	**627**	**224**	**350**	**-126**
Air Force	617	523	161	300	-139
Navy	101	104	63	50	13
Great Britain	**520**	**479**	**327**	**330**	**-3**
Air Force	466	419	302	300	2
Navy	54	60	25	30	-5
Italy	**326**	**309**	**195**	**315**	**-120**
Air Force	324	294	180	300	-120
Navy	2	15	15	15	0
Russia	**4,754**	**3,316**	**1,422**	**1,500**	**-78**
Air Defense	1,380	1,032	320	400	-80
Air Force	2,060	1,270	590	640	-50
Navy	752	635	352	300	52
Strategic	562	379	160	160	0
Sweden	**338**	**296**	**110**	**300**	**-190**
USA	**5,430**	**3,286**	**2,578**	**1,500**	**1,078**
USAF	3,584	2,119	1,608	1,000	608
USN&MC	1,846	1,167	970	500	470
Grand Total	**12,787**	**8,895**	**5,180**	**4,625**	**555**

Source: The Appendix and Table 12.4. Assumes minimum air force inventory of 300 in 2000.

believe that production of many major weapon systems could end permanently within the next decade or two. Conventional arms control talks in Europe over the past 20 years suggest that in a cooperative environment, armed forces can be restructured in ways that build confidence and reduce the risk or war. The thrust of conventional arms control efforts for many years has been to mutually reduce military capabilities for massive, surprise (or short-warning) cross-border attacks—and, by the same token, to increase the effectiveness of defenses against such attacks.

This useful concept can now be applied globally in ways that would reduce the risk of both regional and global war. But this would mean throwing out old assumptions about the appropriate size and character of military forces, and conducting a zero-based (or "bottom-up") assessment of the systems that are particularly useful for defense, and those that are particularly useful for cross-border attack. Limits on the long-range attack capability of air forces—and related limits on the cross-border attack capability of ground forces— would be high on the list of priorities for such a review.

The coming decade, when production, innovation, exports, and threats of major war will be at an unprecedented low, would offer an excellent opportunity for a zero-based review of security policy on the part of the primary arms producers and the other major military powers. This opportunity would be enhanced by a moratorium on arms production and export, while the character and size of future forces are debated, and concepts such as an industrial reserve system are investigated. If a stringent form of non-offensive defense were endorsed during the review, then production of weapons that strengthen offensive capabilities—including long-range, high-performance fighter-attack aircraft—might be halted as part of a new arms control regime.

Another potential obstacle to globally-oriented forms of conventional arms control is the possible opposition of countries like China and India, which are currently seeking to develop military capabilities that lie somewhere between the "great power" level (exemplified by France) and the "superpower" level (exemplified by a mid-point between the United States and Russia). Large Third World countries can match the leading industrial military powers now in quantitative terms, but they will not be able to do so for many years in terms of technology. Thus, China, India, and other Third World nations could easily view such a regime as inherently discriminatory, in a manner analogous to the Nonproliferation Treaty: the "haves" may cut back, but they remain permanently in a position of military advantage, while the "have-nots" are relegated to permanent military inferiority. This potential objection might be overcome if Third World countries were convinced that the nations with the most powerful military forces were cutting back on the size and range of their forces and suspending their continued technological development.

Developing a consensus on a new agenda for conventional arms control will not be easy. But there are encouraging precedents. In the talks on conventional forces in Europe, in strategic nuclear arms control, and in the new chemical weapon convention, intractable issues were resolved with time and hard work. Revamping military forces to stress territorial defense and multilateral peacekeeping and peacemaking will involve a wrenching change—but armies throughout the industrial world have already begun to plan for this change. Energetic, knowledgeable craftsmen and managers will find new ways to preserve industrial know-how without producing weapons not needed for security.

The linked issues concerning reductions in forces and limits on production and trade may be more complex than the topics of other arms control agendas. But the stakes are much higher. Over a decade, several hundred billion dollars could be saved, and new global and regional arms races could be prevented. The role of force in the international system could be transformed. What these changes require—what the post–Cold War world offers and demands—is a willing suspension of disbelief. To develop agreements and practices that institutionalize new East–West and North–South relations we must rethink the most basic concepts of security. The collapse of the world arms market will help us engage in this task.

Appendix

Jonathan Cohen
Andrew Peach

The Primary Arms Producers' Holdings and Production of Combat Aircraft 1993–2010

The following tables give data on the combat aircraft holdings, domestic procurement, and exports of the seven primary producers. Estimates of holdings and domestic procurement are based on information gathered by the authors from various sources, including government documents and interviews. Exports are based on reports of firm orders that appeared in trade journals and other comparable sources. Delivery schedules are based on published reports or have been estimated by IDDS. A complete methodology is given in the *IDDS Almanac 1994* (Cambridge, Mass.: Institute for Defense and Disarmament Studies, forthcoming).

Abbreviations and Conventions

Units: Number of aircraft by projected year of delivery, based on firm and planned orders.

..	Not available or not applicable	ME&NAfr	Middle East and North Africa
Afr	sub-Saharan Africa	Oth	Other
an	Annual	procure	Procurement
atk	Attack	Prod	Producer
Avg	Average	recce	Reconnaissance
CFE	Treaty on Conventional Armed Forces in Europe	R&D	Research and development
		RAF	Royal Air Force (Britain)
E&SEA	East and Southeast Asia	Rec'd	The number of aircraft received by the end of 1992 for that order
ECM	Electronic countermeasures		
EF2000	Eurofighter 2000	SA	South Asia
Eur	Europe	trg	Training
Eur&Can	Europe and Canada	USAF	United States Air Force
EW	Electronic warfare	USN	United States Navy
(L)	Produced under license	USN/MC	United States Navy and Marine Corps
LA	Latin America		

Appendix Table 1. Russia's Holdings and Production of Combat Aircraft 1993–2010

			1993	1994	1995	1996	1997	1998	1999	2000	2001	2002	2003	2004	2005	2006	2007	2008	2009	2010
PLANNED HOLDINGS																				
MiG-21	Air Force	Fighter/attack	200	100	50															
MiG-23	Air Force	Air superiority	520	226	52															
Su-17	Air Force	Attack	230	140	70	30														
MiG-27	Air Force	Fighter/attack	560	480	400	320	240	140	100											
MiG-25	Air Force	Interceptor	220	200	180	160	140	120	100	80	60	40	20							
Su-25	Air Force	Close air support	180	170	160	150	140	130	120	110	100	80	60	50	40	30	20	10		
Su-24	Air Force	Fighter/Bomber	500	490	480	470	460	450	380	300	150	120	80	60	50	40	30	20		
Su-27	Air Force	Fighter/attack	190	190	190	190	190	190	190	190	190	190	190	190	190	190	190	190	160	130
MiG-29	Air Force	Fighter	450	450	450	450	450	450	450	450	450	450	450	450	450	450	450	450	400	360
Su-27M	Air Force	Fighter/attack								60	70	80	90	100	110	120	130	140	150	160
Su-34	Air Force	Fighter/Bomber						10	20	30	40	50	60	70	80	100	120	140	160	180
Su-2?	Air Force	Close air support									10	20	30	40	50	60	70	80	90	100
Total Air Force Active			3,050	2,446	2,042	1,790	1,650	1,530	1,410	1,270	1,090	1,030	980	960	970	990	1,010	1,030	960	930
Su-15	Air Defense	Interceptor	210	150	100	50														
MiG-25	Air Defense	Interceptor	250	230	210	194	178	162	146	124	108	92	76	60	44	28	12			
MiG-23	Air Defense	Air superiority	690	636	582	528	474	420	366	332	296	260	224	188	152	116	80	44	8	
MiG-31	Air Defense	Interceptor	340	340	340	340	340	340	340	340	340	340	340	340	320	300	280	250	220	190
Su-27	Air Defense	Fighter/attack	240	240	240	240	236	236	236	236	236	231	225	220	215	210	205	200	195	190
Total Air Defense Active			1,730	1,596	1,472	1,352	1,228	1,158	1,088	1,032	980	923	865	808	731	654	577	494	423	380
Tu-16	Naval Air	Medium bomber	122	104	86	68	50	32	14											
Tu-22	Naval Air	Medium bomber	71	69	67	63	59	55	51	45	41	36	28	20	12	4				
Tu-95	Naval Air	Strategic bomber	61	60	60	59	58	58	57	56	48	40	32	24	16	8				
Su-25	Naval Air	Close air support	88	83	78	73	68	63	58	51	44	37	30	23	16	9	2			
MiG-27	Naval Air	Fighter/Attack	30	30	28	26	24	22	20	18	16	14	12	10	8	6	4	2		
Su-17	Naval Air	Attack	150	132	114	96	78	60	43	43	25	25	25	20	20	10	10	10	10	10
Tu-142	Naval Air	Strategic bomber	50	50	49	49	48	47	47	46	46	43	40	37	34	31	28	25	22	20
Su-24	Naval Air	Fighter/Bomber	127	124	121	118	115	112	109	104	103	102	100	99	98	97	95	94	93	92
Tu-22M	Naval Air	Medium bomber	213	210	207	204	201	198	195	192	189	186	183	180	175	170	165	160	155	150
Unspecified	Naval Air		10	20	30	40	50	60	70	80	90	100	110	120	130	140	150	160	170	180
Total Naval Air Active			912	862	840	796	751	707	664	635	602	583	560	533	509	475	454	451	450	452

Appendix Table 1. Cont'd

			1993	1994	1995	1996	1997	1998	1999	2000	2001	2002	2003	2004	2005	2006	2007	2008	2009	2010
Tu-16	Strategic Force	Medium bomber	130	106	82	58	34	10												
Yak-28	Strategic Force	ECM	40	40	39	39	39	38	38	37	35	33	31	23	15	7				
Tu-22	Strategic Force	Medium bomber	65	65	65	63	61	59	57	55	50	45	35	25	15	5				
Tu-95	Strategic Force	Strategic Bomber	147	145	144	142	140	138	137	135	123	111	99	87	75	63	51	39	27	20
Tu-22M	Strategic Force	Medium bomber	180	180	172	164	156	148	140	132	131	130	128	127	126	125	123	122	121	120
Tu-160	Strategic Force	Strategic Bomber				20	20	20	20	20	20	20	20	20	20	20	20	20	20	20
Strategic Force Active			562	536	502	486	450	413	392	379	359	339	313	282	251	220	194	181	168	160
Grand Total Active			6,254	5,440	4,856	4,424	4,079	3,808	3,554	3,316	3,031	2,875	2,718	2,583	2,461	2,339	2,235	2,156	2,001	1,922
Various	Air Force	in store	990																	
Various	Air Defense	in store	350																	
Various	Naval Air	in store	160																	
Grand Total Including Stored			7,754																	

	Customer	Ordered	No.	Rec'd	1993	1994	1995	1996	1997	1998	1999	2000	2001	2002	2003	2004	2005	2006	2007	2008	2009	2010
PLANNED DOMESTIC PROCUREMENT																							
Su-27	Air Force	..	..		24																	
MiG-31	Air Defense	..	..		10	10	10	10	10	10	10	10	10	10	10	10	10	10	10	10	10	10
Unspecified	Naval Air	..	..		10	10	10	10	10	10	10	10	10	10	10	10	10	10	10	10	10	10
Su-27M	Naval Air	..	..				10	10	10	10	10	10	10	10	10	10	10	10	10	10	10	10
Su-34	Air Force	..	..							10	10	10	10	10	10	10	10	10	10	10	10	10
Su-2?	Air Force	..	..										10	10	10	10	10	10	10	10	10	10
Total Domestic				..	44	20	30	30	30	40	40	40	50	50	50	50	50	50	50	50	50	50
FIRM ORDERS BY EXPORT (by estimated date of delivery)																							
MiG-27	India (L)	1983	200	117	12	12	12	12	12	12	11											
MiG-29	China	1991	40	0	20	20																
MiG-29	India	1992	20	0		10	10															
MiG-29	Malaysia	1993	18	0		9	9															
MiG-29	Iran	..	60	0			24	24	12			12										
MiG-31	China	1993	48	0		12	12	12	12													
Su-24	China	1990	12	0		12																
Su-24	Iran	..	12	0		2					12											
Su-27	China	1991	72	26		20	26															
Total Russian-built exports		282	26		20	73	79	24	24	12	12	12	0	0	0	0	0	0	0	0	0	0
Total Licensed-produced exports		200	117		12	12	12	12	12	12	11	0	0	0	0	0	0	0	0	0	0	0
Total Export Production			143		32	85	91	36	36	24	23	12	0	0	0	0	0	0	0	0	0	0
Total Domestic Production				..	44	20	30	30	30	40	40	40	50	50	50	50	50	50	50	50	50	50
Grand Total Production				..	76	105	121	66	66	64	63	52	50	50	50	50	50	50	50	50	50	50

Source: "IDDS Almanac 1994." Note: The Su-2? is an unspecified follow-on to the Su-25 that Russia is planning to build. China may order Su-30s instead of MiG-29s or MiG-31s.

Appendix Table 2. United States' Holdings and Production of Combat Aircraft 1993–2010

			1993	1994	1995	1996	1997	1998	1999	2000	2001	2002	2003	2004	2005	2006	2007	2008	2009	2010
PLANNED HOLDINGS																				
B-1	USAF	Bomber	95	95	95	95	95	95	95	95	95	95	95	95	95	95	95	95	95	95
B-2	USAF	Bomber	7	10	13	16	20	20	20	20	20	20	20	20	20	20	20	20	20	20
B-52	USAF	Bomber	118	90	55	55	55	55	55	55	55	55	55	55	55	55	55	55	55	55
F-4	USAF	Defense suppression	129	50	50	50														
F-111	USAF	Long-range attack	148	80	80	75	75	75												
A-10	USAF	Close air support	389	220	220	200	200	200	200	200	200	200	200	200	200	200	127	83	41	
F-117	USAF	Ground attack	58	50	50	50	50	50	50	50	50	50	50	50	50	50	49	43	37	30
F-15A-D	USAF	Air superiority	623	460	410	410	410	410	410	410	410	410	410	410	410	354	256	209	163	119
F-15E	USAF	Long-range attack	195	190	190	190	190	190	190	190	190	190	190	190	190	190	190	190	190	190
F-16	USAF	Multirole	1,822	1,160	1,050	1,025	1,075	1,075	1,075	1,075	1,075	1,075	1,075	1,075	1,075	1,075	1,075	1,075	1,075	1,075
F-22	USAF	Air superiority							12	24	48	72	96	120	144	168	192	216	240	264
Total USAF Active			3,584	2,405	2,213	2,166	2,170	2,170	2,107	2,119	2,143	2,167	2,191	2,215	2,239	2,207	2,059	1,986	1,916	1,848
A-4	USMC	Light attack	52																	
A-6E	USN/MC	Ground attack	304	186	140	70														
EA-6B	USN/MC	EW	114	86	72	50														
AV-8B	USMC	Ground attack	184	189	185	182	174	174	174	167	164	161	158	154	151	148	145	142	140	131
F-14	USN	Air superiority	414	314	276	255	220	220	220	220	220	220	220	220	215	186	163	143	124	103
F/A-18A-D	USN/MC	Multirole	778	825	849	785	756	756	756	756	756	756	756	756	756	756	756	756	756	712
F/A-18E/F	USN/MC	Multirole							12	24	48	72	96	120	144	168	192	216	240	264
Total USN&MC Active			1,846	1,600	1,522	1,342	1,150	1,150	1,162	1,167	1,188	1,209	1,230	1,250	1,266	1,258	1,256	1,257	1,260	1,210
Grand Total Active			5,430	4,005	3,735	3,508	3,320	3,320	3,269	3,286	3,331	3,376	3,421	3,465	3,505	3,465	3,315	3,243	3,176	3,058
Various	USAF	Stored	1,923																	
Various	USN/MC	Stored & training	585																	
Grand Total Including Stored			7,938																	

Appendix Table 2. cont'd

	Customer	Ordered	No.	Rec'd	1993	1994	1995	1996	1997	1998	1999	2000	2001	2002	2003	2004	2005	2006	2007	2008	2009	2010
PLANNED DOMESTIC PROCUREMENT																						
AV-8B	USN	1990-92	51	22	15	14																
F-15E	USAF	1990-92	81	23	29	29																
F-16C/D	USAF	1991-94	192	1	72	48	48	23														
F/A-18C/D	USN	1991-97	240	9	53	53	53	24	24	24												
F/A-18E/F	USN	1997-	24	0							12	12	24	24	24	24	24	24	24	24	24	24
F-22	USAF	1996-	24	0							12	12	24	24	24	24	24	24	24	24	24	24
Total Domestic Procurement			612	55	169	144	101	47	24	24	24	24	48	48	48	48	48	48	48	48	48	48
FIRM ORDERS BY EXPORT (by estimated date of delivery)																						
AV-8B	Spain	1990	8	0			4	4														
AV-8B	Italy	1992	13	0			7	6														
F-15J	Japan (L)	91-95	28	0	6	7	5	5	5													
F-15S	Saudi Arabia	1992	72	0			6	12	24	24	6											
F-15I	Israel	1994	21	0					7	7	7											
F-16C/D	Turkey (L)	84-94	232	114	18	18	18	18	18	18	10											
F-16C/D	Egypt	1987	42	22	20																	
F-16C/D	Egypt (L)	1991	46	0		12	12	12	10													
F-16C/D	Pakistan	1989	71	0	11																	
F-16A/B	Portugal	1990	20	0		20																
F-16C/D	Thailand	1991	18	0	6	6	6															
F-16C/D	S. Korea	1991	48	0		12	12	12	12													
F-16C/D	S. Korea (L)	1991	72	0						18	18	18	18									
F-16A/B	Taiwan	1992	150	0				30	30	30	30	30										
F-16C/D	Greece	1992	40	0					20	20												
F/A-18C/D	Kuwait	1988	40	20	20																	
F/A-18C/D	Switzerland	1991	34	0			17	17														
F/A-18C/D	Finland	1992	64	0				16	16	16	16											
F/A-18C/D	Malaysia	1993	8	0					8													
Total US-built Exports				42	57	38	52	97	117	97	59	30	0	0	0	0	0	0	0	0	0	0
Total Licensed-Produced Exports				114	24	37	35	35	33	36	28	18	18	0	0	0	0	0	0	0	0	0
Total Export Production				156	81	75	87	132	150	133	87	48	18	0	0	0	0	0	0	0	0	0
Total Domestic Procurement				55	169	144	101	47	24	24	24	24	48	48	48	48	48	48	48	48	48	48
Grand Total Production			211	250	219	188	179	174	157	111	72	66	48	48	48	48	48	48	48	48	48	48

Source: "IDDS Almanac 1994." Note: The US has embargoed delivery of Pakistan's F-16 order, and stopped work on the remainder of the Pakistani order.

Appendix Table 3. Great Britain's Holdings and Production of Combat Aircraft 1993–2010

PLANNED HOLDINGS

Type	Service	Role	1993	1994	1995	1996	1997	1998	1999	2000	2001	2002	2003	2004	2005	2006	2007	2008	2009	2010
Hunter	RAF	Maritime attack	6																	
Canberra	RAF	recce/trg	20																	
Buccaneer	RAF	Maritime attack	28																	
Jaguar	RAF	Offensive support	53	53	53	53	53	53	53	53	43	43	29	29						
Harrier	RAF	Offensive support	72	77	85	85	85	85	85	85	84	84	84	84	84	84	84	80	80	80
Tornado F-3	RAF	Air defense	132	102	102	102	102	102	102	102	102	102	102	102	102	102	102	102	102	102
Tornado GR-1	RAF	Attack	169	179	179	179	179	179	179	179	179	179	179	179	179	179	172	154	136	120
EF2000	RAF	Air defense										18	36	54	72	90	108	126	144	162
Total RAF Active			480	411	419	419	419	419	419	419	408	426	430	448	437	455	466	462	462	464
Hunter	Navy	Training	12																	
Sea Harrier	Navy	Multirole	42	42	44	52	60	60	60	60	59	59	59	58	53	48	43	35	30	25
Total Navy Active			54	42	44	52	60	60	60	60	59	59	59	58	53	48	43	35	30	25
Grand Total Active			534	453	463	471	479	479	479	479	467	485	489	506	490	503	509	497	492	489
Various	RAF	Stored	76																	
Hunter	Navy	Stored	12																	
Grand Total Including Stored			622																	

PLANNED DOMESTIC PROCUREMENT

Type	Service	Ordered	No.	Rec'd	1993	1994	1995	1996	1997	1998	1999	2000	2001	2002	2003	2004	2005	2006	2007	2008	2009	2010
Harrier	RAF	1990	13	0		5	8															
Sea Harrier	Navy	1993	18	0			2	8	8													
EF 2000	RAF	..	250	0										18	18	18	18	18	18	18	18	18
Total Domestic Procurement				0	0	5	10	8	8	0	0	0	0	18	18	18	18	18	18	18	18	18

FIRM ORDERS BY EXPORT (by estimated date of delivery)

Type	Customer	Ordered	No.	Rec'd	1993	1994	1995	1996	1997	1998	1999	2000	2001	2002	2003	2004	2005	2006	2007	2008	2009	2010
Hawk	Indonesia (L)	1992	10	0	5	5																
Hawk	Malaysia	1990	18	0		9	9															
Hawk	Oman	1989	12	0	4	4	4															
Hawk	Saudi Arabia	1988	20	0	5	5	5	5														
Tornado IDS	Saudi Arabia	1988	48	0	3	12	12	12	9													
Total UK-built Export				0	12	30	30	17	9	0	0	0	0	0	0	0	0	0	0	0	0	0
Total Licensed-Produced Exports				0	5	5	0	0	0	0	0	0	0	0	0	0	0	0	0	0	0	0
Total Export Production				0	17	35	30	17	9	0	0	0	0	0	0	0	0	0	0	0	0	0
Total Domestic Procurement				0	0	5	10	8	8	0	0	0	0	18	18	18	18	18	18	18	18	18
Total Production				0	17	40	40	25	17	0	0	0	0	18	18	18	18	18	18	18	18	18

Source: "IDDS Amanac 1994."

Appendix Table 4. Italy's Holdings and Production of Combat Aircraft 1993–2010

PLANNED HOLDINGS

			1993	1994	1995	1996	1997	1998	1999	2000	2001	2002	2003	2004	2005	2006	2007	2008	2009	2010
G-91	Air Force	Close air support	58	32	30															
F-104	Air Force	Fighter/Interceptor	120	146	120	108	96	84	72	60	60	60	60	60	40	20				
Tornado ADV	Air Force	Air Defense			12	12	24	24	24	24	24	24	24	24	12	12				
Tornado IDS	Air Force	Multirole	74	74	74	74	74	74	74	74	74	74	74	74	74	74	74	64	54	44
AM-X	Air Force	Close air support	72	92	112	132	136	136	136	136	136	136	136	136	136	136	136	136	136	136
EF2000	Air Force	Multirole													20	40	60	80	100	120
Total Air Force Active			324	344	348	326	330	318	306	294	294	294	294	294	282	282	270	280	290	300
AV-8B	Naval Air Arm	Attack	2	2	9	15	15	15	15	15	15	15	15	15	15	15	15	15	15	15
Grand Total Active			**326**	**346**	**357**	**341**	**345**	**333**	**321**	**309**	**309**	**309**	**309**	**309**	**297**	**297**	**285**	**295**	**305**	**315**
Various	Air Force	Stored	116																	
Grand total Including Stored			**442**																	

PLANNED DOMESTIC PROCUREMENT

	Customer	Ordered	No. Rec'd	1993	1994	1995	1996	1997	1998	1999	2000	2001	2002	2003	2004	2005	2006	2007	2008	2009	2010
AM-X	Air Force 1986	136	52	20	20	20	20	4													
EF2000	Air Force ..	130	0													20	20	20	20	20	20
Total Domestic Procurement			**52**	**20**	**20**	**20**	**20**	**4**							**20**	**20**	**20**	**20**	**20**	**20**

Source: "IDDS Almanac 1994."

Appendix Table 5. Germany's Holdings and Production of Combat Aircraft 1993–2010

			1993	1994	1995	1996	1997	1998	1999	2000	2001	2002	2003	2004	2005	2006	2007	2008	2009	2010
PLANNED HOLDINGS																				
F-4	Air Force	Fighter/ground attack	193	193	183	169	155	140	129	99	67	7								
Alpha Jet	Air Force	Training aircraft	163	163	163	163	163	163	163	163	163	163	163	163	163	114	80	46		
Tornado	Air Force	Fighter/ground attack	237	237	237	237	237	237	237	237	237	237	237	237	237	237	219	197	167	137
MiG-29	Air Force	Fighter	24	24	24	24	24	24	24	24	24	24	24	24	24	24	24	24	24	24
EF2000	Air Force	multirole										20	40	60	80	100	120	140	140	140
Total Air Force Active			617	617	607	593	579	564	553	523	491	451	464	484	504	475	443	407	331	301
Tornado	Naval Air Arm	Ground attack	104	104	104	104	104	104	104	104	104	104	104	104	104	104	104	103	76	63
Grand Total Active			721	721	711	697	683	668	657	627	595	555	568	588	608	579	547	510	407	364

	Customer	Ordered	No.	Rec'd									2002	2003	2004	2005	2006	2007	2008		
PLANNED DOMESTIC PROCUREMENT																					
EF2000	Air Force	...	140	0									20	20	20	20	20	20	20		

Source: "IDDS Amanac 1994." Note: Germany has no stored aircraft.

Appendix Table 6. France's Holdings and Production of Combat Aircraft 1993–2010

PLANNED HOLDINGS

Aircraft	Service	Role	1993	1994	1995	1996	1997	1998	1999	2000	2001	2002	2003	2004	2005	2006	2007	2008	2009	2010
Mirage IIIB/E	Air Force	Fighter/ground atk	39																	
Mirage VF	Air Force	Fighter/ground atk	30	30	15															
Mirage IVP	Air Force	Bomber	15	15	15	15	15	15												
Mirage F1-B/C	Air Force	Air superiority	116	106	94	83	83	68	53	38	23	18								
Jaguar A/E	Air Force	Fighter/ground atk	151	151	151	144	126	108	90	72	54	36	36	18						
Mirage F1-CT	Air Force	Fighter/ground atk	22	32	44	55	55	55	55	55	55	55	55	55	55	37	19			
Mirage F1-CR	Air Force	Reconnaissance	51	51	51	51	51	51	51	51	51	51	51	51	51	51	51	38	26	14
Mirage 2000B/C/-5	Air Force	Air superiority	132	147	150	150	150	150	150	150	150	150	150	150	150	150	150	150	150	132
Mirage 2000N	Air Force	Bomber/ground atk	72	75	75	75	75	75	75	75	75	75	75	75	75	75	75	75	75	75
Mirage 2000D	Air Force	Ground atk/bomber	5	17	32	50	68	83	90	90	90	90	90	90	90	90	90	90	90	90
Rafale C	Air Force	Air superiority						1	1	1	17	33	49	67	85	91	97	103	109	127
Total Air Force Active			**633**	**624**	**627**	**623**	**623**	**606**	**565**	**532**	**515**	**508**	**506**	**506**	**506**	**494**	**482**	**456**	**450**	**438**
Etendard IV	Navy	Recce/trg	18	18	18	18	18	12	6											
F-8E Crusader	Navy	Air superiority	12	12	12	12	12	12	6											
Super Etendard	Navy	Attack	38	38	38	38	38	38	38	38	38	38	38	38	38	36	24	12		
Rafale M	Navy	Air superiority						2	6	12	12	12	12	12	12	24	36	48	60	60
Total Navy Active			**68**	**68**	**68**	**68**	**68**	**52**	**50**	**50**	**50**	**50**	**50**	**50**	**50**	**60**	**60**	**60**	**60**	**60**
Grand Total Active			**701**	**692**	**695**	**691**	**691**	**658**	**615**	**582**	**565**	**558**	**556**	**556**	**556**	**554**	**542**	**516**	**510**	**498**
Various	Air Force	Stored	13																	
Various	Navy	Stored	33																	
Grand Total Including Stored			**747**																	

PLANNED DOMESTIC PROCUREMENT

Aircraft	Customer	Ordered	No.	Rec'd	1993	1994	1995	1996	1997	1998	1999	2000	2001	2002	2003	2004	2005	2006	2007	2008	2009	2010
Mirage 2000N	Air Force	1986	75	64	8	3																
Mirage 2000B/C	Air Force	1982	153	120	15	15	3															
Mirage 2000D	Air Force	1991	90	0	5	12	15	18	18	15	7											
Rafale C	Air Force	1994-	234	0						1			16	16	16	18	18	6	6	6	6	18
Rafale M	Navy	1994-	86	0						2	4	6						12	12	12	12	
Total Domestic Procurement				**184**	**28**	**30**	**18**	**18**	**18**	**18**	**11**	**6**	**16**	**16**	**16**	**18**	**18**	**18**	**18**	**18**	**18**	**18**

FIRM ORDERS BY EXPORT (by estimated date of delivery)

Aircraft	Customer	Ordered	No.	Rec'd	1993	1994	1995	1996	1997	1998	1999	2000	2001	2002	2003	2004	2005	2006	2007	2008	2009	2010
Mirage 2000-5	Tawain	1992	60	0					30	30												
Total Domestic Procurement				**184**	**28**	**30**	**18**	**18**	**18**	**18**	**11**	**6**	**16**	**16**	**16**	**18**	**18**	**18**	**18**	**18**	**18**	**18**
Total Production				**184**	**28**	**30**	**18**	**18**	**48**	**48**	**11**	**6**	**16**	**16**	**16**	**18**	**18**	**18**	**18**	**18**	**18**	**18**

Source: "IDDS Almanac 1994."

Appendix Table 7. Sweden's Projected Holdings and Production of Combat Aircraft 1993–2010

			1993	1994	1995	1996	1997	1998	1999	2000	2001	2002	2003	2004	2005	2006	2007	2008	2009	2010
PLANNED HOLDINGS																				
J-32 Lansen	Air Force	Reconnaissance	32	32	24	16	8													
J-35 Draken	Air Force	Fighter	65	65	59	53	47													
J-37 Viggen	Air Force	Fighter/attack	241	241	241	241	241	235	229	186	158	138	114	90	66	42	18			
J-39 Gripen	Air Force	Multirole		10	20	30	50	70	90	110	130	150	174	198	222	246	270	288	288	288
Total Air Force Active			338	348	344	340	346	305	319	296	288	288	288	288	288	288	288	288	288	288
J-37 Viggen	Air Force	Stored	24																	
Grand Total Including Stored			**362**																	

		Customer	Ordered	No. Rec'd	1993	1994	1995	1996	1997	1998	1999	2000	2001	2002	2003	2004	2005	2006	2007	2008
PLANNED DOMESTIC PROCUREMENT																				
J-39 Gripen	Air Force	1982	140		0	2	8	10	10	20	20	20	20	20	24	24	24	24	24	18

Source: "IDDS Almanac 1994."

Institute for Defense and Disarmament Studies

Randall Forsberg, Executive Director
675 Massachusetts Avenue, Cambridge MA 02139
Tel. (617) 354-4337   Fax (617) 354-1450

Founded in 1979, the Institute for Defense and Disarmament Studies is a nonprofit center for research and education on ways to minimize the risk of war, reduce the burden of military spending, and promote the growth of democratic institutions.

Institute staff members study worldwide military forces and military and arms control policies. The Institute's monthly journal, the *Arms Control Reporter*, published since 1982, is the leading international reference source on arms control negotiations. Other Institute publications include *Soviet Missiles* and *Soviet Military Aircraft* (volumes 1 and 2 of the Institute's *World Weapon Database*); *Strategic Antisubmarine Warfare and Naval Strategy*; *ViennaFax*, a journal of news and analysis on the Vienna talks on reducing conventional forces in Europe; and *Cutting Conventional Forces*.

Since 1990, the Institute's research has focused on four areas of potential international cooperation on security policy: limiting the forces maintained for national defense to non-offensive capabilities and strategies, aimed at defending territorial sovereignty and integrity with little or no threat of attack on other nations; replacing unilateral military intervention with multilateral peacemaking under UN or other nonpartisan auspices; ending the production and export of weapons that can strengthen capabilities for international aggression or cross-border attack, except where such weapons are required for multilateral peacemaking; and strengthening UN and other international institutions for nonviolent conflict resolution.

In 1992 the Institute organized the International Fighter Study, a collaborative effort with scholars from the main arms-producing and arms-importing nations to study ways of restricting the production and export of weapons with long-range attack capability. Other current studies at the Institute concern the implications of increased reliance on multilateral peacemaking for U.S. forces and spending, and the political, ethical, and practical obstacles to an effective UN peacemaking capability. The Institute co-sponsors articles published in the *Boston Review*, which we disseminate in reprints to college teachers, activist leaders, journalists, members of government, diplomats, and independent analysts in the United States and other countries.

Center for Science and International Affairs

William C. Clark, Director
John F. Kennedy School of Government, Harvard University
79 JFK Street, Cambridge, MA 02138
(617) 495-1400

The Center for Science and International Affairs (CSIA) was established in 1973 to advance understanding and resolution of international security problems through a program of research, training, teaching, and outreach. Founded by Paul Doty, a biochemist long involved in arms control, national security, and science policy, CSIA became in 1978 the first permanent research center of Harvard's John F. Kennedy School of Government.

The Center places special but not exclusive emphasis on the role of science and technology in the analysis and design of public policies to address international problems. CSIA's research addresses four interrelated areas: international security affairs, science and technology policy, environment and natural resources, and public policy issues in the Pacific Basin. Current research includes new international security conceptions after the Cold War; nuclear arms control; nonproliferation; U.S. policies toward the former Soviet Union; science and technology policy; information infrastructure; economic competitiveness; technology transfer; global environmental risk management; land use policy; environmental economics; climate change strategies and policies; and interactions among major policy initiatives in Asia and the Americas with the aim of improving decision-making processes in the Pacific region.

Each year the Center hosts a multinational group of approximately 25 scholars from the social, behavioral, and natural sciences. More than 50 Harvard faculty members and 40 adjunct research fellows from the greater Boston area also participate in CSIA activities.

CSIA sponsors seminars and conferences, many open to the public; maintains a substantial specialized library; and publishes a monograph series and discussion papers. The Center's International Security Program, directed by Steven E. Miller, publishes the CSIA Studies in International Security and sponsors and edits the quarterly journal *International Security*.

The Center is supported by an endowment established with funds from the Ford Foundation and Harvard University, by foundation grants, by individual gifts, and by occasional government contracts.